GENDER
AND
AGEING

GENDER AND AGEING

SOUTHEAST ASIAN PERSPECTIVES

EDITED BY
Theresa W. Devasahayam

INSTITUTE OF SOUTHEAST ASIAN STUDIES
Singapore

First published in Singapore in 2014 by
ISEAS Publishing
Institute of Southeast Asian Studies
30 Heng Mui Keng Terrace
Pasir Panjang
Singapore 119614
E-mail: publish@iseas.edu.sg
Website: http://bookshop.iseas.edu.sg

The responsibility for facts and opinions in this publication rests exclusively with the authors and their interpretations do not necessarily reflect the views or the policy of the publisher or its supporters.

ISEAS Library Cataloguing-in-Publication Data

Gender and ageing : Southeast Asian perspectives / edited by Theresa W. Devasahayam.
1. Older people — Southeast Asia.
2. Ageing — Southeast Asia.
3. Gender identity — Southeast Asia.
I. Devasahayam, Theresa W.
II. Workshop on Gender and Ageing in Southeast Asia : Contexts, Concerns and Contradictions (2009 : Singapore)
HQ1064 A9G32   2014

ISBN 978-981-4517-97-3 (soft cover)
ISBN 978-981-4517-98-0 (E-book PDF)

Typeset by International Typesetters Pte Ltd
Printed in Singapore by Markono Print Media Pte Ltd

CONTENTS

LIST OF TABLES AND FIGURES

Tables

Figures

ACKNOWLEDGMENTS

In 2005, the Gender Studies Programme at the Institute of Southeast Asian Studies was established. Since 2009, greater focus was granted to two areas: women's roles in politics, and the social vulnerabilities and impacts felt by specific women groups such as chronically poor women, low-skilled migrant women, sex workers, older women, trafficked women, and internally displaced and refugee women.

Well into its fifth year since its establishment, the programme had seen a series of international conferences, fora, and symposia organized, focusing on a range of topics related to gender such as gender trends in the Southeast Asian region, women and mobility, women's rights, women and politics, and legislative protections for women in marriage. These events were organized with funding from the Konrad Ardenauer Stiftung (KAS). The support the programme had received from KAS throughout these years is a testament to its commitment to the study of women's experiences, interests, and concerns in the Southeast Asian region.

In 2009, the workshop focused on older men and women in Southeast Asia. The topic was selected since ageing has become an issue of immense concern to governments, communities, and families given the growing proportions of older persons in an increasing number of countries in the region. In addition to the workshop, KAS has provided for additional funding for an edited volume to be prepared based on the papers presented at the workshop.

This book is the result of a collective effort of several individuals. As editor of this volume, I would like to thank all the paper contributors for their thoughtful and significant contributions to the research, debates, and discussions around how ageing in the region of Southeast Asia is mediated by gender. All the paper contributors are "experts" on the topic of ageing in the respective countries in which each has had years of experience researching, studying, and investigating the topic. In particular, I am grateful for their commitment to bringing this book project to fruition.

Instead of sending out the entire manuscript for review, as it is the norm for most books, as editor, I decided that each paper in this volume be sent out to country experts working on gender or ageing so that each author receives relevant and appropriate comments and suggestions on their work. Several academics were called upon as anonymous reviewers to undertake this task of reviewing the initial drafts of the respective chapters in this volume, and I also wish to thank each one of them for their willingness to take up the task. There were also academics who had agreed to be discussants at the workshop, and it is in the spirit of gratitude that I would like to acknowledge their input in the ensuing discussions that emerged during the workshop.

Last, I would like to thank the Institute for the opportunity to pursue my interests in gender studies, in particular, Ambassador K. Kesavapany, who encouraged the setting up of the programme, without whom this volume would not have been produced. I would also like to recognize the logistical support provided by Ms May Wong in ensuring that the workshop ran smoothly. In addition, I would like to acknowledge the United Nations Population Fund (UNFPA) for providing funding to the participant at the workshop from Thailand.

Several other individuals have been instrumental in bringing this book to a completion. I wish to acknowledge the assistance of Govind Kurusamy who painstakingly edited and proofread the final manuscript in the weeks leading up to the appearance of the book; Mitchelle Waaras for her editorial input on initial drafts of two chapters; and Bina Gubhaju and Bhakta Gubhaju for checking the tables and figures. Finally, this book could not have come about without Mrs Triena Ong, the previous Managing Editor of ISEAS, who not only took interest in the topic of the book but did everything in her capacity to ensure a speedy appearance of this volume, and Sheryl Sin for her effort in editing the final draft of the book manuscript.

Since the volume includes chapters on most of the countries in Southeast Asia, it could be said to some extent that this book represents a "bible" of gender and ageing in the region. It is my hope that the volume will be of value especially to policy-makers from the countries in the region since research is important to help governments put in place relevant policies to meet the needs of the elderly and to prepare themselves to cope with the increasing dependency ratio of the older persons on the working age population as well as pressures on the public pension system.

Theresa W. Devasahayam
December 2013

CONTRIBUTORS

Theresa W. Devasahayam, Fellow and Researcher-in-charge, Gender Studies, Institute of Southeast Asian Studies

John Knodel, Professor Emeritus, Population Studies Center, University of Michigan and International Staff, College of Population Studies, Chulalongkorn University

Napaporn Chayovan, Associate Professor, College of Population Studies, Chulalongkorn University

Zachary Zimmer, Professor, UCSF School of Nursing, Department of Social and Behavioral Sciences, University of California, San Francisco

Vipan Prachuabmoh, Associate Professor, College of Population Studies, Chulalongkorn University

Bussarawan Teerawichitchainan, Assistant Professor of Sociology, Singapore Management University

Philip Kreager, Senior Research Fellow in Human Sciences, Somerville College and Institute of Population Ageing, Oxford University

Elisabeth Schröder-Butterfill, Lecturer in Gerontology, Centre for Research on Ageing, University of Southampton

Ling How Kee, Director, Centre of Excellence for Disability Studies, Faculty of Social Sciences, Universiti Malaysia Sarawak

Leng Leng Thang, Associate Professor, Department of Japanese Studies, National University of Singapore

Kalyani K. Mehta, Associate Professor, Head, Gerontology Programme, School of Human Development and Social Services, SIM University

Aris Ananta, Senior Research Fellow, Institute of Southeast Asian Studies

Tey Nai Peng, Associate Professor, Department of Applied Statistics, Faculty of Economics and Administration, University of Malaya

Tengku Aizan Tengku Hamid, Director, Institute of Gerontology, Universiti Putra Malaysia

Grace T. Cruz, Professor of Demography, Population Institute, College of Social Sciences and Philosophy, University of the Philippines

Anna Melissa C. Lavares, Member, Demographic Research and Development Foundation

Maria Paz N. Marquez, Associate Professor, Philippine Studies, College of Social Sciences and Philosophy, University of the Philippines

Josefina N. Natividad, Professor of Demography, Population Institute, College of Social Sciences and Philosophy, University of the Philippines

Yasuhiko Saito, Professor, Human Development Science, Nihon University

1

GROWING OLD IN SOUTHEAST ASIA: WHAT DO WE KNOW ABOUT GENDER?

Theresa W. Devasahayam

INTRODUCTION

The world has undergone significant demographic shifts since the second half of the twentieth century. Fertility rates have declined significantly — principally because women have gained greater educational levels — and for many of these women, marriage no longer promises the benefits it once did to earlier generations (Bongaarts 1999; Castles 2003; Jones 2003, 2004, 2007, 2009*b*; Kim 2005). For this reason, marriages are occurring at a later age as young women have found more reasons to resist or at least postpone this rite of passage (Jones 2003, 2004, 2009*a*). Another staggering demographic shift has been demonstrated by the ageing of populations with a doubling in average life expectancy compared with figures from the last century (Kinsella 2009). While these demographic trends have enormous repercussions on the economies of countries, older persons, in particular, have been labelled as a "burden" by governments since they are seen to place hefty demands on healthcare and social security systems and, in turn, to exert higher pressures on the productive population (Mujahid 2006; Mehta 1997*a*). Apart from the economic implications of this trend, the impact of population ageing on national security and the sustainability of families has also been flagged as critical concerns deserving of attention (Jackson and Howe 2008; Kinsella 2009).

One thing for certain is that the perception of older women and men has not been the same in the discourse on ageing populations. The social construction of ageing is distinctly gendered in that men and women have been found to experience life differently in their older age in part because of their gender. First, women have an obvious "demographic advantage" in that they live longer than men. This phenomenon which continues across the life course into old age has led to the coining of the phrase 'feminization of ageing' which suggests that there are greater proportions of older women than men (Kinsella 2009; Gist and Velkoff 1997). Whether experiencing a longer life expectancy is necessarily an advantage to women, however, is far more nuanced since larger proportions of them compared with older men tend to live greater number of years in disability. Owing to their shorter healthy life expectancy and higher survival rates compared with men, this demographic trend in fact serves to reinforce the statement: "women get sick; men die". In this case, this demographic advantage of older women may instead be regarded as a "disadvantage" because their need for formal and informal care increases (Henrard 1996) at an older age, and it is at this time that their health condition becomes burdensome to them (and not to mention the state), especially if healthcare costs are beyond the reach of the individual. However, with greater emancipation as women gain an education and become engaged in wage work, especially as countries become more developed, increasing numbers of women have been able to demand for and afford better healthcare, and in some cases putting themselves on equal par with men, and thereby decreasing the number of years they would spend in disability (Barford, Dorling and Smith 2006).

Second, men and women tend to experience ageing differently in the area of caring. In this regard, older women become caregivers to their husbands while the reverse occurs less often. In the United States, Arber and Ginn (1993) have found that disabled older men on average receive about two-thirds of their personal and domestic care from their own wives while women in a similar situation receive a little more than a quarter of their personal care from their husbands. This is to be expected for two key reasons. First, women tend to marry men who are older than themselves and as their husbands grow older, women invariably take on the role of elder caregivers. Second, this trend of women being primary caregivers of their husbands in old age shows up because of cultural norms. In fact, cultural norms demand women to be the primary caregivers throughout their life course, while men are ascribed the role of breadwinners in the family. In this case, caregiving is bound up with the feminine identity regarded to be at the centre of women's experience of "self". Hence, it is of no surprise that in a study in the United States, it was found that the typical caregiver was a woman providing more than 20 hours of care a week towards an ageing relative (Schumacher, Beck and Marren 2006), and should the role become more intense, it is always the woman who becomes the primary caregiver (OECD 2011). While caregiving may be regarded as a rewarding experience, it may also have a profound negative effect on the woman who becomes the caregiver, potentially affecting her mental health (OECD 2011).

Third, larger proportions of older women are more likely to be "dependent on others" — whether it be spouses, families or the state — more than older men since they would not have worked or would have had interrupted careers as a result of having to provide care towards their families. In this case, being dependent on others has been interpreted as a disadvantage and, in turn, construed as a vulnerability since it signals the lack of savings and the inability to be self-sufficient. Moreover, as a result of not having been engaged in formal employment because of having to provide care towards their own families as well as receiving lower wages compared with men, older women are more likely than older men to slip into poverty or near poverty (Arber and Ginn 1991; Barusch 1994) — a problem that is exacerbated among unmarried as well as divorced women (Gist and Velkoff 1997; Yin 2008). That older women are financially worse off than older men was also found to be the case in Sweden in spite of its well-developed social welfare system. Here, older women were found to be struggling in meeting their basic needs since the country's social security system privileges those who have had stable, long-term labour force engagement, which automatically disadvantages women since many would have spent either fewer years in the labour force compared with men or, for that matter, may not have worked at all because of their caregiving duties (Gummarsson 2002).

Fourth, because there are many more married women who outlive their husbands and survive into old age, the numbers of older women who are more likely to be widowed supersedes that of men (Gist and Velkoff 1997). Nevertheless, among women and men who have survived thus far, their experience of widowhood differs to a significant degree. Widowhood, in fact, has been construed to work to the advantage of women more than men. Among older women, there has been research showing how old age has actually brought on a new sense of autonomy and freedom. Among those who may have been playing the reproductive role during their marriage, many may continue this role into old age as they end up providing care for their own grandchildren after the demise of their husbands (Teo and Mehta 2001). Unless beset by physical impairments, older women lead much stronger "linked lives" in that they are more socially bonded with kin, friends, and neighbours because of the social roles they would have played in various events throughout their life course (Lopata and Levy 2003, p. 4). In contrast, older men have been found to suffer from increasing social disadvantage and isolation compared with older women as they lack strong ties with family members and friends. Others have observed a similar pattern. Chappell (1989), for example, based on research in the United States, discovered that older women have more expressive and supportive bonds and are more intimately connected with others, unlike men who turn to their wives for similar support. Furthermore, older men are unable to turn to wider sources of social support should such support become unavailable from their own family members (Seale and Charteris-Black 2008). In this regard, divorced and never married older men tend to experience greater social isolation than older women of the same marital status. Among them, living alone has the cumulative effect of leading to loneliness, with never married men experiencing the highest levels of loneliness while never married women experiencing the lowest levels of loneliness. Moreover, older men more than older women are more likely to suffer from depression on the demise of their spouses (Victor et al. 2002).

It is clear then from the above selected litany of characteristics differentiating men and women that the experience of ageing is varied across the sexes. Focusing on differentials — both real and potential — between older men and women, feminists have long argued that older women are doubly disadvantaged compared with older men (Arber and Ginn 1995); in a nutshell, they contend that the disadvantages faced by older women are intrinsically entwined with the experiences they have had throughout their life course, whether in the family, education, health, and politics, which further compound their vulnerability to poverty, social deprivation, and poor health in old age (see also Gist and Velkoff 1997; Browne 1998). In other words, the disadvantages older women face are linked to structural and socio-cultural factors which had marginalized them earlier on in life and which then become further pronounced in old age. While this argument may to some degree be compelling, a more nuanced and accurate insight is that older women need not always and in all circumstances be disadvantaged; on the contrary, older men have been found to be disadvantaged in some situations. Thus while we may be taken in by "the images conjured up of ageing woman [as] more derogatory than those of ageing man ... [a] contrast ... due to an equally pervasive sexism", in reality, "older people of both sexes are victims ..." (Jefferys 1996, p. 684). In this case, a more balanced perspective that accommodates both older men's and women's varying vulnerabilities has been proposed, leading some scholars to conclude instead that gender should be treated as a potential rather than a central marker of vulnerability for both older men and women (Knodel and Ofstedal 2003).

Following this conceptual lead, the chapters in this book aim to advance our understanding of the differences between how men and women in Southeast Asia have come to experience ageing. Related to this, the book also aims to uncover if these experiences are unique to older men and women from the region or if similar patterns have been found among older persons in other parts of the world. In other words, are there "cultural scripts" (Mehta 1997b) or "cultural spaces" (Long 2005) particular to this region which would have dictated the ageing trends among both men and women (as cited in Sokolovsky 2009, p. xxiii)?

Focusing the analytical lens on Southeast Asia in an attempt to understand the link between gender and ageing makes for an interesting and important exercise since the region, unlike the rest of Asia or, for that matter, other parts of the world, is marked by a significant measure of gender egalitarianism as expressed in a number of arenas. It has been argued that *adat* (Malay; tradition) and kinship organization have actively formulated the position of women through men in non-hierarchical ways (Wazir Jahan Karim 1992). For example among the indigenous populations, kinship systems found operating in this region are mainly bilateral or matrilineal, with the exception of the northern reaches of Vietnam (Dube 1997) and small pockets of ethnic groups in the Indonesian archipelago where the patrilineal kinship system instead dominates. Moreover, women's position in their families and communities in this region is unlike their counterparts in the rest of Asia. While they may be "dutiful daughters" and "devoted wives", Southeast Asian women enjoy an autonomy, like no other women from the rest of Asia (Atkinson and Errington 1990; Stoler 1977; Strange 1981; Wolf 1990, 1992). For example, unlike in South Asia where the route to remarriage is closed completely to a woman who has lost her husband through death since widowhood is associated with inauspiciousness, widows from Southeast

Asia do not suffer the same plight. A case in point is widow remarriage in Indonesia where women are encouraged to remarry, not necessarily in conformity to the "heterosexual patriarchal family", as argued elsewhere (Wieringa 2012, p. 519), but rather so that they do not become vulnerable to neglect and abandonment. In Kelantan, young widows usually remarried and with ease and no loss of status, while older women seldom remarried because they tended to be less sought after (Douglas Raybeck, personal communication, 20 February 2013). Even in Vietnam, widows are allowed to remarry although it is considered virtuous if they chose to remain faithful to their deceased husbands (O'Harrow 1985).

That men turn over their earnings to their wives who control the household budget is another arena in which Southeast Asian women's autonomy and decision-making power are demonstrated (Li 1989; Sullivan 1994; Swift 1965). In fact, a woman's authority rises with age such that it is not uncommon to find an older woman "slough[ing] off disagreeable chores on daughters or daughters-in-law ... [to] mark ... their increasing authority within the household" (Carsten 1997, p. 78). Moreover in marriage, maternal kin play an important role in the conjugal life of a newly-wed couple as exemplified by the fact that on marriage a couple usually chooses to stay with the bride's kin for a few years until they set up their own household (Jamilah Ariffin 1992; Medina 2001). Daughters, in fact, are held in high regard and never seen to be a financial burden. In matters of property relations, women also enjoy a distinct advantage, especially according to *adat* (Stivens 1996).

In addition, women's autonomy and power are not restricted to the private domain. In Southeast Asia, women exert a strong presence in village markets as entrepreneurs and their earnings have been critical to the maintenance of the family (Alexander and Alexander 2001). In fact among Kelantanese women of Peninsular Malaysia, Raybeck (1980/1981, p. 10) maintains that it is the "middle-aged married woman [who] is usually a more active participant in the economic and social life of the village than is her husband". In embracing economic responsibilities, these women come to assert more strength and assertiveness — traits which become heightened among middle-aged or older women, markedly separating this group from the younger women (Raybeck 1985; Carsten 1997). That widows are not barred from engaging in economic activities is also a testimony to the position they hold in wider society. In Indonesia for example, Wieringa (2012, p. 522) points out how "working outside the house affords them a measure of social respect because they are seen as responsible parents". Moreover, women play prominent roles in indigenous religious rituals as shamans who engage in exorcism, spiritual healing, agricultural magic, and so forth as much as men (Hay 2005). The power these women wield is also demonstrated in their skills in managing ceremonial feasts, and the organization of labour and credit societies as well.

But while women in the region do enjoy a fair amount of power in comparison to their sisters in other parts of the world, this does not mean that there is an absence of overt and covert manifestations of patriarchy (Mazidah Zakaria and Nik Safiah Karim 1986; Ong 1987). In recent times, the region has seen the emergence of fundamentalisms, particularly religious fundamentalisms as exemplified in conservative Islamic teachings. Moreover, it cannot be denied that women continue to face obstacles in entering some spheres in the public domain — a case in point being that of politics (Raybeck 1980/1981). In this case, women's lack of social networks and the unfair practices they encounter which exclude them, as well as religious traditions that reinscribe gender inequality through their teachings serve to tip the balance in favour of men.

Furthermore, gender inequality has been found in other arenas such as in the labour markets driven by neoliberalism. As in many parts of the world, the countries in Southeast Asia have not been shielded from global economic forces. According to AT Kearney, six cities in Southeast Asia — Singapore, Bangkok, Kuala Lumpur, Manila, Jakarta and Ho Chi Minh City — are now among the 66 most globalized cities in the world (AT Kearney 2012). Moreover, the region has long been recognized as a fast developing region in the world accompanied by impressive economic growth indicators. Strong levels of growth have been attributed to high savings rates, the creation of human capital, market reforms, the role of state intervention, cultural ideologies namely the Confucianist ethic, and the emergence of labour-intensive export manufacturing industries (Kaur 2004).

Given that Southeast Asia has undergone immense economic and social changes in recent decades as a result of globalization, it becomes necessary to examine the experience of ageing in light of how global forces have shaped everyday lives. Young women and men have increasingly been drawn away from farm work into the non-farm sectors. Opting to work abroad through labour migration has become part of the narrative of globalization in many places. But large numbers of young women, in particular, have found themselves in low-skilled occupations more than their male counterparts because of possessing lower literacy levels and fewer job-related skills. Moreover, that gender stereotyping continues to persist in the labour sector begs the question of whether wage work presents a site of empowerment for women (Salih and Young 1991 as cited in Elson 1999). For example, upward mobility in the wage work sector has not always been in women's favour (see Elson 1999 for specific examples from South Asia). In fact, often women end up in low-skilled, feminized sectors such as domestic work, nursing and other forms of care work, factory work, sex work, and the service and entertainment industries — sectors that do not pay as much as others dominated by men (Brooks and Devasahayam 2011; Resurrection 2009). That women end up in low-skilled employment sectors that pay much less than low-skilled jobs undertaken by men also suggests that they would have fewer resources when they reach old age. Furthermore, women are more likely than men to be retrenched in times of economic downturn.

Against this backdrop, the book is concerned with the following questions related to gender and ageing in Southeast Asia. These questions include: (a) how do women and men experience old age? (b) do women and men have different means of coping financially and socially in their old age? (c) does having engaged in wage work for longer periods of time serve as an advantage to older men in contrast to older women? (d) does women's primary role as caregiver disadvantage her in old age? (e) what kinds of identities have older women and men constructed for themselves? (f) do women and men prepare for ageing differently and has this been mediated by educational levels? Related to this, does having a higher education make a difference in how one experiences ageing? (g) how does class shape how women and men cope in old age? and (h) what does it mean to be a "single" older person who has lost a spouse through death or has never been married?

In exploring answers to these questions, the chapters in this book, which employ either quantitative or qualitative methods of data collection and analysis, provide interesting insights into how ageing, as experienced by men and women in Southeast Asia, has become tempered by globalization, cultural values, family structures, women's emancipation and empowerment, social networks, government policies, and religion. This compendium is insightful in yet another way since the chapters approach the ageing experience across the sexes from a comparative perspective. Adopting a comparative perspective is useful in two aspects. First, by employing a cross-country analysis, highlighting common themes related to gender and ageing in the different countries in the region, readers gain an understanding of the emergent trends not only in each of the countries but also in Southeast Asia as a whole. Second, the countries in the region of Southeast Asia are analysed in juxtaposition to countries in other regions with the intent of facilitating an understanding of whether the trends in Southeast Asia are similar or dissimilar to the broader trends of gender and ageing found in the rest of the world. To this end, an underlying assumption in this book is that the emergent trends related to gender and ageing in the selected countries chosen for analysis need not necessarily be unique to the region, especially when similar trends have been found in other parts of the world.

MAPPING OUT THE CHAPTERS

Sociologists have long been concerned with class inequalities in educational attainment, especially the failure of working-class children in obtaining education (Haveman and Smeeding 2006). The assumption here is that should education be available across the different classes, it would have the potential of breaking down social inequalities. Feminist research, in contrast, has been concerned with looking at how schooling has perpetuated gender inequalities, for example, how girls end up studying certain subjects while boys read others and how the educational system privileges boys while disadvantaging girls (Abbott, Wallace and Tyler 2005). Whatever the gender gap, one distinct difference in the area of education between the sexes has emerged across the world, that is, that men outnumber women in terms of having received schooling although this trend has gradually reversed especially among the current generations in some developed and developing countries. The gender gap in education in favour of boys over girls, which has been consistently found in many parts of the world, has bolstered the argument that having lower levels of education has been a factor of vulnerability for women, which has a cumulative effect in old age, compared with men who have higher levels of education. As in other parts of the world, Southeast Asia has seen fairly consistent trends in this regard as generally more men than women have attained an education. This trend persists despite the fact that a greater degree of gender equality exists in this part of the world compared with others. In fact, it is normative in the rural areas to think of marriage and motherhood as the destiny for girls. For some Muslim communities, it is unlikely that women will engage in paid employment after marriage and therefore an education may not be highly valued for girls. In part, cultural norms in this case could be used to explain the gender gap in education between older men and women in Southeast Asia.

In Thailand, for example, John Knodel and Napaporn Chayovan in their chapter show that higher percentages of older women than older men have no more than a primary education and a lower percentage have upper secondary or higher education. But this trend only applies to the present cohort of older persons. The authors note that changes in this trend are imminent especially based on projected figures for the next 35 years because of greater numbers of Thai women currently receiving an education — a trend which is expected to occur as countries gain greater momentum in terms of development, coupled with greater numbers of women joining the labour force. Aside from Thailand, other countries in the region also display similar gaps in education. While current cohorts of older persons have lower educational attainment compared to future older cohorts, Aris Ananta shows that in Indonesia, more men than women have been found to have higher educational qualifications — a trend he asserts will continue into the future generation. Surprisingly, a gender gap in education is also evident in the Philippines, as pointed out by Josefina N. Natividad, Yasuhiko Saito and Grace T. Cruz. What is striking about the Philippines is that the difference in educational profile between the sexes is not as pronounced as for the older cohorts in the rest of Southeast Asia. In terms of education, Cambodia represents the outlier in this regard. John Knodel and Zachary Zimmer note that a large majority of elderly men and women have not had formal schooling, affecting literacy levels. Yet among the young old (age 60–64), 84 per cent of men were found to be literate as compared with 29 per cent of women. One probable explanation for this gender gap was that men would have spent some time as monks and as a consequence learnt to read and write.

Beyond these numbers, what would be more important is to ask what then are the implications of the gender gap in education among current and future cohorts of the elderly? In this case, does education empower or translate into empowerment for women? Since education determines labour market outcomes as it enables the individual to attain the desired skills, among older women who have either had lower levels of education or no education compared with their male counterparts, their ability to compete in the labour market diminishes considerably. Moreover, women (and men) benefit from an education since it ensures greater earnings within an occupation which translates into savings and, in turn, becomes critical especially for old-age survival. In this regard, Vipan Prachuabmoh effectively demonstrates in her chapter the extent to which educational levels correlate with preparations for old age in Thailand and, in particular, how having lower levels of education among women puts them at higher risk of not being prepared for old age and how higher levels of education improves their chances in this regard. Among the present cohorts of older persons age 60 and above, she shows how males are more likely than females to have made some old age preparation. The areas in which they would have undertaken some form of preparation concern their physical health, living arrangement, financial security, and arrangement for a caregiver. If women make preparations for old age, however, they tend to be restricted in looking out for their mental health only. Among the near and far away future elderly cohorts (age 18–59), a surprising (or not so surprising) trend has been found in that greater numbers of these women have been found to have made preparations for old age. But this stronger inclination to prepare for old age is bound up with higher levels of education among younger women. In fact, Thailand represents an outstanding example of a country in the region in which girls have been found to be "overachievers" in the education system (Devasahayam 2005). While this may give rise to a "moral panic" in wider Thai society as well as among policy-makers as women's educational success may be seen to challenge male hegemony, for this cohort of future elderly, according to Prachuabmoh's analysis, attaining higher education clearly has its positive outcomes. In comparison with the present cohort of older women, she finds that the future cohort shows a marked difference in their efforts to prepare for old age particularly in terms of financial security and physical health, in addition to their mental health. It may be concluded, thus, that higher levels of education among young females compared to their male counterparts would eventually lead to higher levels of old age preparation among the future generations of older Thai women.

Along the same lines, Bussarawan Teerawichitchainan's chapter highlights the link between levels of education although this time with health outcomes in old age. In contrast to Prabchuabmoh's discussion, Teerawichitchainan's analysis points to how lower levels of education among Vietnamese women have severely disadvantaged them as they have been found to be in poorer health. In fact in Vietnam, a distinct gender gap has been found with half of older women age 60 and above being illiterate and slightly over one-third having had only some primary education, while only about one-fifth had completed primary education.

In contrast among older Vietnamese men, an overwhelming majority have had at least completed basic education evinced by a quarter having finished primary schooling and one-third having some secondary education. Since the cohort of older men has received an education more than their female counterparts, the former is better informed about health-related issues. Moreover, having an education also relates to being economically more well-off compared to those with minimal or no education and, in this case, the Vietnamese men who have had an education would be in a better position to access healthcare and, in turn, enjoy a more improved health status compared with women. In fact, in assessing self-reported health status, Teerawichitchainan found that, more than gender, having had higher levels of education and being financially more solvent have a greater impact on health since these factors lead individuals to be more optimistic about their health status. What in fact her chapter does is to highlight a more nuanced discussion of health disparities based on subjective and objective measures of health. She found that the difference in health disparities that showed up between men and women was a result of a discrepancy between the subjective and objective measures of health rather than an actual difference in health status between the sexes — a trend which has been documented elsewhere in that elderly women were found to assess their own health less positively than older men (Arber and Ginn 1993; Verburgge 1985). Moreover, among the more well-off who have access to economic resources, they are more likely to have greater access to healthcare and, in turn, are more equipped to provide accurate reporting about their health status.

Undoubtedly, Southeast Asia has seen gender gaps closing in the areas of education and health in recent decades, as women gain a stronger foothold in various job sectors, and improve their access to economic resources because of having received an education compared with the earlier generations. Concomitantly, family structures have been changing rapidly resulting from the transformations in women's lives. In spite of fertility rates plummeting and marriage patterns changing as younger people seek to marry later or to abandon the idea of marriage completely (Jones 2003, 2004, 2007, 2009b), a point raised earlier, yet for the majority, marriage remains the norm. But in spite of women taking on the role of financially contributing towards the household through their engagement in wage work, the dominant pattern in Southeast Asian families, as in many other parts of the world, is that women are ascribed the primary role of caregiver and nurturer while men the breadwinner role (Devasahayam and Yeoh 2007). This trend continues into old age when women continue to play the role of caregiver, however, this time to their own spouses. In Thailand, John Knodel and Napaporn Chayovan find that more than half of the men reported that their spouses were their caregivers compared to only 12 per cent of women. Nonetheless, 45 per cent of women residing with their husbands indicated that husbands are their main caregiver. Evidence from Sarawak by Ling How Kee in her chapter shows a similar trend with women more likely to end up playing the role as caregiver whether to their spouses or other men in both formal and informal systems of care. Support initiatives directed by the state or provided by non-governmental organizations to complement and bolster the role of the family as informal carer, however, are almost non-existent. In this case, the family is left with three choices: a woman in the family takes on the primary role of elder caregiver, or she could shift the burden of caregiving to a hired domestic worker, or as a last resort, the family admits the older person to a residential home. The first two scenarios, however, are the most esteemed options, exemplifying the paramount role women play in the organization of care towards an older person while the latter is less popular since it suggests abandonment and neglect.

In fact, in a region where daughters are valued, it is of no surprise that receiving care provided by daughters tends to be the preferred option when children are relied upon for help. John Knodel and Zachary Zimmer find that in Cambodia, daughters play a paramount role in care provision both for older men and women whether currently married or not. Philip Kraeger and Elisabeth Schröder-Butterfill raise a similar point when they describe the preference for the support of daughters among the elderly in Indonesia. While this may be the case across Indonesia, this preference is heightened among the Minangkabau, a matrilineal kinship group from Sumatra, since they look to daughters to take care of the management and continuity of the ancestral property. Among them, therefore, the absence of a daughter through *merantau* (Indonesian; to go abroad) causes anxiety among the elderly. In the case of Sarawakian Chinese, Ling How Kee in her chapter highlights how there are many instances in her research where she has found married daughters returning home or receiving parents into their matrimonial homes to provide respite care for their parents. Yet the role of sons cannot be underestimated, as discussed by Tey Nai Peng and Tengku Aizan Tengku Hamid in their chapter. They show that in Malaysia, sons tend to be the main source of financial support to older persons more than daughters. The vital role of daughters in eldercare has also been documented in other parts of the world aside from Southeast Asia. In the United States, it was found that women more than men expect that their daughters will come to their aid, while daughters have been found to willingly respond to the needs of their mothers (Hogan and Eggebeen 1995). In another study in Belgium, female family members ranging from wives, daughters, and sisters each played a different yet critical role in caregiving of various forms including care provided towards an aged person. In a nutshell, women are "the glue holding social relations together" at every stage of the life course (Bracke, Christiaens and Wauterickx 2008, p. 1348). In a study of three urban locales in China, it was found that daughters provided a higher level of support towards their parents compared with sons, especially if these women had personal resources. These women also chose to coreside with their parents instead of with their husbands' parents, defying patrilineal kinship rules (Xie and Zhu 2006).

As in East Asia, coresidence with adult children is not unheard of in Southeast Asia where it is "often seen as an assurance of care", as Ling How Kee mentions, since adult daughters or sons continue to form an important source of physical care for the elderly. There are two sides to the coin, however, on this issue. While children play an immensely important role in eldercare by ensuring that the material, financial, psychological, and emotional needs of the older person are met, coresidence may also benefit children as they have been found to capitalize on this living arrangement as an economic strategy for survival. An example of this living arrangement was noted by Grace T. Cruz and others who found that in the Philippines, children coreside with the older person rather than the other way around since it is the older person who owns the house and not the children. Having said that, it was found that childlessness was perceived to be a source of anxiety among both older men and women. Philip Kraeger and Elisabeth Schröder-Butterfill present a fascinating example of a childless man from Java whose vulnerability became heightened as a result of not having a spouse or children to care for him. The authors, however, make the interesting point that his vulnerability through the lack of a child to provide care to him is enmeshed with poverty and failed marriages rather than gender identity alone.

Aside from highlighting that women play an integral role as caregivers of the elderly, much of the broader literature on ageing is fixated on showing how women become disadvantaged in old age because of lacking a caregiver in spite of providing care to others for most of their lives. In fact the norm is that more men than women end up citing their spouse as the main caregiver, as it is in the case of Thailand. But it must be emphasized that this trend occurs because of widowhood rather than for reasons of gender alone. For example in Thailand, John Knodel and Napaporn Chayovan show that because women have longer longevity than men — a pattern found around the world as well — living alone is more common among older women than older men while older men are more likely to live only with a spouse than are older women. On whether the absence of a spouse serves to heighten the vulnerability of women, based on the data from Cambodia, John Knodel and Zachary Zimmer unravelled an interesting finding in that widows need not necessarily be disadvantaged, as might be assumed. In fact, they found that those not currently married are more likely to report receiving help and not receiving help but needing it as well as not receiving enough of it compared with those who are married. Among them, men (57 per cent) are more likely to be found in this unfavourable situation compared with women (34 per cent), suggesting that it is the married state rather than gender that bears advantages as men would have sought help from their own spouses should they not have been left widowed (Yin 2008). In the same vein, Teerawichitchainan finds that in Vietnam, regardless of sex, the data highlights that it is the married state that provides a protective cover for older men or women, this time of the older person's health and well-being; in this case, those who are married are more likely to be more positive about their health.

But while living alone may be more common for older women, they need not necessarily be more vulnerable as a result, as mentioned earlier. In fact, based on the rich case studies presented in this volume, women have been found to have stronger social networks which have helped them cope with loneliness, a point which was also raised by others (Allan 1985; Jerrome 1996). Thang Leng Leng argues that while older women in Singapore may fare less positively compared to older men in some respects, the situation may be reversed when it comes to their social well-being. Based on rich data collected from older persons living in low-income, one-room rental apartments in Singapore, she discovered that the older women had more contact with their kin and fictive kin compared with the older men. Among these women, she found that if contact with children was limited, they would instead have maintained considerable contact with their own siblings or whosoever they recognized as good friends. It was the strength of women, such as in social networking with others, which helped them overcome some of their vulnerabilities and enhanced their well-being. In a cultural context dominated by women, Philip Kraeger and Elisabeth Schröder-Butterfill speak to the vulnerability experienced by Indonesian men because of their inability to build social networks. They emphasize that differences in elderly support depend largely on the values and demands of network members. In her chapter on Singapore, Kalyani Mehta also points out that while social support is important for both widows and widowers, she found that the widows she interviewed had stronger support networks and experienced lower levels of emotional and social isolation compared with the widowers in her sample. Hence, she says that while widows are financially "worse off" than widowers, they tend to be "socially" better off than their male counterparts. Such a finding is not unique to Singapore or the region. In the United States, Krekula (2007) found that older women not only had stronger social networks, but also had varying interests compared with older men and, therefore, were able to assert their competence and independence, thereby providing a buffer against loneliness and social isolation. In Southeast Asia, as in the United States, it was primarily children who were the main source of support for the elderly, with widows having greater contact with their children compared with widowers (Ha et al. 2006). This idea is also echoed by Ling How Kee who asserts that women are "accorded a special social position in the family and [in turn] receive reciprocity of support from their children".

For this reason, being financially "worse off" than older men was not necessarily found to be a liability among older women. In the case of Singapore, Thang Leng Leng in her chapter remarks that the same individuals who maintained a more active kin network have also been found to be able to protect themselves against financial hardships. Interestingly, the reverse is also true: because women rely more heavily on children's contributions as a source of income, it is of no surprise that they are more likely than men to be in frequent contact with at least one child. In contrast, John Knodel and Zachary Zimmer found that there was little difference between older men and women in Cambodia in terms of social contact with and material support from children. Besides, very few older persons seem to be deserted by their families. But as the authors point out, these variations may be because of the fact that many older people in Cambodia would have lived difficult lives, having faced harsh circumstances related to war and poverty, and thus older persons irrespective of gender have shown to be equally dependent on the younger generation. But if they are unable to receive support from a child, some older persons have been found to turn to government agencies, as Kalyani Mehta describes in the case of Singapore — a country in the region which underwent the fastest growth, in the proportion of older persons in relation to the larger population, at an unprecedented rate of 4.2 per cent in 1975–2000 (Mujahid 2006). Most of these individuals turn to welfare only because their own children have been struggling financially and have been unable to help. The element of "shame" in this sense has prevented many from seeking help, therefore putting older women more than men at risk of slipping into poverty. In contrast in Indonesia, because children are a significant source of income, childless older persons are particularly vulnerable such that alternative strategies to ensure income protection become imperative for survival. In rural Java, for example, childless couples have resorted to adoption depending on their own socio-economic position and employment through continued patronage and kin support, as well as the charitable support they receive from neighbours, distant kin, and religious institutions (Schröder-Butterfill and Kraeger 2005).

It would seem then that across Southeast Asia, older women are more likely to be dependent on others for survival compared with older men. In this regard, it could be said instead that there are degrees of dependence mediated by the educational level of the elderly person. Ha and her colleagues (2006) found that widows in the United States depended on their children for financial or legal advice and instrumental support although the more educated the widow, the less likely she would be dependent on her children. On this, Kalyani Mehta found in her study in Singapore that older women were more "forthcoming in requesting for help than men", while widowers were less likely to rely on others for financial help because of the fear of being regarded as a failure. Here, the old age cohort of the widows she studied comprised an earlier generation in which not many women would have had high levels of education. Thus, we can expect that current cohorts of women are more likely to mimic their counterparts elsewhere in that they would be less dependent on kin support should they reach old age themselves.

That current cohorts of older women have been found to be dependent on others was revealed in another context. As economies become more integrated as a result of globalization, seeking wage work in the more urban areas of the country or even abroad has increasingly become the norm with growing numbers of younger women (Yeoh, Huang and Gonzalez III 1999; Brooks and Devasahayam 2011; Yamanaka and Piper 2005). Considering households in which there are members employed abroad as overseas contract workers, findings from the Philippines by Grace T. Cruz and others show that about one-fifth of these households receive remittances from children working abroad, with significantly more married older people receiving funds from children overseas and with considerably more older women than men considering these remittances from children abroad as their most important source of income.

Another interesting gendered pattern emerging in these households is that households with only one grandparent revealed that grandmothers are more likely than grandfathers to live with the grandchild and to play the primary role of caregiver and nurturer, especially in the absence of a parent; in households with both grandparents, the trend continues to be marked by a sexual division of labour in which women more than men take on the role of childrearing, including providing care for grandchildren. Usually older women are more likely to find themselves in a "skipped generation" living arrangement more than older men — a trend in Thailand noted also by John Knodel and Napaporn Chayovan. Ling How Kee also relates a similar trend in Sarawak among single mothers who either leave their children with their rural or urban mothers while they work in the urban areas or if they take on work abroad. In the latter two situations, remittances sent home are for both the young and the old.

In fact, remittances are an important source of income more for older women than older men regardless of marital status among those whose children are working abroad. But clearly these older women are not dependent on the remittances they receive solely for their own survival. Rather, many use the remittances they receive for providing care towards their grandchildren. In this case, migrants working abroad do not remit money for altruistic reasons; instead, the remittance is necessary to ensure that the surrogate caregivers and, in this case, the older woman back home continues to provide care for the children of the migrant worker in his/her absence (cf. Secondi, 1997).[1] In a sense, older women are not only at the receiving end but play an integral role at the giving end by constantly providing care to others. This trend reinforces the point made by Agree and others (2005, p. 191) that: "generalized exchange may be more common in societies with higher poverty levels or where the lack of stable market alternatives makes family and friends the main means by which social and economic support is provided". The term "exchange" in this case is most apt because it portrays older persons as active agents contributing to the relationship rather than only receiving resources.[2] Nevertheless, on the part of children working abroad, the practice of transferring resources is linked to the cultural concept of filial piety since expectations of children providing financial support and care towards their ageing parents continue to be strong in the region (Chow 1997).

While studies have highlighted how dependence on others, whether kin or non-kin, tends to be more common among older women, this pattern has been said to occur because older women are more likely to have fewer resources compared with older men. While this may be the case because of having spent fewer years in the labour force — a factor singled out as the reason for why older women are not as financially secure as older men — that this trend has been recorded across Southeast Asia may be indicative of several conditions: shortage of suitable work for women, lack of necessary educational and skill qualifications, and employer discrimination (Mujahid 2006). For example in Thailand, the 2007 Survey of Older Persons found that among those age 60 or above, 26 per cent of women worked compared with 48 per cent of men. Findings from the Philippines according to Josefina N. Natividad, Yasuhiko Saito, and Grace T. Cruz also show a similar trend in that there is high prevalence of working beyond age 60, higher for men than for women although the odds of working consistently decreases as age increases. Indonesia as a case is also no different. Aris Ananta makes the point that the labour force participation of women is much lower than men. But because the social security system is limited or completely non-existent as to be expected for a developing country, working for an income becomes imperative for them as well as their families' survival. Ananta also raises a fascinating point that the statistics for labour force participation for women are markedly lower compared with men because it has become socially acceptable for women to financially depend on their husbands who are expected to be the "rice winners" in the family. But interestingly, this pattern is found across the age groups, thereby suggesting that women have made a choice in deciding whether or not to work and it is a decision they can more easily make because they have husbands whom they can rely on. Thus among women, prioritizing care provision towards their children and having less savings compared with men — because they have not engaged in wage work — need not necessarily be a disadvantage since they can depend on their spouses financially. Conversely, men are not presented with the same choices: they are forced to work in conformity to social expectations of their breadwinner role and, as such, their numbers are much higher than women's in terms of labour force participation.

But should they have worked and the majority would have had, older men are more likely than older women to access pensions as a source of income while for older women, children are by far the most common main source of income. In Cambodia, John Knodel and Zachary Zimmer document that although men are more likely than women to have worked and therefore have a pension income, on a positive note there is little gender difference taking into account other indicators of material well-being such as housing quality, household possessions, and self-assessed economic situation, although as the authors caution, this needs to be "interpreted within the context of widespread poverty" among both men and women. The Malaysian case shows a stark contrast. Tey Nai Peng and Tengku Aizan Tengku Hamid show that older men were more than twice as likely to receive income from their current job and/or pension payment from previous jobs compared with older women. In this case, older women, who make up the majority of the oldest old, are generally more vulnerable than older men because they lack financial resources and, as a result, are more dependent on children and others. That women have less access compared with men to a state-sponsored pension scheme was also found in other countries in the region. In the Philippines, more males are employed, receive pensions, and earn their subsistence from their own earnings from work and farm and, as a result, are less dependent on their children for economic support, as pointed out by Grace T. Cruz and others. In contrast, greater numbers of older women compared with older men consider support from their children as their most important source of income. Interestingly, while women's dependence on children is associated with economic insecurity, these same women report a better profile in terms of household wealth index and overall subjective self-assessed economic status. In contrast in the Thai case, both children and work are almost equally common as sources of financial support for men, thereby reducing men's vulnerability slightly in contrast to the experience of older women.

PROTECTING THE ELDERLY:
THE ROLE OF POLICIES

The feminist contention is that women are oppressed in many spheres of life — an oppression that has a cumulative effect on them which continues into old age. In this case, "the interplay between age and gender has frequently been characterized as a double jeopardy. The combination of sexism and ageism supposedly makes women's ageing more problematic than men's" (Krekula 2007, p. 161). While undoubtedly women have their share of vulnerabilities in old age as discussed earlier in this chapter, these vulnerabilities need to be assessed within the context of globalization, capitalism, and wage work such that the capitalist workplace tends to generate inequality between the sexes rather than emphasize equality which would have been the case if indigenous gender ideologies were operating. But while this factor may in part explain women's share of vulnerabilities, in other areas, older women have been found to have an edge over older men.

The case studies raised in this volume demonstrate poignantly how Southeast Asian men and women in their experience of ageing might have their respective share of vulnerabilities, and the extent to which each sex might be disadvantaged, although differently from the other depending on the context. For example, in the case of widowers, they are less likely than widows to coreside with a child and, as a result, are compelled to cope with loneliness and are less likely than older women to have the option of depending financially on a child. Among men, weaker social networks have the potential of disadvantaging them as the likelihood of not receiving physical care from kin or friends among them is much greater than for older women. What then would the solutions be for this group of men? Perhaps retirement homes or retirement villages may be a possible option, especially if they are generally able to care for themselves. But that such a solution carries with it a hefty price tag may not necessarily make this the most feasible option especially for developing countries in the region. In any case, the right policies targeted at this group of older men become even more important in ensuring that their specific needs are not overlooked.

Older men have been found to be vulnerable in another respect. While they may be financially better off than older women, often assumed to be an advantage they have over older women, being financially more secure because of receiving a pension or because of savings accumulated over a lifetime as a result of having worked does not necessarily protect older men at all times. Because of strong social expectations placed on them as breadwinners of the family, this role expectation is often carried into old age. In fact, older men are more likely than older women to continue to provide shelter and render financial help to adult children who are yet to move out of the household. While throughout their lives older men might have been financially more solvent compared with older women, ironically older men are also more likely to experience more debt than older women although this difference becomes insignificant when controlling for marital status. The most common types of liabilities older men have include personal loans, followed by loans from moneylenders.

Thus, it is not always the case that they are able to financially care for themselves. In this case, eldercare policies should factor in this concern of older men's. For example in Singapore, while this move may be regarded as draconic, the state has made it legal through the Maintenance of Parents Act for older persons to take up a court case against their children who fail to provide them with support. In this case, the law uses "the rhetoric of filial piety to emphasize the principle of familism ... [In doing so] the bill clearly places financial risks and responsibilities not on the community but solely on the individual, i.e., the older person first and then his or her adult children" (Rozario and Hong 2011, pp. 616, 618). Since the Act came into force in 1996, there have been 1,411 applications for maintenance, and of this number, 1,047 maintenance orders were implemented (Lim 2009). Since then, there has been an increase in the number of applications filed from the usual annual rate of 100 with the bulk of applicants being men of Chinese descent, and single parents who either have been divorced or widowed, suggesting that older men more often than older women face neglect by their own relatives.

In spite of the relatively high status women in this region enjoy, two chief concerns arise relating to how well they are able to cope in older age, namely, the absence of a caregiver and the lack of savings. As for older women in Southeast Asia, as with their sisters across the world, their primary role tends largely to be confined to nurturing, indicating that the male as breadwinner and female as caregiver model continues into old age. But among divorced and widowed women in the Western hemisphere who may have neglected their careers to provide care for their children (Arber 2004), the stronger social links women in Southeast Asia would have developed throughout their lifetime serves as a protective measure for them in old age. While the feminist position is that the family is a site for oppression since housework and the caregiving labour a woman puts in are essentially "hidden labour" and never acknowledged as work (Abbott, Wallace and Tyler 2005, p. 231; cf. Oakley 1974*a*; 1974*b*), paradoxically as a Southeast Asian woman gets older, the labour she had provided in her lifetime to others serves to benefit her as she can now turn to her own children for assistance in her old age. Thus, needing a caregiver in old age need not necessarily be considered a liability since it is considered acceptable for older women to turn to children for help particularly with the loss of a spouse through death, as shown in this volume. In fact, their reliance on children ensures that they are financially protected as well, even though they might not have worked or had spent fewer years engaged in wage work compared with men or, for that matter, received less pay for the same work as carried out by men. While this may be interpreted as a lack of independence and security, in societies where the "self" is relational, such as those in Southeast Asia, interpersonal dependence may not necessarily be regarded as a negative trait. Being dependent on others for assistance and rendering help to the elderly who are in need of help continue to be a cultural value largely accepted among the young and old — a value differentiating much of the Western hemisphere from Southeast Asia. To a large extent then it may be said that social networks continue to be relatively strong in Southeast Asian communities in spite of the region's demographic changes, greater emancipation of women, and the impact of globalization felt in this region in recent decades. But herein lies the danger: to assume that these social networks are always operative and can and will never fail is a fallacy given that the size of families are shrinking because fertility rates are dropping; and it is for this reason that it becomes imperative through relevant policies to ensure that no one falls through the cracks.

For example, should an older woman's relatives not be able to render assistance to her because of their own financial struggles, which is more likely to occur in poorer households, or if her relationship with them has not been cordial, she may find herself in a disadvantaged situation. In this case, targeted policies need to be put in place to ensure that the well-being of such older women is protected. Related to this, we may ask what then of the unmarried older woman since it is the unmarried individuals who face potential vulnerability more than their married counterparts because of the lack of a spouse on whom they can depend? As noted elsewhere (Mujahid 2006), it is the unmarried or "single" women who are more likely, as a consequence of not having a spouse, to be less solvent and lack access to care should they fall ill or become disabled. Moreover in some countries such as in male-dominated Vietnam where the patrilineal kinship system operates (Dube 1997), widowhood has been found to pose a "psychological strain" on older women, leaving them to feel more marginalized than if their husbands were still around (Mujahid 2006, p. 17). What of all the single or unmarried women who have had to leave the labour force or take on flexible work to provide care towards their own aged parents? These women are also equally vulnerable as they may not have ample savings for themselves when they reach old age (Devasahayam 2003). Thus in spite of the high status of women in this region, there are women who might slip through the cracks. For these groups of women then, policies targeted at their specific needs are ever more important so that they do not fall behind in their old age.

By way of conclusion, it must be noted that in much of Southeast Asia, the dual factors of strong social expectations on individual behaviour on one hand, and limited state initiatives targeted at the elderly on the other, continue to operate in tandem with each other, reinforcing the family as the primary site of eldercare. The family context presents a site for the complex interplay of factors. Intergenerational exchanges have been found to occur in both directions: while children can expect to receive help such as care provided by their own ageing parents towards their own children (or grandchildren) and at the same time older persons might find themselves to be contributing financially towards their children's well-being in spite of struggling against the odds of survival themselves, there is also the scenario of the filial son or daughter who continues to provide for his/her aged parent — financially, materially, and emotionally — regardless of whether he/she receives anything in return. In both scenarios "the locally existing 'morality' and 'consensus' as to what an old person should be able to expect as a member of the community" remains a powerful force in shaping behaviour towards the elderly (Risseeuw 2001, p. 40). In these two vastly different outcomes, the elderly and the children of aged parents are keenly aware of their roles irrespective of their ages and the circumstances they may find themselves in.

This, however, does not preclude the fact that there should be relevant policies put in place to ensure that all — whether older men or women — are protected regardless of their socio-economic class background. Especially among older cohorts of women, for example, who have not been actively participating in the labour force, regardless of marital status, it is critical that social security schemes apply to them as well so as to meet the financial needs of this group since pensions would guarantee a certain amount of stability and independence (Marianti 2003). By implication then among those not hired in the formal labour sector, a relevant scheme should also be instituted to ensure that these individuals receive a lump sum of money on a monthly or annual basis to use in old age. Particularly unmarried women and men would benefit from this scheme which will ensure that these individuals are not neglected in old age (cf. Pfau and Giang 2008).

Furthermore, we cannot discount the fact that keeping older persons, whether men or women, active in the labour force may yet be another strategy to ensure their well-being and survival. Keeping older persons economically active in the workforce in fact could be a more effective policy strategy in some contexts, especially since people are living longer and the probability of exhausting one's savings is high given the rising rate of inflation. This strategy, however, entails combating age barriers, altering employer behaviour and perceptions, and providing incentives to work longer and for employers to hire retired workers (Walker 2002), although such a remedy is also highly dependent on the health status of the individual. Having said this, especially among those in the lower socio-economic class group, this strategy, among other gains, would help prevent this group from slipping further into poverty. Furthermore, in countries where the social security system put in place has limited coverage, keeping older persons in the labour force may not only be wise but imperative to ensure financial independence among this cohort (Mujahid 2006).

The chapters in this book explicitly show how a range of social factors mediate the experience of ageing. Any policy for eldercare then should be sensitive to the social and cultural environment within which the elderly reside and function. To put it differently, "a well-rounded policy therefore has to seek ways to analyse the ... diverse familial and community settings, and ... varied notions of friendship, intergenerational relations and notions of 'relatedness'" (Risseeuw 2001, p. 32). Since the family continues to be the primary site for eldercare as dictated by social and cultural norms where filial piety continues to define the relationship between the younger and older generations and reinforced by government policy or, for that matter, the lack of relevant state interventions, taking on board "contextual indicators to assess certain cultural norms as well as the settings where these norms are most likely not to be adhered to" becomes paramount in eldercare policy-making so as to ensure that none within the older population will be neglected (Risseeuw 2001, p. 32).

Within this context, the question of gender should arise since ageing impinges on women's lives quite differently from men's, as this volume demonstrates. While it can be expected that gender might surface as a critical intersecting variable in the lives of older persons in some contexts, in others it may not at all or at least not to such a great extent as other factors. In the light of this, since it has been found that men and women require different kinds of assistance as they adapt to life in old age, it follows then that creating services focusing on the specific domains where older men and women are most vulnerable may serve to enhance the effectiveness of the social intervention (cf. Ha et al. 2006). At other times, it becomes critical to decipher how age and gender as an analytical unit "encompass other social positions including race, class and ethnicity" (Calasanti and Slevin 2001; Ginn and Arber 1995;

McMullin 1995, as cited in Krekula 2007, pp. 159–60). In other words, what becomes integral to comprehending women's and men's vulnerability in old age for the purpose of policy-making is identifying and separating the overlapping strands of exclusion linked to class, educational background, marital status, ethnic origin/race, and religion. To this end, understanding the degree to which gender is a critical variable in old age as well as the contexts in which it is significant in the ageing discourse necessitates taking into account a combination of factors, and the purpose of this book is to elucidate this point.

Notes

1. Also to be noted, unlike in patrilineal Taiwan where the transfer activity is focused among lineal kin, Agree and others (2005) have found that in the Philippines, siblings aside from older persons are key benefactors of exchange resources.
2. John Knodel and Chanpen Saengtienchai (2005) make the point that although there are health and welfare benefits for persons living with HIV, the role of parents in support and care should not be underestimated. Elisabeth Schröder-Butterfill (2004, p. 497) compellingly shows how grandparents are not only important in providing childcare and undertaking domestic tasks, but also in playing the role of "economic pillars" in families. See also Zimmer and Kim (2001).

References

Abbott, Pamela, Claire Wallace and Melissa Tyler. *An Introduction to Sociology: Feminist Perspectives*. London: Routledge, 2005.

Agree, E.M., A.E. Biddlecom and T.W. Valente. "Intergenerational Transfers of Resources between Older Persons and Extended Kin in Taiwan and the Philippines". *Population Studies* 59, no. 2 (2005): 181–95.

Alexander, Jennifer and Paul Alexander. "Markets as Gendered Domain: The Javanese *Pasar*". In *Women Traders in Cross-Cultural Perspective: Mediating Identities, Marketing Wares*, edited by L.J. Seligmann. Stanford, California: Stanford University Press, 2001.

Allan, Graham. *Family Life: Domestic Roles and Social Organization*. Oxford: Blackwell, 1985.

Arber, S. "Gender, Marital Status, and Ageing: Linking Material, Health, and Social Resources". *Journal of Aging Studies* 18 (2004): 91–108.

Arber, Sara and Jay Ginn. *Gender and Later Life: A Sociological Analysis of Resources and Constraints*. London: Sage, 1991.

————. "Gender and Inequalities in Health in Later Life". *Social Science and Medicine* 36 no. 1 (1993): 33–46.

————, eds. *Connecting Gender and Ageing: A Sociological Approach*. Buckingham: Open University Press, 1995.

AT Kearney. "2012 Global Cities Index". Available at <http://www.atkearney.com/gbpc/global-cities-index/full-report/-/asset_publisher/yAl1OgZpc1DO/content/2012-global-cities-index/10192> (accessed 20 February 2012).

Atkinson, Jane M. and Shelly Errington. *Power and Difference: Gender in Island Southeast Asia*. Stanford, California: Stanford University Press, 1990.

Barford, A., D. Dorling, G.D. Smith and M. Shaw. "Life Expectancy: Women Now on Top Everywhere". *British Medical Journal* 332 no. 7545 (2006): 808.

Barusch, Amanda S. *Older Women in Poverty: Private Lives and Public Policies*. New York: Springer Publishing Company, 1994.

Bongaarts, J. "Fertility Decline in the Developed World: Where Will It End?". *American Economic Review* 89, no. 2 (1999): 256–60.

Bracke, P., W. Christiaens and N. Wauterickx. "The Pivotal Role of Women in Informal Care". *Journal of Family Issues* 29 no. 10 (2008): 1348–78.

Brooks, Ann and Theresa Devasahayam. *Gender, Emotions and Labour Markets: Asian and Western Perspectives*. London: Routledge, 2011.

Browne, Colette. *Women, Feminism and Aging*. New York: Springer, 1998.

Calasanti, Toni M. and Kathleen F. Slevin. *Gender, Social Inequalities and Aging*. Walnut Creek, California: AltaMira Press, 2001.

Carsten, Janet. *The Heat of the Hearth: The Process of Kinship in a Malay Fishing Community*. Oxford: Clarendon Press, 1997.

Castles, F. "The World Turned Upside Down: Below Replacement Fertility, Changing Preferences and Family-Friendly Public Policy in 21 OECD Countries". *Journal of European Social Policy* 13, no. 3 (2003): 209–27. Available at <http://www.polsci.wvu.edu/faculty/hauser/PS591/CastlesWorldUpsideDown JESP2003.pdf> (accessed 15 December 2012).

Chappell, N. "Health and Helping among the Elderly: Gender Differences". *Journal of Aging and Health* 1, no. 1 (1989): 102–20.

Chow, Nelson. "The Status Quo". In *Untapped Resources: Women in Ageing Societies across Asia*, edited by K. Mehta. Singapore: Times Academic Press, 1997.

Devasahayam, Theresa W. "Organisations that Care: The Necessity for an Eldercare Leave Scheme for Caregivers of the Elderly in Singapore". Asian MetaCentre Research Papers, No. 10. Singapore: National University of Singapore, 2003. Available at <http://www.populationasia.org/Publications/RP/AMCRP10.pdf> (accessed 10 February 2013).

————. "Reproductive Health of Women in Thailand: Progress and Challenges Towards the Attainment of International Development Goals". Bangkok: United Nations Population Fund, 2005.

Devasahayam, Theresa W. and Brenda S.A. Yeoh, eds. *Working and Mothering in Asia: Images, Ideologies and Identities*. Singapore and Copenhagen: National University of Singapore Press and Nordic Institute of Asian Studies, 2007.

Dube, Leela. *Women and Kinship: Comparative Perspectives on Gender in South and South-East Asia*. Tokyo: United Nations University Press, 1997.

Elson, D. "Labor Markets as Gendered Institutions: Equality, Efficiency and Empowerment Issues". *World Development* 27 no. 3 (1999): 611–27.

Ginn, Jay and Sara Arber. "Only Connect: Gender Relations and Aging". In *Connecting Gender and Ageing: A Sociological Approach*, edited by S. Arber and J. Ginn. Buckingham: Open University Press, 1995.

Gist, Yvonne J. and Victoria A. Velkoff. "Gender and Aging: Demographic Dimensions". U.S. Department of Commerce, Economics and Statistics Administration, Bureau of the Census, 1997.

Gunnarsson, E. "The Vulnerable Life Course: Poverty and Social Assistance among Middle-Aged and Older Women". *Ageing & Society* 22 (2002): 709–28.

Ha, J.-H., D. Carr, R.L. Utz and R. Nesse. "Older Adults' Perceptions of Intergenerational Support after Widowhood: How do Men and Women Differ?" *Journal of Family Issues* 27, no. 1 (2006): 3–30.

Haveman, R.H. and T.M. Smeeding. "The Role of Higher Education in Social Mobility". *The Future of Children* 16, no. 2 (2006): 125–50.

Hay, M. Cameron. "Women Standing between Life and Death: Fate, Agency and the Healers of Lombok". In *The Agency of Women in Asia*, edited by L. Parker. Singapore: Marshall Cavendish, 2005.

Henrard, J.C. "Cultural Problems of Ageing especially regarding Gender and Intergenerational Equity". *Social Science and Medicine* 43, no. 5 (1996): 667–80.

Hogan, D.P. and D.J. Eggebeen. "Sources of Emergency Help and Routine Assistance in Old Age". *Social Forces* 73, no. 3 (1995): 917–36.

Jackson, Richard and Neil Howe. *The Graying of the Great Powers: Demography and Geopolitics in the 21st Century*. Washington, D.C.: Center for Strategic and International Studies, 2008.

Jamilah Ariffin. *Women and Development in Malaysia*. Petaling Jaya: Pelanduk Publications, 1992.

Jefferys, M. "Cultural Aspects of Ageing: Gender and Inter-Generational Issues". *Social Science and Medicine* 43, no. 5 (1996): 681–87.

Jerrome, D. "Continuity and Change in the Study of Family Relationships". *Ageing and Society* 16, no. 1 (1996): 91–104.

Jones, G.W. "The 'Flight from Marriage' in South-East and East Asia". Asian MetaCentre Research Paper Series, No. 11. National University of Singapore, 2003. Available at <http://www.populationasia.org/Publications/RP/AMCRP11.pdf> (accessed 15 June 2014).

————. "Not 'When to Marry' but 'Whether to Marry'". In *(Un)tying the Knot: Ideal and Reality in Asian Marriage*, edited by G.W. Jones and K. Ramdas. Singapore: Asia Research Institute and National University of Singapore, 2004.

————. "Delayed Marriage and Very Low Fertility in Pacific Asia". *Population and Development Review* 33, no. 3 (2007): 453–78.

————. "Women, Marriage and Family in Southeast Asia". In *Gender Trends in Southeast Asia: Women Now, Women in the Future*, edited by T.W. Devasahayam. Singapore: Institute of Southeast Asian Studies, 2009*a*.

————. "Recent Fertility Trends, Policy Responses and Fertility Prospects in Low Fertility Countries of East and Southeast Asia". Paper prepared for the Expert Group Meeting on Recent and Future Trends in Fertility. United Nations Population Division, New York, December 2009*b*.

Kaur, Amarjit. "Economic Globalisation, Trade Liberalisation, and Labour-Intensive Export Manufactures: An Asian Perspective". In *Women Workers in Industrialising Asia: Costed, Not Valued*, edited by A. Kaur. New York: Palgrave Macmillan, 2004.

Kim, D.-S. "Theoretical Explanations of Rapid Fertility Decline in Korea". *The Japanese Journal of Population* 3, no. 1 (2005): 2–25. Available at <http://www.ipss.go.jp/webj-ad/Webjournal.files/population/2005_6/kim.pdf> (accessed 25 November 2012).

Kinsella, Kevin. "Global Perspectives on the Demography of Aging". In *The Cultural Context of Aging*, edited by J. Sokolovsky. Westport, Connecticut: Greenwood Publishing, 2009.

Knodel, J. and M.B. Ofstedal. "Gender and Aging in the Developing World: Where are the Men?" *Population and Development Review* 29, no. 4 (2003): 677–98.

Knodel, J. and C. Saengtienchai. "Older-aged Parents — The Final Safety Net for Adult Sons and Daughters with AIDS in Thailand". *Journal of Family Issues* 26, no. 5 (2005): 665–98.

Krekula, C. "The Intersection of Age and Gender: Reworking Gender Theory and Social Gerontology". *Current Sociology* 55, no. 2 (2007): 155–71.

Li, Tania. *Malays in Singapore: Culture, Economy and Ideology*. New York and Singapore: Oxford University Press, 1989.

Lim, P.L. "Maintenance of Parents Act". *Singapore Infopedia*, 2009. Available at <http://infopedia.nl.sg/articles/SIP_1614_2009-11-30.html> (accessed 20 May 2012).

Long, Susan O. *Final Days: Japanese Culture and Choice at the End of Life*. Honolulu: University of Hawaii Press, 2005.

Lopata, Helena Z. and Judith A. Levy. "The Construction of Social Problems across the Life Course". In *Social Problems across the Life Course*, edited by H.Z. Lopata and J.A. Levy. Lanham, Maryland: Rowman and Littlefield Publishers, 2003.

Marianti, Ruly. "'You can Bite it, but It's Tough!' Pensions for Widows in Indonesia". IIAS Newsletter, #32, November 2003. Available at <http://www. iias.nl/iiasn/32/Theme_ECI_pensions_of_widows_in_indonesia.pdf> (accessed 5 February 2013).

Mazidah Zakaria and Nik Safiah Karim. "Women in Development: The Case of an All-Women Youth Land Development Scheme in Malaysia". In *Visibility and Power: Essays on Women in Society and Development*, edited by L. Dube, E. Leacock, and S. Ardener. Delhi: Oxford University Press, 1986.

McMullin, Julie. "Theorizing Age and Gender Relations". In *Connecting Gender and Ageing: A Sociological Approach*, edited by S. Arber and J. Ginn. Buckingham: Open University Press, 1995.

Medina, Belen T.G. *The Filipino Family*, 2nd ed. Diliman, Quezon City: University of the Philippines Press, 2001.

Mehta, Kalyani. "The Impact of the Ageing Revolution on Asian Women". In *Untapped Resources: Women in Ageing Societies across Asia*, edited by K. Mehta. Singapore: Times Academic Press, 1997*a*.

———. "Cultural Scripts and the Social Integration of Older People". *Ageing and Society* 17, no. 3 (1997*b*): 253–75.

Mujahid, Ghazy. "Population Ageing in East and South-east Asia: Current Situation and Emerging Challenges". UNFPA Country Technical Services Team for East and Southeast Asia. Papers in Population Ageing Series, No. 1. Bangkok: United Nations Population Fund, 2006.

Oakley, Ann. *The Sociology of Housework*. London: Martin Robertson, 1974*a*.

———. *Housewife*. London: Allen Lane, 1974*b*.

O'Harrow, Stephen. "Vietnamese Women and Confucianism: Creating Spaces from Patriachy". In *"Male" and "Female" in Developing Southeast Asia*, edited by Wazir Jahan Karim. Oxford: Berg Publishers, 1995.

Ong, Aihwa. *Spirits of Resistance and Capitalist Discipline*. New York: State University of New York Press, 1987.

Pfau, W.D. and T.L. Giang. "Gender and Remittance Flows in Vietnam during Economic Transformation". *Asia Pacific Population Journal* 23, no. 1 (2008): 13–32.

Raybeck, Douglas. "The Ideal and the Real: The Status of Women in Kelantan Malay Society". *Women and Politics* 1, no. 4 (1980/1981): 7–21.

———. "A Diminished Dichotomy: Kelantan Malay and Traditional Chinese Perspectives". In *In Her Prime: A New View of Middle-Aged Women*, edited by J.K. Brown, V. Kerns, and contributors. Massachusetts: Bergin & Garvey Publishers, 1985.

Resurreccion, Bernadette P. "Gender Trends in Migration and Employment in Southeast Asia". In *Gender Trends in Southeast Asia: Women Now, Women in the Future*, edited by T.W. Devasahayam. Singapore: Institute of Southeast Asian Studies, 2009.

Risseeuw, C. "Policy Issues of Inclusion and Exclusion in Relation to Gender and Ageing in the South". *The European Journal of Development Research* 13, no. 2 (2001): 26–48.

Rozario P.A. and S.-L. Hong. "Doing it 'Right' by Your Parents in Singapore: A Political Economy Examination of the Maintenance of Parents Act of 1995". *Critical Social Policy* 31 (2011): 607–27.

Salih, K. and M.L. Young. "Structural Adjustment and Its Impact on Women in Malaysia". In *Women and Structural Adjustment: Selected Case Studies*. London: Commonwealth Secretariat, 1991.

Schröder-Butterfill, E. "Inter-Generational Family Support provided by Older People in Indonesia". *Ageing and Society* 24, no. 4 (2004): 497–530.

Schröder-Butterfill, E. and P. Kraeger. "Actual and *De facto* Childlessness in Old Age: Evidence and Implications from East Java, Indonesia". *Population and Development Review* 31, no. 1 (2005): 19–55.

Schumacher, K., C.A. Beck and J.M. Marren. "Family Caregivers: Caring for Older Adults, Working with their Families". *American Journal of Nursing* 106, no. 8 (2006): 40–49.

Seale, C. and J. Charteris-Black. "The Interaction of Age and Gender in Illness Narratives". *Ageing & Society* 28, no. 7 (2008): 1025–45.

Secondi, G. "Private Monetary Transfers in Rural China: Are Families Altruistic?" *Journal of Development Studies* 33, no. 4 (1997): 487–511.

Sokolovsky, Jay. *The Cultural Context of Aging*, 3rd ed. Westport, Connecticut: Greenwood Publishing, 2009.

Stivens, Maila. *Matriliny and Modernity: Sexual Politics and Social Change in Rural Malaysia*. New South Wales, Australia: Allen and Unwin, 1996.

Stoler, A. "Class Structure, Female Autonomy in Rural Java". *Signs* 3, no. 1 (1977): 74–89.

Strange, Heather. *Rural Women in Tradition and Transition*. New York: Praeger, 1981.

Sullivan, Norma M. *Masters and Managers: A Study of Gender Relations in Urban Java*. Sydney: Allen and Unwin, 1994.

Swift, Michael G. *Malay Peasant Society in Jelebu*. London: Athlone Press, 1965.

Teo, P. and K. Mehta. "Participating in the Home: Widows Cope in Singapore". *Journal of Aging Studies* 15 (2001): 127–44.

The Organisation for Economic Co-operation and Development (OECD). *Help Wanted? Providing and Paying for Long-term Care*. Paris: OECD, 2011.

Verbrugge, L.M. "Gender and Health: An Update on Hypotheses and Evidence". *Journal of Health and Social Behavior* 26 no. 3 (1985): 156–82.

Victor, C.R., S.J. Scambler, S. Shah, D.G. Cook, T. Harris, E. Rink and S. de Wilde. "Has Loneliness amongst Older People Increased: An Investigation into Variations between Cohorts". *Ageing & Society* 22 no. 5 (2002): 585–97.

Walker, A. "A Strategy for Active Ageing". *International Social Security Review* 55 (2002): 121–39.

Wazir Jahan Karim. *Women and Culture: Between Malay Adat and Islam.* Boulder, Westview Press, 1992.

Weiringa, S. "Passionate Aesthetics and Symbolic Subversion: Heteronormativity in India and Indonesia". *Asian Studies Review* 36, no. 4 (2012): 515–30.

Wolf, Diane. "Daughters, Decisions and Domination: An Empirical and Conceptual Critique of Household Strategies". *Development and Change* 21, no. 1 (1990): 43–74.

———. *Factory Daughters: Gender, Household Dynamics, and Rural Industrialization in Java.* Berkeley, California: University of California Press, 1992.

Xie, Y. and H. Zhu. "Do Sons or Daughters give more Money to Parents? Gender and Intergenerational Support in Contemporary Urban China". Report 06-607, Population Studies Center, Institute for Social Research, University of Michigan, 2006.

Yamanaka, Keiko and Nicola Piper. "Feminized Migration in East and Southeast Asia: Policies, Actions and Empowerment". Occasional Paper 11. Geneva: United Nations Research Institute for Social Development, 2005.

Yeoh, B.S.A., Huang, S. and J. Gonzalez III. "Migrant Female Domestic Workers: Debating the Economic, Social and Political Impacts in Singapore". *International Migration Review* 33, no. 1 (1999): 114–36.

Yin, Sandra. "How Older Women Can Shield Themselves from Poverty". Population Reference Bureau, 21 March 2008. Available at <http://www.prb.org/Journalists/Webcasts/2008/olderwomen.aspx> (accessed 12 February 2013).

Zimmer, Z. and S.K. Kim. "Living Arrangements and Socio-demographic Conditions of Older Adults in Cambodia". *Journal of Cross-Cultural Gerontology* 16, no. 4 (2001): 353–81.

2

GENDER AND AGEING IN THAILAND: A SITUATION ANALYSIS OF OLDER WOMEN AND MEN

John Knodel and Napaporn Chayovan

INTRODUCTION

The importance of gender is a major theme in both social research and policy discussions related to population ageing (Mehta 1997 and 2004; Troisi and Pawiliczko 2008; UN INSTRAW 1999). It is a prominent issue in the Plan of Action stemming from the 2002 Second World Assembly on Ageing (United Nations 2002). Typically, the focus is on inequalities that presumably disadvantage older women with respect to their social and economic well-being and their physical and mental health. Rarely are aspects of ageing for which men share vulnerability or are disadvantaged highlighted (Knodel and Ofstedal 2003). Given that the link between gender and ageing likely varies across time and settings, adequate assessments of their interaction need to move beyond assumptions of universal female disadvantage and explore the experiences of both older men and women in specific societal and temporal contexts. The present study contributes to such an effort by comparing the situations of older women and men in contemporary Thailand based on the latest national survey of older persons. It thus brings several previous studies of gender and ageing in Thailand up to date (Knodel 2004; Sobieszczyk et al. 2003; Soonthorndhada et al. 2008). In conformity with the conventional definition used in previous studies, we define the older population as persons age 60 and more years.

THAILAND'S DEMOGRAPHIC, SOCIAL AND ECONOMIC SETTING

Population Ageing

Starting in the late 1960s, Thailand experienced rapid and extensive fertility decline and improvements in life expectancy. By 2005, average life expectancy at birth exceeded 68 years and the total fertility rate was below two children per woman. At the same time, driven primarily by fertility decline, the share of the Thai population age 60 and above more than doubled (United Nations 2009). According to government projections, population ageing will continue at a rapid pace with persons age 60 and older expected to constitute one fourth of the population by 2030 (NESDB 2007). The trend is relatively similar for the older male and female populations although ageing will occur at a modestly faster pace for women than for men.

In common with most other countries, women outnumber men at older ages and especially at more advanced ages. Thus, currently, according to government projections, women constitute 53 per cent of the 60–64 age group but more than 60 per cent of persons age 80 and older. This excess of women over men is expected to modestly increase during the next two decades, particularly among the oldest. However, since very old persons represent only a small share of all older persons, men will continue to represent a large share of Thais age 60 and above, ranging from between 43 per cent and 45 per cent during the 2000–30 projection period.

Social and Economic Context

The vast majority of the Thai population are ethnic Thais, speak some form of the Thai language, and adhere to Buddhism (95 per cent). About 4 per cent of the older population identify themselves as Chinese, and another 9 per cent as mixed Thai and Chinese and are disproportionately concentrated in the urban areas (Chayovan and Knodel 1997). The ethnic Thai majority traditionally favours bilateral descent and inheritance and matrilocal residence although the minority that identify strongly with their Chinese heritage tends to be patrilineal and patrilocal (Henderson et al. 1971; Mason 1992). Generally among ethnic Thais, the child who stays with the parents in old age often inherits the house and perhaps an extra share of the land — a custom generally favouring women given the predominance of matrilocal residence.

As in other Southeast Asian societies, the family traditionally takes the primary responsibility for older people. A norm of filial obligations underlies intergenerational relations (Knodel, Saengtienchai and Sittitrai 1995). Parents also typically continue to feel obliged to ensure the well-being of their adult children and intergenerational exchanges of support and services remain pervasive (Knodel and Chayovan 2008).

During much of the last several decades, Thailand experienced rapid economic growth, although interrupted for several years during the Asian economic crisis that started in mid-1997. As a result, Thailand is currently considered as a lower-middle income nation.

GENDER AND AGEING IN GOVERNMENT POLICY

The Thai government's response to population ageing is relatively recent but increasingly vigorous. Responses include a new national plan on ageing finalized in 2002, the passage of the 2003 Act on Older Persons, and the establishment of organizations to encourage consideration of issues related to older persons in government programmes. Interest in gender issues has also grown recently. The Second Long-term Women's Development Plan (1992–2011) recommends special attention to older women with respect to health and welfare services and calls for a campaign to help women prepare for old age by increasing their self-reliance. Nonetheless, government policies related to ageing are generally gender neutral with issues related to gender and ageing rarely linked.

In 1993, monthly government subsistence allowances for indigent old persons in rural areas were initiated and have subsequently been increased from 200 to 500 baht (approximately 33 baht = US$1 at the time of the 2007 survey). According to official statistics, the numbers receiving the allowances increased steadily from 20,000 to 1,755,666 by 2007 (representing almost one-third of Thais age 60+). This is somewhat above the 25 per cent reporting receipt of allowances in the 2007 Survey of Older Persons (Knodel and Chayovan 2008). No special consideration of gender is specified regarding allocation of allowances and roughly equal proportions of men and women receive them.

Government health benefits are also largely equal for older Thai men and women. Since 1993, free access to most services at government health facilities has been available to all persons age 60 and above not covered by other insurance schemes, such as civil service and social security plans which offer superior benefits. More recently, free government healthcare has been extended in Thailand regardless of age.

Two major government-sponsored plans provide retirement benefits in Thailand: a long-standing (but changing) one that covers government and state enterprise employees, and a recent one that covers employees in private enterprises under the Social Security Act. Because men comprise the larger proportion of government employees, they have some advantage over women for associated retirement benefits. Women, however, are eligible to a share in the retirement benefits as spouses of retired government employees. In 1998, the broader social security scheme initiated a pension fund for employees in private enterprises. Full old age benefits are limited to employees who contribute for at least 15 years and, thus, are not yet available to the current cohorts of older Thais.

DATA SOURCE

The remainder of the present study relies primarily on original tabulations from the 2007 National Survey of Older Persons (NSO 2008). Although the survey covered persons 50 and older living in private households, we restrict consideration to the more than 30,000 persons age 60 and older. Given the large sample size, small differences between men and women are typically statistically significant at standard levels even if they may not be substantively important. The survey relied on direct interviews. However, for 27 per cent of persons age 60 and older covered by the survey, information was provided by a proxy respondent, typically another household member. In 75 per cent of these cases, the reason for a proxy interview was the absence of the older person at the time of interview. Health-related problems among the older persons in the sample were the reason for almost all the remaining proxy interviews. Unless otherwise specified, our analysis includes proxy interviews. For convenience, we use the term respondent even when a proxy provided the information.

Because the survey is limited to private households, older persons in institutional settings are not covered. Thus the small numbers of older persons in old age or nursing homes are omitted. Only a few thousand older persons live in government-sponsored nursing homes. Although accurate statistics on older persons in private establishments are unavailable, the number is likely to be quite modest (Jitapunkul, Chayovan and Kespichayawattana 2002). More importantly, older persons living in religious institutions such as monks and nuns are omitted. According to the 2000 census, 2 per cent of Thai men age 60 and above are monks, a fact that needs to be kept in mind when interpreting results. Information on the number of nuns residing in temples is unavailable.

DEMOGRAPHIC AND SOCIO-ECONOMIC CHARACTERISTICS

Marital Status

Marital status has important implications for many aspects of an elderly person's well-being. Spouses can be primary sources of material, social and emotional support and provide personal care during times of illness or frailty. Thus living with a spouse typically has advantages for older persons. As Table 2.1 shows, few Thai elders never married. Likewise only a small share are separated or divorced or are married but live separately. Age and gender differences, however, are pronounced. The percentage currently married declines sharply with age while the percentage widowed increases commensurately with age, reflecting the impact of mortality on the loss of a spouse combined with declines in remarriage with advancing age.

Among elderly men, 80 per cent are currently married and living with a spouse. Among women, only 44 per cent live with a spouse and even more are widowed. These differences reflect higher male mortality and tendencies for husbands to be older than their wives and their greater tendency to remarry in case of marital dissolution. Among the elderly in their early sixties, substantial gender differences are already apparent in these respects but the difference becomes far more pronounced at older ages. Thus among Thais in their eighties, only 12 per cent of women live with a spouse compared to almost 60 per cent of men.

Number of Living Children

As documented below, adult children remain important providers of material support and other forms of assistance to older age parents. Moreover, coresidence with children and the amount of support from non-coresident children depend in part on the number of children (Knodel, Chayovan and Siriboon 1992; Knodel, Saengtienchai and Obiero 1995; Knodel and Chayovan 2008; Zimmer and Korinek 2008). As Table 2.1

TABLE 2.1
Marital Status and Number of Children, Persons Age 60 and Older, by Gender and Age, Thailand, 2007

	Total	60–64	65–69	70–74	75–79	80+
Marital Status						
% Never married						
Men	1.5	1.4	1.9	0.8	1.7	1.8
Women	3.8	4.5	4.4	3.1	3.1	2.4
% Married, live together						
Men	79.8	87.3	84.4	77.4	66.3	57.7
Women	44.2	58.8	50.2	37.9	33.1	11.6
% Married, live separately						
Men	2.7	2.8	2.0	3.2	2.5	2.9
Women	2.1	3.1	2.2	1.5	1.3	1.7
% Widowed						
Men	14.3	6.8	9.9	16.7	27.6	35.8
Women	46.9	29.1	40.2	55.0	61.0	83.4
% Separated/divorced						
Men	1.7	1.7	1.7	2.0	1.8	1.7
Women	3.0	4.6	3.0	2.5	1.6	0.9
Number of Children						
% With no children						
Men	3.3	4.1	3.0	2.2	3.3	3.6
Women	5.7	6.3	6.1	5.2	4.8	5.2
Mean number among those with children						
Men	4.1	3.4	3.9	4.5	4.9	5.1
Women	4.4	3.8	4.3	4.9	5.0	5.0
Mean number among all						
Men	3.9	3.3	3.8	4.4	4.7	4.9
Women	4.2	3.5	4.0	4.6	4.8	4.7

Note: Children include step and adopted children as well as own biological children.
Source: National Statistical Office (NSO), *Report on the 2007 Survey of Older Persons in Thailand* (original tabulations) (Bangkok: National Statistical Office, 2008).

also shows, only a small minority of older persons in Thailand have no living children. Still, a clear gender difference is evident. Women in each age group are more likely than men to be childless, reflecting the higher percentage of women who never married. However, among older persons with living children, older women average modestly more children than older men. Thus, the mean number of children among all older men and women in each age group is relatively similar. Also similar is the steady rise in the number of living children with each successive five-year age group for both men and women, reflecting the past history of fertility decline in Thailand.

Education

Educational levels and literacy of the Thai population have improved greatly over the past 80 years. As a result, by the time of the 2007 Survey of Older Persons, 85 per cent of men and 69 per cent of women age 60 and older are literate. Formal schooling increased rapidly during the lifetime of the current elderly generation while the gender gap favouring men declined and in recent years reversed (Knodel 1997). As a result, gender differences in educational attainment of future Thai elderly will increasingly differ from those of today. This is clearly revealed by recent projections to 2045 of the educational characteristics of the population 65 and older based on 2000 census data (Hermalin, Ofstedal and Tesfai 2007). As Table 2.2 shows, throughout the entire period covered, women compared to men

TABLE 2.2

Projections of the Educational Characteristics of the Thai Population Age 65 and Older (based on the 2000 census), 2000–45

	% With Primary or Less Education		% With Upper Secondary or Higher Education		Index of Dissimilarity between Educational Distributions by Gender
	Men	Women	Men	Women	
2000	90.1	96.7	4.5	1.6	0.194
2005	88.5	95.9	5.6	2.2	0.167
2010	85.0	94.0	7.5	3.5	0.140
2015	81.9	91.4	9.4	5.1	0.109
2020	78.8	88.7	11.8	7.2	0.100
2025	73.6	84.2	15.1	10.6	0.106
2030	68.4	78.8	18.4	14.3	0.104
2035	63.3	73.0	21.0	17.5	0.097
2040	58.0	66.3	23.4	20.9	0.090
2045	49.6	55.8	26.2	25.4	0.083

Note: The index of dissimilarity equals half the sum of the absolute differences in proportions of men and women at each level of education (using five levels: less than primary, primary, lower secondary, upper secondary, and at least some tertiary).
Source: A.I. Hermalin, M.B. Ofstedal and R. Tesfai, "Future Characteristics of the Elderly in Developing Countries and Their Implications for Policy", *Asian Population Studies* 3, no. 1 (2007): 5–36 (original data provided by authors).

are more likely to have at most a primary education and less likely to have upper secondary or higher education. Overall, the educational profile of the older population will improve considerably especially after 2030, reflecting the major expansion of secondary education that has taken place in Thailand in recent decades (Knodel 1997). Moreover, the consistent decline in the index of dissimilarity indicates that gender differences will decline throughout the period covered by the projection. Thus, although male advantage is still evident in 2045, it is considerably reduced compared to 2000.

HEALTH

Biological processes ensure not only that the risk of mortality increases steadily with age but so do chronic illnesses and the ability to physically carry out activities of daily living. Biological and social processes also shape gender differences in mortality and health. Neither the progression of changing physical well-being with age nor gender differences, however, necessarily remain static over time, especially in light of continuing advances in medical technology and the changing social, economic and physical environments in which people live.

Older Age Mortality

The ultimate measure of health is survival. According to the United Nations, life expectancy at age 60 is estimated at 17.4 years for men and 20.4 for women for the period 2005–10 (United Nations 2007). Moreover, although the United Nations projects longer survival for both older men and women in the future, the gender gap is anticipated to increase from the current female advantage of 3 years to 4 years by 2045–50.

Measures of overall life expectancy, however, do not take into account that among many older persons, some years lived may be in poor health or in a state of disability. The concept of active life expectancy has been developed to take this factor into consideration. Differences between active and overall life expectancy indicate the number of years that one can expect to live in seriously poor health or in disability. Estimates of active life expectancy, however, depend on accurate reporting of disability and health conditions by age and vary with the particular definitions of good health used. Thus, it needs to be emphasized that these figures need to be interpreted with caution.

TABLE 2.3

Life Expectancy (LE), Active Life Expectancy (ALE) and Years with Serious Limitations by Age and Sex, Thailand, 2005/07

Age from Which Life Expectancy is Estimated	Male			Female		
	LE	ALE	Years with Serious Limitation	LE	ALE	Years with Serious Limitation
60	19.34	18.52	0.82	21.66	20.29	1.37
65	16.22	15.39	0.83	17.91	16.51	1.40
70	12.48	11.70	0.78	14.59	13.15	1.44
75	10.31	9.51	0.80	11.57	10.10	1.47
80	8.55	7.64	0.91	8.95	7.40	1.55

Notes: LE Based on Thailand Life Tables 2005–06 from the 2005–06 Survey of Population Change. ALE refers to expected years during which three main activities of daily living (eating, dressing, and toileting) can be performed by self as indicated by the 2007 Survey of Older Persons; years with serious limitation refers to those during which one or more of these activities cannot be performed by self.
Source: 2005–06 Survey of Population Change and *2007 Survey of Older Persons in Thailand* (original tabulations).

Table 2.3 provides recent calculations of active life expectancy defined in terms of years in which a person is able to carry out three basic activities of daily living: eating, dressing, and toileting without assistance. Years with serious limitation refer to those during which one or more of these three activities cannot be performed by self. At almost every age in the elderly age span, both overall life expectancy and active life expectancy are longer for women than for men. However, women will also live with at least one serious limitation for longer durations than men. Thus, at age 60, women can expect to live an additional 21.7 years compared to 19.3 years for men. However, of these years, men will suffer a serious limitation on average of 0.8 years compared to 1.4 years for women. Still, both men and women will live the large majority of their older years in sufficient health to carry out these basic activities on their own without extensive hands-on long-term care.

Physical and Psychological Well-being

Self-assessments of health provide convenient and reasonably valid indicators of overall health (Idler and Benyami 1997). As Table 2.4 indicates, for each age group within the elderly age range, women are less likely

TABLE 2.4
Selected Measures of Physical and Psychological Health, Persons Age 60 and Older, by Gender and Age, Thailand, 2007

	All 60+		60–69		70–79		80+	
	Men	Women	Men	Women	Men	Women	Men	Women
Physical health								
Self-assessed health (% distribution)								
Good or very good	53.2	41.7	61.0	50.0	43.9	32.3	30.1	26.6
Fair	26.7	30.7	24.4	28.3	30.5	34.6	29.4	31.5
Poor or very poor	20.1	27.5	14.6	21.7	25.7	33.1	40.4	42.0
Total	100	100	100	100	100	100	100	100
% Who do not see clearly	15.9	25.0	10.2	15.5	20.8	33.7	39.9	49.3
% Who do not hear clearly	13.0	15.6	6.7	7.8	18.1	20.7	40.5	42.1
% With incontinence problems	13.6	19.8	9.3	15.0	18.3	23.3	28.2	34.9
% Ill during past 5 years	60.5	65.8	57.7	61.1	62.9	70.2	72.9	78.1
Psychological health								
(% sometimes or regularly feeling:)								
No appetite	46.8	56.2	42.1	51.9	52.3	61.3	61.1	64.0
Stressed	42.7	49.4	41.6	47.6	44.4	52.5	44.7	49.3
Moody	42.5	48.0	42.0	46.8	44.0	50.4	40.8	46.7
Hopeless	15.7	20.9	13.6	18.7	18.3	23.0	22.2	27.0
Useless	13.4	18.8	11.5	16.5	15.7	21.0	19.1	24.9
Unhappy	21.3	27.9	19.0	25.4	23.8	30.4	28.2	33.9
Lonely	30.5	38.4	27.3	34.6	33.2	43.0	44.0	45.0

Note: All gender differences are statistically significant at the .01 level except for self-assessed health, hearing, feeling no appetite, stressed, or lonely among those age 80+.
Source: 2007 Survey of Older Persons in Thailand (original tabulations).

than men to assess their health as good or very good and more likely to assess their health as poor or very poor. The percentage who indicate poor or very poor health increases noticeably with age although more so for men than for women. Thus, among Thais age 80 and above, gender differences are modest. Consistent with poorer self-assessments of health, vision and hearing problems, incontinence, and being ill during the past five years are more commonly reported by women than men. Again for both men and women, each of these problems increases with age. The paradox of women reporting worse physical health but also surviving longer than men is a common finding in other populations (Verbrugge 1989). One important part of the explanation is that older men are more prone to fatal diseases and accidents while women are more prone to non-life-threatening illnesses. Table 2.4 also shows that a higher percentage of older women than men report that they experience psychological problems. Women are more likely to lack appetite and to feel stressed, moody, hopeless, useless, unhappy or lonely.

Functional Limitations

One serious consequence of declining health and increased frailty associated with ageing is difficulty with physical movement and in carrying out basic activities of daily living. As functional limitations increase, assistance by caregivers becomes increasingly necessary. Table 2.5 examines a variety of potential disabilities. We define a functional limitation as either not being able to perform the activity or only being able to do so with assistance or an aid. For both men and women, the likelihood of limitations increases substantially with age. Overall, women are more likely to report being limited on each of the activities listed although only relatively small percentages of either men or women are unable to do the three most basic functional activities (eating, dressing, and bathing or using the toilet) by themselves. A female disadvantage holds for all age groups except for the three basic limitations among persons in their sixties. In addition, among all elderly, women are more likely than men to report at least one of the limitations listed and a higher mean number of disabilities.

Care Assistance

The vast majority of respondents (89 per cent of men and 87 per cent of women) in the 2007 Survey of Older Persons indicated that they took care of themselves, implying that they did not need a caregiver.

TABLE 2.5
Functional Limitations, Persons Age 60 and Older, by Gender and Age, Thailand, 2007

	All 60+		60–69		70–79		80+	
	Men	Women	Men	Women	Men	Women	Men	Women
% Reporting having problems doing the following activities								
Eating	2.1	2.4	1.2	0.8	2.5	2.8	6.9	9.7
Dressing	2.6	3.3	1.6	1.2	3.1	3.5	8.5	14.2
Bathing/using toilet	2.8	3.9	1.6	1.6	3.3	3.9	9.7	16.1
Squatting	8.4	15.6	4.4	8.2	12.2	21.0	24.3	38.2
Lifting 5 kilos	18.0	34.2	9.5	19.4	26.2	47.4	50.1	73.0
Walking 200–300 meters	12.1	20.6	5.9	8.9	17.4	28.8	38.7	58.9
Climbing 2 or 3 stairs	9.9	16.6	4.6	7.3	14.6	22.4	31.7	49.0
Using transportation	17.6	32.4	7.8	15.9	26.9	46.6	55.7	77.3
Counting change	7.9	13.1	2.8	4.8	11.7	18.0	30.7	42.1
Any of the above	25.4	44.6	13.4	27.9	38.0	60.9	67.4	85.0
Any basic limitation(a)	3.2	4.2	2.0	1.7	3.5	4.3	17.4	14.8
Mean number of functional limitations listed above	0.81	1.42	0.39	0.68	1.18	1.94	2.56	3.77

Notes: All gender differences are statistically significant at the .01 level except for eating among persons age 60+ and 70–79; dressing and bathing/toileting among persons age 60–69 and 70–79; and any basic limitation among persons age 60–69 and 70–79.
(a) Basic limitations refer to problems with eating, dressing, and bathing or using toilet.
Source: 2007 Survey of Older Persons in Thailand (original tabulations).

Presumably, an inability to independently eat, dress, use the toilet or bathe by oneself signifies the most severe functional limitations and the greatest need for a caregiver to assist on a daily basis. Of respondents who had one or more of these basic limitations, 75 per cent of men and 87 per cent of women indicated they had a caregiver while less than 1 per cent of both men and women indicated that they needed care but did not receive any. Thus, although a large majority of older Thais who most need care say someone provides it, women are somewhat advantaged in this respect.

Table 2.6 indicates that substantial differences are evident between older men and women in terms of who serves as primary caregivers among all who said they received assistance with daily activities. More than half of the men reported that their spouse serves in this role compared to only 12 per cent of women. Much of this difference is attributable to higher levels of widowhood among women, a condition that precludes spouses as caregivers. Among elderly who are currently living with their spouse, the gender difference in the percentage that cite a spouse as the main caregiver narrows considerably. Still even among this group, wives are considerably more likely to serve as primary caregivers for husbands compared with husbands for wives, although for a large

TABLE 2.6

Per Cent Distribution of Caregivers of Persons Age 60 and Older Who Have a Caregiver, by Gender and Marital Situation, Thailand, 2007

			Marital Situation			
			Living with Spouse		Other	
Caregiver	Total					
	Men	Women	Men	Women	Men	Women
Spouse	53.2	11.5	72.1	45.1	1.4	0.0
Son	10.9	12.7	8.6	9.2	17.6	13.9
Daughter	24.4	51.0	15.1	36.5	49.7	56.0
Child-in-law	4.0	8.7	2.0	4.5	9.7	10.2
Other relative	5.8	10.4	1.2	3.3	18.2	12.9
Non-relative	1.6	5.5	1.0	1.4	3.4	7.0
Total	100	100	100	100	100	100
% Cared for by child or child-in-law	39.4	72.5	25.6	50.2	77.0	80.2

Note: Gender differences are statistically significant at the .01 for total and both marital situations.
Source: *2007 Survey of Older Persons in Thailand* (original tabulations).

minority (45 per cent) of women, the husband is their main caregiver. For those not living with a spouse, children are by far the most common primary caregiver with little difference between older men and older women. Among this subset, men are somewhat more likely than women to receive care from a son while women are somewhat more likely to receive care from a daughter.

Risk Behaviours

Gender differences in health and longevity result from both biological and social risk factors. Generally men are more likely than women to engage in risk behaviours that are harmful to health (World Health Organization 2001). As Table 2.7 shows, this difference is pronounced in Thailand with respect to smoking and drinking, which are likely to contribute to the higher male mortality among older Thais. The health implications of alcohol are complex because moderate consumption may be protective of heart disease, while excessive drinking has serious adverse effects (World Health Organization 2001). In Thailand, however, excessive rather than moderate alcohol use is typical (Klausner 1993). At the same time, drinking tends to be occasional. For example, only a modest minority of the men who said they drink alcohol reported drinking regularly. In contrast, women are much more likely than men to report currently chewing betel

TABLE 2.7

Health Risk Behaviours by Gender and Age, Persons Age 60 and Older, Thailand, 2007

Age	% Who Drink Alcohol Sometimes or Regularly		% Who Smoke Sometimes or Regularly		% Who Chew Betel Nut Sometimes or Regularly	
	Men	Women	Men	Women	Men	Women
60–64	48.9	9.2	39.7	5.6	4.0	22.7
65–69	39.1	7.7	40.3	4.1	4.7	27.9
70–74	28.4	5.7	31.0	3.7	6.4	35.4
75–79	23.8	4.1	31.3	2.5	8.7	40.9
80+	12.4	2.5	22.1	2.9	12.4	44.7
Total	36.4	6.8	35.8	4.2	5.9	31.2

Note: All gender differences are statistically significant at the .01 level.
Source: *2007 Survey of Older Persons in Thailand* (original tabulations).

nut, a mild narcotic associated with mouth and throat cancer. Among them, most said they do it on a regular basis (Reichart 1995). For both men and women, the percentage who drink and the percentage who smoke virtually decline with each successive age group, likely reflecting the relinquishing of these behaviours as one ages. In contrast, the sharp increase in the percentage who chew betel nut with age is likely primarily a cohort effect reflecting declines in betel nut chewing during the period when respondents were coming of age.

LIVING ARRANGEMENTS

In Thailand, as in most of Southeast Asia, living with or nearby adult children, typically in a stem family configuration, has been a predominant pattern that traditionally played a central role in the context of family support (Cowgill 1968, 1972). Older Thais often see coresidence as crucial to their own well-being (Knodel, Saengtienchai and Sittitrai 1995). In contrast, living alone is usually viewed as a disadvantage associated with less frequent interpersonal interactions and increased chances that urgent needs for assistance in case of an acute health crisis or accident will go unnoticed. Living alone may even signify desertion by others. Living together with only a spouse in a two-person household is seen as less problematic since a spouse can provide emotional and material support and personal care. Coresidence can benefit both generations although often parents eventually reach ages where they are largely dependent on others for care and support.

Literal coresidence, as measured by the percentage of older persons who live in the same household with one or more of their children, has been steadily declining in Thailand, from 77 per cent in 1986 to 59 per cent in 2007. Still most older Thais continue to live with their children. When situations in which a child lives next door are taken into account, then 71 per cent of the 60 and older population either lived with or adjacent to a child in 2007 (Knodel and Chayovan 2008).

As Table 2.8 shows, although relatively few older Thais live alone, and only a modest proportion lives only with their spouse, gender differences are apparent. Living alone is more common among women while men are more likely to live only with a spouse. These overall gender differences are a function of marital status differences. The percentage of men and women who live only with a spouse is similar among married persons who live together and men are actually more likely than women to live alone among the elderly not living with a spouse (30 per cent vs. 16 per cent). Gender differences with respect to coresidence or the combined

TABLE 2.8
Selected Measures of Living Arrangements, by Gender and Marital Situation, Persons Age 60 and Older, Thailand, 2007

			Marital Situation			
			Living with Spouse		Other	
	Total					
Per Cent Living:	Men	Women	Men	Women	Men	Women
Alone	6.0	8.9	d.n.a.	d.n.a.	29.8	16.0
Only with spouse	21.3	12.3	26.6	27.8	d.n.a.	d.n.a.
With any child	57.4	60.9	57.5	56.1	57.1	64.7
With or next to any child	69.0	72.3	69.5	69.6	67.0	74.5
With any ever-married child	36.5	44.4	33.4	37.0	42.2	50.0
With an ever-married son	13.9	16.2	13.5	14.0	15.7	18.0
With an ever-married daughter	23.2	29.7	22.1	24.8	27.6	33.6
In a "skipped generation" household	14.7	13.9	16.9	16.9	6.4	11.6

Notes: "Skipped generation" households are those with one or more grandchildren but no married child or child-in-law. Within the total column, all gender differences are statistically significant at the .01 level except for skipped generation households; within living with spouse column only gender differences in living with any married child and with any married daughter are statistically significant at the .01 level; within the other marital situation column all gender differences except living with married son are statistically significant at the .01 level.
d.n.a. = does not apply.
Source: *2007 Survey of Older Persons in Thailand* (original tabulations).

percentage that live with or adjacent to children among all elderly and among elderly living with a spouse are minimal. Among older persons not living with a spouse, however, women are modestly more likely than men to be coresident or live adjacent to a child.

Coresidence with ever-married children reflects a mature stage of intergenerational living arrangements in which children often support rather than depend on parents. In line with the matrilocal tendency among ethnic Thais, more elders live with a married daughter than a son, a feature that is particularly pronounced among older women, especially those not living with a spouse (Knodel, Chayovan and Siriboon 1992).

A living arrangement involving older persons of particular interest is the so-called "skipped generation" household, that is, situations in which grandparents live together with dependent grandchildren in the absence of adult children. The main cause leading to skipped generation households in Thailand is out-migration of adult children, typically to find employment, but who leave their own young children behind (see Chapter 12, this volume). In the present study, skipped generation households are defined as those with one or more grandchildren but with no married child or child in-law present. Previous research revealed both increases in migration of adult children and a substantial increase in the skip generation households among elderly Thais between 1994 and 2007 (Knodel and Chayovan 2008). As Table 2.8 also shows, there is little difference in the percentage of older men or women in skipped generation households. However, the fact that skipped generation households are more common among women than among men who are not living with a spouse, suggests that the presence of a grandmother is more crucial than the presence of a grandfather for leaving grandchildren behind.

SOCIAL CONTACT WITH CHILDREN

Maintaining contact with children who leave the household is an important source of social and emotional well-being for elderly parents, especially if no children remain with them or live nearby. In recent years, the dramatic increase in access to telephones, especially cellphones, has greatly expanded the ability to keep in contact with absent children. In addition, transportation system improvements facilitate the ease of visits. Results in Table 2.9 make clear that only rarely do elderly parents with non-coresident children not see any during the year and that this differs little between mothers and fathers. If parents are living together, visits typically would be to both. More revealing, however, is that among those parents who do not live with their spouse (i.e. who are widowed, separated, divorced or live separately), gender differences in the frequency of visits with non-coresident children are minimal.

Overall, almost two-thirds of elderly Thais with non-coresident children maintain at least monthly telephone contact and over a third have weekly phone contact with minimal evident gender difference. E-mail contact is still extremely rare between elderly Thais and non-coresident children regardless of the gender of the parent.

A common concern in the popular media in Thailand, based largely on anecdotal evidence, is that migration of adult children is leaving large numbers of elderly parents deserted, especially in rural areas. Presumably parents who live with or adjacent to a child also see a child on a daily basis. For other parents, frequency of contact with children can be judged through information on visits, phone calls or provision of remittances. Summary measures included in Table 2.9 are based on a combination

TABLE 2.9

Frequency of Contact with Non-Coresident Children during Past Year, Parents Age 60 and Older, by Gender and Marital Situation, Thailand, 2007

| | Total | | Marital Situation | | | |
| | | | Living with Spouse | | Other | |
Per Cent Living:	Men	Women	Men	Women	Men	Women
Among parents with at least one non-coresident child						
% Who had visits from one or more						
Daily or almost daily	23.6	24.8	23.0	25.8	25.9	23.9
At least weekly	37.1	38.4	36.5	39.1	39.6	37.9
At least monthly	55.2	56.6	54.2	56.8	59.3	56.3
At least once during year	83.9	84.1	83.7	84.1	84.4	84.1
% who had phone contact with one or more						
Daily or almost daily	12.5	11.6	13.6	13.4	8.0	10.1
At least weekly	36.2	33.0	38.8	36.5	25.4	29.9
At least monthly	66.0	62.0	68.9	67.4	53.7	57.3
At least once during year	71.2	66.9	73.9	71.6	59.8	62.8
% who had e-mail contact						
Any during year	0.6	0.3	0.7	0.4	0.0	0.2

Summary measures of desertion among all parents

% With less than monthly contact	3.5	3.1	3.3	2.9	4.3	3.3
% With less than monthly contact and under 5000 baht remittances	2.3	1.9	2.2	1.8	2.7	2.0
% With less than monthly contact and no remittances	1.3	0.8	1.2	0.7	1.8	1.0
% With no contact during year	1.4	1.2	1.3	1.2	1.7	1.2
% With no contact and under 5000 baht remittances	1.0	0.9	0.9	0.9	1.3	0.8
% No contact and no remittances	0.6	0.4	0.5	0.4	1.2	0.5

Notes: Within the total column, gender differences are statistically significant at the .01 level for weekly, monthly and yearly telephone contact; within the with spouse column gender, differences are statistically significant at the .01 level for daily, weekly and monthly visits and for yearly telephone contact; within the other marital situation column, gender differences are statistically significant at the .01 level for all levels of telephone contact. Summary measures are based on combined information on coresidence, adjacent living, visits or phone calls with any child and remittances. Gender differences in the summary indicators are statistically significant at the .01 level only for the per cent with less than monthly contact and no remittances in each column.

Source: 2007 Survey of Older Persons in Thailand (original tabulations).

of this information and provide objective assessments of the extent of "desertion". In general, only about 3 per cent of older age parents have less than monthly contact with any child and only 1 per cent report that they had no contact with any of their children in the past year. Thus, regardless of gender, few older age parents in Thailand appear to be completely deserted.

SOURCES OF MATERIAL SUPPORT

Sources of Income

According to the 2007 Survey of Older Persons, 48 per cent of men and 26 per cent of women age 60 or older worked during the previous week. Previous research clearly documents that the percentage who worked declines steadily with age for both sexes (Knodel and Chayovan 2008). Interpretation of gender differences regarding work need to take into account that work in the survey includes unpaid family work but excludes domestic chores within the household. Also, whether working at older ages can be construed as an advantage or disadvantage depends on the reasons for working and how it is viewed by those involved.

Although important, work is but one of a number of possible sources of income for older aged Thais. As Table 2.10 indicates, children are by far the most common source of income regardless of gender of the older person. One's own work is distinctly the second most common source of income for men but for women, there is no single pronounced second most common source. Overall, 20 to 30 per cent indicate they receive income from each of several sources including work, elderly allowances, spouse, and some combination of interest, savings, and rent.

Among the married elderly who live with a spouse, women are considerably more likely than men to report a spouse as a source of income (48 per cent vs. 30 per cent). Presumably, this reflects the higher level of economic activity among men (see Chapters 10 and 11, this volume). Women are modestly more likely than men to report children and relatives as sources of income and minimal gender difference is evident in receipt of elderly allowances. While men are more likely to report pensions, fewer than 10 per cent do so, reflecting the high proportions of elderly Thais whose main occupation was in farming or otherwise outside the formal sector.

Table 2.10 also examines the main source of income. Several striking gender differences are apparent. Overall, among the older population, children are by far the most common main source of income for women

TABLE 2.10

Sources of Income and Main Source of Income, Persons Age 60 and Older, by Gender and Marital Situation, Thailand, 2007

			Marital Situation			
			Living with Spouse		Other	
	Total					
	Men	Women	Men	Women	Men	Women
% Receiving Income from the following Sources						
Work	51.0	27.2	55.5	35.1	33.0	20.9
Pension	8.5	2.9	8.7	3.0	7.5	2.8
Elderly allowance	23.1	25.5	20.6	18.3	33.0	31.2
Interest/savings/rent	33.8	30.1	35.0	32.0	29.1	28.6
Spouse	24.8	22.1	30.3	48.1	3.1	1.4
Children	79.5	85.3	79.8	85.6	78.2	85.0
Relatives	9.5	12.3	7.3	7.7	17.9	16.0
Other	1.3	1.7	1.2	1.2	1.5	2.2
Main Source of Current Income						
Work	41.4	18.8	45.2	24.6	26.7	14.1
Pension	6.6	2.5	6.7	2.5	6.2	2.5
Elderly allowance	2.5	3.0	1.8	1.4	5.3	4.4
Interest/savings/rent	3.0	2.7	3.1	2.9	2.6	2.6
Spouse	3.8	7.9	4.6	17.6	0.5	0.3
Children	40.8	61.5	38.0	50.4	52.0	70.2
Other relatives	1.4	2.9	0.2	0.3	6.2	5.0
Other	0.4	0.6	0.3	0.3	0.5	0.9
Total	100	100	100	100	100	100

Note: All gender differences are statistically significant at the .01 level except for per cent receiving income from relatives and from other under both with spouse and other marital situation columns and elderly allowance and interest/savings/rent under the other marital situation column.
Source: 2007 Survey of Older Persons in Thailand (original tabulations).

while for men, children and work are almost equal in this respect. Children and work account for the main sources of income for about four-fifths of older persons regardless of gender. Pensions are more often the main income source for older men than for older women. Among married older persons living with spouses, women are far more likely than men to cite their spouse as their main source. Among older persons who do not live with a spouse, children are the most common main source of income for both men and women although even more so for women.

Family Support

Children can be an important source of material support. Results in Table 2.11 show receipt of money separately for coresident and non-coresident children with results based on parents who have at least one

TABLE 2.11
Material Support from Children during the Past Year, Parents Age 60 and Older, by Gender and Marital Situation, Thailand, 2007

	Total		Living with Spouse		Other	
	Men	Women	Men	Women	Men	Women
% Who received money from coresident children among parents with at least one coresident child						
Any money	65.4	78.0	63.5	72.2	72.8	81.9
At least 5,000 baht	33.5	38.7	33.9	38.7	31.8	38.7
% Who received material support from non-coresident children among parents with at least one non-coresident child						
Money						
Any money	75.4	81.6	75.1	80.6	76.4	82.5
At least 5,000 baht	48.8	52.3	49.5	53.9	45.6	50.8
Food						
Daily or almost daily	16.3	19.0	14.7	17.4	23.0	20.5
At least weekly	32.7	36.3	31.9	35.8	36.3	36.8
At least monthly	52.9	57.4	52.6	57.7	54.0	57.2
Goods or clothes						
At least monthly	16.3	18.9	16.1	17.8	16.8	19.9
At least once during year	79.7	83.2	80.1	83.6	77.9	83.0

Note: All gender differences are statistically significant at the .01 level except for per cent receiving food weekly under the other marital situation column and per cent receiving goods under the total and other marital situation columns.
Source: *2007 Survey of Older Persons in Thailand* (original tabulations).

child of the relevant type. Provision of food and goods were only asked in relation to non-coresident children in the 2007 survey. A substantial majority of coresident parents received money during the year from at least one coresident child and one-third received at least 5,000 baht in total. Regardless of marital situation, mothers are somewhat more likely than fathers to receive money from coresident children. Receipt of money from non-coresident children is somewhat more common than from coresident children, especially with respect to larger amounts. Again mothers are favoured compared to fathers both among parents who live with their spouse and among those who do not (i.e. who are widowed, separated, divorced or live separately) (see Chapter 12, this volume).

Receipt of food from non-coresident children is very common in Thailand although often provided only during occasional visits and is typically of symbolic value. Regular provision of food is less usual and can be a meaningful source of material support. Receipt of food on a regular basis is modestly more common for elderly women than men. Receipt of clothing or goods at least occasionally is also very common but on a far less frequent basis than food. Although such gifts may be only a symbolic gesture, unlike food, a single gift sometimes is an item of significant value. Mothers are only slightly more likely to receive such help than are fathers.

SUPPORT AND SERVICES PROVIDED BY OLDER PERSONS

Older aged Thais not only receive services and material support but also contribute to exchanges within the family. The 2007 Survey of Older Persons indicates that the flow of money from parents to coresident and non-coresident children is far less common than in the reverse direction. Still to the extent they exist, older age fathers are more likely than mothers to provide children with money. For example, among coresident parents 60 and older, 17 per cent of fathers and 8 per cent of mothers had given their coresident children some money in the prior year and 9 per cent of fathers and 3 per cent of mothers had given at least 5,000 baht. Monetary support to non-coresident children is even less common but fathers are more likely than mothers to provide such help. Thus, among parents with non-coresident children, 8 per cent of fathers and 4 per cent of mothers had given a non-coresident child some money in the prior year and 5 per cent of fathers and 3 per cent of mothers had given at least 5,000 baht.

Indirect material support from older age parents is much more common than monetary support. Just over three-fourths of coresident parents 60 and older own the residence and, thus, provide shelter for the children who live with them. According to the 1995 Survey of the Welfare of Elderly in Thailand, coresident fathers were more likely than mothers to be the owner of the residence (original tabulations by authors).

Older age parents as grandparents often assist with the care of grandchildren, from both coresident and non-coresident children, thus freeing the parents of the grandchildren to engage in economic activity outside the home. In some cases, the grandparents may virtually take full responsibility for much of the upbringing of grandchildren from migrant children. This is already suggested from the information on the skipped generation households presented above. The 2007 Survey of Older Persons in Thailand collected direct information on grandchild care. As Table 2.12 shows, over 40 per cent of both older men and women live with at least one minor aged grandchild and one-fourth have coresident minor age grandchildren whose parents are absent. Among the elderly, overall, there is little gender difference in this respect. However, in situations where only one grandparent is in the household, grandmothers are more likely than grandfathers to live with a minor grandchild, especially when the grandchild has no parent present. In cases where minor age grandchildren are present but whose parents are absent, grandmothers are more likely than grandfathers to be responsible for their care, regardless of the marital situation of the grandparents. Still, among those who are married and living together, it is quite common for both grandparents to share the care. It is also true that in a sizable proportion of cases, the grandparents are not the main caregiver for the grandchildren.

With respect to financial support, in the large majority of cases of grandchildren with absent parents, the grandchild's own parents are primarily financially responsible for the child. This undoubtedly reflects an ability to send remittances by adult children who migrated elsewhere to find employment (Knodel et al. 2007). Among the small minority in which the grandparents are responsible, grandfathers appear to be somewhat more likely to be financially responsible than grandmothers except in cases where the grandparent is not living with a spouse.

TABLE 2.12
Presence of Coresident Minor Age Grandchildren and their Care and Support, Persons Age 60 and Older, Thailand, 2007

| | Total | | Marital Situation | | | |
| | | | Living with Spouse | | Other | |
	Men	Women	Men	Women	Men	Women
Among All Persons Age 60 and Older						
% With coresident minor age grandchild	41.7	44.9	43.8	45.4	33.5	44.5
% With coresident minor age grandchild whose parents are absent or dead[a]	25.4	25.2	27.9	28.7	15.2	22.5
Among Persons Age 60 and Above with Coresident Minor Age Grandchild whose Parents are Absent or Dead						
% Caring for grandchild						
Self	12.5	33.9	10.8	25.3	25.2	42.6
Spouse	22.2	4.1	25.3	8.0	0.0	0.2
Self and spouse	20.7	12.1	23.6	23.7	0.0	0.4
% Financially supporting grandchild						
Self	6.2	5.5	6.3	3.2	6.0	7.9
Spouse	2.4	1.8	2.7	3.5	0.0	0.1
Self and spouse	7.1	3.9	8.1	7.7	0.0	0.0
Parent of child	82.3	85.2	81.3	83.2	89.7	87.0

Notes: Minor age grandchildren are under age 18. All gender differences are statistically significant at the .01 level except per cent with coresident minor age grandchild whose parents are absent or dead under the total column and living with spouse column and per cent with coresident minor age grandchild under the living with spouse column.

[a] Because of ambiguity in the survey questionnaire, a small number of cases with only adult grandchildren may be included in this category.

Source: 2007 Survey of Older Persons in Thailand (original tabulations).

MATERIAL WELL-BEING
Income, Assets, Debt and Financial Assistance

Table 2.13 presents measures of income and assets of persons age 60 and above. The top panel shows the percentage distribution of persons 60 and older according to their reported average annual income in Thai baht. The second panel shows the percentage distribution according to the value of their property and savings. Property includes gold, expensive possessions, house and land. Interpreting gender differences in income among married persons is complicated since spouses likely share benefits from each other's incomes. While access to income does not necessarily imply decision-making and control over resources, in Thailand, wives typically control household budgets (Knodel, Chamratrithirong and Debavalya 1987). Likewise with ownership of assets, each partner in a marriage may benefit from the assets regardless of which spouse owns it. Among those not living with a spouse, gender comparisons are far less ambiguous since no spouse shares income or assets with the respondent.

Overall, the percentage distribution of older persons by income favours men. Women are more concentrated than men in the lower income categories and less in the higher income categories. When distribution of men and women not living with a spouse are compared however, there is far less difference and men are actually more likely than women to fall into the lowest income category. Somewhat similar patterns are evident for the distribution by the combined value of property and savings. Overall, men show a more favourable distribution but again this pattern is absent among those not living with a spouse. Since among couples, spouses are likely to benefit from each other's income and assets, these findings do not necessarily reflect a disadvantage in material well-being for women.

The economic situation of the household also depends on the extent of debt and the ability to gain assistance in case severe financial difficulties arise. As the third panel of Table 2.13 shows, overall, slightly more than half of both older men and women live in households that are debt free. Among those who live with a spouse, there is also little gender difference in terms of debt but among those not living with a spouse, a modestly higher proportion of women live in households where some members are in debt. Men are more likely, however, to be themselves in debt or to share debt with another household member than are women. For women in households in debt, the debt is generally the responsibility of some other members. This pattern is particularly pronounced among older persons who live with a spouse and thus suggests that husbands rather than wives

TABLE 2.13

Per Cent Distributions of Persons Age 60 and Older According to Average Annual Income, Value of Property and Savings (in Thai baht), Debt, and Availability of Someone to Help if Financial Assistance was Needed, by Gender and Marital Status, Thailand, 2007

	Total		Marital Situation Living with Spouse		Other	
	Men	Women	Men	Women	Men	Women
Annual income						
Under 10,000	13.9	19.1	10.8	14.4	26.2	22.8
10,000–29,999	32.3	37.2	32.6	37.3	31.0	37.1
30,000–99,999	35.8	30.4	37.2	33.6	29.9	27.9
100,000+	18.0	13.3	19.4	14.7	12.8	12.2
Total	100	100	100	100	100	100
Value of property and savings						
None	26.6	35.0	24.2	32.6	36.3	36.9
Under 100,000	23.6	24.9	23.3	24.5	24.4	25.2
100,000–399,999	26.8	23.4	28.3	24.8	20.8	22.3
400,000–999,999	16.0	11.6	16.6	12.2	13.6	11.1
1,000,000+	7.0	5.2	7.5	5.9	4.9	4.6
Total	100	100	100	100	100	100

TABLE 2.13 (Cont'd)

| | Total | | Marital Situation | | | |
| | | | Living with Spouse | | Other | |
	Men	Women	Men	Women	Men	Women
Debt in household						
Self only	14.6	7.1	15.5	4.5	11.0	9.2
Other member only	19.7	30.9	18.2	30.0	25.8	31.6
Self and other	14.7	9.1	16.9	13.8	5.9	5.4
No one in debt	51.0	52.9	49.4	51.7	57.3	53.8
Total	100	100	100	100	100	100
Could someone provide financial assistance if needed						
Yes	77.0	75.5	78.5	78.2	71.3	73.3
No	8.8	9.1	8.4	8.2	10.3	9.8
Unsure	14.2	15.4	13.2	13.6	18.4	16.9
Total	100	100	100	100	100	100

Note: All gender differences for income, value of property and savings, and debt are statistically significant at the .01 level; gender differences with respect to availability of assistance are statistically significant at the .01 level only under the total column.
Source: 2007 *Survey of Older Persons in Thailand* (original tabulations).

tend to be responsible for household debt. If these debts are incurred in terms of household businesses such as borrowing for agricultural inputs, the gender difference in who is responsible for debt may reflect traditional gender roles in such matters as well as the higher level of economic activity among men compared to women.

As the last panel of Table 2.13 shows, over three-fourths of both older men and women indicated that someone would be available to provide financial assistance in case it was needed. Regardless of marital situation, gender differences are largely absent.

Housing Quality, Household Possessions and Self-Assessed Economic Well-Being

As evident from Figure 2.1, gender differences are minimal among older Thais with respect to the quality of housing, as measured by living in

FIGURE 2.1

Gender Differences among Persons Age 60 and Above in Housing Quality and Household Possessions, Thailand, 2007

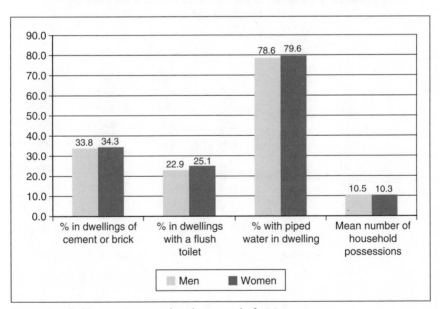

Notes: Household possession score based on a total of 19 items.
Gender differences in flush toilet and mean number of possessions are statistically significant at the .01 level.
Source: *2007 Survey of Older Persons in Thailand* (original tabulations).

dwellings constructed of cement or brick, that have a flush toilet, and that have piped water inside the dwelling. Each of these housing characteristics is superior to their alternatives and, thus, reflects better economic standing. Likewise, there is minimal difference between older men and women in the mean number of household possessions based on a simple count. These household possessions include appliances, transportation vehicles, and other items that make daily living more convenient.

The 2007 Survey of Older Persons asked respondents to judge the sufficiency of their income and their satisfaction with their financial situation. As Figure 2.2 shows, regardless of marital situation, gender differences are almost non-existent and accord reasonably well with the more objective measures of material well-being reviewed above. Moreover, there is virtually no relationship between marital situation and self-assessed economic well-being. Analyses of national surveys conducted in 1994 and

FIGURE 2.2

Gender Differences among Persons Age 60 and Above in Self-Assessed Income Sufficiency and Financial Satisfaction, Thailand, 2007

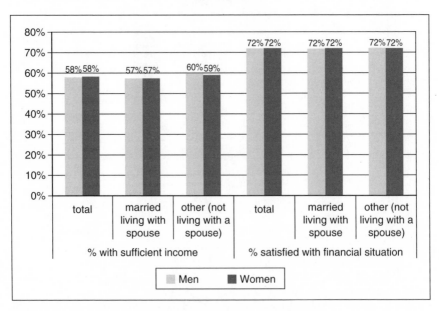

Note: No gender difference is statistically significant at the .01 level.
Source: *2007 Survey of Older Persons in Thailand* (original tabulations).

1995 produced quite similar findings with respect to perceived economic well-being (Sobieszczyk, Knodel and Chayovan 2003). Thus, while being in an intact marriage is likely to provide important social support and may be critical for meeting caregiving needs, it appears to confer little advantage for an elderly person with respect to his or her self-perceived material well-being.

DISCUSSION AND CONCLUSIONS

The foregoing analyses suggest that there are both significant similarities and differences in the situation of older men and women in Thailand. On a number of measures of current physical and psychological health, however, older Thai women appear to be worse off than men. Nevertheless, older Thai women live longer and thus are advantaged on the most crucial measure of health. In part because of this survival advantage, older Thai women are significantly more likely than men to experience marital dissolution through widowhood. Gender differences in educational opportunities in the past have resulted in lower levels of literacy and educational attainment among the current generation of older women. This education gender gap, however, is declining as new cohorts for whom the gender gap is reduced move into the elderly age span. Women are also more likely to live alone, although this is largely a function of gender differences in marital status.

There are also gender differences that do not necessarily convey disadvantage. For example, older Thai women are less likely to be economically active and more likely to depend on children or relatives as their main source of income. The latter reflects their lower economic activity and their greater likelihood to be non-married, a situation associated with greater economic dependence on adult children. Other differences are apparent in which older Thai men are disadvantaged. In part related to their higher mortality, older men have worse health risk behaviours regarding smoking and drinking. Also, among older persons with no spouse present, men are less likely than women to coreside with a child. Men are also less likely than older women to receive money from a child and more likely to experience debt.

Older men and women also assist their adult children. Older women as grandmothers are more likely than grandfathers to care for minor-aged grandchildren whose parents are absent. However, consistent with their higher level of economic activity, older men are more likely to provide financial assistance to both coresident and non-coresident children, although only a modest minority do so.

On numerous measures of well-being, older Thai men and women are relatively similar. Social contact with children differs little between fathers and mothers and few of either sex are deserted by all their adult children. Perhaps most striking is that older men and women are similar in their material well-being as measured by the quality of their housing, the number of household possessions, self-assessed adequacy of income, and satisfaction with financial situation. Although women living with a spouse disproportionately report lower personal income and wealth than men, as wives they likely benefit from their husbands' income and wealth. Among older persons not living with a spouse, older women fare at least as well as men. Moreover, self-assessed material well-being does not differ by marital situation. Hence, in this respect, the higher levels of widowhood among older women do not appear to disadvantage them. At the same time, it is important to recognize that substantial proportions of the older population in Thailand are still quite poor regardless of gender. Less than two-thirds of both men and women 60 and older say they consistently have sufficient income and over one-fourth report that they are dissatisfied with their financial situation.

Marital status often mediates gender differences in well-being among older persons (see Chapter 5, this volume). In some cases, analysis of gender in conjunction with marital status reveals that certain groups face particular disadvantage in old age. For instance, women who do not have a coresident spouse are significantly less likely than their male counterparts to have access to pensions. Also, given the past sharp fall in fertility rates in Thailand, future cohorts of older persons will have far fewer children available to provide support. Because older women, and particularly non-married older women, tend to be more dependent than men on children, they may constitute a disproportionate share of those who will be most in need of government financial assistance.

References

Chayovan, Napaporn and John Knodel. *A Report on the Survey of the Welfare of the Elderly in Thailand*. Bangkok: Chulalongkorn University, 1997.

Chayovan, Napaporn, John Knodel and Siriwan Siriboon. "Thailand's Elderly Population: A Demographic and Social Profile Based on Official Statistical Sources". Comparative Study of the Elderly in Asia. Research Report No. 90-2. Population Studies Center, University of Michigan, 1990.

Cowgill, Donald O. "The Social Life of the Aged in Thailand". *The Gerontologist* 8 (1968): 159–63.

———. "The Role and Status of the Aged in Thailand". *Ageing and Modernization* (1972): 91–101.

Feith, H. and A. Smith. "Indonesia". *Southeast Asia: Documents of Political Development and Change* (1970): 99–110.

Henderson, John W., Helen A. Barth, Judith M. Heimann, Philip W. Moeller, Rinn-Sup Shinn, Francis S. Soriano, John O. Weaver and Eston T. White. *Area Handbook for Thailand.* Washington, D.C.: U.S. Government Printing Office, 1971.

Hermalin, A.I., M.B. Ofstedal and R. Tesfai. "Future Characteristics of the Elderly in Developing Countries and their Implications for Policy". *Asian Population Studies* 3, no. 1 (2007): 5–36.

Idler, E.L. and Y. Benyami. "Self-rated Health and Mortality: A Review of Twenty-Seven Community Studies". *Journal of Health and Social Behavior* 36 (1997): 21–37.

Jitapunkul, Sutthichai, Napaporn Chayovan and Jiraporn Kespichayawattana. "National Policies and Long Term Care of Elderly in Thailand". In *Ageing and Long-Term Care: National Policies in the Asia Pacific*, edited by D.R. Phillips and A.C.M. Chan. Singapore: Institute of Southeast Asian Studies, 2002.

Klausner, William J. "The Drunkard: Challenge and Response". In *Reflections on Thai Culture.* Thailand: Sayam Samakhom, 1993.

Knodel, John. "The Closing of the Gender Gap in Schooling: The Case of Thailand". *Comparative Education* 33, no. 1 (1997): 61–86.

———. "Older Women in Thailand: Are They Really Worse Off Than the Men?". In *Untapped Resources: Women in Ageing Societies Across Asia*, 2nd ed., edited by K. Mehta. Singapore: Marshall Cavendish Academic Press, 2004.

Knodel, John, Aphichat Chamratrithirong and Nibhon Debavalya. *Thailand's Reproductive Revolution: Rapid Fertility Decline in a Third World Setting.* Madison: University of Wisconsin Press, 1987.

Knodel, John, S. Chanpen and W. Obiero. "Do Small Families Jeopardize Old Age Security? Evidence from Thailand". *BOLD* 5, no. 4 (1995): 13–17.

Knodel, John, S. Chanpen and W. Sittitrai. "The Living Arrangements of Elderly in Thailand: Views of the Populace". *Journal of Cross-Cultural Gerontology* 10 (1995): 79–111.

Knodel, John, Jiraporn Kespichayawattana, Suvinee Wiwatwanich and Chanpen Saengtienchai. "Migration and Inter-generational Solidarity: Evidence from Rural Thailand". UNFPA Country Technical Services Team for East and Southeast Asia. Papers in Population Ageing Series, No 2. Bangkok: United Nations Population Fund, 2007.

Knodel, John and M.B. Ofstedal. "Gender & Ageing in the Developing World: Where Are the Men?". *Population and Development Review* 29, no. 4 (2003): 677–98.

Knodel, John and Napaporn Chayovan. "Population Ageing and the Well-being of Older Persons in Thailand". UNFPA Country Technical Services Team for East and Southeast Asia. Papers in Population Ageing Series, No 5. Bangkok: United Nations Population Fund, 2008.

Knodel, John, N. Chayovan, and S. Siriboon. "The Impact of Fertility Decline on Familial Support for the Elderly: An Illustration from Thailand". *Population and Development Review* 18, no. 1 (1992): 79–102.

Mason, K.O. "Family Change and Support of the Elderly in Asia: What Do We Know?". *Asia-Pacific Population Journal* 7, no. 3 (1992): 13–32.

Mehta, Kalyani. *Untapped Resources: Women in Ageing Societies*. Singapore: Times Academic Press, 1997.

———., ed. *Untapped Resources: Women in Ageing Societies Across Asia*, 2nd ed. Singapore: Marshall Cavendish Academic Press, 2004.

National Economic and Social Development Board (NESDB). *Population Projections for Thailand, 2000–2030*. Bangkok: National Economic and Social Development Board, 2007.

National Statistical Office (NSO). *Report on the 2007 Survey of Older Persons in Thailand*. Bangkok: National Statistical Office, 2008.

Reichart, P.A. "Oral Cancer and Precancer Related to Betel and *Miang* Chewing in Thailand: A Review". *Oral Pathology and Medicine* 24 (1995): 241–43.

Sobieszczyk, T., J. Knodel and N. Chayovan. "Gender and Well-Being among the Elderly: Evidence from Thailand". *Ageing & Society* 23, no. 6 (2003): 701–35.

Soonthorndhada, Amara, Rossarin Gray, Kusol Soonthorndhada and P.K. Viswanathan. "Elderly women in Thailand: Roles and Position". In *The Elderly Women in Asia: Her Roles and Position*, edited by J. Troisi and A.L. Pawiliczko. Malta: United Nations International Institute on Ageing, 2008.

Troisi, Joseph and Ann L. Pawiliczko, eds. *The Elderly Women in Asia: Her Roles and Position*. Malta: United Nations International Institute on Ageing, 2008.

United Nations. *Report of the Second World Assembly on Ageing. Madrid, 8–12 April 2002*. Publication A/CONF.197/9. New York: United Nations, 2002.

———. *World Population Prospects: The 2008 Revision*. New York: United Nations, 2009.

———. *World Population Ageing 2007*. New York: United Nations, 2007.

United Nations International Research and Training Institute for the Advancement of Women (INSTRAW). *Ageing in a Gendered World*. Santo Domingo, Dominican Republic: INSTRAW, 1999.

Verbrugge, L. "The Twain Meet: Empirical Explanations of Sex Differences in Health and Mortality". *Journal of Health and Social Behavior* 30, no. 3 (1989): 282–304.

World Health Organization (WHO). *Men, Ageing and Health*. Publication WHO/NMH/NPH/01.2. Geneva: World Health Organization, 2001.

Yang, Tracy. "Crisis, Contagion, and East Asian Stock Markets". ISEAS Working Papers on Economics and Finance No. 1. Singapore: Institute of Southeast Asian Studies, 2002.

Zimmer, Z. and K. Korinek. "Does Family Size Predict Whether an Older Adult Lives With or Proximate to an Adult Child in the Asia-Pacific Region?" *Asian Population Studies* 4, no. 2 (2008): 135–59.

3

GENDER AND WELL-BEING OF OLDER PERSONS IN CAMBODIA

John Knodel and Zachary Zimmer

INTRODUCTION

Today's population of older Cambodians lived through an exceptionally traumatic period of history during their adult years. Prolonged civil strife starting in the 1960s eventually led to the complete take over of the country by the brutal Khmer Rouge regime in 1975. During their four-year rule, political violence, severe food shortages, and lack of medical care resulted in the deaths of as much as a fourth of the population (Heuveline 1998). Many who died were the children or spouses of today's older-aged population. Social dislocation, continuing political conflict, pervasive poverty, and an AIDS epidemic took their toll during the succeeding years resulting in further losses of family members. These events potentially threaten the core family support of older persons in a country that is among the poorest in Asia and where formal channels of assistance are minimal (Knodel 2007; Zimmer et al. 2006).

Population ageing is at an early stage in Cambodia with less than 6 per cent of the current total population being 60 or older, the lowest proportion of elderly of all the countries in Southeast Asia (Mujahid 2006). The low proportion of elderly in the population has resulted in the general lack of attention to issues related to older persons by the Cambodian government and most international agencies. Nevertheless, over one in four households or around 27 per cent has at least one member who is 60 or older.[1] With recent prodding by UNFPA and HelpAge International, ageing is beginning to emerge as an issue on the government's agenda, although efforts are modest and mostly appear to be in the planning stages (Office of the Council of Ministers 2007; UNESCAP 2007).

Gender issues in general have received some attention in Cambodia, although the focus almost exclusively concerns the interests of women. Again this is in part, if not in the main, in response to the prompting and support of international agencies (UNIFEM et al. 2004; UNDP Cambodia 2008). Specific concerns about older persons, however, are virtually absent in the discourse concerning either gender or ageing. The extensive gender assessment conducted on behalf of international agencies makes almost no mention of the needs or situation of either older men or women (UNIFEM et al. 2004). In part, this lack of attention results from the paucity of relevant research on the topic of ageing for Cambodia. Yet, as detailed below, understanding issues concerning gender and ageing is particularly pertinent for Cambodia given the unusually large predominance of women in the older population.

The present study helps redress the lack of relevant research on gender and ageing. It provides an overview of the situation of older men and women in Cambodia with respect to a variety of dimensions that relate to their well-being. The primary data source, and one uniquely suited to the purpose, is the 2004 Survey of Elderly in Cambodia (SEC), a representative survey of 1,273 persons 60 and older conducted in Phnom Penh and the five largest provinces. We also draw on the nationally representative 2004 Cambodian Inter-censal Population Survey (ICDS) and 2005 Demographic and Health Survey (DHS).[2] In all cases, we present original tabulations. While our study is primarily descriptive, we hope it will provide a solid empirical foundation for more analytical treatments of the subject that can interpret the findings in relation to the nature of the social order in Cambodian society in general, and the place of gender within it, in particular.

COUNTRY SETTING

Cambodia is one of the world's "least developed countries" and ranks low on the Human Development Index (UNAIDS 2006). Much of Cambodia's human capital was depleted during the rule of the Khmer Rouge and its aftermath. During the Khmer Rouge reign, educated and professional persons were badly treated and subjected to targeted executions (de Walque 2005). Others died of pervasive starvation and disease. Many took flight as refugees during and after the Khmer Rouge rule and never returned. Although the Khmer Rouge were dislodged from national power by forces from Vietnam at the end of 1978 and early 1979, they maintained a presence in parts of the countryside. Significant civil strife continued during the ten-year period of occupation by Vietnam and several years after. UN-sponsored elections in 1993 helped restore some semblance of normality, although factional fighting at times among coalition partners undermined political stability.

In recent years the economy has improved, fuelled by economic growth driven largely by an expanding garment sector and tourism. Still, over 80 per cent of the population lives in rural areas and most depends on agriculture for their living. Moreover, the future of economic growth in Cambodia is uncertain given the global economic crisis currently unfolding, and the uneven nature of recent economic success coming from only a couple of industries (CIA 2008; PRB 2008).

Culturally, the population is relatively homogeneous with respect to ethnic and religious composition. Approximately 90 per cent of the population identifies itself as ethnic Khmer, and 95 per cent profess Theravada Buddhism. According to the extensive Cambodia gender assessment by international agencies, despite decades of turmoil, hierarchical notions of power and status within the society persist, conditioning social relations and relegating women to lower status than men (UNIFEM et al. 2004). The extent of which such a sweeping generalization of women's position in Cambodian society, however, is contentious and ignores the considerable complexities discussed in the academic literature (e.g. Jacobson 2006; Ledgerwood 1995; Lee 2006).

SOCIO-DEMOGRAPHIC CHARACTERISTICS

United Nations' estimates (United Nations 2009) indicate that in 2000, fewer than 600,000 of the almost 13 million Cambodians were age 60 and older. The projections anticipate, however, a rapid growth of the older population, reaching almost four million by 2050, with their population share rising to 16 per cent. Still, population ageing in Cambodia will be well behind that anticipated for the region as a whole where 23 per cent of the population is projected to be age 60 and older by 2050.

Predominance of Women

In most countries, women exceed men at older ages because of female advantage in survival chances throughout the life span. This excess is unusually pronounced in Cambodia as a result of the disproportionate share of men who died during the long period of civil strife and especially during the Khmer Rouge period (de Walque 2005). Figure 3.1 clearly illustrates this feature of Cambodia's 2005 older age population, defined as those age 60 and above, based on UN estimates. The ratio of women to men in older ages in Cambodia far exceeds that in either neighbouring Thailand or Southeast Asia overall. Moreover, as Figure 3.1 also shows, this unusual imbalance also holds for Cambodians in their fifties, that is, the age group that will be entering the older age span during the following decade.

At the same time, UN projections indicate that the magnitude of the female majority among the 60 and older population is expected to diminish considerably over time. By mid-century, women are projected to constitute only 54 per cent of the older population compared to 64 per

Figure 3.1
Female Sex Ratio by Age Group, Cambodia, Thailand and Southeast Asia, 2005

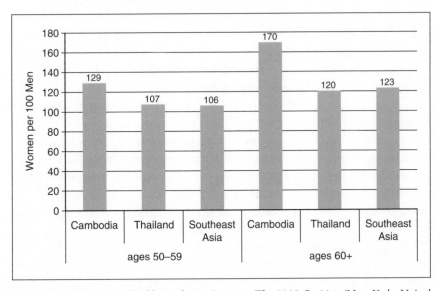

Source: United Nations, *World Population Prospects: The 2008 Revision* (New York: United Nations, 2009).

cent in 2000. This substantial decrease is the result of upcoming cohorts who have not been subject to the distorting influence of the unusually high male mortality associated with past civil strife. In contrast, UN projections anticipate only modest change in the sex imbalance for Southeast Asia as a whole, while the percentage of females among the older population is not anticipated to differ between 2000 and 2050 — being at 55 per cent in both years (UN 2009). Thus by 2050, Cambodia's proportion of older persons should resemble other countries in the region in this respect and will no longer be an exception.

Marital Status and Living Children

An elderly person's marital status has important implications for well-being (see Chapters 2 and 5, this volume). Spouses can be primary sources of material, social and emotional support and provide personal care during times of illness or frailty. Thus, living with a spouse typically has advantages for older persons. According to the 2004 ICDS, less than 1 per cent of men and less than 2 per cent of women age 60 and above were never married and fewer than 2 per cent of men and 4 per cent of women were then separated or divorced. Far more striking gender differences are evident with respect to the per cent currently married or widowed. The large majority of elderly men (86 per cent) compared to only 48 per cent of elderly women are currently married. In contrast, only 11 per cent of men compared to 46 per cent of older women are widowed. This difference reflects a combination of higher male mortality, a tendency for men to marry women younger than themselves, and higher remarriage rates among men than women. The gender difference in the percentage of those married and widowed hold for all old age cohorts but is particularly pronounced among the oldest. Among those age 80 and above, only 32 per cent of women in contrast to 63 per cent of men are currently married while the reverse percentages hold for widowhood.

Adult children are important sources of social and material support as well as personal care for their older age parents in most Southeast Asian countries. Beyond this, coresidence with children and living nearby depend in part on the number of children available (Zimmer and Korinek 2008). Data from the SEC indicate that only 1 per cent of older men and 5 per cent of women are childless. Family size remains large among elderly Cambodians who have children, although men on average have more children than women (5.6 versus 4.4).

Loss of Spouses and Children in the Past

As noted above, Cambodian elders of today lived through a historical period characterized by severe social dislocation, wide-scale civil conflict, and political violence, resulting in the death of many family members. The most traumatic period was between 1975 and early 1979 when up to a fourth of the population perished during the Khmer Rouge rule. Adult mortality was particularly high for men (de Walque 2005). Thus, it is of interest to examine gender differences among today's elderly with respect to the loss of spouses and children in the past, particularly in relation to the Khmer Rouge years.

As Table 3.1 indicates, large shares of today's elders lost a spouse during their lifetime. However, the percentage of elders who lost their spouses is twice that for women than men. Loss of a spouse because of

TABLE 3.1

Per Cent of Persons Age 60 and Above Who Experienced Deaths of Spouses and Deaths of Children Age 11 or Older by Sex, Cause of Death, and Period of Death in Relation to Khmer Rouge (KR) Rule, Cambodian Elders, 2004

Cause	Period	Loss of a Spouse		Loss of a Child Age 11+	
		Men	Women	Men	Women
All causes [a]	All periods	30.9	67.8*	42.8	52.5*
	Pre KR	8.0	12.9*	4.6	6.2
	During KR	5.9	23.1*	19.5	32.4*
	Post KR	19.5	33.8*	25.9	23.3
Violence [b]	All periods	2.1	16.6*	20.1	31.0*
	Pre KR	0.2	0.8	1.8	1.9
	During KR	1.9	15.5*	16.1	28.0*
	Post KR	0.0	0.3	2.6	1.9
Illness	All periods	27.3	45.4*	21.9	23.8
	Pre KR	7.4	8.9	2.0	4.3*
	During KR	2.9	5.9*	3.6	4.6
	Post KR	18.6	31.1*	18.0	17.0

Notes: Pre KR = 1970–75; During KR = 1975–79; post KR = 1979–2004.
[a] includes violence, disappearance, illness, accident and other causes
[b] includes violence and disappearance
* Women significantly different from men at p < .05.
Source: 2004 Survey of Elderly in Cambodia (original tabulations).

violence is largely concentrated during the Khmer Rouge years and is confined mainly to deaths of husbands rather than wives. Overall, the loss of spouses to illness is considerably more common than the loss to violence. During the Khmer Rouge years, deaths of men and thus of husbands were actually more commonly attributable to violence than to illness

Table 3.1 also examines the per cent of today's elders who lost a child in the past. Results are shown for the loss of children age 11 and above since violent deaths are largely restricted to this age upwards. Both men and women attributed large shares of the deaths of their children age 11 and above to violence with most such deaths occurring during the Khmer Rouge period. Despite the period lasting only four years, substantial proportions of both elderly men and women lost at least one child during those years. Men were somewhat less likely than women to report losing a child. The difference is mainly attributed to difference in losses because of violence during the Khmer Rouge period. This difference could arise because men were more likely to be victims of violence than were women. Hence, in areas where Khmer Rouge violence was severe, the survival chances of women over men would have been substantial. In contrast, where the violence was less common, women's survival advantage would be more modest. Thus, men who survived the Khmer Rouge period would be more likely than women to come from areas where violent death was less of a risk not only for themselves but also for children. Unlike violent deaths, there is not a large difference in the proportion of men and women who reported losses of children age 11 and above owing to illness.

Education and Literacy

Substantial gender differences in education were pervasive in Cambodia in the past and especially during the time when the current older population was of school-going age. As Table 3.2 clearly shows, based on the 2005 Cambodia DHS, differences in formal education are stark between elderly men and women in Cambodia. Over three-fourths of women received no formal schooling compared to only slightly more than one-fourth of men. Thus, the percentage of men who attained each level of education shown is higher than that of women.

For both men and women, the proportion with no education increases substantially with age. At the same time, very large gender differences are apparent at every age within the elderly age span. Even among women in the younger elderly years, the substantial majority never attended school.

TABLE 3.2

Educational Attainment by Gender and Age, Cambodia, 2005

Age	% With No Education		% With any Primary Education (Incomplete or Complete)		% With Any Secondary or Higher Education	
	Men	Women	Men	Women	Men	Women
60–64	15.9	58.4	59.6	36.1	24.5	5.5
65–69	20.7	77.6	60.1	20.0	19.2	2.4
70–74	35.8	86.8	49.5	11.6	14.6	1.6
75–79	37.8	94.2	52.1	5.5	10.1	0.3
80+	44.5	91.7	45.9	8.3	9.6	0.0
Total	25.9	77.3	55.8	20.1	18.3	2.7

Source: National Institute of Public Health, National Institute of Statistics [Cambodia] and ORC Macro, *Cambodia Demographic and Health Survey 2005* (Phnom Penh, Cambodia and Calverton, Maryland: National Institute of Public Health, National Institute of Statistics and ORC Macro, 2006).

Gender differences are extremely pronounced with respect to the percentage who received secondary or higher education. But only a modest minority of either men or women received secondary or higher education. Thus, while there is a striking gender contrast in education, neither elderly men nor elderly women in Cambodia have much formal schooling.

As a result of the lack of education, older women are far less likely than men to be literate, particularly at the oldest ages. According to the 2004 ICDS, only 9 per cent of women age 80 and above compared to 64 per cent of men are literate. Even among those age 60–64, literacy rates are only 29 per cent for women compared to 84 per cent for men. One explanation for the higher literacy rate of elderly men compared to elderly women is that a substantial proportion of elderly men may have spent some time as monks in the pagoda where they learnt to read and write — a privilege that was not available to women.

HEALTH

Indicators of Health

A common, almost universal, paradox with respect to gender and health found in many settings is that older women live longer than men but prevalence rates of morbidity based on cross-sectional data are higher for women. Past research indicates that this is also true in Cambodia among the older population. Zimmer (2006) provides estimates of both overall life expectancy and "active life expectancy" for the older population. The latter refers to the number of years that will be lived in a functionally healthy or "active" state, that is, without disability. Overall life expectancy at age 60 for men is 15.0 compared to 17.0 for women, a female advantage of two years. At the same time, the extra years of life that women live in Cambodia are mostly disabled or "inactive" years. For men at age 60, 11.9 of their remaining years are spent "active" and 3.1 "inactive", compared to 12.2 and 4.8 for women. Thus, 1.7 of the 2.0 year advantage for women is time spent in a disabled state. In sum, while women live longer, active life expectancy for men and women is nearly the same.

From the cross-sectional data, women were found to experience more years of "inactive" life resulting from higher prevalence of disability. The first panel of Table 3.3 presents the percentage of those reporting four activity of daily living (ADL) limitations — tasks that individuals need to do in order to personally maintain themselves without assistance (for example, getting up from a lying down position, eating, bathing, and dressing), as well as the percentage of those reporting at least one ADL limitation. Here, persons experiencing at least one ADL limitation are often considered to be "disabled".

TABLE 3.3
Health Indicators among Persons Age 60 and Above, by Gender, Cambodia, 2004

	Men	Women
Unweighted N	463	810
1. ADL limitations		
Getting up from lying down	15.2	21.3*
Eating	7.2	9.7
Bathing	7.2	9.1
Dressing	5.9	6.4
At least one ADL limitation	19.1	25.8*
2. Serious functional limitations[a]		
Lifting	27.1	47.2*
Walking	22.9	40.5*
Climbing	19.1	32.5*
Crouching	16.6	28.5*
Grasping	9.8	17.0*
At least one functional limitation	37.8	61.9*

	Men	Women
Unweighted N	**463**	**810**
3. Other selected health problems		
% Reporting poor self-assessed health[b]	64.4	78.7*
% Reporting not seeing well without glasses	64.1	65.4
% Reporting not hearing well without a hearing aid	31.4	30.6
Mean number health symptoms[c]	7.1	7.7*
4. Indicators of emotional well-being[d]		
Per cent in last month who report:		
feeling not at all happy	34.9	43.2*
had difficulty sleeping most of the time	34.7	36.6
not able to eat most of the time	15.3	20.7*
feeling depressed most of the time	7.8	15.4*
feeling unsuccessful with life most of the time	4.3	6.5
feeling lonely most of the time	4.0	12.5*
Mean number of negative emotional well-being responses	1.01	1.35*
5. Indicators of satisfaction[d]		
Per cent who are very or somewhat satisfied with:		
family relationships	49.3	52.8
housing situation	44.2	51.8*
respect received from younger generation	23.0	28.9
life overall	38.2	42.4
Mean number of satisfied responses	1.59	1.94*

Notes:
* Women significantly different from men at p < .05.
[a] A serious limitation refers to having a lot of difficulty or cannot do.
[b] does not include 37 proxy respondents
[c] count of number of the following reported within last month: headache, vomiting, fever, diarrhea, skin problem, chest pain, joint pain, dizziness, back pain, trembling hands, stomach ache, breathing problem, coughing, loss of bladder control, weakness
[d] proxy respondents excluded
Source: 2004 Survey of Elderly in Cambodia (original tabulations).

The second panel in Table 3.3 shows the percentage of those reporting more general functional limitations. These are tasks that relate to basic bodily movements: lifting things above one's head, walking 200 metres, climbing a flight of stairs, crouching, and grasping things with fingers. We report the percentage among those having "serious" difficulties with these tasks (that is, having much difficulty or being completely unable to do the task). While having a functional limitation can lead to an ADL limitation, the link is not necessarily definitive. Thus, a greater proportion of elderly will report the former rather than the latter

(Freedman, Martin and Schoeni 2002). This is apparent in the results. As for gender differences, a significantly higher percentage of women report these limitations. Overall, about 38 per cent of men report at least one serious functional limitation compared to 62 per cent of women.

Several other indicators of physical health are presented in the third panel of Table 3.3. Respondents in the SEC were asked to rate their overall health as very good, good, fair, poor or very poor. The percentage of those assessing their health as poor or very poor is statistically higher for women. There is little gender difference in either the percentage of those reporting impaired vision or hearing. The SEC also asked about whether respondents had experienced a series of fifteen health 'symptoms' within the last month. These are not chronic conditions but could relate to specific health disorders. For instance, the symptoms included headaches, vomiting, and fever. Based on the results in Table 3.3, women reported an average of 7.7 of these symptoms compared to 7.1 for men — a difference that is statistically significant.

The fourth and fifth panels of Table 3.3 examine emotional health. Panel 4 shows six items selected and translated from the standard CES-D depression scale, which has been used frequently in the United States to indicate levels of depression (Radloff 1977). Panel 5 consists of four questions related to life satisfaction: satisfaction with family relationships, housing, respect received from the younger generation, and overall life. Results of individual items, and summary measures, are shown. Women are more likely to report each of the depressive symptoms but are also more likely to give favourable responses to the satisfaction items. This presents somewhat of a paradox and makes it difficult to draw a conclusion regarding gender differences in psychological well-being. Possibly, clinical levels of depression are actually higher among older women in Cambodia but this is compensated for by the presence of strong inter-personal relationships and higher levels of network support that result in higher levels of life satisfaction. Alternatively, men may be more hesitant to report depressive symptoms as it goes against the culturally-defined masculine image.

Care Assistance

Respondents who reported at least one ADL limitation can be considered to have a disability and to require assistance in completing tasks necessary for self-maintenance. For this reason, for this subset of older persons, having someone who provides care and assistance can be particularly important for well-being. Respondents who reported an ADL limitation were asked additional questions about whether they received help in conducting daily tasks. Table 3.4 summarizes the situation regarding receipt of personal assistance according to gender and marital status. Division by marital status is critical since the spouse, where available, is likely to play a vital caregiving role. The absence of a spouse may, therefore, be a distinct disadvantage. Since women are more likely to be widowed than men, they may be disadvantaged with respect to receiving care. Given that results are conditioned on having at least one limitation, the sample sizes are relatively small. Thus, we omit reporting statistical significance, and results should be considered only suggestive.

It was also found that a little under half of both men and women with limitations receive personal assistance. Despite women being more likely to be widowed, there is not much evidence that they have a care-receiving disadvantage. A little less than a quarter of both men and women not receiving help report needing help, while around two-fifths of both sexes who receive help report that the help is not enough. Results differ somewhat by marital status. While those not currently married are more likely to report receiving help, they are also more likely than those married to report not receiving help but needing it and not receiving

TABLE 3.4

Care Assistance among Persons Age 60 and Above Who Have an ADL Problem or Functional Limitation, by Gender, Cambodia, 2004

	Total Sample		Currently Married		Other[a]	
	Men	Women	Men	Women	Men	Women
Unweighted N	75	203	47	28	28	175
% Who received help	45.9	49.7	34.8	43.8	75.0	52.0
% Not receiving help who report that they need help	21.2	24.5	17.8	29.6	42.9	22.2
% receiving help who report that they do not receive enough	40.0	36.7	28.0	45.0	57.1	34.2

Notes:
[a] Other includes widowed, separated, divorced, and never married in this table and all subsequent tables
Source: 2004 Survey of Elderly in Cambodia (original tabulations).

adequate help. Among those not currently married, men are more likely to be in this unfavourable situation. For instance, about 57 per cent of the not currently married men who receive help report they do not receive enough compared to about 34 per cent of women.

Additional questions asked include those receiving help, who provides the help and who the main caregiver is (results not shown in table). The general pattern of responses suggests that both men and women receive considerable personal help from daughters and grandchildren, while married men also receive a substantial amount of help from their spouse. The daughter is particularly important for both genders and for both currently married and others. In total, 60 per cent of men and 65 per cent of women report receiving help from a daughter, while 40 per cent of men and 50 per cent of women report the daughter as the single main source of personal assistance.

Risk Behaviours

The SEC asked respondents about tobacco smoking and betel nut chewing.[3] Table 3.5 shows a clear gender pattern in these behaviours.

TABLE 3.5
Per Cent Engaging in Risk Behaviours among Persons Age 60 and Above, by Gender and Rural/Urban Residence, Cambodia, 2004

| | All Regions | | Urban[a] | | Rural[a] | |
	Men	Women	Men	Women	Men	Women
N (unweighted)	463	810	81	181	382	629
Smoking						
currently smokes	68.4	14.7*	39.5	3.7*	70.7	16.1*
smokes daily	61.5	11.7*	35.9	2.4*	63.7	12.8*
ever smoked	88.5	18.6*	63.2	6.1*	90.5	20.2*
Betel nut chewing						
currently chews	5.7	63.9*	5.1	34.1*	5.9	67.6*
chews daily	2.9	57.4*	2.6	29.3*	3.0	60.8*
ever chewed	8.4	71.2*	7.7	41.5*	8.4	74.7*

Notes:
* Women significantly different from men at p < .05.
[a] Urban includes city of Phnom Penh. Rural includes semi-rural peripheral areas of Phnom Penh and rural areas in other provinces.
Source: 2004 Survey of Elderly in Cambodia (original tabulations).

Men are by far more likely to be smokers while women are by far more likely to chew betel nut. The SEC also asked frequency of these behaviours and past behaviours for respondents who were not currently engaged in them. Most male smokers and female chewers engaged in these behaviours daily. The percentage of men who said they ever smoked is very high in comparison to women, while the opposite association exists for betel nut chewing. There is also a difference in tendencies by place of residence. While the gender differentials are generally maintained in both rural and urban areas, such high risk behaviour tends to be more prevalent in rural areas.

Living Arrangements

Many aspects of well-being of older persons are influenced by their living arrangements. In the Asian context, living together with an adult child, and specifically in Cambodia especially with a daughter, has been the traditional pattern (Kato 2000). While household composition is the most common indicator of living arrangements, the meaning and implications of particular configurations can be ambiguous. For example, such measures do not encompass information about others who live nearby but who may still play an important role in the lives of elderly members (Knodel and Saengtienchai 1999). Although measures of the living arrangements based on household composition can be suggestive, they need to be interpreted cautiously.

With that said, coresidence with one or more adult children often meets the needs of both generations. In contrast, living alone likely leads to less frequent interpersonal interactions and, hence, potential feelings of loneliness. Also, there is a greater chance that urgent needs for assistance created by an acute health crisis or accident will go unnoticed longer than if others are present in the household. Living only with a spouse in the absence of children is generally viewed as less problematic since a spouse can be a principal source of emotional and material support and provide personal care during illness or frailty.

The vast majority of older Cambodians live with at least one child and even higher shares live with or next to a child. Regardless of marital status, men are modestly more likely than women to live with a child. In part this reflects the fact that more women are childless than men. When living with a child is conditioned on having at least one living child, the difference contracts.

One type of living arrangement involving older persons of particular interest is the "skipped generation" household, that is, situations in which grandparents live together with dependent grandchildren but in the absence of any of their adult children who have either migrated or died (see Chapter 2, this volume). In the present study, skipped generation households are defined as those with one or more grandchildren but no resident married child or child-in-law. Overall, older women are modestly more likely than men to live in skipped generation households but the difference is not statistically significant. Still, this likely reflects contrasting gender roles with respect to childcare. This could explain why gender differences do not show up for married persons (since a woman is also present in cases of married men), but do for respondents who are not currently married.

Coresidence does not necessarily imply the parents are primarily dependent on the children in the household. Especially when the children are not yet married, the opposite may be true. Coresidence with ever-married children reflects a more mature stage of intergenerational living arrangements that evolve after single children leave the household or marry and take adult responsibilities. Thus, coresident married children are likely to play more important support roles.

Older Cambodians are far more likely to live with a married daughter than a married son, reflecting a traditional matrilocal tendency among Cambodians. In contrast to the gender difference with respect to coresidence with children in general, women are more likely than men to coreside with an ever-married child (conditioned on having an ever-married child). The difference is much reduced, however, once marital status is controlled.

Table 3.6 summarizes living arrangements based on the SEC. Since the sample was limited to private households, it does not cover elders living in institutional settings. While old-age homes in Cambodia are almost non-existent, some elderly live in temples and, are thus excluded from the sample. Unfortunately, little systematic information is available on the extent to which the elderly live in temples. As the results show, living alone is rare among Cambodian elders, although more common among women than men. In contrast, living only with a spouse is more common among men reflecting gender differences in marital status. Among current married older Cambodians, more women than men live only with their spouse but because so many more women than men are not currently married, for the total population of elders, the reverse is true.

TABLE 3.6

Selected Measures of Living Arrangements, by Gender and Marital Status among Persons Age 60 and Above, Cambodia, 2004

	Total		Currently Married		Other	
	Men	Women	Men	Women	Men	Women
Among all elderly, per cent living						
Alone	0.8	5.0*	—	—	4.3	7.2
Only with spouse	7.2	4.1*	8.8	13.2	—	—
With any child	84.7	76.1*	83.7	73.0*	89.0	77.5*
With or next to a child	87.0	77.8*	86.3	74.8*	90.1	79.1*
In a "skipped generation" household[a]	11.4	14.1	11.5	11.5	11.0	15.3
Among elderly with at least one child of the specified type, per cent living with						
Any child	85.4	80.4*	84.4	76.5*	90.0	82.1
An ever-married child of either sex	53.7	66.7*	49.0	56.6	74.1	71.3
An ever-married son	15.2	18.2	13.2	15.0	24.6	19.8
An ever-married daughter	49.6	60.5*	45.9	49.5	65.7	65.6

Notes:

* Women significantly different from men at p < .05.

[a] A "skipped generation" household is one in which there is a coresident grandchild but no coresident ever married child or child-in-law.

Source: 2004 Survey of Elderly in Cambodia (original tabulations).

Social Contact with Children

Maintaining contact with children who leave the household is important for the social and emotional well-being of many older persons, especially if no children live nearby. Only a relatively small minority of older parents (5 per cent of men and 6 per cent of women) do not have at least one child in the same village, and in most cases in the same household, as the living arrangements results indicated. Less than 3 per cent of older age parents of either sex have all their children living outside the province in which they live.

Research in neighbouring Thailand has shown that the rapid spread of cell phones there in recent years has greatly increased the ability of parents and migrant children to keep in contact (Knodel and Saengtienchai 2007; Knodel et al. 2007). This may also be happening in Cambodia. Information on visits but unfortunately not on telephone contact with non-coresident children is available in the 2004 SEC. However, only 16 per cent of respondents lived in a household with either a cell or landline phone at that time; hence, telephone contact would have been still fairly limited. Based on information about each non-coresident child, 33 per cent see their parents on a daily basis, reflecting the fact that many live next door or very near to their parents. Approximately half of non-coresident children see their parents at least weekly and almost two-thirds see their parents at least monthly while only less than one-fifth of the non-coresident children see their parents at least once a year. Thus, generally Cambodian parents and many of their children who live outside the household tend to be in relatively frequent contact. Moreover, the frequency of visits between children and their parents, irrespective of whether these are their fathers or mothers, is very similar.

If we combine information on visits with coresidence, and assume parents see a coresident child daily, results indicate that few Cambodian older age parents do not have contact with at least one of their children on a relatively frequent basis. Moreover, 97 per cent of both mothers and fathers see at least one child at least monthly and none of the fathers and only 2 per cent of the mothers did not see a child at least once a year. Moreover, even among the few parents who did not see a child at least yearly, just over half reported that they received money or a gift from a child during the previous year. Thus, very few Cambodian elderly parents are completely deserted by all their children.

Sources of Material Support

The official retirement age in Cambodia for civil servants ranges from 55 to 60 depending on the level of the position. Employees of some private firms may also be subject to compulsory retirement ages. However, for the vast majority of the population that is mostly engaged in agriculture or is self-employed in the informal sector, there is no particular age at which work ceases. Even those who are compelled to retire at a specific age may continue to work at a different job. Nevertheless, there are numerous reasons that lead older Cambodians to disengage from economic activities as they grow old, including decline in the physical strength required by farming in which the majority is engaged.

The 2004 ICDS distinguished between being employed (including self-employment) in economic activities and doing housework. Overall, just over two-thirds of older men were reported being employed compared to just over two-fifths of older women who were substantially more likely to report being engaged in housework than men. However, even if housework is treated as work, a substantially higher percentage of older men than women worked during the prior year (73 per cent versus 55 per cent). The percentages of both older men and women who are not working increases rapidly with age so that 80 per cent of men and 88 per cent of women among those age 80 and above report being neither employed nor doing housework. Unless they have sufficient savings or investments of their own, elders who are no longer economically active end up becoming dependent on others for material support.

Given that men are much more likely to be economically active in older ages than women, it is not surprising that in the SEC, far more older men report they receive income from work than do women (47 per cent versus 27 per cent). For both men and women, however, the percentage of those reporting self-income from work is lower than the percentage of those reporting themselves as working. This indicates that a fair proportion of the economic activity of older persons is for non-paid employment such as subsistence farming.

Income is far less common from pension, rent or investment, or welfare compared to work. Men are more likely to report that they receive pension income (8 per cent versus 1 per cent) while 6 per cent of both men and women report income from rent or investment. The fact that pension income is far more common among men than women reflects the substantial gender gap during the lifetime of the current elderly in civil service and private enterprises that provide pensions. Income from welfare is extremely rare for the elderly for either sex (0.4 per cent for men and 1.0 per cent for women).

Although older persons may receive income from several sources, some are more important than others. SEC respondents were asked to identify who was the main person who supported their household as well as which source was the most important for their own support. As Table 3.7 shows, the majority of both older aged men and women say that their children are the main contributors to overall household support. For the total elderly population, this is true for a greater share of women than men (see Chapter 12, this volume). However, when marital status is controlled, little gender difference is apparent for either the currently married or others. Overall, elderly Cambodians who are not currently married are substantially more likely than those who are married to cite their children as the main contributor to their household support. Since more women are not currently married than men, children are more often a main source of support for women overall. Among those for whom children are not the main source of support, the respondent, the respondent's spouse, or both together are the main contributors to their household.

Results on the main source of the respondent's own support largely mirror the findings with respect to who the main contributor to the household is. Children are again cited as the most important source and for the overall elderly population, children are more commonly mentioned by women than men (see Chapter 12, this volume). Again this difference is a function of marital status differences since children are less likely to be the main source of support for currently married elders than others and women are more likely not to be currently married. The second most important source of support was the respondent's own or spouse's economic activity. Among the total population of older persons, this is far more common as a main source of support for men than women but again differences are minimal once marital status is controlled.

In much of the developing world including Southeast Asia, intergenerational exchanges of material support is an integral part of the family system and particularly crucial for the welfare of elderly parents (World Bank 1994). As noted above and as previous analyses have shown, children are the main source of support for the majority of Cambodian elders (Zimmer et al. 2008). Material support can be in the form of money and through gifts of food and other goods. In the SEC, respondents were asked about the contributions made to them by each of their children in terms of money, food or clothing, and general support of the household during the previous year.

TABLE 3.7

Main Source of Support and Main Contributor to Household Support, by Gender and Marital Status, Persons Age 60 and Above, Cambodia, 2004

	Total		Currently Married		Other	
	Men	Women	Men	Women	Men	Women
Main contributor to supporting household (% Distribution)						
Self	11.3	10.2	10.7	5.1	13.8	12.5
Spouse	9.4	5.1	11.2	15.7	(a)	(a)
Self and spouse	21.1	6.6	25.8	21.3	0.0	0.0
Children	55.1	71.6	50.1	54.0	77.7	79.5
Other	3.1	6.4	2.1	3.8	8.5	8.0
Total	100	100	100	100	100	100
Statistical significance at .05 level		yes		yes		no
Main source of support (% Distribution)						
Work (own or spouse)	41.9	19.5	47.5	37.7	17.0	11.2
Children or children-in-law	53.0	70.8	47.7	52.5	76.6	78.9
Other family members	1.8	5.8	0.7	3.8	6.4	6.7
Non-family sources	3.3	3.9	4.1	5.9	0.0	3.2
Total	100	100	100	100	100	100
Statistical significance at .05 level		yes		yes		no

Note: (a) A small number of non-married persons who reported their spouse as their main contributor to supporting the household included in the category "other".

Source: 2004 Survey of Elderly in Cambodia (original tabulations).

Table 3.8 summarizes the percentage of older aged Cambodians who receive assistance from children. The type of support provided by a child and the use to which it is put may differ according to whether or not the child lives with the parent. For example, money or food provided by coresident children may be mainly to cover communal household needs rather than for the parent's own use. This is less likely to be so for support from non-coresident children. Thus, results are shown separately for contributions from coresident and non-coresident children, as well as for all children combined.

Based on these results, the vast majority of elderly parents report that a child contributes to the support of the household, provides some money, and provides some food or clothing. However, the amount of support is typically quite modest. Only about one-fourth of elderly parents reported that they received combined contributions of money and food or clothing during the previous year worth at least US$25. In general, women are more likely than men to report receiving support, especially from coresident children. This may reflect the tendency for women to manage the household budget, a common pattern in Southeast Asia, and help explain why gender differences in receipt of material support from children are pronounced only among married respondents. Since married respondents may be sharing the contributions with their spouses, it is not clear that women benefit more than men, even though overall they are more likely to be the recipient.

Older aged parents may also provide material support to their children. In two-thirds of the cases where parents and children coreside, the parents own the dwelling and, thus, are providing living quarters for coresident children. In half of these cases, the house is owned jointly by husband and wife but among the remainder, a mother is more likely the owner than a father, reflecting the dominance of women among elders who have become widowed. The SEC also asked if respondents gave their children money, food or goods in the past year. The results indicate that parents are far less likely to provide material assistance to their children than the reverse. To the extent gender differences are apparent, men are more likely to provide support than are women. This may reflect the greater likelihood that older aged men are more likely to have cash income through work or pensions than older women. Overall, 8 per cent of men and 4 per cent of women report providing amounts of support valued at US$25 or more to any child. Support is far more common to coresident children than to non-coresident children. Only 2 per cent of men and 1 per cent of women reported giving US$25 of material aid to any non-coresident child.

TABLE 3.8
Receipt of Material Support from Children during Past Year, by Gender and Marital Status, Persons Age 60 and Above, Cambodia, 2004

	Total		Currently Married		Other	
	Men	Women	Men	Women	Men	Women
From any child (among elders with living children)						
Support of household	89.6	91.2	88.7	86.6	93.5	93.1
Money	94.5	93.6	94.4	93.3	94.6	93.8
Food/clothes etc.	82.8	87.3*	81.7	86.7	87.1	87.5
Money and/or food/clothes worth $25+	24.1	27.8	23.4	28.6	28.0	27.4
From any coresident child (among elders with coresident children)						
Support of household	79.0	91.6*	74.9	83.0*	96.4	95.3
Money	78.2	80.4*	67.1	76.0*	89.3	90.9
Food/clothes etc.	62.3	79.2*	58.4	67.4*	78.6	84.1
Money and/or food/clothes worth $25+	15.6	19.1	13.7	14.5	22.9	21.1
From any non-coresident child (among elders with non-coresident children)						
Support of household	61.7	63.2	64.4	65.2	49.4	62.3*
Money	89.2	90.2	90.0	95.7*	85.5	87.7
Food/clothes etc.	72.7	76.3	73.1	82.4*	71.1	73.5
Money and/or food/clothes worth $25+	14.8	19.2*	15.3	24.8*	13.1	16.4

Note: * = statistically significant at the .05 level.
Source: 2004 Survey of Elderly in Cambodia (original tabulations).

ECONOMIC WELL-BEING

Assets and Debt

Table 3.9 provides information on assets and debt of older Cambodians. Since spouses may jointly benefit from each other's assets, results regarding asset ownership are presented both in relation to the respondents themselves and the combined situation with their spouse. Most older Cambodians either own their dwelling units by themselves or jointly with a spouse. Overall, women themselves are more likely than men to be the owner of the house while men are more likely to jointly own their house with a spouse. When marital status is controlled, the gender differences diminish or largely disappear, although among the not currently-married elders, women are less likely than men to own the house.

With respect to other assets, men are more likely than women to own land and livestock while women are more likely to own jewellery (which presumably includes gold, a traditional form of savings). Very few elderly Cambodian men or women have bank accounts. At the same time, men are more likely to be in debt than women, although this is limited to those who are married. Thus, while the husband may be responsible for the debt, it may still detract from the wife's economic well-being as well. In any event, very low percentages see debt to pose as a serious burden for them.

Housing Quality and Household Possessions

Besides assets, housing quality and possessions associated with the household are important reflections of material well-being. Regardless of ownership, all members are likely to benefit from better housing and the presence of items that make living more convenient. Moreover, the presence of household possessions reflects the overall economic status of the household.

Figure 3.2 examines both housing characteristics and household possessions. Women are somewhat more likely than men to live in a house that has electricity but gender differences in other respects are minimal. Both men and women are almost equally likely to live in a house with a finished floor, a better-quality roof, and a flush toilet. Thus, overall major gender differences are lacking with respect to housing quality. Differences in the percentage of elderly Cambodian men and women who live in households with the possessions shown are minimal and exhibit no consistent pattern. Thus, there appears to be gender equality in this respect as well.

TABLE 3.9
Assets and Debt by Gender and Marital Status, Persons Age 60 and Above, Cambodia, 2004

	Total		Currently Married		Other	
	Men	Women	Men	Women	Men	Women
% Own house						
Self only	19.7	37.7*	9.6	4.4*	64.8	52.6*
Spouse only	5.8	1.7*	7.1	5.0	—	—
Self and Spouse jointly	53.9	21.7*	66.0	69.4	—	—
% Own land						
Self	25.5	14.3*	28.4	8.8*	20.3	15.4
Self or spouse	28.3	16.0*	32.7	19.1	—	—
% Own livestock						
Self	41.3	22.0*	42.5	34.9	36.3	16.2*
Self or spouse	47.1	23.3*	49.5	39.3*	—	—
% Having bank account						
Self	0.1	0.5	0.1	0.9	0.0	0.3
Self or spouse	0.3	0.5	0.3	0.9	—	—
% Having jewelry						
Self	13.4	27.0*	14.7	27.1*	7.8	27.0*
Self or spouse	28.8	28.0	33.5	30.1	—	—
% In debt	26.3	19.9*	28.4	21.2*	16.3	19.2
% For whom debt is a serious burden	5.2	3.9	5.8	5.2	2.3	3.4

Note: * = statistically significant at the .05 level.
Source: 2004 Survey of Elderly in Cambodia (original tabulations).

Figure 3.2
Housing Quality Indicators and Household Possessions among
Persons Age 60 and Older by Gender, Cambodia, 2004

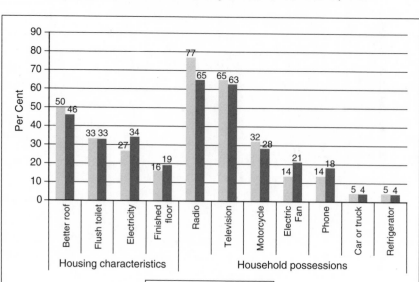

Note: Only the differences in electricity, radio and fan are statistically significant at the .05 level.
Source: 2004 Survey of Elderly in Cambodia (original tabulations).

Summary Measures

Information on characteristics of the dwelling unit and the presence of household possessions can be combined into a single overall wealth score using principal component analysis that provides an objective measure of the economic well-being (Filmer and Pritchett 2001). Other questions in the SEC provide subjective judgements. Respondents rated their own economic status relative to others in the community and also indicated the sufficiency of their income and their satisfaction with their economic situation. An overall self-assessed economic well-being score was derived by combining responses to these three questions. In addition, interviewers were asked to judge the economic status of the household on a five-point scale based on the appearance of the respondent's house. In order to facilitate interpretation of these three measures, the scores have

TABLE 3.10

Objective and Subjective Summary Measures of Economic Well-being, by Gender and Marital Status, Persons Age 60 and Above, Cambodia, 2004

Measure of Economic Well-being (expressed as mean percentile)	Total		Currently Married		Other	
	Men	Women	Men	Women	Men	Women
Wealth score based on house characteristics and household possessions	50.5	49.7	51.7	49.4	45.1	49.9
Self-assessed economic well-being score	50.5	49.7	51.0	52.1	48.1	48.6
Interviewer assessed economic status score	52.7	48.2*	54.0	51.4	47.2	46.8

Note: * = statistically significant at the .05 level.
Source: 2004 Survey of Elderly in Cambodia (original tabulations).

been converted to percentiles such that higher percentiles signify better economic well-being. The mean percentile scores are presented for men and women in Table 3.10.

Based on this information, overall, there is little gender difference in the mean scores for either the objective wealth score or subjective self-assessed economic well-being. However, interviewers rated the socio-economic status of women respondents somewhat lower than men with the difference being statistically significant. The overall difference in this measure, however, is largely attributable to the fact that interviewers rated not currently married respondents to have a lower wealth score than those who are currently married. Within the two marital status categories, that is, for both married men and women, statistically significant differences are absent. Thus, on both the objective and subjective summary measures, there is little substantial difference in economic well-being between elderly Cambodian men and women.

DISCUSSION AND CONCLUSIONS

This study represents the first systematic assessment of the relation between gender and well-being of older persons in Cambodia in terms of health, demographic, social support, and economic indicators. Given the unusually pronounced numerical dominance of women among the elderly population, the Cambodian context is particularly interesting for such an assessment. This unusual excess of older women over men is the legacy of a past history of civil unrest and violence that particularly took male lives, resulting in the current generation of older women being far more likely than the surviving men to have experienced the loss of a spouse during the period of civil disturbances.

The results of our analyses reveal both differences and similarities between elderly men and women. On some measures, older Cambodian women clearly face disadvantages compared to their male counterparts. They are far less likely to be currently married and, thus, to have a spouse to provide social and material support and assistance. Elderly women are also far less educated than men and far less likely to be literate, although even for men, educational levels are quite low.

Gender differences are apparent on numerous aspects of health but do not consistently favour one sex over the other. Elderly women report poorer self-assessed health than men and more symptoms of illness, but seeing and hearing problems are reported fairly equally. Elderly women are also more likely to suffer from physical functioning problems. At the same time, previous research indicated that the overall level of disability among both older men and women in Cambodia is extremely high in comparison to other countries, likely because of high levels of poverty among the population (Zimmer 2006, 2008). Older men suffer lower survival rates than women although most of the extra years experienced by women after age 60 are lived with a disability.

Both older men and women engage in risk behaviours. Older men are more likely to smoke while women are more likely to chew betel nut. Most likely, the risk behaviours of men are more serious and, thus, contribute to their higher mortality. Women are more likely to report depressive symptoms, but are also more likely to report satisfaction with life. Men and women with physical limitations appear equally likely to have unmet caregiving needs.

Women are more likely than men to live alone, although only a small minority does so. Women are also less likely to coreside with a child, in part, because they are more likely to be childless. Among elders who have married children, women are more likely to coreside with one and, thus, be in a situation where a mature adult child is available to provide assistance within the household.

Several gender differences are evident that do not necessarily convey advantage or disadvantage. Older women are less likely than men to be in the labour force and more likely to depend on children as their main source of income (see Chapters 10, 11 and 12, this volume). The latter is related to the fact that women are not only less likely to be economically active but also comprise a larger proportion of not currently-married older persons who are most dependent on their children for material support. Men are more likely to have debt but only among those who are married and, thus, the debt may disadvantage their spouses as well. Men are more likely to provide material support to children although rarely in substantial amounts.

On several important dimensions of well-being, little association with gender was found. Elderly fathers and mothers differ little in terms of social contact with children. Few elderly parents of either sex appear to be deserted and a large majority receives some material support from their children. Older men and women also appear similar in their material well-being as measured by housing quality, household possessions and self-assessed economic situation, even though men are more likely to report income from work and pensions. While the lack of major gender differences in material well-being is encouraging, it must be interpreted within the context of widespread poverty among both elderly Cambodian women and men.

In sum, both gender differences and similarities exist across several critical dimensions of well-being of older persons in Cambodia. While a conclusive advantage or disadvantage existing for either men or women was not found, there are variations in characteristics and circumstances in which both may be advantaged or disadvantaged. Recognition of these specific contexts can be useful for understanding the unique needs of men and women in a country in which many older people have lived difficult lives, having faced harsh circumstances related to war and poverty.

Notes

1. See 2005 Cambodia Demographic and Health Survey (original tabulations by authors).
2. Detailed descriptions of the surveys are provided in John Knodel et al., *Older Persons in Cambodia: A Profile from the 2004 Survey of Elderly*, Research Report 05-576 (Ann Arbor, Michigan, Population Studies Center, 2005); National Institute of Statistics, *Cambodia Inter-Censal Population Survey 2004: General Report* (Phnom Penh: United Nations Population Fund, 2005); and National Institute of Public Health, National Institute of Statistics [Cambodia] and ORC Macro Cambodia, *Demographic and Health Survey 2005* (Phnom Penh, Cambodia and Calverton, Maryland: National Institute of Public Health, National Institute of Statistics and ORC Macro, 2006).
3. This is a mild narcotic plant associated with mouth and throat cancer (Reichart 1995).

References

Central Intelligence Agency (CIA). "The World Factbook: Cambodia, 2008". Available at <www.cis.gov/library/publications/the-world-factbook/geos/cb.html> (accessed 20 December 2008).

de Walque, D. "Selective Mortality during the Khmer Rouge Period in Cambodia". *Population and Development Review* 31, no. 2 (2005): 351–68.

Filmer, D. and L.H. Pritchett. "Estimating Wealth Effects without Expenditure Data — or Tears: An Application to Educational Enrollments in States of India". *Demography* 38, no. 1 (2001): 115–32.

Freedman, V.A., L.G. Martin and R.F. Schoeni. "Recent Trends in Disability and Functioning among Older Americans: A Critical Review of the Literature". *Journal of the American Medical Association* 288, no. 24 (2002): 3137–46.

Heuveline, P. "'Between One and Three Million': Towards the Demographic Reconstruction of a Decade of Cambodian History (1970–79)". *Population Studies: A Journal of Demography* 52, no. 1 (1998): 49–65.

Jacobson, Trudy. *Women, Time and Power in Cambodia*. Honolulu: University of Hawaii Press, 2006.

Kato, Elizabeth U. "Ageing in Cambodia: Tradition, Change and Challenges". In *Ageing in the Asia-Pacific Region*, edited by D.R. Phillips. New York: Routledge, 2000.

Knodel, John. "Poverty and the Impact of AIDS on Older Persons: Evidence from Cambodia and Thailand". *Economic Development and Cultural Change* 56, no. 2 (2007): 441–75.

Knodel, John and C. Saengtienchai. "Studying Living Arrangements of the Elderly: Lessons from a Quasi Qualitative Case Study Approach in Thailand". *Journal of Cross-Cultural Gerontology* 14, no. 3 (1999): 197–220.

―――. "Rural Parents with Urban Children: Social and Economic Implications of Migration on the Rural Elderly in Thailand". *Population, Space and Place* 13, no. 3 (2007): 193–210.

Knodel, John, Jiraporn Kespichayawattana, Suvinee Wiwatwanich and Chanpen Saengtienchai. "Migration and Inter-generational Solidarity: Evidence from Rural Thailand". UNFPA Country Technical Services Team for East and Southeast Asia. Papers in Population Ageing Series, No. 2. Bangkok: UNFPA, 2007.

Knodel, John, Souvan Kiry Kim, Zachary Zimmer and Sina Puch. "Older Persons in Cambodia: A Profile from the 2004 Survey of Elderly". Research Report 05-576. Ann Arbor, Michigan: Population Studies Center, 2005.

Ledgerwood, J.L. "Khmer Kinship: The Matriliny/Matriarchy Myth". *Journal of Anthropological Research* 51, no. 3 (1995): 247–61.

Lee, Susan Hagood. *Rice Plus: Widows and Economic Survival in Rural Cambodia*. New York: Taylor and Francis, 2006.

Mujahid, Ghazy. "Population Ageing in East and South East Asia: Current Situation and Emerging Challenges". UNFPA Country Technical Services Team for East and Southeast Asia. Papers in Population Ageing No. 1. Bangkok: UNFPA, 2006.

National Institute of Public Health, National Institute of Statistics [Cambodia] and ORC Macro. *Cambodia Demographic and Health Survey 2005*. Phnom Penh, Cambodia and Calverton, Maryland: National Institute of Public Health, National Institute of Statistics and ORC Macro, 2006.

National Institute of Statistics. *Cambodia Inter-Censal Population Survey 2004: General Report*. Phnom Penh: United Nations Population Fund, 2005.

Office of the Council of Ministers. Secretariat of the Committee on Population and Development. *Population Aging in Cambodia: Planning for Social Protection*. Phnom Penh: UNFPA, 2007.

Population Reference Bureau (PRB). *2008 World Population Data Sheet*. Washington, D.C.: Population Reference Bureau, 2008.

Radloff, L.S. "The CES-D Scale". *Applied Psychological Measurement* 1, no. 3 (1977): 385–401.

Reichart, P.A. "Oral Cancer and Precancer related to Betel and Miang Chewing in Thailand: A Review". *Oral Pathology and Medicine* 24 (1995): 241–43.

United Nations. *World Population Prospects: The 2008 Revision*. New York, United Nations, 2009.

UNAIDS. *2006 Report on the Global AIDS Epidemic*. Geneva, UNAIDS, 2006.

UNDP Cambodia. Project Fact Sheet 01/2008 (Project no. 00037213) — Partnership for Gender Equity. Phnom Penh, Cambodia: United Nations Development Programme, 2008.

United Nations Economic and Social Commission of Asia and the Pacific (UNESCAP). "Country Report: Review and Appraisal of the Progress on Implementation of the Madrid International Plan of Action on Ageing (MIPAA) in Kingdom of Cambodia". Paper presented at High-Level Meeting on the Regional Review of the Madrid International Plan of Action on Ageing (MIPAA), Macao, China, 9–11 October 2007. Submitted by the Royal Government of Cambodia. Available at <www.unescap.org/ESID/psis/meetings/AgeingMipaa2007/Cambodia.pdf> (accessed 3 August 2010).

UNIFEM, WB, ADB, UNDP and DFID/UK. *A Fair Share for Women: Cambodia Gender Assessment*. Phnom Penh, Cambodia: UNIFEM, WB, ADB, UNDP, DFID/UK, 2004.

World Bank. *Averting the Old Age Crisis*. New York: Oxford University Press, 1994.

Zimmer, Z. "Disability and Active Life Expectancy among Older Cambodians". *Asian Population Studies* 2, no. 2 (2006): 133–48.

———. "Poverty, Wealth Inequality and Health among Older Adults in Rural Cambodia". *Social Science and Medicine* 66, no. 1 (2008): 57–71.

Zimmer, Z., J. Knodel, S.K. Kim and S. Puch. "The Impact of Past Conflicts and Social Disruption in Cambodia on the Current Generation of Older Adults". *Population and Development Review* 32, no. 2 (2006): 333–60.

Zimmer, Z. and K. Korinek. "Does Family Size Predict Whether an Older Adult Lives with or Proximate to an Adult Child in the Asia-Pacific Region?" *Asian Population Studies* 4, no. 2 (2008): 135–59.

Zimmer, Z., K. Korinek, J. Knodel and N. Chayovan. "Migrant Interactions with Elderly Parents in Rural Cambodia and Thailand". *Journal of Marriage and Family* 70 (2008): 585–98.

4

PREPARATIONS FOR OLD AGE AND SOCIAL PARTICIPATION OF PRESENT AND FUTURE OLDER PERSONS IN THAILAND: GENDER DIFFERENCE[1]

Vipan Prachuabmoh

INTRODUCTION

Rapid population ageing in many Asian countries including Thailand has led to increasing public concern about the vulnerability of the elderly. In addition, gender has been identified as a factor that might worsen the situation among older women, especially their quality of life. The processes of socialization, socio-economic development, as well as cultural setting are likely to have a cumulative impact on their life course, especially during old age. In particular, gender differences may lead to differing ability between men and women in preparing themselves for quality ageing. Insufficient or poor preparation for old age may degrade the quality of life as well as the ability of older people to contribute to society. Past studies tended to investigate the factors influencing preparation for old age, but rarely linked the preparation process with active ageing.

According to the World Health Organization, "active ageing" has been defined as the process of optimizing opportunities for health, participation and security in order to enhance quality of life as people age (World Health Organization 2002). In this sense, the word "active" refers to the ability to be physically active by participating in the labour force as well as by continuing participation in social, economic, cultural, spiritual, and civic affairs. Active participation in social activities by older persons not only increases their quality of life in terms of maintaining their autonomy, independence, and dignity, but also promotes intergenerational relationships and increases their contribution towards sustainable development in an ageing society.

This chapter presents gender differences in the preparation for old age and investigates the relationship between preparation for old age and active ageing among the present and future cohorts of male and female elderly in Thailand.

DATA SOURCES

Two sets of national surveys have been used for the analysis in this chapter. The first data set is the 2007 National Survey on Older Persons in Thailand conducted by the National Statistical Office. The study involved a nationally representative survey of 56,022 adults age 50 years and above selected by way of a stratified sampling procedure, stratified by 76 provinces (National Statistical Office 2008). Although the 2007 Elderly Survey covered persons age 50 and above living in private households, the present analysis has been limited to 30,427 elderly age 60 years and above. The second data set used is that of the national survey of people age 18–59 about their knowledge and attitude towards older persons. It was also conducted by the National Statistical Office in collaboration with the College of Population Studies and the Ministry of Social Development and Human Security in the same year, that of 2007. In this survey, there were 9,000 completed interviews with 18–59 year old respondents selected by a stratified sampling procedure differentiated by regions (National Statistical Office 2007). In order to facilitate a comparison with the 2007 elderly survey, the 18–59 year old survey also included some similar questions. While the former survey provides data on the present elderly, the latter survey offers information on future cohorts of the elderly. Thus, use of the two survey data sets enables a comparison between the present and future cohorts of elderly with regards to their old age preparation and social participation.

PREPARATIONS FOR OLD AGE

Because of worldwide trends towards an ageing society in this century and the challenges of sustainable social and economic development, preparations for old age or later stage of life is tied up with achieving a good quality life for the elderly and for national development as a whole (United Nations 1996).

Like many other Asian countries, the main support and insurance system for the elderly in Thailand is still the family or children (Chayovan and Knodel 1997; Prachuabmoh and Mithranon 2003; National Statistical Office 2008). Knodel and Chayovan (2008) have pointed out that about four-fifths of the elderly receive some income from children regardless of the gender of the older person. However, children seem to be the main source of income for women, while support from children as well as work are the main sources of income for men.

In the context of globalization and rapid demographic changes, there is an increasing concern about the erosion of family support systems as a result of a reduction in the number of children available to provide support for aged parents (Prachuabmoh and Chayovan 2000; Prachuabmoh and Mithranon 2003). Although the impact of a rapid fertility decline on the family support system in Thailand is likely to be less severe than in countries where preference for a male child is strong, globalization processes may weaken traditional norms as support from family in all probability diminishes. Since both formal and informal systems of support for the elderly have some limitations, it is important that individuals take responsibility to prepare themselves for quality ageing.

The analysis in the next section will begin by exploring the level and trends of preparation for old age, followed by examining the types of preparation, the age when preparations for old age start, and the differentials in each type of preparation.

Level and Trends

The 2007 elderly and the 18–59 year old surveys have been utilized for analysing the level and trends of preparation for old age of present and future cohorts of the elderly. Preparation for old age in this chapter is defined as having prepared for at least one out of the five below-mentioned areas before reaching the age of 60. Respondents were first asked about whether they had thought about making each individual type of preparation. Those who answered "yes" were further asked if they had actually made each type of preparation. Although the types of preparation for old age inquired about in the two surveys differed slightly (that is, the 18–59 year old survey contains more questions on types of preparation), for comparative purposes, the analysis undertaken in this investigation is limited to the five types of preparation that were focused on in both surveys. The five types are: finances, living quarters, physical health, psychological health, and arrangement for caregiver.

Based on the two questions, namely, whether the respondent had thought about preparing for old age and if he/she had actually made preparations for each of the five types, three possible answers may be classified for each type: (1) preparations have been made; (2) thought about it but not made any preparations as yet; and (3) never thought about it nor made any preparations. Respondents who said they had made preparations of a particular type were classified as having prepared for that type. Moreover, the 2007 Elderly Survey also inquired about the age the respondents first started making preparations for old age. Thus respondents in the elderly survey who reported to have started preparing for old age only after the age of 60 were classified as not having made any preparations for old age.

The results in Table 4.1 reveal that about 57 per cent of the present elderly (60 and above) made some kind of preparation for old age. Compared with the results of the 1986 survey — Socioeconomic Consequences of the Aging Population in Thailand (SECAPT) — the proportion of the elderly who have made some preparation was found to have increased from less than half (about four out of 10 elderly) to more than half in the current cohort. Although, the trend in the preparation has increased over time, about 43 per cent of the present elderly did not make any specific preparation for this stage of their life. In addition, the results indicate that male elderly made slightly more types of preparation than female elderly (see Table 4.1).

When considering the proportion of which age groups from that of less than 20 to more than 80 prepared for old age (see Table 4.2), the results show very interesting trends. The proportion who made some preparation increases steadily from 63.5 per cent in the 20–29 age group to 85.5 per cent in the 50–59 age group and then it starts consistently dropping from age 60 and above (that is, from 64.0 per cent among the age group 60–69 to 40.3 per cent among the age group 80+). Such trends seem to reflect that those approaching older age start preparing themselves in some aspects more than the present and the distant future elderly cohorts. For the distant future elderly cohorts, even though they view preparation for old age as an important issue, it was found that several of them did not yet make any preparations. This may be because they see their current stage of life as still being rather far from old age.

TABLE 4.1

Percentage Distribution of Persons Age 18–59 and 60+ according to Number of Preparations Made and Mean Number of Preparations by Age and Gender

Number of Types Prepared for	18–39*			40–59*			60+**		
	Males	Females	Total	Males	Females	Total	Males	Females	Total
0	33.4	28.7	30.9	18.8	16.6	17.7	41.5	44.7	43.3
1–2	32.6	32.1	32.3	33.0	31.2	32.1	15.5	14.9	15.0
3–5	34.0	39.2	36.9	48.1	52.2	50.3	43.3	40.4	41.7
Total	100.0	100.0	100.0	100.0	100.0	100.0	100.0	100.0	100.0
Mean	1.8	2.0	1.9	2.5	2.6	2.6	2.1	1.9	2.0

Note: Five types of preparation namely finances, living quarters, physical health, psychological health, and arrangement for caregiver are examined in Table 4.1.

Sources: * National Statistical Office (NSO), *The National Survey of the 18–59 Year-Old on Their Knowledge and Attitude towards Older Persons* (original tabulations) (Bangkok: National Statistical Office, 2007).

** National Statistical Office (NSO), *2007 Survey of Older Persons in Thailand* (original tabulations) (Bangkok: National Statistical Office, 2008).

TABLE 4.2
Per Cent Who Made Preparations for Old Age by Age and Gender

Age	% Who Prepared for Old Age		
	Males	Females	Total
<20	50.7	63.6	57.1
20–29	62.5	64.2	63.5
30–39	72.3	77.5	75.1
40–49	78.7	80.6	79.7
50–59	84.0	86.8	85.5
Total for future elderly (age 18–59)	*74.1*	*77.3*	*75.8*
60–69	65.3	63.0	64.0
70–79	49.3	47.2	48.1
80+	42.5	39.0	40.3
Total for present elderly (age 60+)	*58.5*	*55.3*	*56.7*

Sources: National Statistical Office (NSO), *The National Survey of the 18–59 Year-Old on Their Knowledge and Attitude towards Older Persons* (original tabulations) (Bangkok: National Statistical Office, 2007) and National Statistical Office (NSO), *2007 Survey of Older Persons in Thailand* (original tabulations) (Bangkok: National Statistical Office, 2008).

It was also found that both gender and age seem to have some impact on old age preparation. Among the present cohorts of older persons, males are more likely than females to have made some old age preparation, while among both near and far away future elderly cohorts, women demonstrate higher proportions that have made some preparation for old age (see Table 4.2).

It is also interesting to explore how many types of preparation were made. As mentioned earlier, the 18–59 year old survey questionnaire included more items of types of preparations for old age than the elderly survey. For comparative purposes, since this study is limited to the five types of old age preparations that were similar in both surveys, the mean number of prepared areas was calculated for both the present and future elderly. The respondents who made preparations in all the five types were given a score of one, while the highest score was five and the lowest was zero.

Table 4.1 presents the percentage distribution of persons age 18–59 and 60+ according to number of preparations made and the mean number of prepared areas for old age by age and gender. The results indicate that the mean number of types of preparation has a curvilinear relationship with age. Such a pattern still appears when gender is included. In addition, the results show that men in the present cohort of the elderly made slightly more types of preparation than women, while women of future cohorts of age 18–59 years tend to make slightly more types of preparation than men.

Start Age for Making Preparations for Old Age

In the elderly survey, the older persons were asked about the age at which they started preparing for old age (see Table 4.3). From the frequency distribution it can be seen that about one-third of the present elderly started preparing for old age at the age 50–59 years. Similarly, the mean age of starting preparation for old age is about 50 years, which is rather late. In addition, there is no gender difference in the starting age of preparation among the present cohort of the elderly.

In the national survey of the people age 18–59 on knowledge and attitude towards older persons, respondents were asked at what age one should start preparing for old age. Table 4.4 shows the percentage distribution of this group of people according to their views about the appropriate age to start preparing for old age by age and gender. Compared to the present elderly, the future elderly are likely to make preparations at an earlier age for both sexes. The highest percentage for the appropriate age at which one needs to start preparing for old age was found in the age group of 30–39 (34 per cent). On comparing the responses of respondents age 18–39 with those age 40–59, the younger

TABLE 4.3

Per Cent Distribution of Persons Age 60 and Above according to the Age They Started Preparing for Old Age and Mean Age of Starting with Old Age Preparation, by Gender

Age Started Making the Preparation	Males	Females	Total
Not prepared	21.9	23.2	22.6
60+	19.6	21.4	20.6
50–59	33.8	33.2	33.5
40–49	16.3	14.6	15.4
30–39	6.9	6.1	6.4
<30	1.6	1.5	1.5
Total	100.0	100.0	100.0
Mean Age at which one started preparing for old age among the elderly who made preparations	50.2	50.8	50.5

Sources: National Statistical Office (NSO), *The National Survey of the 18–59 Year-Old on Their Knowledge and Attitude towards Older Persons* (original tabulations) (Bangkok: National Statistical Office, 2007) and National Statistical Office (NSO), *2007 Survey of Older Persons in Thailand* (original tabulations) (Bangkok: National Statistical Office, 2008).

TABLE 4.4

Per Cent Distribution of Persons Age 18–59 according to the Perception of the Appropriate Age to Prepare for Old Age by Age and Gender

Appropriate Age to Start Preparing for Old Age	Total			Males			Females		
	Total	18–39	40–59	Total	18–39	40–59	Total	18–39	40–59
Need not prepare	3.7	3.7	3.7	3.9	4.3	3.6	3.5	3.2	3.8
60+	4.5	6.0	3.0	4.3	6.3	2.4	4.7	5.7	3.6
50–59	7.3	6.0	8.6	6.8	5.2	8.3	7.7	6.5	8.9
40–49	29.7	24.3	35.1	29.6	23.7	35.3	29.8	24.7	34.9
30–39	33.6	34.4	33.0	33.7	34.3	33.1	33.6	34.5	32.8
<30	21.2	25.8	16.6	21.7	26.3	17.4	20.7	25.3	16.0
Total	100.0	100.0	100.0	100.0	100.0	100.0	100.0	100.0	100.0

Sources: National Statistical Office (NSO), The National Survey of the 18–59 Year-Old on Their Knowledge and Attitude towards Older Persons (original tabulations) (Bangkok: National Statistical Office, 2007) and National Statistical Office (NSO), 2007 Survey of Older Persons in Thailand (original tabulations) (Bangkok: National Statistical Office, 2008).

age group tends to view a younger age as an appropriate age to start old age preparation. One-third of the 18–39 age group reported that the appropriate age is 30–39, followed by before the age of 30 (about 26 per cent), while 35 per cent of the 40–59 age group viewed age 40–49 as the most appropriate age to start preparations for old age. Although the future elderly tended to start making preparations at an earlier stage of life than the present elderly, some types of preparation such as finance and physical health should start in their early years such as during their working life or even from childhood onwards.

Types of Preparation

Five types of preparation were included (finances, living quarters, physical health, arrangements for caregiving, and turning to religion or studying the Dhamma) in both the 2007 elderly and 18–59 year old surveys. Table 4.5 presents the percentage for each type of preparation based on age and sex. The area with the highest proportion of preparation by the present elderly is physical health (44 per cent), followed by mental or psychological health. In fact, approximately 44 per cent of elderly reported turning to religion or studying the Dhamma as a form of mental or psychological preparation for old age. This was followed by preparation for living quarters (38.9 per cent), securing old age finances (38.5 per cent), and arranging for a caregiver (34 per cent), respectively. These results reveal relatively similar areas of preparation to the previous study conducted in 1995 using SWET data set, which indicated that the Thai elderly have a tendency to prepare for psychological and physical health more than economic security (Chayovan and Knodel 1997). A possible explanation could be that the economic hardships faced during one's work life may be an obstacle to saving as well as preparing financially for one's future (Chayovan 2005). Moreover, a majority of Thai elderly still expect and do receive an income from children as a main source of support (Knodel and Chayovan 2008).

One point that should be noted is that this study found that the elderly who prepared for ageing after the age of 60 had not made any preparations for ageing before the age of 60. However, the results with regards to the proportion that prepared for each type of old age preparation may include those who started preparing only after the age of 60, especially in the area of turning to religion. About two-thirds (the data are not shown in the table) of the present elderly reported that they made preparations by turning to religion. However, on excluding those

TABLE 4.5

Per Cent Who Made Each Type of Preparation for Old Age among Persons Age 18–59 and Age 60 and Above by Age Group and Gender, Thailand, 2007

Type of Preparation	Age 18–39*			Age 40–59*			Age 60+**		
	Males	Females	Total	Males	Females	Total	Males	Females	Total
A. Financial preparation/savings	49.9	56.9	53.7	60.8	61.9	61.4	41.5	36.0	38.5
B. Living quarters	30.3	34.1	32.4	43.8	47.9	46.0	41,8	36.6	38.9
C. Physical health	45.4	48.4	47.0	56.6	57.4	57.1	45.4	42.9	44.0
D. Arrangement for caregiver	29.9	32.5	31.3	44.7	48.3	46.6	35.2	33.7	34.0
E. Turning more towards religion/Studying the *dhamma*	27.2	32.2	30.1	42.9	46.8	45.0	43.3	44.2	43.8

Sources: * National Statistical Office (NSO), *The National Survey of the 18–59 Year-Old on Their Knowledge and Attitude towards Older Persons* (original tabulations) (Bangkok: National Statistical Office, 2007).
** National Statistical Office (NSO), *2007 Survey of Older Persons in Thailand* (original tabulations) (Bangkok: National Statistical Office, 2008).

who prepared only after the age of 60, the proportion preparing for old age by turning to religion reduces to only about 44 per cent.

When looking at the gender difference, the results show that men are more likely than women to prepare for matters concerning physical health, living quarters, financial security, and arrangements for a caregiver. In contrast, women have a tendency to make slightly more preparations for mental health (see Table 4.5). This may be because of the traditional norms and gender roles that assign the role of breadwinner of the family to the men. Therefore, men may consider preparation for old age in the areas of physical health and finance as an important assurance for themselves and their family (Chayovan 2005).

In comparison to the present elderly, the future elderly tend to prepare more for the areas of financial security and physical health rather than mental health. Such a trend appears in both the distant future and near elderly cohorts (age 18–39 and age 40–59). This may be because of the influence of globalization towards a capitalist economy, which in turn has led them to be more concerned about financial security. In addition, the implementation of the Second National Plan on the Elderly may have had the effect of enhancing awareness among the future elderly in the areas of health promotion and economic assurance for old age (see Table 4.5).

It is worth noting that future cohorts of older women have been preparing for old age at a higher or slightly higher proportion than men in all five aspects of financial security, physical health, living quarters, arrangements for caregiving, and turning more towards religion. Such a shift towards a higher level of women's preparation for old age may reflect the change in social norms related to traditional gender roles along with the increasing opportunities in society. In other words, extending the number of years in school for both men and women, higher opportunities for females to participate in the labour force, late marriages, as well as a reduction in the number of children being given birth to might have been significant contributing factors leading to an increase in the number of females preparing for old age.

DIFFERENTIALS IN PREPARATION FOR OLD AGE

In this section, the relationship between gender and preparation for old age is being examined. The descriptive data in the previous sections show that, to some extent, gender appears to have some influence on the preparation for old age. The logistic regression analysis is used to further examine this relationship.

To determine if there is any association between gender difference and preparation for old age, each type of preparation is considered for each individual model as shown in Tables 4.6 and 4.7. The dependent variables are dichotomous: whether preparation has been made in each area or not. Gender is used as an independent variable in every model, while controlling for age, education, place of residence, and income. The independent variables included in the model are quite limited since the logistic regression model for both present and future elderly cohorts should have similar independent variables for comparison purpose. Moreover, there are some differences in the independent variables that are used for the present and future cohorts because data for each cohort are from separate surveys. For the present elderly, income refers to personal income during the past year, while for the future elderly, income refers to household income per month. In addition, both income and place of residence of the present elderly cohorts are based on current characteristics. The 2007 elderly survey does not provide information on past income or economic status and place of residence. Hence in this section, we have to assume that the current income and place of residence are proxy for past economic status and place of residence.

For the present cohort of the elderly (age 60+), results of the logistic regression in Table 4.6 show that in all kinds of preparation (financial, living quarters, physical health, arrangements for caregiving, and turning toward religion/studying the Dhamma), gender has a statistically significant impact, although the magnitude of differences is rather small. Females are less likely to make preparations in the area of finance and living quarters than males. In contrast, females are more likely to prepare in the area of mental health, physical health, and arrangements for caregiving. This is consistent with the previous findings that men were more likely than women to make preparations concerning finance, while women tended to turn closer to religion than did men (Chayovan and Knodel 1997). This may be partly explained by a man's traditional role of being economic provider for the family, while managing the home and nurturing the children are considered a woman's responsibility. Therefore, men tend to be concerned more about financial matters and, thus, have the ability to earn and save more than women (see Chapters 10 and 11, this volume).

The age of the present elderly is also statistically significant in relation to the types of preparation for old age. For all types of preparation, the older the elderly, the likelihood that they have made any preparations before this stage of life substantially decreases. This may be because

TABLE 4.6

Logistic Regression: Odds Ratio of Making Each Type of Preparation for Old Age in Relation to Gender and Other Background Characteristics of the Present Elderly

Background Variables	Financial Preparation	Living Quarters	Physical Health	Arrangement for Caregiver	Turning More towards Religion/ Studying the Dhamma
	Odds Ratio	Odds Ratio	Odds Ratio	Odds Ratio	Odds Ratio
Female vs. male	.949***	.912***	1.037***	1.020***	1.168***
Age 70–79 vs. age 60–69	.759***	.716***	.623***	.830***	.705***
Age 80+ vs. age 60–69	.579***	.584***	.502***	.669***	.503***
Income	1.265***	1.182***	1.148***	1.114***	1.111***
Rural vs. Bangkok	1.239***	1.404***	.980***	.932***	1.629***
Provincial urban vs. Bangkok	1.427***	1.404***	1.057***	.995***	1.537***
No education vs. primary education	.834***	.927***	.867***	.916***	.840***
Secondary and higher vs. primary education	2.091***	1.711***	1.888***	1.332***	1.501***
–2 Log Likelihood	8,796,551.6	9,050,457.3	9,235,516.4	8,887,800.1	9,380,943.1

Note: $*p < .05$; $**p < .01$; $***p < .001$.
Source: National Statistical Office (NSO), *2007 Survey of Older Persons in Thailand* (original tabulations) (Bangkok: National Statistical Office, 2008).

of a lack of awareness on the significance of preparation for old age among older generations and the persistence of traditional norms that the elderly may receive and rely on the support of children rather than be self-reliant.

Income has a direct positive relationship with the probability of preparing for old age, when controlling for gender, age, place of residence, and education. This may be because those who have a higher income tend to have better economic status and for this reason, they can save or have more financial security.

Place of residence also has a significant impact on the probability of preparing for old age. The elderly who reside in rural areas and provincial urban areas are more likely to prepare for old age in the areas of finance, living quarters, and mental health, as compared to those living in Bangkok. This may be because of the higher living expenses in Bangkok which make it difficult for its residents to save money. Furthermore, those who reside in rural areas and provincial urban areas have been found to have a higher level of faith and commitment to religious institutions than those living in Bangkok.

Another interesting finding is that the elderly who live in rural and other urban areas are less likely than those living in Bangkok to make preparations for caregivers. This is probably because of stronger family and community ties in rural and other urban areas as compared to that in Bangkok. As a result, elderly from the rural and other urban areas may be less anxious about who will take care of them in their old age.

Education also plays a significant role in preparing for old age. The elderly with no education are less likely to make any specific type of preparation for old age as compared to those with primary education. In contrast, those with secondary education are more likely to prepare for all the types of preparation than those with primary education.

Logistic regression is also used to investigate the relationship of probability of preparation for old age and gender and other background characteristics of the future elderly (see Table 4.7). In contrast to the findings for the present elderly, the results for the future elderly reveal that females are more likely than males to prepare for finance, living quarters, physical health, caregivers, and mental health. This may be because of social and cultural changes that have now provided women with the opportunity to be more involved in public matters.

Age is another factor that has statistically significant influence on types of preparedness for old age. Compared to those below the age of 30, those who are in the age group of 50–59 demonstrate a higher

TABLE 4.7

Logistic Regression: Odds Ratio of Making Each Type of Preparation for Old Age in Relation to Gender and Other Background Characteristics of the Future Elderly

Background Variables	Financial Preparation Odds Ratio	Living Quarters Odds Ratio	Physical Health Odds Ratio	Arrangement for Caregiver Odds Ratio	Turning More towards Religion/Studying the Dhamma Odds Ratio
Female vs. male	1.241***	1.221***	1.121**	1.166***	1.233***
Age 30–39 vs. age <30	1.630***	1.597***	1.441***	1.514***	1.337***
Age 40–49 vs. age <30	2.117***	2.136***	1.867***	2.052***	1.816***
Age 50–59 vs. age <30	2.472***	3.289***	2.463***	3.220***	3.256***
Household income	1.193***	1.061***	1.081***	1.029*	1.024
Rural vs. Bangkok	1.358***	1.198**	1.579***	1.178*	1.690***
Provincial urban vs. Bangkok	1.311***	1.191*	1.455***	1.068	1.301***
No education vs. primary education	.759	.713*	.705*	.805	.885
Secondary and higher vs. primary education	1.451***	1.224***	1.374***	1.086	1.215***
–2 Log Likelihood	11,817.0	11,725.4	12,200.0	11,707.5	11,523.4

Note: *p < .05; **p < .01; ***p < .001.
Source: National Statistical Office (NSO), *The National Survey of the 18–59 Year-Old on Their Knowledge and Attitude towards Older Persons* (original tabulations) (Bangkok: National Statistical Office, 2007).

probability of preparing for old age in all types. In particular, the magnitude of difference between the two cohorts in terms of preparation of living quarters, mental health, and arrangements for caregiving is quite large. These results reflect that people tend to engage in more preparation as they approach old age.

In addition, future older persons who are residing outside Bangkok and have secondary education show a higher probability of preparing for old age. Such a relationship emerges in all types of preparation.

Social Participation of Present Elderly and Gender Difference

Being a member of various groups and participation in community and other social activities reflect exposure to external social life and is typically viewed as one of the important aspects of active ageing. This part of the analysis is limited to the present elderly because relevant information is not available in the 18–59 year old survey. According to the elderly survey, respondents were asked if they were a member of a group and participated in activities of each of the seven groups: elderly club, funeral, cooperative, village scout, occupational, and housewife, and community/village. In this chapter, "social participation" is measured by whether the elderly participated in any of these activities during the past year, regardless of their membership.

Levels of Social Participation

Table 4.8 presents the percentage of those who participated in each type of social activity among persons age 60 years and above by gender. The results reveal that a majority of the elderly did not participate much in social activities among the seven groups, except for community or village activities (71.8 per cent). The participation level ranges from 1.9 per cent in the occupational group to 39.8 per cent in the funeral group. When considering whether or not the elderly have participated in any of the seven listed activities in the last year, the results reveal that 75.4 per cent of the older persons participated in activities of at least one of the seven groups. However, if community activities are excluded, the level of social participation in any of the other six groups drops to about 50 per cent.

Caution should be taken when interpreting these results because most of the community activities that the elderly are involved in tend to be

TABLE 4.8
Per Cent Who Participated in Each Type of Social Activity among Persons Age 60 and Above by Gender

Participated Activities	Males	Females	Total
Elderly club activities	21.4	21.1	21.2
Funeral group activities	42.2	37.8.	39.8
Cooperative group activities	18.1	13.1	15.3
Village scout group activities	2.9	1.6	2.2
Occupational group activities	2.2	1.6	1.9
Housewife group activities	1.9	5.2	3.7
Community/village activities	73.7	70.3	71.8
Participation in any of the seven activities	77.4	73.9	75.4
Participation in any of the six activities (excluding community activities)	52.1	47.5	49.6

Source: National Statistical Office (NSO), *2007 Survey of Older Persons in Thailand* (original tabulations) (Bangkok: National Statistical Office, 2008).

religious or entertainment-oriented and are normally organized during special occasions such as "elderly day" or New Year celebrations. These activities seem to happen once or twice a year or are specifically arranged for the elderly and may be the reason for why participation levels in community/village activities have been reported to be the highest. In addition, some elderly persons, while being members of various groups, did not participate in any activities because the groups they were affiliated with did not organize or host any activities in the past year. For example, although about 65 per cent of the elderly are members of at least one of the six groups, namely elderly club, funeral, cooperative, village scout, occupational, and housewife groups (data not shown), about 52 per cent of them did not participate in any of the activities of these groups in the past year as a result of the groups not organizing any activities. Therefore, the lower level of social participation of the elderly may not necessarily stem from their lack of interest or their physical limitations or socio-economic problems, but because of the weak management of these groups.

Gender Difference in Social Participation

Types of activities

For every type of group activity, except for the housewife group, older men show a higher proportion of participation, especially in community/village, funeral, and cooperative groups (see Table 4.8). The gender differences in social participation may be said to reflect differences in traditional gender roles and the sexual division of labour within the family wherein men have played the role of breadwinner, while women have been responsible for household chores as well as playing a supportive role to their husbands. A point that needs to be highlighted here is that although older women are less likely to participate in social activities as compared to men, it does not mean that they contribute less to others and society. Several of them, while taking on the main responsibility of managing household chores and supporting other family members, also participate in social activities.

PREPARATIONS FOR OLD AGE AND SOCIAL PARTICIPATON: GENDER DIFFERENCES

This section aims to investigate the relationship between preparations for old age and social participation and to explore whether there are any differences between elderly men and elderly women in this regard. The hypothesis here is that those who engage in a greater number of types of preparation for old age are more likely to have a higher potential to participate in social activities of every group.

Binary logistic regression has been used for analysing the factors influencing each type of social participation of the present elderly. Gender, number of types of preparation for old age, and other background variables including age, education, current place of residence, marital status, income, number of channels from which news is received, perceived health status, and level of feelings of despair or a feeling of life as having no value are used as independent variables. Activities of six groups: community/village, elderly club, funeral, cooperative, occupational, and village scout groups, are treated as dependent variables.

When controlling for other independent variables in multivariate analysis, the results have been changed from bivariate analysis. While elderly men are more likely to participate in funeral, cooperative, and village scout-related group activities, elderly women are more likely to participate in community/village activities and elderly clubs. However, there is no gender difference in participation in the occupational group. These findings seem to reflect that elderly men tend to participate in social activities related to financial investment or accumulation. For example, those who participate in funeral and cooperative groups need to contribute some money or pay a fee as a member of the group in order to receive benefits. The reason for men's involvement in such activities more than women may be because they can afford the fees to engage in these activities because of having participated in the labour force. Therefore, the present cohort of elderly men seem to be interested and can afford to participate in social activities where financial contribution is required more so than elderly women. Moreover, some activities such as village scout groups tend to be male-oriented.

This finding also indicates that gender difference has some effect on active ageing as reflected by types of social participation. The present cohort of older women is less likely to participate in certain types of social activities compared to older men. This may be because of the traditional socialization roles, cultural norms, and division of labour that enables men to play a more active role in social or public circles while women are relegated largely to family and home engagement roles.

Another variable that has a significant effect on the types of social activities in which one participates is the number of types of preparation for old age. The more preparations made for old age, the more likely that the elderly would participate in social activities. This pattern appeared in all six activities considered. This may be because those who are more prepared for old age tend to be better-off in terms of health and finance. This in turn leads to more independence and higher dignity among the elderly as well as increases the likelihood among them to participate in various social activities. For most types of activities, the older the elderly, the less likely they are to participate in social activities, except for the elderly club and village scout activities which seem to have a curvilinear relationship with age.

One of the significant findings is that the elderly who reside in Bangkok have less probability of participating in all kinds of activities compared to those who reside in rural areas. This may be because of weaker social ties, more individualistic values in mega cities, the urban lifestyle, and an unfriendly environment for the elderly living in Bangkok, such as an inconvenient transportation system and lack of adequate appropriate infrastructure.

Besides these, other factors included in the model also show statistically significant influence on the types of social participation. For example, those who are more exposed to the news and are able to access information from various media channels tend to have better physical health, do not feel a sense of despair, have received basic primary education, are married, and are more likely to participate in almost all types of social activities than those who have the opposite characteristics. In addition, it is interesting to find that those with a higher income have a tendency to participate

TABLE 4.9

Logistic Regression: Odds Ratio of Participating in Activities of Each Group in Relation to Gender and Other Background Characteristics of the Present Elderly on Their Social Participation

Background Variables	Community/ Village Activities Odds Ratio	Funeral Group Odds Ratio	Elderly Club Odds Ratio	Cooperative Group Odds Ratio	Occupational Group Odds Ratio	Village Scout Group Odds Ratio
Female vs. Male	1.035***	0.936***	1.043***	0.868***	1.004	0.700***
Age 70–79 vs. 60–69	0.773***	0.880***	1.345***	0.644***	0.798****	1.068***
Age 80–89 vs. 60–69	0.425***	0.592***	0.992*	0.313***	0.296***	0.351***
No. of aspects prepare before old age	1.168***	1.117***	1.058***	1.114***	1.122***	1.185***
No. of channels of received news	1.185***	1.211***	1.212***	1.198***	1.417***	1.354***
Perceived health status	1.203***	1.091***	1.086***	1.085***	1.248***	0.964***
Feeling despair	0.752***	0.843***	0.762***	0.837***	0.666***	0.808***
Primary vs. No education	1.293***	1.156***	0.832***	1.545***	0.883***	0.896***
Secondary vs. No education	0.691***	0.827***	0.749***	1.725***	0.629***	0.553***
Bangkok vs. Rural	0.092***	0.066***	0.170***	0.070***	0.049***	0.022***
Provincial urban vs. Rural	0.456***	0.460***	0.861***	0.400***	0.846***	1.152***
Single vs. marriage	0.548***	0.524***	0.718***	0.588***	0.602***	0.614****
Divorce/Separate/Widow vs. Marriage	0.842***	0.875***	1.062***	0.877***	0.846***	0.724***
Annual income	0.957***	0.891***	0.949***	1.036***	1.060***	1.103***
2 Log Likelihood	6,994,166.1	8,371,353.7	6,830,167.8	5,324,478.6	1,137,210.3	1,311,857.1

Note: *p < .05; **p < .01; ***p < .001.
Source: National Statistical Office (NSO), 2007 Survey of Older Persons in Thailand (original tabulations) (Bangkok: National Statistical Office, 2008).

less in almost all community activities, funeral groups, and elderly clubs as compared to those with lower income. This may be because some of these activities, such as community activities and funeral groups, are more likely to attract those with a lower income rather than those with a higher income.

CONCLUSIONS AND RECOMMENDATIONS

Rapidly moving towards an ageing society is a big challenge for the well-being of the elderly and the sustainable development of a country. Gender differences and inequality become major issues that make the situation in an ageing society much more complicated. In the case of Thailand, the problem of gender inequality is not as serious as in some other Asian countries which have norms favouring men and a gender preference for sons. In the present times, the processes of socio-economic development as well as globalization create more opportunities for Thai women. Women enjoy more opportunities to receive education, participate in the labour force, and work in the formal employment sectors. Fertility decline has also reduced the burden of childcare and has given women more opportunities to participate in other activities. One shifting trend is that females in the future cohorts of the elderly are more likely to make old age preparations than men.

Preparations for old age among the future cohorts of elderly of both sexes in Thailand appears to be more positive as they are likely to start earlier than the present elderly. However, the expected age of preparation is still after the age of 30–40 which is already in the middle stage of life. Several types of preparation have to start from childhood, such as for one's physical and mental health as well as financial security, and these need to be attended to over time. Both present and future elderly have been found to have only made preparations for old age in one or two areas on average; thus, not all the areas that need to be addressed for old age preparation have been covered. Therefore, the government should create more awareness and provide incentives for all Thais to prepare themselves for quality ageing from childhood itself through both formal and informal education. Given limited national income and resources, the policy should not focus only on materialistic provision. Such support may not be able to serve the rapidly growing number of elderly thoroughly and equally. It is best to encourage self-dependency and dignified living. For the next decade, the government should also focus on expanding the coverage of old-age financial security systems, promoting personal savings, and strengthening the national pension system.

Although financial or material preparation is important for old-age survival, making non-material or mental and physical health preparation is equally important. Further improvement of health promotion and services are still needed in order to minimize the period of dependency or disability in old age. In addition, information and activities on self-preparation and self-care for healthy ageing should be incorporated into the curriculum or courses in both formal and informal education.

It is worth noting that findings in this study show that the elderly who reside in Bangkok are less likely to prepare for old age than those in other urban and rural areas. These findings are consistent with the findings from the project, *Setting-Up the System for Monitoring and Evaluation of the Second National Plan for Older Persons*, which employed both quantitative and qualitative data. This latter study found that the elderly in Bangkok were less active in preparation for old age than those residing in rural areas because of weaker community networks, economic problems, and an inconvenient transportation system. Moreover, it also found that the proportion who did not receive monetary welfare among older persons who were poor and without adequate sources of support was highest in Bangkok (Prachuabmoh et al. 2008). The findings also suggest that the elderly who are living in poverty in Bangkok need urgent support from both the Bangkok Metropolis Administration and the national government.

Results of this study also reveal that the older generations or present elderly who prepared themselves for old age are more likely to participate in various types of social activities. Among future generations, the trend in active ageing in terms of participation in social activities may also change because of the shift in the trend of female preparation for old age. It is also expected that a higher level of old age preparation among young females compared to their male counterparts may narrow the gender gap in social participation. Further research, however, is needed for assessing the trends of preparations in old age and the social participation among men and women in Thailand.

Note

1. The author would like to express her sincere thanks to Professor John Knodel, Associate Professor Napaporn Chayovan, and Assistant Professor

Bussarawan Teerawichitchainan for their insightful comments and suggestions on an earlier draft of this chapter.

References

Chayovan, Napaporn. "Preparation for Old Age among Thai Adults and Elderly" (in Thai). *Proceedings of the Annual Meeting of the Thai Population Association*, 19–20 November 1992.

————. "Policy Implications for Old-Age Economic Support of Changes in Thailand's Age Structure: A New Challenge". *Population, Resources, and Development: Riding the Age Waves* 1 (2005): 157–80.

Chayovan, Napaporn and John Knodel. "A Report on the Survey of the Welfare of the Elderly in Thailand". Publication 248/97. Bangkok: Institute of Population Studies, Chulalongkorn University, 1997.

Knodel, John and Napaporn Chayovan. "Gender and Ageing in Thailand: A Situation Analysis of Older Women and Men". Report 08-664. Ann Arbor: Population Studies Center, University of Michigan, 2008.

National Statistical Office (NSO). *The National Survey of the 18–59 year-old on Their Knowledge and Attitude towards Older Persons*. Bangkok: National Statistical Office, 2007.

————. *2007 Survey of Older Persons in Thailand*. Bangkok: National Statistical Office, 2008.

Prachuabmoh, V. and P. Mithranon. "Below-Replacement Fertility in Thailand and Its Policy Implications". *Journal of Population Research* 20, no. 1 (2002): 35–50.

Prachuabmoh, V. and N. Chayovan. "Consequences of Low Fertility and Policy Responses in Thailand". *Low Fertility and Policy Responses to Issues of Aging and Welfare* (2000): 246–72.

Prachuabmoh, Vipan, Napaporn Chayovan, Malinee Wongsit, Siriwan Siriboon, Busarin Bangkaew and Chanette Milintangul. *The Project on Setting-Up The System for Monitoring and Evaluation of the Second National Plan for Older Persons (2002–21)*. Bangkok: Thanwa Printing, 2008.

United Nations. *Lifelong Preparation for Old Age in Asia and the Pacific*. New York: United Nations, 1996.

World Health Organization (WHO). *Active Ageing: A Policy Framework*. Geneva: World Health Organization, 2002.

5

GENDER AND HEALTH STATUS AMONG OLDER ADULTS IN VIETNAM[1]

Bussarawan Teerawichitchainan

INTRODUCTION

Over the last decade, the growing size of Vietnam's older population has prompted the government to pay more attention to the well-being of this group (Bui et al. 2000; Nguyen 1998; VCPFC 2002). The proportion of Vietnamese adults age 60 and above is projected to rise substantially from 8 per cent in 2000 to 13 per cent in 2025 and over 25 per cent by the mid twenty-first century (United Nations 2007*a*). Female old-age vulnerability has been placed in the forefront of government-funded social programmes to improve the living standards of the old (HelpAge 2007; Mitchell and Khuat 2000; United Nations 2002, 2007*b*). Influenced by the dominant policy discourse on gender and ageing, Vietnamese policy-makers are concerned that older women would be more susceptible than men to various forms of hardship because they tend to experience socio-economic disadvantage in early life and to be widowed in older years (Giang and Pfau 2007*a*; Ofstedal et al. 2003).

Recently the disproportionate policy focus on older women's vulnerability has been increasingly criticized for its lack of consistent evidence and for its dismissal of men's potential disadvantages (Knodel and Ofstedal 2003).

For example, while women might be inferior to men in the labour market, they are not necessarily more vulnerable in later life since female elders tend to be more protected socially by family and kin network support. These criticisms also extend to the prevailing perspective on gender and health equity which posits that women are more likely than men to have poor health at older ages. The issue is particularly relevant to Vietnam's recent efforts to address the healthcare needs of its older population. While healthcare provision for the elderly, especially for female elders who are less likely to receive pension and health insurance, has been discussed widely in the public sphere, little is known about the extent to which health status in older years varies by gender and what mechanisms lie behind male-female differences (Thanh Nien News 2009; Vietnam News 2008).

To shed light on these questions, this chapter analyses nationally representative data from the 2001–02 Vietnam National Health Survey (VNHS) to examine gender differentials in two important indicators of old-age health status: (1) self-assessed health; and (2) incidence of hypertension — one of the most common risk factors for cardiovascular disease which is one of Vietnam's leading causes of death (WHO 2004a).

Specifically, the chapter investigates whether gender differences in these two health indicators are influenced by the differential socio-economic characteristics and health-related behaviours of older men and women. Furthermore, since gender differences in morbidity can be explained not only by biological and behavioural differences between men and women but also by how illnesses are differentially recognized and reported by each gender (Verbrugge 1989), the study includes both subjective and objective measures of hypertension to explore the patterns of how Vietnamese men and women report an illness episode might have differed from their health outcomes observed objectively. Based on these multi-dimensional measures of health statuses, this chapter contributes to timely discussions about older Vietnamese women and to clarify which segments of Vietnam's older population are most in need of the country's limited public healthcare resources.

BACKGROUND

The dominant perspective on gender, health, and ageing asserts that older women are more likely than older men to experience poor health (both physical and mental), more illness episodes, greater difficulty in physical activities, and more disabilities (Arber and Ginn 1991; Nathanson 1975). This influential view is derived primarily from research in developed societies and has not yet been examined systematically in the context of Vietnam. To date, a growing body of research on ageing in Vietnam has paid inadequate attention to the health status of the Vietnamese elderly. Social science studies tend to focus on socio-economic well-being in older years, whereas health research is likely to examine health conditions in childhood and adult years rather than in older adulthood. To fill this research gap, this chapter addresses the question of whether gender is an appropriate marker for differences in health status among Vietnam's older population.

The review of the literature indicates that there are three broad groups of factors that explain gender differences in health in older years: biological, behavioural, and reporting biases (Verbrugge 1989). First, the biological argument posits that gender health differences are attributable to male and female differences in biological predispositions. A biological component to the sex differentials in mortality and morbidity has been extensively documented so much so that there is a tendency to interpret male survival disadvantage as being natural and to view females' longer life expectancy as exposing women to more years of ill health (Knodel and Ofstedal 2003). Critics point to the need of ageing research on health disparities to examine gender-specific influences that disadvantage men with regards to survival and those that contribute to women's disadvantage in health status.

Second, the behavioural approach argues that male-female health outcomes in older years can be accounted for by gender normative roles, socio-economic characteristics, and personality traits, including gender variations in labour force participation, lifestyle practices, health practices (for example, doctor visits), and psychological state. To address this approach, the author is mindful about the historical and societal contexts of Vietnam that shape the life course of men and women and, in turn, their health and well-being. For example, while Vietnamese women's smoking habits tend to be frowned upon, there was no such social disapproval for men resulting in significant gender divide in tobacco use in Vietnam (Hoang et al. 2006). Furthermore, Vietnam's wars between the 1960s and 1970s might have had long-term impacts on the physical and psychological health of the current cohorts of older Vietnamese men who were massively inducted into the military and exposed to combats earlier in their life course. In addition, the country's recent shift from a collective to a market economy has been accompanied by health-sector reforms that included the imposition of user fees at public health facilities (World Bank 2001). Since health benefits accrue more often to men who are more likely to be veterans or to work in the public sector, the health reforms may have had adverse impact on women's healthcare because they are not likely candidates for pension or health insurance coverage in older years (Goodkind et al. 1999). Nonetheless, female disadvantage might be mediated by the fact that family members, especially children, play a pivotal role in providing support for both male and female elders (Friedman et al. 2003; Ofstedal et al. 2003). Social scientists find little or modest gender differences in socio-economic well-being of older adults in Vietnam and assert that factors such as location of residence appear to be more important in explaining old-age vulnerability than gender (Friedman et al. 2001; Knodel and Truong 2002).

The third argument indicates that gender differences in health are an artifact of how men and women differ in their reporting of illnesses rather than any observed clinical reality. This perspective posits that older women tend to be more aware of their health problems and/or more willing than men to report them. While this hypothesis has been tested quite extensively in the context of western societies (e.g., Anson et al. 1993; Davis 1981), it has rarely been applied to the populations of less developed countries because of a lack of subjective and comparable objective measures of health status in large scale data sets. Therefore, in the context of developing countries, the effects of reporting biases on gender health disparities have yet to be established.

Past studies demonstrate that neither biological, behavioural, nor reporting arguments are dominant in the sense that anyone explains all or most of the variations in gender health differentials among older people. This chapter does not aim to test these hypotheses but rather considers combined effects of all three approaches when addressing gender differences in health status among older Vietnamese. More specifically, this chapter examines the extent and nature of gender differentials in health status in older years, focusing on how the effects of gender vary across the measures of health used. Second, it assesses how gender health differences can be explained by older men's and women's demographic, socio-economic, and health-related behavioural characteristics. Using objective and subjective measures of health, this research addresses the question of whether male-female variations in reporting of ill health might contribute to observed gender differences in health outcomes and discusses whether the policy emphasis on female health vulnerability at older ages is justified in the case of Vietnam.

DATA

Conducted by the Ministry of Health and General Statistics Office, the Vietnam National Health Survey (VNHS) is a population-based nationally representative sample data set that provides a unique resource for addressing gender differences in health status at older ages. Data are derived from a three-stage, stratified, cluster random probability sample of 36,000 households containing nearly 160,000 individuals from 1,200 communes nationwide. Because of a sampling design that produced unequal probabilities of cluster selection, the analyses have been adjusted for clustering and stratification effects. Furthermore, the author restricts the sample to adults age 60 and above (N=15,214).

The VNHS household questionnaire was designed so that one individual considered by the household to be the most informed about health and expenditures of household members was designated as the key informant.[2] Information on chronic illnesses, including hypertension, was derived from direct interviews with the individuals or the people who knew most about these episodes. However, interviewers also accepted responses from key informants if it was difficult to have direct interviews with the individuals (that is, household members) (Bales 2003). In addition, each sample household was visited by an anthropometrist who implemented the health check questionnaire. Anthropometrists took a measurement of each household member's weight and height. For members age 15 and above, blood pressure was also taken. Since anthropometric measures require anthropometrists to meet the individuals directly, questions regarding self-assessed health and health-related habits were also probed during the occasion.

MEASURES OF HEALTH STATUS

One of the VNHS's most distinct features is its rich information that permits a construction of multiple measures of health status. This study focuses on two health indicators: self-assessed health and incidence of hypertension. What follows is the description of how each health status indicator was operationalized in this research.

Self-assessed health is a respondent's subjective evaluation of his/her own health.[3] Respondents were asked directly by an anthropometrist: "In general, how do you feel about your health?" To rate their health, respondents might answer very good, good, average, weak, or very weak. In the analyses, the author combines older adults who rated their health "very good" and "good" as "above-average". About 0.2 per cent of the elderly in the sample, who were reported too frail to answer the question during the interview, was coded as "very weak". About 5 per cent of older adults rated their health as above-average, 43 per cent average, 47 per cent weak, and 6 per cent very weak.

The VNHS contains information that permits a construction of subjective and objective measures of hypertension among older Vietnamese adults. The first measure is derived from the household survey in which the incidence of hypertension was subjectively reported for each household member by the individuals themselves (and occasionally by key informants). It is arguable that the presence of hypertension required a medical diagnosis and was not merely based on subjective assessment of disease. However, this self-reported measure is subject to individuals' recognition of the medical condition and the fact that the individual received a blood pressure screening in the first place. According to this measure, approximately 23 per cent of older adults were reported to have had hypertension.

The second measure is an objective assessment of hypertension, which is based on blood pressure readings taken during the health-check survey. Anthropometrists were instructed to monitor three readings of blood pressure from each eligible household member.[4] In assessing whether an older adult had hypertension, the author averages the three readings. Older adults are classified as not having hypertension if their average blood pressure readings were less than 140/90 mmHg. If their blood pressure levels were 140/90 mmHg or greater, they are categorized as having hypertension. According to this measure, nearly half of all older adults (48 per cent) in the sample showed a sign of developing hypertension at the time of the survey.

DESCRIPTION OF PREDICTOR VARIABLES

The VNHS provides data on demographic and socio-economic characteristics and information regarding individuals' health-related behaviours such as smoking and alcohol consumption. Table 5.1 presents the distribution of older adults in the sample by each independent variable used in this study. Descriptive statistics are presented for all older adults and separately for male and female populations. Results from tests of significance are reported to indicate whether the differences observed between older men and women for each independent variable is statistically significant.

TABLE 5.1

Descriptive Statistics, Characteristics of Older Adults Age 60 and Older in the VNHS Sample

Variable Description	All (N=15,214)	Male (N=6,236)	Female (N=8,978)	Sig.
	Proportion			
Age				
60–69	0.55	0.59	0.53	**
70–79	0.33	0.32	0.34	
80+	0.12	0.09	0.13	
Current marital status				
Currently married	0.62	0.86	0.46	**
Widowed	0.36	0.13	0.51	
Divorced/Never married	0.02	0.01	0.03	
Location of residence				
Urban	0.23	0.23	0.22	n.s.
Rural	0.77	0.77	0.78	
Region of residence				
Red River Delta	0.27	0.26	0.28	n.s.
Northern Uplands	0.13	0.13	0.12	
Central	0.28	0.28	0.27	
South	0.32	0.33	0.32	
Education				
Illiterate	0.32	0.11	0.46	**
Less than primary	0.34	0.31	0.35	
Primary	0.18	0.25	0.13	
At least some secondary	0.16	0.32	0.06	
Household economic status				
Poor	0.14	0.14	0.15	n.s.
Less poor	0.43	0.43	0.42	
Well off	0.43	0.43	0.43	
Tobacco use				
Never smoked	0.64	0.22	0.93	**
No longer smoke	0.13	0.29	0.02	
Smoking regularly	0.23	0.49	0.05	
Alcohol consumption				
Not drinking regularly	0.82	0.62	0.95	**
Regular consumption	0.18	0.38	0.05	

Note: **Difference between male and female is significant at $p < 0.01$; n.s. = not significant p-value.

Source: Vietnam Ministry of Health and General Statistics Office, *Results of Vietnam National Health Survey 2001–2002* (Hanoi, Vietnam: Medical Publishing House, 2003).

Women account for 59 per cent and men 41 per cent of all older adults in the sample. As in almost all countries, women represent a greater share of older populations largely because of their longer life expectancy. Age is incorporated into the analysis as a categorical variable indicating whether a respondent's age was 60–69, 70–79, or 80 and above at the time of survey. More than half of older adults were below age 70; one third between ages 70–79; and the remaining 12 per cent were age 80 and older. The age distributions of older men and women show statistically significant differences. Among the oldest old (age 80 and above), the proportion of women is higher than that of men. This is relevant because age is hypothesized to have a strong influence on the health status of older adults.

Furthermore, the analyses employed a categorical variable indicating whether a respondent was married, widowed, or divorced/never married at the time of survey. Over 60 per cent of older Vietnamese in the sample were married, whereas one third was widowed. Proportions of older adults who were divorced or never married were very small (2 per cent). There are significant gender differences in marital status. While 86 per cent of older men were reportedly married, less than half of their female counterparts remained so. Half of older women were widowed, compared to only 13 per cent of men. Evidence indicates that marital status is an important indicator of elderly living arrangement and old-age support. In particular, marriage provides significant protection for the socio-economic well-being of older adults in Vietnam (Knodel et al. 2000; Giang and Pfau 2007*b*). Therefore, I hypothesized marital status to have significant impact on health outcomes of older adults.

Besides demographic attributes, household characteristics are incorporated in the analyses. First, location of residence is a dummy variable indicating whether an older adult resided in an urban or rural area at the time of the survey. About three quarters of older people live in rural areas and the rest in urban areas. In addition, since Vietnam's economic development varies greatly by regions, region of residence is incorporated as a categorical variable indicating which region of Vietnam a respondent resided in, including the Red River Delta, Northern Uplands, Central, and South. Slightly over a quarter of older adults lived in the densely-populated region of the Red River Delta; 13 per cent resided in the Northern Uplands which include northeastern and northwestern provinces; 28 per cent were from the Central region, including the Central Coasts and Central Highlands. One third of older adults resided in the rapidly developed southern regions of the Mekong River Delta and Southeast. Tests of statistical significance show no distinct differences between male and female elders with regards to the location and region of their residence. The author expects Vietnamese elders from urban and more developed regions such as the Red River Delta or the South to have better health status than their counterparts from remote, rural, and less developed areas in the Northern Uplands and the Central regions.

In the analyses, education is measured as a categorical variable indicating whether an individual was illiterate, had some primary schooling, finished primary education, or had at least some secondary schooling. Older women in Vietnam were significantly disadvantaged compared to men with regards to their educational attainment. Nearly half of the older women in the sample were illiterate, whereas slightly over one-third had some primary education. Only about one-fifth of female elders completed primary education. An overwhelming majority of older Vietnamese men were literate. A quarter of them finished primary schooling and one-third had some secondary education. Education is expected to positively affect old-age health and well-being and to mediate gender differences in health outcomes because not only are well-educated individuals better informed about health and healthcare but they are also likely to be economically well-off, which are in turn positively related to health status (see Chapter 4, this volume).

In addition, household wealth is incorporated as a categorical variable, indicating whether a respondent's household economic status was considered poor, less poor, or well-off. Given Vietnam's recent health reforms that led to the increasing privitization of its healthcare system, the author expects older adults from economically well-off households to enjoy better health status than those with fewer economic resources. In the VNHS, household wealth is defined by per-capita expenditure. Households were stratified into five per-capita household expenditure quintiles of equal size defining relative living standards in the population (Bales 2003). Households in the lowest quintile are classified as "poor", while the second and third lowest quintiles are categorized as "less-poor" and the top two quintiles as "well-off". About 14 per cent of older adults in the sample came from poor households, 43 per cent from less-poor, and the rest from well-off households. Table 5.1 suggests that older men and women in the sample were not significantly different with regards to their household economic status.

The analyses also incorporate health-related behaviours, including tobacco use and alcohol consumption, to control for their effects on health outcomes at older ages. While researchers have yet to reach consensus regarding the long-term effects of alcohol consumption on the physical and mental health of older adults, it has been well established that smoking compromises the quality of life and health in old age (e.g., Strandberg et al. 2008). In this research, I expect alcohol consumption and tobacco use to negatively affect the health status of the elderly. In the analyses, tobacco use is measured as a categorical variable indicating whether an older adult never smoked, smoked in the past but no longer smoked, or continued to smoke at the time of the survey.[5] Table 5.1 shows a significant difference between older men and women in tobacco use. While most women (93 per cent) never habitually smoked in their lifetime, only one-fifth of men were non-smokers. Half of male elders remained a regular smoker and about a third no longer smoked at the time of the survey. Furthermore, the analyses measured alcohol consumption as a dummy variable indicating whether an individual drank at least one can/bottle of beer or 100 ml of liquor at least once a week. Like tobacco use, older women and men in Vietnam are significantly different in alcohol consumption. Nearly 40 per cent of elderly men reported to have been regular drinkers, compared to only 5 per cent among women.[6]

DESCRIPTIVE ANALYSES RESULTS

Figure 5.1 describes trends in self-assessed health among older adults by gender and age groups. Results indicate three distinct patterns. First, older men and women differed significantly in how they rated their health. For every age group, female elders reported a negative assessment of their health more often than their male counterparts. For example, among older adults in their sixties, 44 per cent of women and 35 per cent of men rated their health as weak. Likewise, there were greater proportions of male than female elders who felt rather positive about their health. Fifty-five per cent of men in their sixties rated their health as average, whereas half of the female counterparts felt the same way.

Consistent with evidence found in other settings, the second pattern shown in Figure 5.1 is that older Vietnamese adults had a tendency not to rate their health as extremely positive. Relatively small proportions of the sample assessed their health as above-average. While more males, especially those in their sixties, felt good about their health compared to female elders, the gender differences are rather modest. A similar trend is observed for a very negative assessment of health. Very small proportions of older adults reported that their health was very weak with the exception

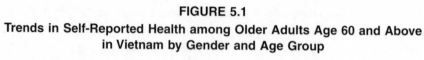

FIGURE 5.1

Trends in Self-Reported Health among Older Adults Age 60 and Above in Vietnam by Gender and Age Group

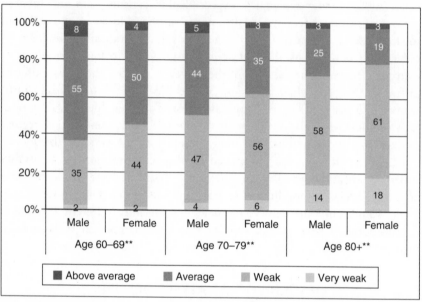

Note: ** Difference between male and female is statistically significant at p < 0.01.
Source: Vietnam Ministry of Health and General Statistics Office, *Results of Vietnam National Health Survey 2001–2002* (Hanoi, Vietnam: Medical Publishing House, 2003).

of the oldest old. One of the most striking findings is that a negative assessment of health increases considerably as an older person ages. This is consistent for both genders. For instance, proportions of older women reporting weak health increased from 44 per cent among those in their sixties to 56 and 61 per cent respectively among female elders in their seventies and eighties. Among the oldest old, nearly four-fifths of women and three-quarters of men rated their health as below-average.

Figure 5.2 presents proportions of the elderly with hypertension by gender and age group. The estimates are reported based on two measurements of hypertension, including subjective (left panel) and anthropometric measures (right panel). By and large, regardless of how one measured hypertension, results demonstrate no statistically significant gender differences in the prevalence of hypertension among older adults in Vietnam. There were two exceptions: (1) the incidence of hypertension among the elders in their sixties based on subjective reporting, and (2) among the oldest old based on the anthropometric

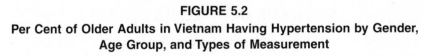

FIGURE 5.2

Per Cent of Older Adults in Vietnam Having Hypertension by Gender, Age Group, and Types of Measurement

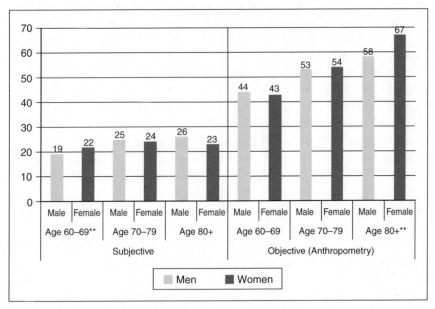

Note: ** Difference between male and female is statistically significant at p < 0.01.
Source: Vietnam Ministry of Health and General Statistics Office, *Results of Vietnam National Health Survey 2001–2002* (Hanoi, Vietnam: Medical Publishing House, 2003).

measure. In both instances, there were greater proportions of older women than men with signs of developing hypertension.

Findings indicate large discrepancies between prevalence of hypertension based on the subjective measure and those derived objectively from the health-check survey. For both genders and all age groups examined, the anthropometric measure of blood pressure indicated twice higher incidence of hypertension than the estimates based on self-reports. Furthermore unlike trends in self-assessed health shown in Figure 5.1, percentages of hypertension based on the subjective measure did not show any upward trends by age. On the contrary, the incidence of hypertension derived from direct blood pressure readings demonstrated a linearly increasing trend by age. Slightly over 40 per cent of elders in their sixties were found to develop high blood pressure disease. The percentages rose to over 50 per cent among male and female elders in their seventies. Among the oldest old, 58 per cent of men and 67 per cent of women had blood pressure levels that suggested hypertension.

MULTIVARIATE ANALYSES RESULTS

While the descriptive analyses provide some compelling findings on gender differentials in self-assessed health and hypertension, they have not yet taken into account demographic and socio-economic differences observed among older Vietnamese men and women (see Table 5.1), which might have affected their health outcomes. Within the multivariate framework, the author used binary logistic regressions to estimate the effect of gender on various indicators of health status at older ages, net of the influences of older adults' background characteristics. Research questions addressed here include: Do older women experience ill health more frequently than men? How do the gender differentials vary by the measures of health status used? Are the observed relationships between gender and each health status modified after an introduction of other covariates? To what extent do demographic and socio-economic attributes of older adults influence their health outcomes? Do reporting biases exist and how do they affect observed gender health differentials?

In the analysis shown in Table 5.2, the author uses binary logistic regression models to estimate the odds ratios that older persons assess their health status negatively (i.e., weak and very weak) versus rating their health positively (i.e., average and above-average). The analyses consist of five additive models. The first model presents self-assessed health as a function of gender; Model 2 incorporates a respondent's age and marital status; Model 3 adds household location and region of residence; Model 4 includes a respondent's education and household economic status; and the last model incorporates a respondent's tobacco use and alcohol consumption.

The exponentiated coefficients are shown in Table 5.2 as the ratio of the odds of rating one's health below-average for each category, relative to the comparable odds of reference category for each covariate. For example, in Model 1, the reference category of female elders had a standard odds ratio of 1.00. Male elders had the odds ratio of 0.61 suggesting that they were about 40 per cent less likely than their female counterparts to rate their health below-average. Moreover, according to Model 2, older adults in their seventies had the odds ratio of 1.83, indicating that they had 83 per cent greater likelihood of reporting poor health compared to those in the reference category (those in their sixties).

Findings indicate that older men were persistently less likely than their female counterparts to assess their health negatively. Although gender gaps in self-assessed health became narrower after an introduction of other covariates, the gender effect remained statistically significant. Other individual characteristics associated with the decreased likelihood of reporting poor health include marital status,[7] educational attainment, and household wealth status. Holding other characteristics constant, older adults whose marriage remained intact at the time of the survey were less likely than those who had never been married or had experienced marital dissolution to rate their health as below-average. Proxies for socio-economic status, such as education and household wealth, were linearly associated with negative assessments of health. Older adults who were better educated and those whose families were economically well-off tended to be more optimistic about their health status, compared to those with lower socio-economic status.

Consistent with Figure 5.1, multivariate results show that age was a strong determinant of self-assessed health. Net of other effects, the likelihood of rating one's health status as below-average increased considerably as an individual aged. Furthermore, rural residents tended to report poor health more often than those in urban areas. This was also the case for older adults living outside the Red River Delta. Those in the South consistently assessed their health more negatively than their counterparts in other regions. In addition, it was found that risky health behaviours such as smoking did not have any independent effects on how the elderly in Vietnam rated their health status; yet, older adults in the sample who reported regular alcohol consumption were significantly less likely to rate their health status as below-average.

Analogous to the analysis presented in Table 5.2, Table 5.3 uses binary logistic regression models to estimate the effects of gender and other covariates on the odds that the Vietnamese elderly reported having hypertension. Results demonstrate no gender differences in hypertension when the medical condition was self-reported. While the coefficient in Model 1 suggests that elder males were less likely than their female counterparts to report having hypertension, gender differentials became statistically insignificant once other variables such as age and marital status were introduced in Model 2.

Compared to gender, socio-economic characteristics and demographic attributes appeared to be more robust predictors of self-reported hypertension. According to this subjective measure, the odds of hypertension incidence increased, as older persons aged. Meanwhile, the elderly who had neither been married nor experienced marital dissolution were persistently more likely than those whose marriage remained intact at the time of the survey

TABLE 5.2

Binary Logistic Regression (Coefficients Expressed as Odds Ratios) Indicating that the Respondent Rated Their Health as Below-Average: Older Vietnamese Adults Age 60 and Above

Individual and Household Characteristics	Model 1		Model 2		Model 3		Model 4		Model 5	
	Odds Ratio	Std. Error	Odds Ratio	Std. Error	Odds Ratio	Std. Error	Odds Ratio	Std. Error	Odds Ratio	Std. Error
Male (Female=ref)	0.61***	0.02	0.69***	0.026	0.68***	0.03	0.79***	0.03	0.89*	0.05
Age (60–69=ref)										
70–79			1.83***	0.068	1.87***	0.07	1.72***	0.06	1.69***	0.06
80+			4.07***	0.243	4.27***	0.26	3.70***	0.23	3.57***	0.23
Currently married (Widowed/Divorced/Never Married=ref)			0.79***	0.031	0.83***	0.03	0.84***	0.03	0.84***	0.03
Urban (Rural=ref)					0.73***	0.03	0.90**	0.04	0.89**	0.03
Region of residence (Red River Delta=ref)										
Northern Uplands					1.43***	0.08	1.24***	0.07	1.26***	0.07
Central					1.78***	0.09	1.66***	0.08	1.61***	0.8
South					2.04***	0.09	2.07***	0.09	1.96***	0.09
Education (Illiterate=ref)										
Less than primary							0.80***	0.04	0.79***	0.04
Primary							0.71***	0.04	0.71***	0.04
At least some secondary							0.60***	0.04	0.60***	0.04

	(1)		(4)		(8)		(14)		(17)	
Household economic status (Poor=ref)										
Less poor							0.83**	0.05	0.81***	0.04
Well off							0.56**	0.03	0.55***	0.03
Tobacco use (Never Smoked=ref)										
No longer smoke									1.13	0.07
Smoking regularly									1.05	0.06
Regular alcohol consumption (Not drinking regularly=ref)									0.58***	0.03
df	1		4		8		14		17	
Log likelihood	−10,388.541		−9,926.490		−9,769.262		−9,628.669		−9,571.396	
Number	15,214		15,214		15,214		15,214		15,214	

Note: * Significant at $p < 0.05$; ** Significant at $p < 0.01$; *** Significant at $p < 0.001$. Ref=reference category.

Source: Vietnam Ministry of Health and General Statistics Office, *Results of Vietnam National Health Survey 2001–2002* (Hanoi, Vietnam: Medical Publishing House, 2003).

TABLE 5.3

Binary Logistic Regression (Coefficients Expressed as Odds Ratios) Indicating that the Respondent Reported Having Hypertension: Older Vietnamese Adults Age 60 and Above

Individual and Household Characteristics	Model 1 Odds Ratio	Model 1 Std. Error	Model 2 Odds Ratio	Model 2 Std. Error	Model 3 Odds Ratio	Model 3 Std. Error	Model 4 Odds Ratio	Model 4 Std. Error	Model 5 Odds Ratio	Model 5 Std. Error
Male (Female=ref)	0.91*	0.03	0.98	0.04	0.98	0.04	0.84	0.04	1.01	0.06
Age (60–69=ref)										
70–79			1.19***	0.05	1.19***	0.05	1.31***	0.06	1.26***	0.06
80+			1.06***	0.06	1.09	0.07	1.28***	0.08	1.21**	0.08
Currently married (Widowed/Divorced/Never Married=ref)			0.82***	0.04	0.86**	0.04	0.84***	0.04	0.84***	0.04
Urban (Rural=ref)					1.62***	0.07	1.36**	0.05	1.34***	0.06
Region of residence (Red River Delta=ref)										
Northern Uplands					0.51***	0.04	0.58***	0.04	0.59***	0.05
Central					0.92	0.05	1.00	0.06	0.99	0.06
South					1.76***	0.09	1.82***	0.09	1.79***	0.09
Education (Illiterate=ref)										
Less than primary							1.16***	0.06	1.15**	0.06
Primary							1.32***	0.09	1.29***	0.09
At least some secondary							1.70***	0.13	1.67***	0.13

	(1)		(2)		(3)		(4)		(5)	
Household economic status (Poor=ref)										
Less poor							1.45***	0.11	1.40***	0.10
Well off							1.85***	0.14	1.79***	0.14
Tobacco use (Never Smoked=ref)										
No longer smoke									1.17*	0.08
Smoking regularly									0.79***	0.05
Regular alcohol consumption (Not drinking regularly=ref)									0.62***	0.04
df	1		4		8		14		17	
Log likelihood	−8,182.064		−8,159.862		−7,850.941		−7,761.069		−7,711.156	
Number	15,214		15,214		15,214		15,214		15,214	

Note: * Significant at p < 0.05; ** Significant at p < 0.01; *** Significant at p < 0.001. Ref=reference category.
Source: Vietnam Ministry of Health and General Statistics Office, *Results of Vietnam National Health Survey 2001–2002* (Hanoi, Vietnam: Medical Publishing House, 2003).

to be identified with hypertension. Moreover, high education, better-off economic status, and residence in urban areas or more economically developed regions such as the Red River Delta or the South were associated with greater odds of self-reported hypertension. Another interesting, yet perplexing, finding shown in Table 5.3 is diverse effects of risky health-related habits on the odds of hypertension. While former smokers were slightly more likely than non-smokers to report experiencing high blood pressure, the incidence of hypertension was significantly less frequent among current tobacco users and regular alcohol consumers than among elders who neither smoked nor drank habitually.

Table 5.4 presents results from binary logistic regression models estimating the determinants of objective hypertension (based on blood pressure readings). Although male and female elders did not significantly differ when incidence of hypertension was self-reported (see Table 5.3), findings from Table 5.4 suggest that there were modest gender differences in the incidence of hypertension when it was measured objectively. Other characteristics being equal, older Vietnamese men experienced greater likelihood of having abnormally high blood pressure than did their female counterparts (Model 5).

In addition to gender, other important individual attributes that were associated with elevated risks of hypertension include age and location of residence. According to this objective measure, there was a linear relationship between age and incidence of hypertension found in the anthropometry survey. Model 5, for instance, suggests that the likelihood of hypertension among elders age 80 and above was higher than that of those 60–69 by over twofold. Meanwhile, urbanites were 22 per cent more likely than rural residents to be diagnosed with hypertension. Furthermore, results in Table 5.4 indicate strong effects of marital status on hypertension incidence. Marital dissolution and non-marriage among the elderly appeared to aggravate the risk of high blood pressure.

Risky health-related behaviours demonstrated varied, yet inconsistent, influence on hypertension. Tobacco use was associated with lower odds of hypertension, whereas regular alcohol consumption significantly aggravated the risks of having high blood pressure. Unlike prior multivariate analyses, The author does not find the net effects of regions of residence, education, and household wealth when hypertension was measured using anthropometric tools. The only exception was observed among older adults in the South who experienced lower odds of having high blood pressure than those from the Red River Delta.

TABLE 5.4

Binary Logistic Regression (Coefficients Expressed as Odds Ratios) Indicating that the Respondent's Average Blood Pressure Reading Suggested Hypertension: Older Vietnamese Adults Age 60 and Above

Individual and Household Characteristics	Model 1		Model 2		Model 3		Model 4		Model 5	
	Odds Ratio	Std. Error	Odds Ratio	Std. Error	Odds Ratio	Std. Error	Odds Ratio	Std. Error	Odds Ratio	Std. Error
Male (Female=ref)	0.93	0.03	1.06	0.04	1.06	0.04	1.03	0.04	1.15**	0.06
Age (60–69=ref)										
70–79			1.43***	0.05	1.44***	0.05	1.46***	0.05	1.46***	0.06
80+			2.10***	0.11	2.10***	0.11	2.14***	0.12	2.12***	0.12
Currently married (Widowed/Divorced/Never Married=ref)			0.77***	0.03	0.76***	0.03	0.76***	0.03	0.76***	0.03
Urban (Rural=ref)					1.26***	0.04	1.23**	0.05	1.22***	0.05
Region of residence (Red River Delta=ref)										
Northern Uplands					0.99	0.05	1.00	0.05	0.99	0.05
Central					0.87***	0.04	0.88***	0.04	0.91	0.04
South					0.79***	0.04	0.79***	0.04	0.82***	0.04
Education (Illiterate=ref)										
Less than primary							0.98	0.04	0.97	0.04
Primary							1.06	0.06	1.05	0.06
At least some secondary							1.06	0.07	1.04	0.07
Household economic status (Poor=ref)										
Less poor							0.96	0.05	0.96	0.05
Well off							1.04	0.06	1.02	0.06

TABLE 5.4 *(cont'd)*

Individual and Household Characteristics	Model 1 Odds Ratio	Model 1 Std. Error	Model 2 Odds Ratio	Model 2 Std. Error	Model 3 Odds Ratio	Model 3 Std. Error	Model 4 Odds Ratio	Model 4 Std. Error	Model 5 Odds Ratio	Model 5 Std. Error
Tobacco use (Never Smoked=ref)										
No longer smoke									0.86*	0.05
Smoking regularly									0.75***	0.04
Regular alcohol consumption (Not drinking regularly=ref)									1.19***	0.06
df	1		4		8		14		17	
Log likelihood	−10,538.552		−10,352.773		−10,316.719		−10,310.227		−10,291.869	
Number	15,214		15,214		15,214		15,214		15,214	

Note: * Significant at p < 0.05; ** Significant at p < 0.01; *** Significant at p < 0.001. Ref=reference category.
Source: Vietnam Ministry of Health and General Statistics Office, *Results of Vietnam National Health Survey 2001–2002* (Hanoi, Vietnam: Medical Publishing House, 2003).

DISCUSSION AND CONCLUSIONS

Based on nationally-representative data from the VNHS, this chapter examines the determinants of two important health indicators among older adults in Vietnam: self-rated health and incidence of hypertension. In particular, it evaluates whether gender is a significant marker of later-life health vulnerability, after male-female differentials in socio-economic characteristics, health-related behaviours, and patterns in health reporting are taken into account. Additionally by using subjective and comparable objective measures of ill health, this research represents one of the few studies in non-western contexts that addresses how health reporting might have influenced observed health outcomes at older ages and thereby, gender differentials in health status.

While older women are more likely to be vulnerable because of their survival to later ages and widowhood (United Nations 2002, 2007b), the present study extends this dominant policy perspective by showing nuances of gender health disparities and factors other than gender that lead to health vulnerability in older years. Evidence demonstrates a complex picture of how actual health statuses and perception about health can differ for male and female elders. First, when an encompassing measure of health status such as self-rated health was examined, results indicate that older women persistently assessed their health more negatively than their male counterparts. This perhaps reflects that the measure draws on the elders' overall perception of well-being, which may be influenced by mental health and fatigue. Vietnamese women might have felt more exhausted because of greater expectations imposed on them by family, community, and society in terms of fulfilling their economically productive roles as well as domestic duties. This perhaps leads to women's negative self-ratings of health and well-being. Well beyond the scope of this study, one could further investigate this hypothesis with time use data.

Moreover when a more specific health outcome such as incidence of hypertension was considered, the effects of gender were different and diverse. For self-reported hypertension, the author does not find any significant gender differentials. However when direct blood pressure readings were taken from the elderly, not only do results show that the incidence of hypertension was much higher than the self-reported measure, but evidence also indicates that older men were more likely to be diagnosed with hypertension. The discrepancy in subjective and objective measures indicates biases in self-reported ill health among older adults in Vietnam. It also implies older men's tendency to fail to recognize that they had high blood pressure. Such failure could harm their health and adversely affect their survival in later ages.

In addition to varied effects of gender, socio-economic status is a powerful predictor of health status among older people in Vietnam. Elders who were better educated and came from wealthier households tended to rate their health more positively than those with lower education and inferior economic status. Contrary to self-rated health, results indicate that the rich and well-educated are more likely to report hypertension. However, this does not necessarily mean that they were less healthy. The evidence is rather indicative of better perception and more accurate reporting of the illness among this segment of the population. This is perhaps because they had greater awareness of hypertension and access to health examination. When hypertension was determined objectively based on blood pressure readings, the effects of socio-economic status disappears. Findings suggest that upper social status might provide older Vietnamese adults a certain optimism regarding their health status which also equips them with greater access to health screening possibly leading to more accurate reporting and, in turn, better care and health outcomes. This evidence also echoes widespread concerns regarding rising health inequality and the adverse impacts of recent health-sector reforms on the health of the poor.

Older adults' age and marital status are two demographic factors that significantly determine health status in later life. Recent data indicate that life expectancy at birth in Vietnam is 75 for females and 71 for males (United Nations 2007a), whereas estimates for healthy life expectancy are considerably lower — 63 years for females and 60 years for males (WHO 2004b). Evidence indicates that the health status of the elderly deteriorates considerably as one gets older. For all measures of health examined in these analyses, the oldest old were more likely to report and be identified with ill health than their younger counterparts. Regardless of gender and age, marriage appears to consistently provide protective influences on health and well-being (see Chapter 12, this volume). Consistent with the literature, the author finds that the elderly whose marriage remained intact were more positive about their health, less likely to report hypertension, and were less frequently diagnosed with high blood pressure. The net effects of marital status are consistent and rarely changed with an introduction of other covariates in the analyses.

While the effects of household wealth, marital status, and age on health in older years tend to be one-directional, the influences of location of residence are multifaceted. Urban residents rated their health more positively than rural counterparts. Yet, they were more likely to have hypertension based on both subjective and objective measures of blood pressure. Two explanations are plausible. First, older adults in urban areas generally had greater access to health screening than rural residents, particularly in the context of Vietnam's health reforms. Second, given the country's market transition and recent economic success, residents in towns and cities were perhaps more exposed to affluent lifestyles and diets, thus leading to greater risks of hypertension (Ala et al. 2004).[8]

Not only are older adults' demographic and socio-economic characteristics taken into account, but this study also considers the effects of their health-related behaviours. On the one hand, results reveal mixed effects of smoking on the measures of health status under investigation. The analyses show no net effects of smoking on self-assessed health but they reveal that smoking was associated with decreased odds of being diagnosed with hypertension. On the other hand, older adults who consumed alcohol regularly tended to evaluate their health positively and less frequently reported hypertension. However when blood pressure readings were taken, results indicate that alcohol consumers were about 20 per cent more likely than non-drinkers to be identified with hypertension. While the relationships between these risky habits and health outcomes pointed out here are compelling, they should be considered as tentative because of how arbitrary "regular" tobacco use and alcohol consumption were defined in the VNHS questionnaire. Furthermore, this evidence also suggests the biases associated with self-reporting. Smokers and drinkers might be less likely to visit doctors and, hence, have no knowledge about their blood pressure and, thus, tend to make guesses instead (and here, guesses that were optimistic).

Findings from these analyses demonstrate that gender is but one of several dimensions that differentiate health in later life. In identifying older Vietnamese people who are most likely to be unhealthy and vulnerable, not only should researchers and policy-makers be mindful about how women are more likely to be widowed, which in turn has an impact on mortality and morbidity. But researchers and policy-makers should also look beyond gender. Differential effects of gender across various health measures suggest that female health vulnerability may not necessarily be warranted in the case of Vietnam. While this study may be restricted to only a few measures of health, the analyses consistently show age, marital status, education, household wealth, location of residence, smoking, and alcohol consumption to be important predictors of health outcomes among older adults. As Vietnam's health sector has become increasingly privatized, the health of the disadvantaged elderly is of particular concern. They tend to be more pessimistic about their health and appear to have less awareness of health risks such as hypertension, and limited access to health screening. In addition to looking beyond gender, this study points out the importance of reporting on observed health outcomes in older years. Future studies will benefit from incorporating more objective assessments and biomarkers of health status among older adults.

Notes

1. The author is grateful for the insightful comments from Kim Korinek, Josefina N. Natividad, and an anonymous reviewer. I acknowledge the permission granted by the Ministry of Health, Vietnam for using the Vietnam National Health Survey.
2. Approximately 37 per cent of the main respondents were male while the rest (63 per cent) were female. They were mostly either heads of the household or spouses of the household head. The author expects that the gender of the key informant affects neither health assessment rated by the older adults themselves nor biometric measures of health.
3. For this variable, there are 362 cases (2.4 per cent of the total sample) that had missing values, mainly because they were not present during the implementation of the health-check questionnaire. These missing cases are excluded from the analysis.
4. Anthropometrists were unable to read blood pressure from approximately 2.8 per cent of the older adults in the sample households.
5. In the VNHS, any household members age six and above were asked if they had smoked 100 cigarettes in their whole life. If they did, these smokers would be asked further if they smoked at least seven cigarettes in a week on average. For those who smoked less than seven cigarettes in a week, they were also asked if they had quit smoking.
6. In the analysis not shown here, smoking and drinking are negatively associated with household wealth among older men. Education is negatively related to smoking; yet, it is positively associated with older men's drinking habit. Among older women in Vietnam, both education and household wealth are negatively associated with smoking and drinking but the correlations are not strong.
7. In multivariate analyses, since a very small proportion of older adults in the sample were never married or divorced (2 per cent), they were combined with elders who were widowed. The dummy variable of marital status reflects older adults with intact marriage versus those whose marriage were dissolved or who were never married.

8. Interpreting the effects of region of residence on the health of older adults in
    Vietnam is more complicated because results do not show consistent patterns
    across the three measures of health status. For example, for self-reported
    health, findings indicate that residents of the Red River Delta were more
    optimistic about their health than those in other regions of Vietnam. When
    hypertension was determined using the anthropometric measure, regional
    differences were not significant, with the exception of those from the south
    who were less likely than Red River Delta residents to be diagnosed with
    hypertension.

References

Ala, L., G. Gill, R. Gurgel and L. Cuevas. "Evidence for Affluence-Related
    Hypertension in Urban Brazil". *Journal of Human Hypertension* 18 (2004):
    775–79.

Anson, O., E. Paran, L. Neumann and D. Chernichovsky. "Gender Differences
    in Health Perception and Their Predictors". *Social Science & Medicine* 36,
    no. 4 (1993): 419–27.

Arber, Sara and Jay Ginn. *Gender and Later Life: A Sociological Analysis of Resources
    and Constraints*. London: Sage, 1991.

Bales, Sarah. *Technical Documentation for The Vietnam National Health Survey
    2001–02*. Hanoi, Vietnam: Ministry of Health and Statistics Sweden
    International Consulting Office, 2003.

Bui, The Cuong, Si Anh Truong, Daniel Goodkind, John Knodel and Jed
    Friedman. "Vietnamese Elderly amidst Transformations in Social Welfare
    Policy". In *Aging in the Asia-Pacific Regions: Issues and Policies*, edited by
    D.R. Phillips. London: Routledge, 2000.

Davis, M.A. "Sex Differences in Reporting Osteoarthritis Symptoms: A Socio-
    Medical Approach". *Journal of Health and Social Behaviour* 22, no. 3 (1981):
    129–37.

Friedman, J., D. Goodkind and S.A. Truong. "Work and Retirement among the
    Elderly in Vietnam". *Research on Aging* 23, no. 2 (2001): 209–32.

Friedman, J., J. Knodel, T.C. Bui and S.A. Truong. "Gender Dimensions of
    Support for Elderly in Vietnam". *Research on Aging* 25, no. 6 (2003):
    587–630.

Giang, Thanh Long and Wade D. Pfau. "The Elderly Population in Vietnam
    during Economic Transformation: An Overview". In *Social Issues under
    Economic Transformation and Integration in Vietnam, Volume 2*, edited by
    T.L. Giang. Hanoi: The Publishing House of Social Labor, 2007*a*.

————. "Patterns and Determinants of Living Arrangements of the Elderly in
    Vietnam". In *Social Issues under Economic Transformation and Integration in
    Vietnam, Volume 2*, edited by T.L. Giang. Hanoi: The Publishing House of
    Social Labor, 2007*b*.

Goodkind, D., S.A. Truong and T.C. Bui. "Reforming the Old-Age Security in Vietnam". *Southeast Asian Journal of Social Science* 27, no. 2 (1999): 139–62.

HelpAge International. "Age Demands Action in Vietnam: Progress on Implementation of the Madrid International Plan of Action on Aging", 2007. Available at <http://www.helpage.org/Resources/AgeDemandsActionbriefings> (accessed 17 March 2009).

Hoang, V.M., N. Ng, S. Wall, H. Stenlund, R. Bonita, L. Weinehall, M. Hakimi and P. Byass. "Smoking Epidemics and Socio-Economic Predictors of Regular Use and Cessation: Findings from WHO STEPS Risk Factor Surveys in Vietnam and Indonesia". *The Internet Journal of Epidemiology* 3, no. 1 (2006). Available at <http://www.ispub.com/journal/the-internet-journal-of-epidemiology/volume-3-number-1/smoking-epidemics-and-socio-economic-predictors-of-regular-use-and-cessation-findings-from-who-steps-risk-factor-surveys-in-vietnam-and-indonesia.html#sthash.tduBLnEX.dpbs> (accessed 3 March 2013).

Knodel, J., J. Friedman, S.A. Truong and T.C. Bui. "Intergenerational Exchanges in Vietnam: Family Size, Sex Composition, and the Location of Children". *Population Studies* 54, no. 1 (2000): 89–104.

Knodel, J. and M.B. Ofstedal. "Gender and Aging in the Developing World: Where Are the Men?" *Population and Development Review* 29, no. 4 (2003): 677–98.

Knodel, J. and S.A. Truong. "Vietnam's Older Population: The View from the Census". *Asia-Pacific Population Journal* 17, no. 3 (2002): 5–22.

Mitchell, Suzette and Khuat Thu Hong. *Gender Briefing Kit Vietnam*. Hanoi: UNDAF, 2000.

Nathanson, C. "Illness and the Feminine Role: A Theoretical Review". *Social Science and Medicine* 9, no. 2 (1975): 57–62.

Nguyen, Kim Lien. "Government Policy on Helping the Elderly in Vietnam". *Mekong Basin Initiative on Aging*. Chiang Mai, Thailand: HelpAge International, 1998.

Ofstedal, Mary Beth, Erin Reidy and John Knodel. "Gender Differences in Economic Support and Wellbeing of Older Asians". *Population Studies Center Research Report* 03-350. Ann Arbor, Michigan: University of Michigan, 2003.

Strandberg, A., T. Strandberg, K. Pitkala, V. Salomaa, R. Tilvis and T. Miettinen. "The Effect of Smoking in Midlife on Health-Related Quality of Life in Old Age: A 26-Year Prospective Study". *Archives of Internal Medicine* 168, no. 18 (2008): 1968–74.

Thanh Nien News. "Healthcare Lacking for Elderly: Says Official", 7 January 2009. Available at <http://www.thanhniennews.com/healthy/?catid=8&newsid=45217> (accessed 7 January 2009).

United Nations. *Report of the Second World Assembly on Aging. Madrid, 8–12 April 2002*. United Nations, Publication A/CONF.197/9. New York: United Nations, 2002.

————. *World Population Prospects: The 2006 Revision*. New York: United Nations, 2007*a*.

————. *First Review and Appraisal of the Madrid International Plan of Action on Aging: Preliminary Assessment*. United Nations, Publication *E/CN.5/2008/7*. New York: United Nations, 2007*b*.

Verbrugge, L. "The Twain Meet: Empirical Explanations of Sex Differences in Health and Mortality". *Journal of Health and Social Behaviour* 30, no. 3 (1989): 282–304.

Vietnam Committee for Population, Family and Children (VCPFC). *Report for the Fifth Asia-Pacific Population Conference*. Bangkok, Thailand: United Nations Economic and Social Commission for Asia and the Pacific (UNESCAP), 2002.

Vietnam Ministry of Health and General Statistics Office. *Results of Vietnam National Health Survey 2001–2002*. Hanoi, Vietnam: Medical Publishing House, 2003.

Vietnam News. "Big State Budget for Healthcare Vital to Vietnam's Wellbeing", 31 May 2008. Available at <http://english.vietnamnet.vn/social/2008/05/785876/> (accessed 17 March 2009).

World Bank. *Growing Healthy: A Review of Vietnam's Health Sector*. World Bank Report No. 22210-VN. Hanoi: World Bank, 2001.

World Health Organization (WHO). *The Global Burden of Disease: 2004 Update*. Geneva: World Health Organization, 2004*a*.

————. *World Health Report 2004*. Geneva: World Health Organization, 2004*b*.

6

AGEING AND GENDER PREFERENCES IN RURAL INDONESIA

Philip Kreager and
Elisabeth Schröder-Butterfill

Over the last two decades, gender has moved steadily up the agenda of interdisciplinary population studies, beginning with a number of early programmatic statements (Mason 1993; Greenhalgh 1994; Obermeyer 1995), and continuing via substantial collections (e.g. Bledsoe, Lerner and Guyer 2000) and in-depth studies (Basu 1992; Bledsoe 2002; Johnson-Hanks 2006). The increasing focus among demographers over the same period on consequences of demographic transition has made the conjunction of two themes — ageing and gender — inescapable. Demographic data at the national level readily show potentially significant economic and social differentials between men and women, and these data have been used to make a general case for important gender disadvantages in later life, particularly for women. The impact of disadvantages, by implication, accumulates across the life course. Thus, in Indonesia, women's disadvantage is found in variables like the years of education they receive, their income stream, whether they participate equally in formal sector employment, enjoy equity in marriage choices, and have equal access to pensions (Malhotra

1991; Rudkin 1993; Adioetomo and Eggleston 1998; Kevane and Levine 2003; Samosir, Tuhiman and Asmanedi 2004). The accumulative effects of these differences, however, are less clear. Women participate extensively in intergenerational transfers, leading some commentators to conclude that gender differences in support provision for older people are "practically non-existent" (Frankenberg and Kuhn 2004, p. 27). General patterns of economic and social change in which elders receive support from both sons and daughters, and which often give particular emphasis to daughters' roles in providing personal care, continue to follow tradition. In other words, most elders appear to find that both daughters and sons deliver — even though some gendered aspects of the life course, and elders' expectations about gendered kinds of support, remain unequal.

Generalized statements of gender disadvantage or advantage, no matter how systematic the survey data on which they rely, can only take us part of the way to understanding whether and how gender differences actually impact on later life. A critical review of the literature by Knodel and Ofstedal (2003), in underscoring this point, has done the field three important favours. First, the authors emphasize that attention to context is a necessary and unavoidable component of social and demographic explanation. We cannot simply assume that aggregate differentials apply uniformly in the diverse settings and circumstances in which people live. Second, and more particularly, they highlight the capacity of socio-economic differences to condition and override the importance of gender. For example, disadvantages that individual women or men face may be attributed less to gender *per se* than to the impact of poverty and social hierarchy on whether family networks function successfully as redistributive mechanisms. In consequence, aggregate gender disadvantages in education or access to healthcare may not impact significantly on older women if family networks consistently enable them to gain access to modern sector services. Third, Knodel and Ofstedal (2003) argue convincingly that until contextual and structural factors are taken into account, an emphasis on the disadvantage to one or another gender is premature. Exploration of patterns of female and male disadvantage provides a more balanced approach.

Two assumptions underlying their critique deserve note. One is that they take the existence of major cultural and economic differences as a given, and expect there to be much variation — undoubtedly within, as well as between, societies — in patterns of gender disadvantage and advantage. At least, the potential importance of such differences needs to be checked empirically before general patterns of gendered disadvantage are asserted. Second, study of variation requires methodologies that examine underlying processes, and thereby inform and complement survey data. While surveys tell us about aggregate statuses and outcomes, they do not actually observe the family and community mechanisms that give gender and other differentials their meaning and impact.

This chapter draws on the longitudinal ethnographic and demographic field study of three communities representing major Indonesian ethnicities (Javanese, Sundanese, and Minangkabau), located in three of the five provinces that, since 1990, have reported more than 7 per cent of the population over the age of 60. Comparative ethnographic study supported by panel surveys enables us to establish contexts and variations in family and community support for older people, and the advantages and disadvantages that may accrue in consequence to older men and women. Similar patterns of socio-economic stratification exist in the three communities, which have an important bearing on elderly well-being, notably by influencing the supply of children, family network size and structure, and intergenerational exchanges. Following a brief introduction, in which the communities and research methodology are described, the chapter notes two contrasting preference structures that differentiate gender in the communities. Gender has a marked structural significance in matrilineal societies, like the Minangkabau, that is not manifest for the Javanese and Sundanese. Case studies then illustrate some aspects of these structures. The chapter concludes with a brief look to the future, by considering the expectations of current working age generations about their own later lives, and the limitations of relying exclusively on aggregate data to assess their likely policy needs.

AGEING IN INDONESIA

Beginning in April 1999, a joint Indonesian and British research team has studied the populations of three communities: Kidul in East Java, Citengah in West Java, and Koto Kayo in West Sumatra.[1] The family systems in the two communities on Java are characterized by nuclear/bilateral patterns, while the Minangkabau population of Koto Kayo is matrilineal. The proportions of adult children reported in 2000 as no longer resident in the community (46, 45 and 75 per cent, respectively) give some idea of the active engagement of family networks in regional, national and international economies (Kreager 2006). Since most migrants are of younger ages, the level of migration tends to increase the proportion of the population age 60 and above: 11, 10 and 18 per cent of the respective communities are over the age of 60, noticeably higher than the 7 per cent normal in their respective provinces (Ananta, Anwar and Suzeti 1997). Each community is characterized by a mixed family economy, drawing on income from migrants, employment in local government, and services and small-scale manufacturing, while also retaining the traditional economic base in agriculture and local markets. All communities are predominantly Muslim. Languages spoken in the home are respectively Javanese, Sundanese, and Minangkabau, with most speakers competent in the national language, Bahasa Indonesia. Interviews were conducted in more than one language in each site.

To begin with, a brief overview of findings from the research project *Ageing in Indonesia* will help to define the contexts in which gender differences matter. A key starting point is the contrast between the matrilineal extended family system of the Minangkabau, and the nuclear family systems, backed up by bilateral kindreds, characteristic of the two Javanese sites. These contrasting kin and family logics entail: (1) strikingly different norms defining intergenerational support; and (2) a categorical emphasis on the position of daughters in the matrilineal system that has no equivalent in the less formal, preferential attitudes of the Javanese populations to gender. We will discuss the Javanese sites first, before turning to the Minangkabau population in West Sumatra.[2]

Strata, Networks and Gender in Javanese Communities

In the two Javanese sites, family norms may be characterized as a balance entailing generational independence in a context of mutual support in which elders commonly take the major role (Kreager and Schröder-Butterfill 2008). On the one hand, couples in later life prefer to live on their own, with at least one adult child living nearby, and with regular and if possible frequent contacts with other children living away from the village. This pattern is substantially realized, as on average family networks experience numbers of younger generation members who are "lost to the system" — that is, out of contact, and not contributing materially to family networks — at levels of one child or less (Kreager 2006, p. 41). On the other hand, where coresidence with children is found, it often reflects either economic vulnerability or lack of independence in the young adult generation (and hence continuing dependence on elderly parents), or the fact that the youngest child has yet not left home. Dependence of the younger adult generation on the old is often consequent on their divorce or lack of employment; further dependence takes the form of a "skipped generation" household in which elders are raising and covering costs of grandchildren that their own children have left with them while working away from the community (Schröder-Butterfill 2004a). Coresidence, in short, provides no reliable indicator of elderly dependence, and may well indicate the opposite.

Values of independence favoured by the Javanese have a double character, manifest in many aspects of daily life. On the positive side, older people wish to remain active in family and social life, and generally succeed in doing so. Gainfully employed throughout most of their later lives, and sometimes with the help of small pensions, they remain net contributors to the economy, even when families no longer strictly require them to do so. The continuing employment of elders reflects the dependence of their identity and reputation on continuing participation in intergenerational exchanges. For example, analysis of the 2000 household survey in the East Javanese site showed that, for family networks including older members, two-fifths of all families engaged in balanced exchanges between generations — "balanced" here denoting not a strictly equal monetary value of goods and services, but reciprocity. In the 2005 survey, this proportion had increased to nearly one-half (Kreager and Schröder-Butterfill 2008). Of course, as elders' physical disabilities increase, their material contribution normally lessens, but even small contributions are recognized as maintaining status. Part-time agricultural labour or factory work, and assistance in children's households, enable elders to participate as expected in family and community rituals. Even if the income gained or saved is small, it remains important in matters of personal and collective esteem. The "exchanges" in question may, to take a common example, enable elders to give out of their own pockets, and as a matter of course, sweets and small favours to grandchildren.

On the negative side, elderly vulnerability emerges where elders' declining material contribution to families coincides with overall family poverty, manifest in limited network size and useful connections, and scarce assets in land or other material resources. Households in lower socio-economic strata show the greatest strain.[3] A quarter of elderly people are net receivers of support from children, some 80 per cent of whom belong to poorer strata: support, usually confined to food and/or companionship, does not provide an adequate safety net, for example in the event of a health crisis. Even in families not facing poverty, elders' sheer physical frailty (particularly incontinence and an inability to carry out basic activities of daily living (ADL)) involves inevitable loss of reputation. The inability to contribute in any way to family or wider exchanges equates to loss of social status, especially where dependence is on charity coming from without the family.[4] The potential downside of normative values of independence and balance of generations here becomes plain: unlike joint family systems (prevalent in much of mainland Asia), or stem family systems (as in Thailand), family networks do not explicitly and normatively designate a particular child as responsible for eldercare late in life or for other circumstances of their vulnerability. In Javanese communities, ties between elders and particular children or grandchildren are preferential: they evolve in the context of personal relationships over the life course and, thus, are vulnerable to the usual ups and downs experienced by members of different generations.

The preferential character of Javanese elderly support patterns may give a strategic significance to gender, especially to the role of spouses and daughters, but not in a sense that overrides the more fundamental role of family networks and of normative values of reciprocity governing them. This situation is most evident in the case of adoption: childless elders in better-off strata are much more likely to be able to find nieces or other female kin to adopt, explicitly with the intention of their providing personal care and companionship in later life (Schröder-Butterfill 2004b). Clearly, in a family system that emphasizes generational independence, the role of spouses — male or female — is the usual first port of call for assistance for livelihood or personal care. Given the predominance of women among the elderly, men are, as in most societies, on average more likely to have a spouse on whom to rely. Serious male vulnerability nonetheless arises from inadequate networks — especially where there is a lack of female support in the network — as will be demonstrated in the case studies below.

The preferred residential pattern, in which some children are "near" while others reside "away" at ever-greater distances, provides a second and potentially crucial back-up for widows, widowers, the unmarried, and frail elderly couples. Intimate personal care is provided normally by daughters or daughters-in-law, and elders in almost all cases will express a preference for having a daughter living near to them (Schröder-Butterfill and Fithry 2014). The advantage of the "some near/some away" residential pattern is that in most cases, a number of members of a family network can be found to provide meals, companionship, or personal care — but arrangements are often mutable, depending on who is available.[5] A kind of division of family labour enables children and sometimes other kin to share support responsibilities — some providing food or companionship because they are at hand to do so, others making less continuous contributions during visits or emergencies (such as contributing to hospital costs) (Schröder-Butterfill 2005). The reality, nonetheless, is that levels of migration and alienation within the family network make primary or exclusive reliance on daughters impossible for many people, some or all of the time. Norms of generational independence and reciprocity imply that the needs and demands of both younger and older generations must be balanced, if possible. In practice, elders have no special priority.

Strata, Networks and Gender: Minangkabau

Minangkabau society has developed a sophisticated migration-based economy for more than a century, making it an integral part of the wider Southeast Asian economy. Koto Kayo, as is typical of traditional Minangkabau communities, has a local economic base in agriculture, with almost 90 per cent of households drawing part of their subsistence from rice and other locally grown foodstuffs, while many also engage in cultivation of crops like coffee and cinnamon for the market (Indrizal 2004). Most of the village's wealth, however, is the product of labour migration (*rantau*) associated particularly with trade in cloth and clothing across the Indonesian archipelago. Upwards of two-thirds of young adults are away from Koto Kayo at a given point in time (Kreager 2006). *Rantau* is at once a commercial strategy for generating wealth for oneself, one's lineage, and the community. It is also a crucial *rite de passage*. Young men who do not establish themselves successfully on *rantau* cannot attain full respect and position in the community. With time, flows of migrants from the community have established lineage networks and resident communities in major cities like Jakarta and Bandung, and this facilitates the entry of new migrants into successful trade and other employment. It has also enabled women to participate in *rantau* activities, not only as property owners and wives, but as major traders in their own right. Networks are the basis of major flows of remittances, supporting annual or more frequent visits to the home community and support for local community projects. Active networks in this way reinforce or improve family status, as well as building and sustaining ties through local Islamic and political associations. The Minangkabau became "transmigrants" — that is, a people with a permanent material and cultural basis in more than one place in the Indonesian archipelago.

This close identification of individual, family, and community identity with success on *rantau* results in a very different normative structure of intergenerational relations than observed in the Javanese communities. Key evidence of a family network's success and solidarity is elderly parents' ability to rely on a combination of remittances and local practical support, rather than having to continue to work. Quite unlike rural Java, dependence in later life is a source of satisfaction and respect. Where Javanese elders emphasize their own continuing contributions (even where they are also receiving material support from children), Minangkabau elders emphasize contributions of the younger generation, even where local agricultural income means they can survive comfortably on their own. Both as an ideal and in practice, the emphasis on support from children is strong. For two-thirds of elders, net intergenerational exchanges flow predominantly upwards from the younger generation (including, as appropriate in a matrilineal society, support from nephews and nieces). The second round of the household survey, following up the situation of the oldest old, showed that this pattern intensifies to almost nine-tenths of elders over age 70 (Kreager and Schröder-Butterfill 2008).

As in the Javanese sites, the strategic importance of gender is conditioned by relative socio-economic status and the size and constituency of networks. Gender, however, plays a much more profound role within these constraints, as would be expected in a matrilineal society. The 4.8 million Minangkabau in Indonesia form the world's second largest matrilineal population, and the organization of descent and inheritance follows prescriptive rules in which rights and property pass from mothers to daughters, and women take major roles in the management of family affairs in conjunction with their brothers. Men thus look to their sisters' children as heirs, although they are also likely to have strong (if less formalized) ties to their own children. Normative preference is for the senior female to live in the matriline's ancestral home (*rumah gadang*), with the daughter who will succeed her. The husband of the senior female, and the daughter's husband, live as "honoured guests" in the *rumah gadang*; their major family and material interests are in the property and *rumah gadang* of their sisters, and this gives them an inevitably ambivalent status in relation to their wives' matriline — especially as the senior female's brother takes the major formal and practical role in decision-making. The prescriptive nature of matrilineal descent is perhaps most evident in the emphasis on links between mothers and daughters: a matriline without daughters faces no future, and kinship here is referred to as "lost" (*keluarga punah*). Sons cannot inherit and pass on property and, indeed, a matriline without daughters is considered childless no matter how many sons — and successful ones — it may have (Indrizal 2004).[6] Childlessness affects 7 per cent of older people, but a further 17 per cent lack surviving female offspring (Indrizal, Kreager and Schröder-Butterfill 2009).

The prescriptive character of matrilineal descent carries a number of structural entailments that can make gender differences problematic, both for men and women. One is a kind of *de facto* childlessness, a situation in which, for example, all daughters decide to remain permanently away from the *rumah gadang*, preferring their lives on *rantau*. Although distant family members may be found to maintain ancestral properties, the lack of a daughter resident in the *rumah gadang* is a disgrace. A second liability is the structural vulnerability of older men without wives, whether on account of divorce, the wife's death, or non-marriage.

While the prescriptive character of female descent gives rise to critical constraints in some matrilines, the situation is clearly easier in the majority of households where the continuity of the matriline is not endangered. A senior female without daughters may have a sister with daughters, one of whom is prepared (and will reap considerable advantages) by assuming the mantle of senior female on the death of her aunt. Most daughters (who are not in line to become senior female) and sons are less constrained by the matrilineal rule; their residence in households near the *rumah gadang* or being permanently away on *rantau* is less of an issue, assuming (as is the commonly observed norm) that their remittances, visits, and continuing support towards the family and community keeps them within the family orbit.[7] The pattern of "some children near/ some away", which we noted in the case of Javanese communities, also characterizes support patterns in Koto Kayo. Here, although daughters are fundamental to matrilineal ideology and practice, daily support for older people comes normally from *both* sons and daughters, varying according to their capacities and their point in *rantau* development and, in this respect, intergenerational exchanges resemble the preferential pattern observed in the Javanese communities.

DISCUSSION

The observation, cited earlier, by Frankenberg and Kuhn (2004, p. 27), that in Indonesia gender differences in support provision for older people are "practically non-existent", was based on national-level surveys. We are now in a position to interpret this assertion more carefully. On the one hand, it may be taken as broadly true, as both daughters and sons are actively engaged in support of their elders. While elders commonly express a desire for their daughters' support, particularly in personal matters, their preference is no less to have a number of children of both sexes actively engaged.[8] Support is part of a long term and diverse body of exchanges that take place across the life course. The family networks that characterize inter-generational support appear to function in a way that permits flexibility — they include both sons and daughters as well as continuing elderly support of younger generations, and allow for changes in support roles according to the possibilities and needs of both generations (and, also, of grandchildren). The preference among elders for daughters' involvement, in short, is not pursued single-mindedly, or without due allowance for the preferences of the daughters themselves — which inevitably embrace more than issues of support for ageing parents.

On the other hand — and as Frankenberg and Kuhn (2004) are no doubt well aware — to say that gendered patterns of support effectively do not exist is a radical simplification of a complex set of realities. The fact and value of a daughter's involvement and care is a general sociological phenomenon in thousands of Indonesian communities, such as those described in this chapter. This is true whether expressed as a preference or, as in the matrilineal case, a prescription that stipulates that the very continuity and reputation of a family absolutely require a daughter to take the primary role at the centre of the matriline. What is at issue in all of these cases is not only the importance of gender as encompassing a set of values in Javanese, Sundanese, and Minangkabau cultures, but the inevitable heterogeneity of practice in these communities, which means that gender preferences are realized (or not) in different ways among several values, and are subject to varying constraints. Not everyone manages to have the children they prefer actually care for them in old age, or do so all of the time. Alternative arrangements are inevitably necessary. The presence of these alternatives, and the fact that many, or even most, elders may have to make do with them, does not lessen the importance of the gendered values in question. Norms are only achieved some of the time, and this may enhance their value, rather than lessen it.

As we have noted, actual flows of intergenerational support, whether from sons or daughters, are mediated by socio-economic status and network behaviour. Members of current elder generations who belong to better-off strata and more successful networks are, particularly in Java, both more likely to have surviving children and to be better able to adopt young people successfully to look after them.[9] In contrast, one of the several consequences of the prescriptive character of matrilineal succession in the Minangkabau case is that a lack of daughters cannot be alleviated by economic or social success. The following brief case studies are intended to illustrate how family systems in these cultures cope — with varying success — when they run up against constraints on the availability of support, particularly where that support involves a normative gender preference. We will consider, in turn: (1) coping with childlessness and *de facto* childlessness; and (2) male vulnerability in the absence of a spouse and/or children.

Vulnerability in Javanese, Sundanese, and Minangkabau societies does not necessarily arise from a lack of children, or of daughters or sons. Adoption (often of siblings' children) and remarriage provide alternative routes to children in the Javanese communities. In the logic of the matrilineal system, a sister's children are equivalent to a woman's own children, as they belong to the same matriline, can inherit ancestral property, and are able to perpetuate both line and property. Indeed, no distinction is made in kin terms between a woman's own children and the children of her sister, both being referred to simply as *anak* (child). Children will refer to their matrilateral aunts as *mandeh ketek* ("small mother", if the aunt is junior to the mother) or *mandeh gadang* ("big mother", if the aunt is senior). A woman without children can thus take a positive and respected place in the family as classificatory mother of her sister's children, and it is to these children that she will look for assistance should she need it (van Reenen 1996).

Problems arise, as noted earlier, either where there are no daughters prepared to return permanently from *rantau* and assume matrilineal responsibilities in the *rumah gadang*, or where sisters also lack children. In the former, children's regular remittances and return visits to the village ensure adequate levels of material support for most elders. However, the psychological insecurity arising from an absence of children locally, and the threat of an empty *ruamah gadang*, cannot be underestimated. This is particularly felt by elderly women whose daughters are all away, since they look to one of these daughters to take over the management and continuity of ancestral property. The case of Asnima exemplifies the paradox of, on the one hand, having many and successful children, while on the other, feeling lonely, vulnerable and "childless" because none are locally available. Asnima, age seventy-five, is the youngest of eight siblings and the only sister. She descends from a line of clan headmen (*penghulu datuk*), now including one of her sons. She has seven sons and two daughters. All are married and living in migration sites. Both daughters married non-Minangkabau. The oldest has a successful permanent job in Jakarta. The other daughter, married to an Acehnese, recently moved to Padang, a good three hours away from Koto Kayo. For the time being, Asnima can look after the *rumah gadang* and family lands. She is financially secure, because her children regularly support her and she has income from the lineage rice fields. None of this, however, can reduce her fears about the future presence of her lineage in the village. Asnima often visits her children, but will not consider settling permanently with them. Living with a son is not, in any case, an option, since this violates Minangkabau norms and would reflect badly on her daughters. If she had her own way, Asnima would raise the only granddaughter she has via her daughters, because it will ultimately be that granddaughter's responsibility to continue the matriline. Asnima nowadays occupies the ancestral home on her own, although sometimes a young, unrelated woman keeps her company at night, helps her with cooking and takes care of her when she is ill.

Asnima's situation illustrates the contrary impacts of migration: on the one hand, *rantau* continues guaranteed support and social standing; on the other, these strengths co-exist with the genuine threat of the end of the matriline in the community. Thus far, most ancestral homes are occupied, although some, like Asnima's, are rather quiet. In less prosperous communities, many *rumah gadang* are abandoned or fall into disrepair. When frailty or ill health makes personal assistance necessary, women like Asnima face a choice between two courses of action, neither of which preserves self-esteem or public face: accepting help from a non-relative, or leaving the ancestral home to be with a daughter who has moved away.

A contrasting example, in which a woman with many children is left *de facto* childless, can be drawn from the narrative of Rumiati who hails from Citengah, the West Javanese research village. Rumiati is a widow in her late seventies with eight children. Of the eight, one died in infancy, and Rumiati also lost an adult daughter in childbirth, which left her a baby girl to raise. Despite working hard as an agricultural labourer, she needed to sell half of the small amount of land she possessed to assist several children on transmigration to Sumatra and Kalimantan. A further sale provided a "loan" (never repaid) to her granddaughter to help her start up a business as a trader. The granddaughter was also given the larger half of Rumiati's house after her marriage. None of the five children who left have ever returned or sent money, not even the daughter who left her first-born son in Rumiati's care. One daughter now lives nearby, but is poor and relies on sharecropping on the remainder of her mother's land to survive. Rumiati's present income from agricultural labour has to support her and her coresident grandson, still at school.

The absence of local, supportive children in both Asnima's and Rumiati's cases are instances of migration gone wrong from the older generation's point of view. Neither, despite the undoubted assistance they provided their children, have any child at hand on whom they can rely near the end of their lives. Yet the two cases also highlight important differences between Minangkabau and Javanese communities. In Java, parents are expected to assist adult children to become independent, often to the limits of their ability, and to step in if necessary even after children have left home. This does not obligate children to provide reciprocal flows of support to elderly parents, as it does in Koto Kayo. In Koto Kayo, young grandchildren were never left with grandparents, whereas in Java, it is not unusual for grandparents to be left in charge of grandchildren when the middle generation migrates, without this eliciting regular or adequate remittances (Schröder-Butterfill 2004b). This latter responsibility, however, provides Rumiati with a small compensation not possible for Asnima: she retains the presence of the granddaughter whom she raised, and any (albeit modest) assistance she may need, whether in the form of cooked food or care in illness, is likely to come from her granddaughter. Despite Asnima's much greater material well-being, her ability to organize her later life in a way that carries out local norms (i.e. which successfully involves a daughter or granddaughter in her home) remains less than Rumiati's.

Turning now to examples of male vulnerability, the example of Jamain shows how Minangkabau elders whose lineage faces extinction, and who have failed to create adequate ties within the matrilineal system, experience severe insecurity and loss of status. They have no safety net of support late in life of the kind that Minangkabau lineages normally provide. Atypically for men from Koto Kayo, Jamain only briefly took part in labour migration and returned unsuccessful. His two marriages were childless, ending in divorce. The second earned him disapproval from fellow villagers for marrying a woman from outside the village. Jamain's older brother has four children, but in accordance with the structure of Minangkabau society, their first loyalties lie with their mother's matriline. It is to his sister and her offspring that a man normally turns for support. Unfortunately, the sister also remained childless, and recently died. Jamain now relies on a sympathetic neighbour and on less sympathetic fellow villagers, who unwillingly give him money when he begs. Begging lowers Jamain's status and dignity, and deviates strongly from expected Minangkabau behaviour. The lack of daughters in his extended family network means that Jamain's matriline is doomed to extinction. Since his sister died, Jamain can at least live in his ancestral house and benefit from the production of family rice land. Eventually, the house with its land will fall to a distant, collateral line.

Given the logic of Minangkabau kinship organization, in which connections may be traced to increasingly distant but inclusive units of kin, relatives sharing responsibilities can normally be identified by going back several generations. In the eyes of other villagers, had Jamain conducted himself in a manner more in keeping with the ethos of the Minangkabau people, someone from such a collateral line might well have stepped in to help. Equally, money sent back to the village by successful migrants, distributed by the mosque, would have been more forthcoming.

A comparable case of male vulnerability in the absence of a spouse and/or children comes from Kidul in East Java. Lubis has no children of his own, but gained four stepchildren by two marriages, including two daughters. He also helped to raise two boys belonging to a neighbour. None of his stepchildren continue to live locally. Lubis' family was very poor, often without regular work, but small sums of money from one of the 'raised' boys, and occasional gifts from his stepchildren, have helped him to get by. In 2002, Lubis's second wife left him to live with one of her daughters, leaving him to rely chiefly on a neighbour and a nephew (the son of his first wife's sister) for his meals. The situation quickly deteriorated when Lubis fell and became bedridden. For a short time, one stepdaughter visited and sent money, but day-to-day care was available only from the neighbour and the nephew. Neither was prepared to continue providing intensive support for long, especially as Lubis's condition worsened. Against his will, he was taken to the home of a distant relative in a neighbouring city who, although possessing nominal rights to inherit Lubis's house, had not been in contact for many years. Lubis died shortly thereafter, and his wish to be returned to Kidul for burial was ignored.

Both Lubis and Jamain are examples of older men who reach the end of their lives with all but non-existent support networks. Poverty, unsuccessful marriages, and childlessness combine powerfully to limit their options, even in Lubis's case in which there were numerous stepchildren, and of both sexes. In both cases, none of the alternatives to having children (such as having more distant kin, neighbours, or stepchildren) proved comparable to care by one's own child or spouse, and the quality of care and the extent to which care could be sustained were likewise lessened. Those who took responsibility for looking after Lubis, if only for a time, were the people who happened to be nearby and to have a modest tie of some kind to him. From the outside, the attitude of Lubis's stepchildren, or Jamain's brother's children, may seem uncaring — but it is a reminder that support is a relationship built up over time via networks; values like gendered care, or sustained care, are secondary to the structure of ties a life course does, or does not, create. To the extent that men are less likely to build enduring networks in Indonesian communities, their vulnerability tends to be greater.

CONCLUSIONS

The subject of gender, as it emerged in late twentieth-century social demography, has commonly been approached as a potential marker of disadvantage, particularly as experienced by women. In the Indonesian case, at least, we have seen that, even where gender differences serve as powerful mechanisms of individual and group identity, intergenerational relationships and flows of support are guided by flexible network arrangements that in most cases secure support of both sons and daughters. There are, moreover, major differences in the way Indonesian cultures configure gender, which we have summarized and contrasted very briefly as *preferential* (for support from daughters, in the Javanese and Sundanese communities) and *prescriptive* (the Minangkabau maintain a powerful gender ideology emphasizing female lines of descent, inheritance, and family arrangement in which preferences regarding ongoing material support nonetheless rely on both sexes). In sum, gendered support, while important to older people's perception of their situation, and often in the patterns of assistance they actually receive, is not determinant of levels of support or of the diverse network arrangements by which family and community networks respond to elderly needs.

Gender undoubtedly poses a dilemma for demography, and for ageing research more generally. While important, gender differences, as they influence intergenerational relations and patterns of support, commonly resist reduction to the value of a variable. As Knodel and Chayovan show in this volume, similarities in the situation of older men and women on many dimensions are often more dominant than clear contrasts. Variables often tend to point in conflicting directions. Economic variables like the distribution of household income may show little difference between genders (see Chapter 2, this volume), while other and closely related ones, like labour force participation (see Chapters 10 and 11, this volume), do show such differences. The influence of regional and ethnic variations is likely to complicate interpreting national level patterns in such variables; national survey data often appear, at best, to be a kind of composite of several regional, ethnic, and other patterns of behaviour, and are therefore unlikely to describe any one of them adequately. And relative economic situations, as they pertain to elderly well-being, will need to be interpreted in light of evidence that older women are more adept networkers than men.

The difficulty, of course, enters long before modelling techniques are applied, in the customary simplifications employed in collecting and compiling data, and in the way classes of data are then taken as proxies for difficult-to-get-at multi-dimensional phenomena, like gender. By way of conclusion, it may therefore be interesting to look at some survey data on the three communities described in this chapter, to see what happens when description and analysis attempt to shortcut the heterogeneity of gender support patterns. We shall take current and projected living arrangements as a case in point, since demography and ageing research have long emphasized their significance.

It could be argued, for example, that residential arrangements, to the extent that they indicate older people's desires and access to support, may provide a relatively simple and efficient measure of disadvantage. Thus, if residence is an accurate proxy for the extent to which older people are successful in realizing preferences for assistance from a child of one gender, then we can use measures of residence patterns as indicators of gender-related advantage or disadvantage. Does such an approach stand up to scrutiny?

Table 6.1 gives percentages of elders' living arrangements, in three groups: *independent* (including those living alone, with spouse, or with dependent unmarried or young descendants); *with an adult female descendant* (a married daughter, an adult non-married daughter, or a married granddaughter); or *with an adult male descendant* (a married son, adult non-married son, or married grandson). The pattern in the table of gender-specific coresidence with children or grandchildren reflects in a general way the contrasting status of daughter preference across the three communities. A closer look at the table, however, drawing on the evidence presented above, shows that the relative advantage or disadvantage of elders, and whether support really depends on gender differences, are not tied consistently to residence.

TABLE 6.1
Living Arrangements of Older People in 2005 (by Per Cent)

	Kidul	Citengah	Koto Kayo
Independent	37.7	61.6	47
Adult female descendant	26.5	23	53
Adult male descendant	35.8	15.4	0
Total	100	100	100
No. of elders	53.0	52.0	49

Source: Ageing in Indonesia Household Survey (2005) (authors' data).

Beginning with Koto Kayo, where we would expect the strongest evidence of daughter preference, we see that living with a son or grandson never occurs, while the prescriptive importance of living with a coresident daughter holds good in over half of households. The evidence clearly supports the norm in which one daughter should remain in the ancestral property of her matriline. The situation of the nearly one-half of elders who do not coreside with their daughters, however, is more difficult to interpret. As the case studies given above indicate, "independent" encompasses several sub-groups. The 47 per cent not currently co-residing with daughters are not a uniform block of people, identifiable as not conforming to residential norms. Their current residence arrangements reflect the developmental character of kin networks, and the many different needs and opportunities networks address. Once we take into account network patterns between households, then "independent" and "coresident" cease to be discrete categories.

One sub-group within the "independent" category is composed of elders with all children away on *rantau* who have, or believe they have, the firm commitment of a daughter who will return to the *rumah gadang*. There is, however, another sub-group, to which Asnima (see case study above) belongs, that does not have any such commitment. Upward support flows from sons and daughters, however, are ample for both of these sub-groups, so that neither is subject to economic disadvantage — quite the contrary. Economic advantage is thus not tied to key gender differences for either sub-group — even though the implication for households whose daughters refuse to return from *rantau* is extinction. There are still further sub-groups, moreover, including elders like Jamain (again, see case study above), who are demographically disadvantaged because they do not have children and are economically disadvantaged because they lack *rantau* support; yet, as noted in Jamain's case, his demographic disadvantage need not have left him so economically weak if he had participated in normative exchanges during his lifetime. There exists, in short, yet another sub-group of elders without children who are nonetheless economically well-off, on account of matrilineal patterns of exchange.

For Koto Kayo, then, Table 6.1 provides at best a very crude picture of gender preferences and possible related disadvantage, even though there is a strong pattern of coresidence with daughters for half of the population. Coresidence is but one phase of network patterns, and one that occurs for some elders, but not others; half of the community is currently not in coresidence, but this is a diverse set of sub-groups not consistently related to economic or demographic disadvantage. Data on actual networks and on how and why they change over time is thus crucial to interpreting residential arrangements, and testing whether residence is an adequate proxy for gender disadvantage.

The need for contextual evidence on network behaviour as well as conventional survey measures to establish whether there is a clear link between disadvantage and gender is even more pronounced for the two communities on Java. From Table 6.1 we can see that Citengah is much more successful (61.6 per cent) in observing the preference for elders living independently than is Kidul (37.7 per cent). Living with a son, however, describes between one-sixth and one-third of households in the two communities, and predominates over coresidence with daughters in Kidul. Once again, however, knowledge of how networks give rise to sub-groups within these categories fundamentally changes our understanding of what they mean. Two points stand out. One is that calling an elderly person or couple "independent" just because they live alone often disguises major network support, for example, from a son or daughter resident elsewhere in the community (perhaps merely next door). Likewise, instances in which elders continue to give support to adult children not living with them go unrecognized. The other, in Kidul, is that coresidence with a son or daughter frequently describes a household strongly dependent on its elderly members, not one in which elders are net recipients of assistance. Within the coresident categories in Kidul, the percentage of households in which elders live with a married son or married daughter is the same (20.8 per cent), and these are sub-groups in which there is much more likely to be a balanced flow of support between generations. The remaining sub-groups within these categories

TABLE 6.2
Who Do You Hope to Live With in Old Age?

	Kidul	Koto Kayo	Citengah
Alone/with spouse	16.2	0.0	9.5
Any child/all children/only has one child	22.1	0.0	34.9
Specific child: daughter	25.0	64.5	54.0
Specific child: son	10.3	0.0	1.6
Other relatives (nephew, niece, grandchild)	2.9	4.8	0.0
Don't know	23.5	30.7	0.0
No. of respondents	68.0	62.0	63.0
Youngest child	19.1	3.2	15.9

Source: Ageing in Indonesia Household Survey (2005) (authors' data).

(living with an adult non-married child, or married grandchild) are likely to be households in which elders provide most of the material support; they are, in fact, more like "independent" households that continue to have unmarried younger descendents.[10] Not only is there no reliable link here between residence, gender, and disadvantage, it is clear that static residence data, whether at a given point or points in time (the exercise can also be carried out for the 2000 round of the household survey), cannot on their own be relied upon without more fundamental evidence of network processes.

If we ask adults who are not yet elderly what living arrangements they would prefer in old age (see Table 6.2), their responses likewise return us to the current state of play in family networks, since preferences expressed for residence with or near a child of a given gender depend on actual and potential network relationships. Daughter preference is, once again, strongest for Koto Kayo: the nearly one-third in the community who responded "don't know" live predominantly in households in which there is not yet a daughter. The percentages preferring coresidence with a daughter in Kidul (25 per cent) and Citengah (54 per cent) are the highest in these communities, but co-exist with substantial sub-groups in which living in other arrangements is preferable. Clearly, where childbearing is unfinished, and where the future material success, location of residence, and marriage patterns of children are unknown, answering this question becomes very hypothetical.[11] Once again, in communities in which inter-generational exchanges between households, continuing involvement of elders in the family economy, and the involvement of several children in support flows over time, are all normative, respondents answering this survey question are, in effect, being asked to make a complex set of assumptions about how their family networks will play out over time. As we have seen, in the contemporary situation in the three communities, preference for daughters as a social fact coexists with other components of family networks and changing constraints on them. Gendered support is not a variable that can be isolated as a determinant of behaviour (unless the whole complex of factors could somehow be identified in a way that enabled their interaction with gender to be controlled). Attempts by means of proxies to define the importance of gender as a key variable in support patterns are, therefore, likely to understate its role in many, if not most, older people's lives.

Notes

1. Village data presented in this chapter were collected in the research project, *Ageing in Indonesia, 1999–2007*, with the generous support of the Wellcome Trust and the British Academy. We are grateful to Edi Indrizal and Tengku Syawila Fithry, our colleagues at Andalas University, Padang, who conducted the field research at the West Sumatran field site, and to our colleagues Vita Priantina Dewi and Haryono, at the Center for Health Research, University of Indonesia, Depok, who conducted the field research in West Java. Extended fieldwork of up to a year's duration, together with return visits, enabled development of comparable quantitative and qualitative databases. Semi-structured interviewing achieved substantial coverage of the elderly, between 80 and 97 per cent in the communities; repeated in-depth interviews were conducted with between 20 and 60 elderly in each site, complemented by in-depth interviews with one or more other adult family members in most cases. Collection of life histories enabled mapping of kin networks, checked by observation of exchanges over time. Fieldwork also made possible observation of local events, and enabled familiarity with problems and adjustments to changing circumstances that make up much of people's daily lives. Randomized surveys of household economy and inter-household exchanges with 50 "young" households and 50 "elderly" households in each of the three communities then served two important functions: they substantiated differences in social and economic status within and between networks which shape family and community responses to older people's needs; and they enabled quantitative analysis of the role of support from absent network members. Two survey rounds, in 2000 and 2005, were accompanied by in-depth follow-up interviews. Randomized health surveys were also carried out in both rounds. This combined qualitative and

quantitative methodology means that data were collected from many elderly respondents in several forms (observation, surveys, semi-structured and in-depth interviews), enabling quality checks on data and the identification and exploration of differing interviewees' interpretations of events and relations.

2. In view of the similarity of Javanese and Sundanese family patterns, and for ease of reference, both communities will here be referred to simply as Javanese.

3. Socio-economic strata in the three sites were defined by aligning economic differences revealed in the surveys with local terms of reference that people used in the course of in-depth interviews to describe their own and others' relative social position. No explicit scheme of social classification is normative in the communities, but four distinctions recur in everyday speech: (1) wealthy; (2) comfortable; (3) getting by; and (4) dependent on charity. A more detailed account of the strata is given in Kreager (2006, pp. 8–9).

4. Sophisticated community institutions in many cases exist to provide food and monetary support to the very poor (Schröder-Butterfill 2006; Kreager 2009). This aspect of support is not differentiated in terms of gender, and thus falls outside the current topic.

5. Employing non-family members to provide care for elderly parents is considered shameful, although bringing in poorer, more distant kin to provide services (and quietly providing the material incentives to do so) is an option available for some better-off families.

6. The contrast to patrilineal family systems lacking heirs underscores the prescriptive nature of matrilineal descent. Men without sons in a patrilineage may take further wives, either by divorcing the current wife or (where permitted) via polygyny, in order to obtain male offspring. A woman who may be fertile, but is unable to bear daughters, generally has no parallel option of obtaining daughters via remarriage. In contrast to Java, adoption is also not considered an acceptable solution (cf. Kreager and Schröder-Butterfill 2007).

7. Between 66 and 93 per cent of Minangkabau migrants contribute remittances or other support to their elders, depending on strata; the lower figure, which refers to the wealthiest strata, reflects the fact that at any one point in time only some children may be contributing; percentages for the other three strata are at least 87.5 per cent (Kreager 2006).

8. However, it should be noted that older Minangkabau men without wives, where they have reached physical disability that restricts carrying out basic life tasks, will express a preference for male personal care (Schröder-Butterfill and Fithry 2012).

9. On historical demographic factors that influence the shortage of children in current older cohorts, see Schröder-Butterfill and Kreager (2005); on the generality of this pattern outside Indonesia, see Kreager (2004); a good review of demographic patterns of childlessness affecting these cohorts at the provincial level is given by Hull and Tukiran (1976).

10. If we adjust the percentages in Kidul to reflect this (for example, by transferring all households characterized by dependent adult non-married children and married grandchildren to the "independent" elder categories), then the percentage of "independent" in Kidul rises much closer (57.7 per cent) to that of Citengah.

11. A sizeable minority expressed preferences that blur preference for residence with or near a daughter with residence with or near the youngest child (19 per cent in Kidul, 16 per cent in Citengah) (see Table 6.2); a further ambiguity is that stated preferences for living with a daughter may for some respondents not reflect a preference for daughters, but a preference for living with a particular child who happens to be a daughter.

References

Adioetomo, S.M. and E. Eggleston. "Helping the Husband, Maintaining Harmony: Family Planning, Women's Work and Women's Household Autonomy in Indonesia". *Journal of Population* 4, no. 2 (1998): 7–31.

Ananta, Aris, Evi N. Anwar and Diah Suzenti. "Some Economic Demographic Aspects of Ageing in Indonesia". In *Indonesia Assessment: Population and Human Resources*, edited by G.W. Jones and T.H. Hull. Canberra, Singapore: Australian National University and Institute of Southeast Asian Studies, 1997.

Basu, Alaka. *Culture, the Status of Women and Demographic Behaviour: Illustrated with the Case of India*. Oxford: Oxford University Press, 1992.

Bledsoe, Caroline. *Contingent Lives: Fertility, Time and Aging in West Africa*. Chicago: University of Chicago Press, 2002.

Bledsoe Caroline, Susan Lerner and Jane Guyer. *Fertility and the Male Life Cycle in the Era of Fertility Decline*. Oxford: Oxford University Press, 2000.

Frankenberg, E. and R. Kuhn. "The Implications of Family Systems and Economic Context for Intergenerational Transfers in Indonesia and Bangladesh". *California Center for Population Research On-Line Working Paper Series*, 2004. Available at <http://escholarship.org/uc/item/6xn029cj> (accessed 5 November 2013).

Greenhalgh, Susan. "Anthropology Theorizes Reproduction: Integrating Practice, Political Economic and Feminist Perspectives". In *Situating Fertility*, edited by S. Greenhalgh. Cambridge: Cambridge University Press, 1994.

Hull, T. and Tukiran. "Regional Variations in the Prevalence of Childlessness in Indonesia". *Indonesian Journal of Geography* 6, no. 32 (1976): 1–25.

Indrizal, Edi. "Problems of Elderly without Children: A Case-study of the Matrilineal Minangkabau, West Sumatra". In *Ageing Without Children: European and Asian Perspectives*, edited by P. Kreager and E. Schröder-Butterfill. Oxford: Berghahn, 2004.

Indrizal, Edi, Philip Kreager and Elisabeth Schröder-Butterfill. "Old-age Vulnerability in a Matrilineal Society: The Case of the Minangkabau of Sumatra, Indonesia". In *The Cultural Context of Aging: Worldwide Perspectives*, 3rd ed., edited by J. Sokolovsky. London: Praeger, 2009.

Johnson-Hanks, Jennifer. *Uncertain Honour: Modern Motherhood in an African Crisis*. Chicago: University of Chicago Press, 2006.

Kevane, Michael and David I. Levine. "The Changing Status of Daughters in Indonesia". Working Paper C03-126. Center for International and Development Economics Research, University of California, Berkeley, 2003.

Knodel, J. and M.B. Ofstedal. "Gender and Aging in the Developing World: Where are the Men?" *Population and Development Review* 29, no. 4 (2003): 677–98.

Kreager, Philip. "Where Are the Children?". In *Ageing Without Children: European and Asian Perspectives*, edited by P. Kreager and E. Schröder-Butterfill. Oxford: Berghahn, 2004.

————. "Migration, Social Structure and Old-Age Support Networks: A Comparison of Three Indonesian Communities". *Ageing & Society* 26, no. 1 (2006): 37–60.

————. "Ageing, Finance and Civil Society: Notes for an Agenda". In *Older Persons in Southeast Asia*, edited by E. Arifin and A. Ananta. Singapore: Institute of Southeast Asian Studies, 2009.

Kreager P. and E. Schröder-Butterfill. "Gaps in the Family Networks of Older People in Three Indonesian Communities". *Journal of Cross-Cultural Gerontology* 21 (2007): 1–25.

————. "Indonesia against the Trend? Ageing and Inter-generational Wealth Flows in Two Indonesian Communities". *Demographic Research* 19, no. 52 (2008): 1781–1810.

Malhotra, A. "Gender and Changing Generational Relations: Spouse Choice in Indonesia". *Demography* 28, no. 4 (1991): 549–70.

Mason, Karen O. "The Impact of Women's Position on Demographic Change during the Course of Development". In *Women's Position in Demographic Change*, edited by N. Federici, K.O. Mason and S. Sogner. Oxford: Oxford University Press, 1993.

Obermeyer, C.M. "Islam, Women, Politics: The Demography of Arab Countries". *Population and Development Review* 18, no. 1 (1995): 33–60.

Rudkin, L. "Gender Differences in Economic Well-being among the Elderly of Java". *Demography* 30, no. 2 (1993): 209–26.

Samosir, Omas Bulan, Hendratno Tuhiman and Asmanedi. "Socio-economic Conditions of the Elderly". In *Empowerment of Indonesian Women: Family, Reproductive Health, Employment and Migration*, edited by S.H. Hatmadji and I.D. Utomo. Jakarta: University of Indonesia, Demographic Institute, 2004.

Schröder-Butterfill, E. "Inter-generational Family Support Provided by Older People in Indonesia". *Ageing & Society* 24, no. 4 (2004*a*): 497–530.

————. "Adoption, Patronage, and Charity: Arrangements for the Elderly Without Children in East Java". In *Ageing Without Children: European and Asian Perspectives*, edited by P. Kreager and E. Schröder-Butterfill. Oxford: Berghahn, 2004*b*.

————. "The Impact of Kinship Networks on Old-Age Vulnerability in Indonesia". *Annales de Démographie Historique* 2 (2005): 139–63.

————. "The Role of Religious and Secular Community Institutions for Elderly People's Welfare in Rural Indonesia". Paper given at the Cambridge Group for the Study of Population and Social Structure, October 2006.

Schröder-Butterfill, E. and P. Kreager. "Actual and *de facto* Childlessness in Old-Age: Evidence and Implications from East Java, Indonesia". *Population and Development Review* 31, no. 1 (2005): 19–56.

Schröder-Butterfill, E. and T.S. Fithry. "Care Dependence in Old Age: Preferences, Practices and Implications in Two Indonesian Communities". *Ageing & Society* 34, no. 3 (2014): 361–87.

7

EXPLORING THE EXPERIENCES OF OLDER MEN AND WOMEN IN CAREGIVING AND CARE-RECEIVING IN SARAWAK, MALAYSIA[1]

Ling How Kee

INTRODUCTION

The issue of "care for" and "care by" older people has strong gender dimensions. Older women, extending the traditional role of caregiver and homemaker, tend to predominate as caregivers. Research has shown that as the life expectancy of older women surpasses that of men, they are more likely to provide care for their spouses rather than to receive it (ARROWs for Change 1999; UNESCAP 1991). Moreover, it has been documented that grandparenting is a role increasingly thrust upon older women by the younger generation of women entering the workforce because of the lack of suitable childcare facilities and services (Gray 2005; Ling 2007). However, in terms of receiving care, older women are found to be at the losing end, even to the extent of becoming vulnerable to neglect and abuse (Aitken and Griffin 1996; Whittaker 1995).

Research has also drawn attention to the possibility that older men may experience similar vulnerabilities to older women or in some aspects be even more disadvantaged (Knodel and Ofstedal 2003). Research has also shown that care of older people is strongly influenced by cultural norms, traditions of inheritance and exchange, and by different government services and income support systems. Generally, there is a difference between the way care is provided to older people in developed and developing economies, and in Southeast Asian regions, as much as in the rest of Asia, more emphasis has been placed on the family (Liu and Kendig 2000).

With an increasing ageing population in Sarawak, Malaysia, a culturally diverse society undergoing rapid urbanization, care of older persons is an issue that merits examination. This chapter explores the experiences of older men and women as caregivers and care-receivers in both formal and informal systems of care. Drawing on the findings of a larger study called *Ageing in Sarawak: Needs, Impact and Emerging Issues* (Social Development and Urbanisation Council 2005), this chapter examines the impact of gender on caregiving and care-receiving, taking into consideration rural/urban variations, socio-economic differences and, where relevant, ethnicity. The chapter concludes with recommendations for a broader spectrum of care programmes, drawing attention to areas of emerging need while concurrently considering gender, ethnic, and regional differences.

AGEING IN SARAWAK

The study on *Ageing in Sarawak: Needs, Impact and Emerging Issues* was commissioned by the Ministry of Social Development and Urbanisation, Sarawak in 2004 and completed in 2005. The aim of the study was to examine the impact of ageing and to identify issues and concerns for older people and their families, and to suggest and make recommendations to the government and NGOs on policy and relevant programmes for the ageing population of Sarawak. Three Divisional Administrative areas, namely Kuching, Sibu, and Miri were chosen as the principal research sites. Within these sites, different regions — towns and villages — were selected in order to cover urban, semi-rural, and rural settings. Based on a proportionate stratified sampling procedure, and taking into consideration the total population in each district and division, a sample of 600 respondents, comprising 318 women and 282 men, was selected and interviewed using a pre-tested questionnaire. The questionnaire was designed to gather information on the demographic characteristics of the respondents, their socio-economic status, their physical and mental well-being, their activities of daily living (ADL), their level of independent living, as well as the help and services needed. To further explore experiences of ageing, in-depth interviews were conducted with 30 older women and 48 older men accessed from residential homes, service agencies and in the community using a purposive sampling method in line with the qualitative research approach (Miles and Huberman 1994; Silverman 2010). Representatives from six Older Persons' Organizations and informal self-help or social groups were also interviewed. In addition, data pertaining to issues of care were elicited from 30 formal caregivers, and 8 women informal carers through a focus group interview.

The study observed a steady increase in the ageing proportion of the population over the last twenty years. The Sarawak Department of Statistics' population census data recorded a total population growth from 1.351 million in the year 1980 to 1.658 million in 1990, and to 2,065 million in 2000. The proportion of the ageing population in terms of number and percentage of the total population in the last two decades is shown in Table 7.1.

Based on the table, there has been a steady increase of 8.03 per cent of the ageing population (55 and above)[2] in 1980 to 8.39 per cent in 1990 and further increasing to 8.81 per cent in 2000.

In terms of gender, the number of older women, consistent with the feminization of ageing internationally, is greater than that of older men. The population census in 2000 showed that 9.6 per cent of the female population was over 55 compared with 7.97 per cent for males in 2000 (Social Development and Urbanisation Council 2005). It is interesting to note it was only in the 1990s that the number of older women began to exceed that of older men. In 1980, the older male population was marginally higher at 8.1 per cent compared with 8.0 per cent for females. In 1990, there were 8.8 per cent for women compared with 8.0 per cent for men, and in 2000 the number of women increased to 9.7 per cent compared with 8.0 per cent for men. As Tan and Masitah (1997) observed, prior to 1970 the lower

TABLE 7.1
Population Age 55 and Above of Sarawak, 1980 to 2000

Year	Number of Older Population (in thousands)	Total Population (in thousands)	Percentage
1980	108.3	1,351.1	8.03
1990	141.7	1,657.8	8.39
2000	181.9	2,065.0	8.81

Source: Department of Statistics, Malaysia (Sarawak Branch), *Yearbook of Statistics* (Sarawak: Department of Statistics, 2002).

number of older women compared with men was largely because of higher female mortality as a result of high maternal mortality levels at that time. Since then, better medical and health services, specifically greater knowledge and easier availability of reproductive and maternal healthcare including access to family planning, have enabled more women to live until old age. Not surprisingly, of the 22.7 per cent of respondents who were 75 years and above, the majority were women. Based on the 2010 life expectancy estimate for males calculated at 74.3 years and females at 78.3 years (Department of Statistics, Malaysia 2011), older women have been found to outnumber older men. This trend is likely to continue in years to come. This suggests a need to address specific issues confronting older women when planning programmes and services for older people, particularly when the data suggest that older women may experience greater disadvantages (Ling 2007). However, the findings of the study also indicate the need for considering the varying impact of gender on ageing. The question is, therefore, not whether older women are more vulnerable than older men, but rather the way socio-economic differences and role expectations across gender impact upon older persons' later lives. The current older population, coming from a generation who have lived their lives in traditional gender roles which relegate men to the economic sphere and women to the domestic sphere, provides an interesting comparison between older women's and men's experiences of caregiving and care-receiving.

The discussion in the following sections is based on both quantitative and qualitative data, the latter presented by case vignettes. These vignettes are intended to be illustrative and exploratory, drawing attention to areas of concern which require further research.

GENDER ROLES, SOCIO-ECONOMIC, AND INCOME DIFFERENCES

While not discounting variations in women's position across the different ethnic communities, in general, the traditional gender role model of man as breadwinner and woman as caregiver in the family has been the norm until recent years. Comparison of previous occupations between older men and women clearly reflects this gender role differentiation. As shown in Figure 7.1, nearly half of the older women, 49 per cent, identified themselves as housewives followed closely by 42 per cent who said that they were self-employed. Of these self-employed groups, the common occupations mentioned were farmers, hairdressers, dressmakers, and bakers. Only 5 per cent of the elderly women interviewed had been employees in the government sector and 2 per cent were employees in the private sector. In contrast, 36 per cent of older men were previously government employees and 10 per cent were private sector employees, as Figure 7.2 shows. The 49 per cent who were self-employed were mainly in small-scale agricultural businesses, subsistence farming or carpentry; and interestingly, 1 per cent stated they were engaged in housework.

FIGURE 7.1
Women's Previous Occupations

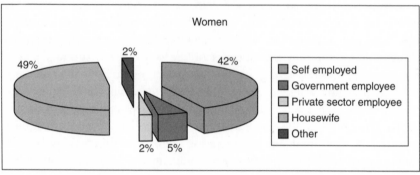

Source: Social Development and Urbanisation Council, *Ageing in Sarawak: Impact, Needs and Emerging Issues* (Kota Samarahan, Sarawak: Centre for Technology and Consultancy, Universiti Malaysia Sarawak, 2005).

FIGURE 7.2
Men's Previous Occupations

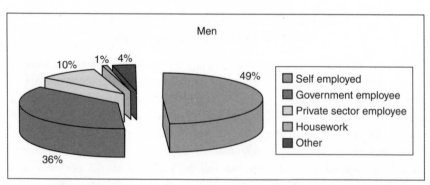

Source: Social Development and Urbanisation Council, *Ageing in Sarawak: Impact, Needs and Emerging Issues* (Kota Samarahan, Sarawak: Centre for Technology and Consultancy, Universiti Malaysia Sarawak, 2005).

TABLE 7.2
Income Distribution by Gender

| | Gender | | |
Monthly Income	Male	Female	Total
Don't know	53	104	157
Less than RM200	40	68	108
RM201–RM400	34	52	86
RM401–RM600	33	39	72
RM601–RM800	32	16	48
RM801–RM1000	23	15	38
RM1,001–RM2,000	45	16	61
RM2,001–RM3,000	11	3	14
RM3,001 and above	10	2	12
Missing figure	1	3	4
Total	282	318	600

Source: Social Development and Urbanisation Council, *Ageing in Sarawak: Impact, Needs and Emerging Issues* (Kota Samarahan, Sarawak: Centre for Technology and Consultancy, Universiti Malaysia Sarawak, 2005).

The fact that women dominate the unpaid workforce is reflected in the level of income. From Table 7.2, it is evident that most of the elderly women fall into the lower income group with a monthly income of less than RM200. The number of women having a monthly income which exceeded RM601 was much fewer than men. In addition, over 32 per cent of them (104) stated that they did not know their income as many did not receive any cash income. This is in contrast to only 18 per cent of men (53) who said that they did not know their income. The low or lack of income of older women is indicative of their socio-economic status and their low participation rate in the formal employment sector.

As shown in Figure 7.3, the low monthly income of women corresponds with their lower level of formal education. Seventy-two per cent of the older women in the research had no formal education as compared with only 31 per cent of older men. This is not surprising for women of their generation as parents at that time prioritized the education of sons over daughters. Traditional parents believed that daughters did not need to go to school because ultimately they would be married off and become housewives.

Moreover, women's access to formal schooling should be considered within the context of different developmental phases of the Malaysian education system. The attitude against girls going to school began to lose ground by the pre-Second World War period, as the number of girls going

FIGURE 7.3
Educational Level of Women and Men (by Percentage)

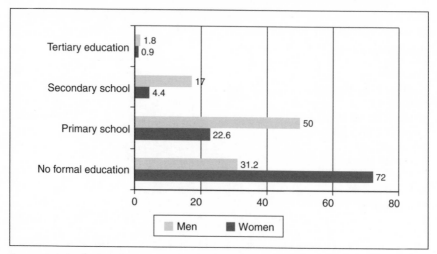

Source: Social Development and Urbanisation Council, *Ageing in Sarawak: Impact, Needs and Emerging Issues* (Kota Samarahan, Sarawak: Centre for Technology and Consultancy, Universiti Malaysia Sarawak, 2005).

to school rose again in the 1970s, and then maintained a steady increase in the 1980s, showing a parallel rate with the enrolment of boys (Jamilah 1992). In Sarawak, education in the colonial era was very much associated with missionary work. However, although missionary girls' schools such as St. Mary and St. Theresa had existed in Kuching for over 150 years, they were only accessible to girls from elite families.

FAMILY AND INFORMAL CARE FOR THE OLDER PEOPLE

Family and informal care is generally understood to consist of physical and emotional assistance provided to an older person by family, friends or neighbours on an unpaid basis. Brody (2004) discusses four categories of informal care: (1) practical tasks such as helping with daily personal care and household assistance; (2) providing emotional support; (3) financial assistance; (4) mediation with formal and informal organizations such as hospitals, care support services, and domiciliary nursing. In the context of Southeast Asia in which universal pension and income support scheme are lacking, financial support provided by children to older persons is often a reflection of care and should be considered as a category of informal care.

Furthermore, remittances sent by adult children who are working or who have migrated overseas to ageing parents in their home countries can be considered a way of caring from afar. A study by Lazzarini (2009) showed Filipinos who work/reside in Australia continue their caregiving by sending remittances home.

Living Arrangements and Care

Living arrangements of older people can be considered an indicator of care, with the general assumption that those who are living with children are being cared for (DaVanzo and Chan 1994). In the ageing study, we found that the majority of older persons, 41.2 per cent (247), to be living with their spouse and children. This was followed by 37.2 per cent (223) who live with their children only, and 8.8 per cent (53) with their spouse only. This is followed closely by 6.8 per cent (41) who live in other extended family situations such as with parents, brothers and sisters, grand-children, and other relatives. A total of 4.2 per cent (25) of the respondents live alone, and this is distinguished from another 1.8 per cent (11) who live alone but with family close by, whether in a longhouse or the village setting.

In trying to ascertain whether living together with family ensures a certain level of social and financial support for older persons, data analysis found 89 per cent of the respondents saying that they spent time with their families daily, and received assistance from family members whenever needed. This is high but surprisingly not consistent with the figure of 94 per cent who are living in a different form of family situation, suggesting that a number of older persons who, although living with family members, are not receiving the care and support needed.

TABLE 7.3
Living Arrangements

Living Arrangements	Frequency	Percentage
Stay alone	25	4.2
Stay alone but with family close by	11	1.8
Stay with spouse only	53	8.8
Stay with children only	223	37.2
Stay with spouse and children	247	41.2
Stay in other extended family situations	41	6.8

Source: Social Development and Urbanisation Council, *Ageing in Sarawak: Impact, Needs and Emerging Issues* (Kota Samarahan, Sarawak: Centre for Technology and Consultancy, Universiti Malaysia Sarawak, 2005).

Quantitative data do not show any difference between the care received by older men and women who are in a family although several case studies have indicated that older women may have a greater need for support in areas of transportation, healthcare, and dealing with official matters. As women were relatively homebound in their younger days, they have not been able to keep up with the fast-changing environment around them which has become more bureaucratized and complex. This is particularly difficult for older women who did not have the opportunity to go to school, or who had gone to school in English or Chinese but are illiterate in the national Malay language, which was only made the official medium of instruction in schools in the mid-1980s. Older women from indigenous minority communities, who recently migrated to towns following their children, are most disadvantaged, as illustrated by the situation of Madeline.[3]

> At 73, Madeline reluctantly migrated from a small village in Marudi to live with one of her married sons in Miri three years ago when her husband passed away. While both her son and daughter-in-law worked during the day, she helped to look after their two pre-school children. She is totally dependent on the use of modern technology including a telephone. Using public transportation is also a struggle for her. Venturing out of her home in the outskirts of Miri into the bustling city is a totally alien and overwhelming experience for her. Her isolation is compounded by her lack of proficiency in any of the languages commonly used in Miri.

Madeline's case highlights the faulty assumption that older persons living with children have their needs taken care of.

The case of Ruth is another which suggests that older persons may be neglected even though they may be living with their families.

> 74-year-old Ruth, a member of one of the Orang Ulu communities, was widowed in her sixties. All her four children had married and lived far away so she moved to stay with her eldest son and his wife in their low-cost home. Her son worked during the day and she claimed that her daughter-in-law did not pay her any attention. She has to prepare her own food, take care of her own laundry, and was not given any money for buying necessities. She has been told by her daughter-in-law not to leave the house or mix with the neighbours. She also wanted more of her regular medicine but the family had not attended to this. She has high blood pressure, backache, 'nerve pain', and prolonged coughs.

Madeline's and Ruth's situations bring to the fore two questions: first is the question of who provides care for the older persons and whether there are any gender differences; and second is the issue of vulnerabilities and gender. In the following paragraphs, the author attempts to answer these two questions.

Who Cares for Whom?

Traditionally in all major cultures in Sarawak, the care of older people falls on the shoulders of women. Daughters and daughters-in-law play important roles in the care of the elderly in a family. Among certain ethnic groups, particularly the Chinese, it is the norm for daughters-in-law to care for her parents-in-law. While filial piety is much lauded and indeed a source of social support for older people, this kind of care arrangement often imposes stress and strain on the caregivers and on the relationships between older women and daughters-in-law, between husbands and wives and the rest of the family (Chee 2004). Families who are financially better off are able to engage a domestic helper to help ease the pressure, particularly when the older persons become infirm; however, this often presents new sets of problems and when the family can no longer cope, residential care is resorted to.

Qualitative data and focus group interviews with a group of women informal carers confirmed that many of the older women are indeed carers for their spouses, including some who have been widowed. Mui Na, for example, spoke of how her elderly mother cared for her father for four years after he had a debilitating stroke. The demands were heavy and she was concerned for her mother's well-being as well as her father's (now deceased), and wondered if the strain of caring had contributed to her mother's subsequent health problems.

There were, however, several narratives which revealed that there was reciprocity of care between older couples, refuting the assumptions that men "do not engage in carework". One of them, Mei Ling, described vividly how her two parents, both in their mid-eighties, oscillate between carer and patient to each other. At the time of the interview, she shared how the care she provided towards her mother during a short but worrying illness had taken a toll on her father who had just recovered from a hospital admission.

The experiences of this group of women also disproved two general assumptions. First, is the idea that men do not provide caring; these women confirmed that their brothers contributed a great deal to the caring — practically, financially, and emotionally. Very often, the physical care needed for older men entailed the close assistance of sons rather than daughters or daughters-in-law. A recent study conducted among the urban Chinese community in the capital city of Kuching supported this observation (Chung 2012). Second, is the assumption that daughters do not provide care to their parents once they are married since parents coreside with son(s) in keeping with Chinese tradition. There are many instances where married daughters return home or receive their parents into their matrimonial homes to provide respite care towards their parents. A third assumption which is refuted is that children who stay apart do not provide care to their parents (see Chapter 2, this volume). The experiences of Mui Na and Mei Ling proved that often, children living apart from parents made frequent trips over varying distances to visit and care for their parents. In the case of Mui Na, it is an hour's plane trip from Kuching to Sibu and for Mei Ling a two hour's plane trip from Kuching to Miri.

NEGLECT AND ABUSE: GENDER DIFFERENCES

The experiences of Magdeline and Ruth discussed in the earlier section support the existing literature which points to older women's greater vulnerabilities to neglect and abuse (Aitken and Griffin 1996; Whittaker 1995). As little research on elder abuse has been carried out in Malaysia and it is very much a hidden problem, there is no indicative data to show whether women are indeed more vulnerable or not to elder abuse. While Ruth is one case example in this study, another case of an older man seems to suggest that ageing and ageism may be an "equalizer" in terms of gender in that both women and men are open to abuse or neglect in later life, especially when the older person possesses disabilities and is forced to depend on others, as shown in several recent studies in western countries (Kosberg 1998, 2007; Pritchard 2001). Tang, in his mid-seventies, claimed he was neglected and abandoned by his family. He had been a sailor in his younger days, and later worked in the construction industry. Because of failing health in his later years, he stopped work and tried to earn a living as a property broker. Two years ago, he suffered a stroke, and although he recovered, it left him disabled and confined to a wheelchair. Tang said that he came to be seen as a burden to his family and his presence was unwelcomed by his son with whom he already had a strained relationship. As Tang's two married daughters were unable to take him in (one living with her in-laws, and the other in a low-cost housing flat with her husband and two small children), he was finally admitted to an old age home run by a charitable society, after a long wait of six months.

Tang's situation resonates with some studies in developing countries which found that older men from lower economic backgrounds without savings or assets may be more vulnerable to neglect or abuse. A study on Thailand by Knodel and Chayovan (see Chapter 2, this volume) indicates that among older persons with no spouse present, men are less likely than women to coreside with a child. Men are also less likely than older women to receive money from a child. Several studies in Mexico observed that older men's former role as economic providers does not make them "desirable co-residents by their children and other relatives" and those "who lack resources are unlikely to realize their hopes of future reciprocity via-a-vis their children" (Gomes and Montes de Oca 2004, p. 236; see also Varley and Blasco 2000). This becomes apparent when we compare Tang's situation with his wife's, who is happily living with their son. Mrs Tang, 69 years old, lives with her son and his wife who have three children age 13, 11, and 8. Her son runs a small sundry business and her daughter-in-law works as a clerical assistant in a company. Tang's wife has been the childminder for all the grandchildren since they were born and there is a strong bond between her and the grandchildren.

The point to highlight here is that the caregiving relationship between older women and their family can be considered as one of exchange and reciprocity. By extending their role as care providers in their later life, older women are securing economic assistance and family support from their children. Men, in contrast, who have hitherto been involved in the economic sphere as breadwinner for the family, face the possibility of having no role when they reach old age since they are no longer employable.

RECIPROCITY AND EXCHANGE:
TO CARE AND BE CARED FOR

The case of Tang, who, despite having a son, is living in an old age home, is often considered a disgrace among the Chinese community steeped in the tradition of filial piety. The tradition of caring for one's elders is equally strong across the ethnic groups in Sarawak, and coresidence with children is often seen as an assurance of care. However, what emerged from the ageing study is that care of older persons is not unilateral; instead very often, the older persons are providing care and financial support to their children. Table 7.4 shows that a total of 54 per cent of respondents (324)

TABLE 7.4
Family Roles by Gender

Family Roles	Women	Men	Total
Head of family	12.6% (76)	28.8% (173)	41.5% (249)
Grandparenting	10.6% (64)	1.8% (11)	12.5% (75)
Total	23.3% (140)	30.6% (184)	54.0% (324)

Source: Social Development and Urbanisation Council, *Ageing in Sarawak: Impact, Needs and Emerging Issues* (Kota Samarahan, Sarawak: Centre for Technology and Consultancy, Universiti Malaysia Sarawak, 2005).

are involved either in grandparenting or as the head of the family. It is interesting to note that 41.5 per cent of them said they are head of the family (*ketua keluarga*) and this includes 12.6 per cent of women (76). In terms of grandparenting, more women, 10.6 per cent, identified with that role compared with men (1.8 per cent). Further examination shows that those who stated grandparenting as the role they played in the family were mostly those who are the primary care providers for their grandchildren whereas those who identified themselves as heads of family were those who have children — including married children — who continue to live with them. Partly out of cultural expectations, and partly for economic reasons, it is still not uncommon for younger married couples to choose to live with one of their parents.

Older women's role in providing care for grandchildren warrants further discussion (see Chapters 2 and 12, this volume). First, the increasing participation of younger women in the workforce has meant that childcare is no longer the exclusive work of the mother. Childminding services have been a burgeoning business area in the last two decades. However, for young babies, there is a preference for care in the home. This is particularly so in the case of younger couples who enter the lower rung of the job market who are not able to afford childcare services even with a dual income, and instead turning to the "free labour" provided by older women. Second, it is not uncommon for couples who have migrated from the rural areas to towns to fill the labour force needs of the light and service industry sectors, and then to have their mothers move to the town with them solely to help look after the grandchildren. Third, it is not uncommon for single mothers to leave their children with their rural mothers while they work in the urban areas (Hew 2003). Another familiar situation is when adult children work outside Sarawak and they leave their children to be cared for by their parents. In the latter two situations, remittances sent home are for both the young and the old.

While caring for the young offers a way for the older women to be cared for, the form and quality of care they receive in return varies depending on a number of factors. Elsewhere the author has discussed how grandparenting enhances their social role for some older women, particularly if they are in good health and support networks are available, but for others it is a source of stress and burden; for yet another group, it confines them to their children's homes which are not their own, adding to their isolation and alienation (Ling 2007).

Living Alone

What about older persons who live alone? Does that reflect a state of neglect? A closer examination of those who live alone found that they come from a range of different age groups including two who are between 80 and 84 years old. In terms of their income, the majority are from income groups of below RM800, with only five who are from the income group of RM801 and above. Sixteen of them come from rural areas, eight from urban, and only one from a semi-urban area. Older people living alone, particularly those in the rural areas, most often do so because their children have left for work or marriage in another town or even moved or migrated to another country. The two case examples below show very contrasting situations. Aminah, a 76-year-old woman, who lives alone in a small remote village in the Miri Division since her husband's death ten years ago, typifies the neglected ones as a result of urbanization. Her two married sons found employment in Miri and settled there. She has hardly any contact with them and does not even remember the last time they visited. Neither does she have any idea of how many grandchildren she has. Her younger sister who lives nearby is her only source of help in times of need. She receives a meagre sum of RM130 a month from the Welfare Department under the Elderly Persons Assistance Scheme (*Skim Bantuan Orang Tua*) and some support in the form of food and kind from the local community, especially during major festivals. She suffers from high blood pressure, a circulation problem in arms and legs, and haemorrhoids. She requires supportive devices such as spectacles, a walking cane, and dentures. At the time of the interview, Aminah presented her life in old age as one of sadness and loneliness. In stark contrast to Aminah is Mrs Chong, a 65-year-old retired primary school headmistress, who lives alone in a double-storey house in Kuching. Her two married children have migrated to Australia and her husband chose to go with them. She is an active church member, and since retirement nearly ten years ago, she has been involved in teaching Sunday School. She enjoys gardening and reading, two activities for which she now has the time. She owns a car and with a pension of RM2,000 and being free of child support responsibility, she, in her own words, has "more than enough" to meet her needs.

Mrs Chong's case shows that for some older persons living alone is a matter of choice, indicating that it is possible that good health and sound financial standing provide them with social and economic independence, a trend noted in one recent study in China (Xie and Yan 2001). In addition, she represents a small percentage of women in her era, more likely urban Chinese, who are able to benefit to some extent, from the provision of better educational facilities and parental support.

The foregoing discussions highlight that the care and living arrangements of older persons warrant the development of formal services to supplement care available from traditional providers, as Sarawak undergoes urbanization, and because traditional support networks appear to be weakening and the family is shrinking in size as well as family members increasingly living further apart (Ling 2009). This is the focus of the next section.

FORMAL CARE OF OLDER PERSONS

In the main, formal care for older persons comprises income support, residential care, and senior citizens' centres. Support schemes from the state or NGOs, to complement and supplement care within the family, are almost non-existent.

Income Support Schemes

Table 7.5 shows the respondents' sources of income which provide a glimpse into the financial circumstances of older persons. Apart from the 36.5 per cent who derived income from their employment, 22.0 per cent lived on pensions and slightly more than 10 per cent had received gratuities. Less than 2 per cent received Workmen's Compensation SOCSO (Social Security Organisation) payments, and about 3.7 per cent received retrenchment benefits. Almost 6 per cent of respondents were receiving financial aid from the Social Welfare Department in their own name, and 2.2 per cent were living with one family member who received assistance from that department.

TABLE 7.5

Distribution of Respondents by their Sources of Income

Sources	Frequency	Percentage
Financial Aid from charitable organizations	5	0.8
Workmen Compensation SOCSO	8	1.3
Financial Aid from Welfare Department	13	2.2
Other sources	16	2.7
Retrenchment benefit	22	3.7
Gratuity	63	10.5
Rental/interest from investment	129	21.5
Retirement pension	132	22
Employment	219	36.5
Assistance from family members	397	66.4
No response	27	4.5

Source: Social Development and Urbanisation Council, *Ageing in Sarawak: Impact, Needs and Emerging Issues* (Kota Samarahan, Sarawak: Centre for Technology and Consultancy, Universiti Malaysia Sarawak, 2005).

In Sarawak, as in the rest of Malaysia, only civil servants receive a life-long pension after retirement, and the mandatory age of retirement was raised to 60 years old. This pension, upon the death of the former civil servant, can be transferred to his/her immediate next-of-kin. As Ong (2002) notes, a pension as a social security benefit is enjoyed by less than 1 per cent of the Malaysian population. A more extensive scheme is the Employees Provident Fund (EPF) made mandatory by law under the Employees Provident Fund Act 1991 (Act 452). However, although the EPF was introduced over fifty years ago, it was, until 1991, not mandatory; it excludes workers who are employed on a part-time or temporary basis, and the wage limit for eligible contributors of RM400 a month (raised to RM500 in 1963) renders many low-income earners ineligible (Lee 2001). Moreover, contributing to EPF is not compulsory for people who are self-employed; in Sarawak, this means many older persons engaged in the informal sector are excluded. Those in small, home-based businesses or in subsistence farming are also not able to benefit from the scheme (Caraher 2003). Older women, whose participation in the labour force has been in the domestic and informal sector in their prime productive years are, therefore, even less likely to receive any form of old age security support.

In terms of the financial assistance schemes available to older persons in need, the State Welfare Department operates a *Skim Bantuan Orang Tua* (Older Persons Assistance Scheme) in which eligible older persons receive a monthly assistance of RM130. It is, however, a stringently means-tested scheme, only for those who are in dire need, covering the needs of those who are without family support, are abandoned or disabled. The 2.2 per cent of respondents receiving assistance from the Welfare Department, despite an overwhelming 44 per cent of them receiving an income of RM200 and below, is indicative of the nature of this scheme. Again, older women who have a spouse are less likely to receive financial assistance in their own right, as it is more often given to their husbands.

The problems faced by older persons from low-income groups are particularly pressing when support from their children is not forthcoming either because of physical distance or the latter's own economic constraints. While there are also charitable organizations, usually religious-based, rendering assistance to needy older persons, these are often subsistence in nature, providing only food or "in kind". Faced with this, older people have two options: those who are migrants from the rural areas may choose to return to the village if their health permits, or they may seek admission to a residential home.

Residential and Nursing Homes

The espoused tradition of caring for one's elders is usually equated with providing care within the family home; admission into a residential care setting is often equated with abandonment and is strongly frowned upon. The admission criteria of existing residential homes reflect this cultural norm, restricted only to those who are destitute with no next-of-kin.

There are two government-run residential homes *(Rumah Seri Kenangan)*, one in the capital city Kuching and the other in Sibu. Admission criteria restrict access to those who are considered destitute (although in recent years the criteria have become more flexible) and are not infirmed; if the resident becomes invalid later, they are transferred to a convalescent block. It is interesting to note that *Rumah Seri Kenangan* Kuching was in fact a pauper home set up in 1932 by the Chinese community catering for single male migrants from China; it was later handed over to the government. Today, both homes receive applications from older people of various ethnic backgrounds, including some from minority indigenous communities.

Apart from the government homes, there are several homes run by charitable organizations, reflecting community recognition of the need to provide alternative care for older people. Responding to the emerging needs of older persons who are infirmed and require extensive support beyond the ability of the family, several private nursing homes have been established since the 1990s. Residential care of the elderly is no longer a state or NGO affair. This provides an option for older people from middle and upper income families to be cared for in a residential setting, when previously the admission criteria to the two state-run government homes were limited to those from low-income families and who were physically ambulant. Recognizing this trend, the Federal government has extended the Care Centre Act 1993 to Sarawak to regulate private home operators.

In terms of gender breakdown, an interesting observation is that men in the homes outnumbered women until recently. Apart from the fact that single Chinese men constituted the majority of the resident population prior to the 1980s, this phenomenon may well have been contributed to by the longer life expectancy of men until the 1980s, as discussed earlier. Another observation is that older women tended to be more capable of independent living in their own familiar setting, or be more likely to be taken in than older men to live with their children in later life, if they had not been living together previously. Further research is needed to ascertain gender differences and residential care.

In the main, government-run residential homes are more ethnically diverse, raising questions about provision to meet cultural diversity, and communication between staff and residents. There is a tendency for homes to cater to members of the dominant culture, either in terms of the residents or of the staff or owner, leaving the minorities feeling their own cultural preferences are either not understood or are ignored. It was also evident that the range of assistance was limited for people with special needs (for example, among those who are visually/hearing impaired or who have suffered post-stroke communication problems). When their needs were not fully met or in some instances not understood, it was considered that their needs had not been recognized. In comparison, homes run by voluntary charitable bodies are more Chinese-dominated, and tend to have more user participation than either the government-run homes or the private nursing homes.

Day Centres

The Day Centres for older people have been very popular in the last twenty-five years. There are centres initiated and run by the Social Welfare Department or Medical Department, and others by community organizations or Senior Citizen Associations. The setting up of these centres demonstrates recognition that social interaction is an essential part of living, and that for older persons, a venue needs to be provided to facilitate this.

Many of these centres are well equipped with facilities for exercises and games, with funding from either government departments or voluntary organizations. Visits to these centres conveyed a picture of active ageing, with older persons engaging in a range of activities: table tennis and dancing, *tai chi*, and many other types of indoor activities. Those who attend these centres are usually those who are in good health and who have been leading an active social life, whether in their working life or in some other religious or community-based involvement. Gender differences in participation in these day centres are not obvious; however, many of the centres, especially those at the hub of the city tend to be dominated by the Chinese communities. Concerns have been expressed for those from ethnic minority groups who are newcomers to the urban settings who, because of the lack of an established social network, and language and cultural barriers, are limited in their opportunities for social interaction. Of greater concern is when isolation and loneliness affect older persons' mental well-being. For example, cursory observation revealed that there are men from ethnic minority groups spending time in public places on their own, and some are seen to engage in excessive drinking. The question of healthcare including mental health for older persons arises here.

Healthcare

Specialized geriatric services under the Health Department are at its infancy in the country, beginning in 1997 when the Federal Ministry of Health formed a National Council of Health for the Elderly and, subsequently, a nationwide Elderly Health Care Programme (Tengku Aizan and Nurizan Yahya 2008). In relation to this, several health centres have formed Senior Citizen Clubs which conduct recreational, social, and health activities for their members. Similar to the Senior Citizen Service centres but under the auspices of the Social Welfare Department, these centres have become popular meeting places for senior citizens who initiate their own activities, as the members are autonomous in their decision-making.

Overall, the study found that a substantial number of respondents suffered from one or more of the following: hypertension, heart disease, arthritis, hearing impairment, and impaired vision (particularly cataracts), tuberculosis, and gastric problems. This finding is consistent with other studies done in different parts of Malaysia (Chen 1987*a*; Siop 2003;

Tracy and Tracy 1993; Zaiton Yassin and Terry 1990). However, questions should be raised as to whether, or rather, to what extent, this trend can be attributed to the kind of work in which the elderly have been engaged during their young and adult life. In addition, poor nutrition in younger life, the inaccessibility to proper healthcare in rural areas, and lower purchasing power, that may have exacerbated the poor health condition of the elderly, are also concerns. The findings of the study did not permit detailed analysis comparing the health status of men as against women, but it is speculated that this cohort of older women may have suffered more negative repercussions from the historically less-developed healthcare facilities.

In addition, a glimpse of respondents' self-reported well-being shows that some 63 per cent of women reported symptoms of insomnia, loneliness, depression, and anxiety, whereas considerably fewer men reported these conditions. Whether or not this may be because of men being less willing to admit emotional problems remains an area requiring further attention for both older men and women in Sarawak (Chen 1987*b*; Teoh, Rosdinom Razali and Normah Che Din 2001).

CONCLUSIONS

The caregiving and care-receiving experiences of older men and women in Sarawak highlight several pertinent issues, indicating the need to develop a range of programmes and schemes to either provide alternative care, or to strengthen the care of older persons within the family and community. This chapter has drawn attention to one pattern of care: that care has been more of an "either in the family" or "in the residential homes" option. Public services or schemes to bolster the role of the family as an informal care provider and to enable older persons — regardless of gender, ethnicity, and socio-economic background — have remained underdeveloped.

Generally, both older men and women from higher socio-economic strata, regardless of gender and ethnicity, are able to have a choice of the system of care which best suits their needs. However, there has been increasing evidence to suggest that families are overextended, and given greater mobility and the smaller size of families, the need for the development of professional domiciliary and nursing care is a matter of urgency. While there are facilities for meeting the social and recreational needs of older people, day-care support for the non-ambulant is almost non-existent.

Based on the findings of this study, while older women are more likely to be economically dependent, there is evidence that where they are able to provide caregiving to grandchildren, alongside the increasing labour force participation of younger women (their daughters or daughters-in-law), they are accorded a special social position in the family and receive reciprocity of support from their children. In contrast, older men, more so for those from lower income groups, are more vulnerable when they lose the role of economic provider in the family. The traditional role of being the economic provider and the "stern" father has taken its toll in family relationships, with the result that, in the event of older men's disability or dependence, they may be more vulnerable to neglect or more likely to be admitted to residential homes.

Moreover, urbanization and greater human mobility have led to older people being left behind, particularly in the rural areas. In cases where adult children are struggling to make ends meet, remittances are hard to come by, rendering older people vulnerable to neglect. There is a need for social support and social protection schemes to be developed for older people and for financial assistance to be granted to women in their own right. Special attention requires to be paid to ethnic minorities in rural regions and to those who have migrated to towns, following their children.

Notes

1. The author wishes to acknowledge the Ministry of Social Development and Urbanisation, Sarawak for permission to publish the findings of the study in this chapter. She is also grateful to Professor Dr Spencer Empading Sanggin, the lead researcher, as well as Gill Raja and Zuraidah Abdul Rahman, the other team researchers, for their work in the larger study. Special thanks also go to Professor Jonathan Parker for his comments on an earlier draft of this chapter.
2. The Ageing study defined those 55 and above as an older person. While it was recognized that the recent National Policy for the Elderly defined those who are 60 and above as elderly, following the World Health Organization's categorization, in this study the starting point was extended downwards to coincide with the government's lowest official retirement age of 55. A younger starting point is also justified, as life expectancy in developing countries is lower than in developed nations. Estimated life expectancy in Malaysia in 2004 is 69.29 years for men and 74.81 for women.
3. All names used are pseudonyms.

References

Aitken, Lynda and Gabriele Griffin. *Gender Issues in Elder Abuse*. London: Sage Publication, 1996.

ARROWs for Change. "Feminisation of Aging in Asia-Pacific: Health Implications". *Arrows for Change* 5, no. 2 (1999): 12.

Brody, Elaine, M. *Women in the Middle: The Parent Care Years*, 2nd ed. New York: Springer Publishing Company, 2004.

Caraher, K. "Malaysia: Approaches to Income Security in Old Age". *Social Policy and Society*, no. 2 (2003): 295–304.

Chee, Pei Ying. "Tekanan dan Isu-Isu Timbul yang Dihadapi Oleh Anak Menantu Perempuan dalam Penjagaan Ibu Bapa Mertua Masyarakat Cina". Unpublished Final Year Project. Bachelor of Social Sciences (Social Work), Universiti Malaysia Sarawak, Malaysia, 2004.

Chen, P.C.Y. "The Health of the Aging Malaysian: Policy Implications". *Medical Journal of Malaysia* 42, no. 3 (1987*a*): 146–55.

———. "Psychosocial Factors and the Health of the Elderly Malaysian". *Annals of the Academy of Medicine* 16, no. 1 (1987*b*): 10–14.

Chung, Raymond. "The Experiences of Caregivers for Older Persons among Chinese Community in Urban Kuching, Sarawak". Unpublished dissertation. Master of Environment Management (Development Planning), Universiti Malaysia Sarawak, 2012.

DaVanzo, J. and A. Chan. "Living Arrangements of Older Malaysians: Who Coresides with their Adult Children?". *Demography* 31, no. 1 (1994): 95–113.

Department of Statistics, Malaysia (Sarawak branch). *Yearbook of Statistics*. Sarawak: Department of Statistics, 2002.

Department of Statistics, Malaysia. "Jadual Hayat Ringkas Malaysia 2008–10", 2011. Available at <http://www.statistics.gov.my/portal/images/stories/files/LatestReleases/abridged/Jadual_Hayat_Ringkas_Malaysia_2008-2010.pdf> (accessed 2 March 2013).

Gomes, Cristina and Veronica Montes De Oca. "Ageing in Mexico: Family, Informal Care and Reciprocity". In *Living Longer: Ageing, Development and Social Protection*, edited by P. Lloyd-Sherlock. United Nations Research Institute for Social Development, London and New York: Zed Books, 2004.

Gray, A. "The Changing Availability of Grandparents as Carers and Its Implications for Childcare Policy in the UK". *Journal of Social Policy* 34, no. 4 (2005): 557–77.

Hew, C.S. "The Impact of Urbanisation on Family Structures: The Experience of Sarawak, Malaysia". *Sojourn: Journal of Social Issues in Southeast Asia* 8, no. 1 (2003): 110–38.

Jamilah Ariffin. *Women and Development in Malaysia*. Petaling Jaya: Pelanduk Publications, 1992.

Knodel, J. and M.B. Ofstedal. "Gender and Ageing in the Developing World: Where Are the Men?" *Population and Development Review* 29, no. 4 (2003): 677–98.

Kosberg, J.I. "Abuse of Elderly Men". *Journal of Elder Abuse and Neglect* 9, no. 3 (1998): 69–88.

————., ed. *Abuse of Older Men.* Binghamton, New York: Haworth Press, 2007.

Lazzarini, Iris G. "Intergenerational Financial Transfers: Filipino Migrants Caring for Parents Overseas". Unpublished Ph.D. thesis. School of Social Work and Human Services, University of Queensland, Australia, 2009.

Lee, Hock Lock. *Financial Security in Old Age: Whither the Employees Provident Fund of Malaysia?* Subang Jaya, Malaysia: Pelandok Publications, 2001.

Ling, How Kee. "Elderly Women's Experiences of Urbanization". In *Village Mothers, City Daughters: Women and Urbanization in Sarawak*, edited by Hew C.S. Singapore: Institute of Southeast Asian Studies, 2007.

————. "Urbanization and the Ageing Community in Sarawak". In *Older Persons in Southeast Asia: An Asset*, edited by E.N. Arifin and A. Ananta. Singapore: Institute of Southeast Asian Studies, 2009.

Liu, T. William and Hal Kendig, eds. *Who Should Care for the Elderly? An East-West Value Divide.* Singapore: Singapore University Press, 2000.

Miles, Matthew B. and A. Michael Huberman. *Qualitative Data Analysis: A Source Book.* 2nd ed. Thousand Oaks, California: Sage, 1994.

Ong, Fon Sim. "Ageing in Malaysia: A Review of National Policies and Programmes". In *Ageing and Long Term Care: National Policies in the Asia-Pacific*, edited by D.R. Phillips and A.C.M. Chan. Singapore: Institute of Southeast Asian Studies & Canada: International Development Research Centre, 2002.

Pritchard, Jacki. *Male Victims of Elder Abuse: Their Experiences and Needs.* London: Jessica Kingsley Publishing, 2001.

Silverman, David. *Doing Qualitative Research.* 3rd ed. London: Sage, 2010.

Siop, Sidiah. *Health Needs of Older People in a Semi-Urban Village in Malaysia.* Kota Samarahan: Universiti Malaysia Sarawak, 2003.

Social Development and Urbanisation Council. *Ageing in Sarawak: Impact, Needs and Emerging Issues.* Kota Samarahan, Sarawak: Centre for Technology and Consultancy, Universiti Malaysia Sarawak, 2005.

Tan Poo Chang and Masitah Mohd. Yatim. "Old Age Financial Security for Women in Malaysia". In *Untapped Resources: Women in Ageing Societies Across Asia*, edited by K. Mehta. Singapore: Times Academic Press, 1997.

Tengku Aizan Hamid and Nurizan Yahya. "National Policy for the Elderly in Malaysia: Achievements and Challenges". In *Ageing in Southeast and East Asia*, edited by Lee H.G. Singapore: Institute of Southeast Asian Studies, 2008.

Teoh Hsien-Jin, Rosdinom Razali and Normah Che Din. "Mental Health of the Malaysian Elderly: Issues and Perspectives". In *Mental Health in Malaysia: Issues and Concerns*, edited by A. Haque. Kuala Lumpur: University of Malaya Press, 2001.

Tracy, M.B. and P.D. Tracy. "Health Care and Family Support System of Functionally Impaired Rural Elderly Men and Women in Trengganu, Malaysia". *Journal of Cross-Cultural Gerontology* 8 (1993): 35–48.

United Nations Economic and Social Commission for Asia and the Pacific (UNESCAP). *Status of Elderly Women in Asia and the Pacific Region*. Bangkok: UNESCAP, 1991.

Varley, A. and M. Blasco. "Intact or in Tatters? Family Care of Older Women and Men in Urban Mexico". *Gender and Development* 8, no. 2 (2000): 47–55.

Whittaker, T. "Violence, Gender and Elder Abuse: Towards a Feminist Analysis and Practice". *Journal of Gender Studies* 4, no. 1 (1995): 35–45.

Xie X., and X. Yan. "Adult Children Taking Care of their Ageing Parents: A Multiple-Case Study on Caregivers Perspectives". *International Social Work* 11, no. 2 (2001): 52–64.

Zaiton Yassin and R.D. Terry. "Health Characteristics of Rural Elderly Malay Females in Selected Villages in Negeri Sembilan". *Medical Journal of Malaysia* 45, no. 4 (1990): 310–18.

8

AN "ACTIVE AGEING" APPROACH TO LIVING ALONE: OLDER MEN AND WOMEN LIVING IN RENTAL FLATS IN SINGAPORE[1]

Leng Leng Thang

INTRODUCTION

Studies on gender and ageing have generally established that with the "feminization of ageing", older women face more vulnerabilities than older men. In Singapore, the 2004 AWARE-TSAO Foundation Report on Women and Income Security in an ageing Singapore population found that Singapore is similarly affected with this phenomenon, as shown in the sex ratio for age groups in Singapore. The 2000 Singapore census shows that the sex ratio increases drastically from 1.061 (females per 1,000 males) for those age 60–69 years to 1.72 (females per 1,000 males) for those age 80–89 years. Older women face more vulnerabilities pertaining to health and finances. In terms of health, older women have higher needs for long-term care (Chia et. al. 2008). As a survey in a nursing home in Singapore shows, 70 per cent of its residents are female, with the majority single, widowed, and above the age of 75 (Yap et. al. 2003).

There is also a larger number of older women compared to older men living in one- or two-room public housing flats, which suggests a higher level of poverty among them. Most of the above mentioned older women are either single, widowed, divorced or separated. Older women tend to have fewer financial means as compared to older men as childcare has kept them out of the workforce for a greater number of years. Moreover, they tend to be lowly educated, with only 10 per cent of women age 60 and above receiving education beyond primary school level.[2] Similarly, a study of the retirement needs of elderly Singaporeans concluded that older women face severe inadequacy in retirement financial needs — a posited 12 per cent higher than that for older men (Chia 2008, p. 36). These reports highlight the plight of older women. As Tsao Foundation's report of the study states: "The situation of older women in the future looks grim as there are fewer siblings to share the financial cost of care giving. Moreover, the older woman is likely to be widowed and frailer due to longer life span and old age disabilities."

However, is this necessarily so in situations where both older men and women are experiencing the same structural vulnerabilities? In urging for a more gender-balanced perspective in studies of population ageing and gender, Knodel and Ofstedal (2003, p. 681) highlighted "the general lack of recognition given to the wide variation in cultural, political, and socioeconomic contexts that determine both gender relations and old-age support and the likelihood that their interrelationships will differ across the settings within which they play out".

With a gender balanced perspective in mind, this chapter thus attempts to understand whether differences in gender would mediate the experiences of older persons who are of similar age, ethnicity, health concerns, living arrangements and socio-economic circumstances. The chapter explores the above question through the framework of "active ageing", adopting WHO's (2002, p. 12) definition of active ageing where "active aging is the process of optimising opportunities for health, participation and security in order to enhance quality of life as people age." The active ageing approach is based on the recognition of the human rights of older people and the principles of independence, participation, dignity, care, and self-fulfilment. In adopting a life course perspective of ageing, the approach perceives "active" beyond just the ability to be physically active or to participate in the labour force, recognizing that retirees and those who are ill or live with disabilities can remain active contributors to their families, peers, communities, and nation. Here, "health" is also defined beyond physical well-being to include mental and social well-being. Hence, the study on "active ageing" among older persons in this context not only includes but also extends beyond the conventional notion of physical activity. More specifically, the chapter will discuss how older persons maintain "active ageing" through the following: first, the extent of their social and mental activities and well-being seen through their connections with the outside world, such as their kin and other social networks, which include the significance of the availability of social services such as neighbourhood link centres (NL), and other community help in promoting active ageing; second, the role of religion; and third, their efforts in keeping physically active such as through exercise and other means.

Research on older people who live alone have shown that compared with older persons who live with their families, they tend to have limited access to informal sources of support. For instance, Chou and Chi (2000) compared elderly people in Hong Kong who lived alone with those who lived with others, and pointed out that those who lived alone reported smaller social networks of relatives and receiving less instrumental and emotional support. Elsewhere in Larsson's and Silverstein's (2004) study on Swedish elderly persons age 81 to 100 years old, living arrangements emerged as the main factor differentiating the extent of the use of public and informal care. Particularly, older persons living alone tended to receive less formal and informal care compared to those residing with others, resulting in social isolation (Klinenbery 2002, 2005; Findlay 2003). Older persons living alone are also shown to have higher tendency towards suffering from depression and other mental health problems, thus prompting suicide attempts (Chou, Ho and Chi 2006; Kua and Hong 2003; Chan, Ng and Niti 2006). It is thus helpful to examine the extent to which older people living alone create strategies to achieve social, mental, and physical well-being so as to help them to cope with problems that may accompany their circumstance of living alone, such as social isolation.

DATA COLLECTION

The data for the chapter is derived from a larger on-going qualitative study on older people living alone in Singapore. For this chapter, the author focuses on fieldwork data from a specific geographic confine: older persons living alone in low-income, one-room rental apartment blocks, in the central part of Singapore. Fieldwork was conducted in the latter half of 2008. We gained access to the respondents through the introduction of the neighourhood link centre located on the first level of the block. Interviews, conducted in the homes of the older persons, usually lasted between 90 to 150 minutes per respondent. The informal interviews which were recorded were conducted either in Mandarin or in Chinese dialect such as Hokkien or Cantonese. Participant observations were also carried out at the activity centre and the surrounding areas of the apartment block to observe the daily flow of life in the community. Although the number of respondents was small, the author managed to seek information from them regarding the other residents who also lived alone in the same apartment block. This information provided a more comprehensive understanding of the living conditions of older people living alone and their interpersonal dynamics.

Profile of Respondents

This chapter focuses on 10 older residents (3 females and 7 males) residing in the same apartment block (see Table 8.1 for a brief profile of the respondents). They share the same ethnicity, age group, and socio-economic characteristics. All of them live alone and are Chinese ages between 65 and 88 years. Among the female respondents, two are single and one is widowed. Among the seven male respondents, three are single, two divorced, and two widowed. The male respondents who are single attributed their single status to poverty and low education which prevented them from achieving the expected norm of marrying.

TABLE 8.1
Respondents (Female #)

Respondent	Age	Financial Support	Religion	Marital Status	Educational Level
A#	67	Relatives	Buddhist	Single	Primary
B#	68	Work income	Christian	Single	NA
C#	73	Children	No religion	Widow	Secondary
D	67	Public assistance	Buddhist	Single	Primary
E	71	Public assistance	Buddhist	Divorced	NA
F	65	Odd job earnings	Buddhist	Single	Secondary
G	82	Public assistance	Christian	Widower	Primary
H	88	Public assistance	Buddhist	Single	Primary
I	71	CPF savings	Christian	Divorced	NA
J	72	Child	Buddhist	Widower	Primary

For the single older women, poor health seemed the main reason deterring them from getting married. All but two had retired from paid work by the time this study was conducted. Four men rely on public assistance (PA) ($330 per month at the time of study). Three (one man and two women) rely on their siblings or children, while one uses his CPF savings to support himself. Of the two who are working, female respondent B has a part-time job where she works three times a week, and male respondent F takes up odd job employment where he works when he is asked to. They earn a monthly income roughly the same amount as the PA payout.

The Public Assistance Scheme in Singapore provides welfare assistance to Singapore citizens who require long-term financial assistance as a result of old age, sickness or disability and who have no family available to provide the support. In 2008, about 3,000 Singaporeans were PA recipients.[3] They receive free medical treatment, subsidized rentals and utilities, as well as rebates for service and conservancy charges, besides a monthly subsistence sum.

It is inevitable for health to be a main concern among the older persons. The respondents have a variety of health concerns, ranging from the more common forms of chronic diseases found among older persons such as hypertension, diabetes, and high cholesterol, to heart, lung, kidney, eye problems, asthma, and problems with legs. All are on some form of regular medication. Despite their health problems, these older persons are all capable of managing their daily life in a lone dwelling. An 88-year-old male respondent H, the oldest in the study who has limited mobility, relies on help from neighbours to clean his flat and bring him meals every day. Except for respondent H, the rest claim that they have visited their doctors regularly for medication and treatment, with help from PA and full medical subsidies. For those who are not PA recipients, many were able to obtain medical subsidies and concession payments owing to old age and their low or "no income" status. The procedure for obtaining such a subsidy is usually done through the help of social workers' and doctors' recommendations, after which they seek renewal of concessions and subsidies through community centres.

After a brief discussion about the context of living alone among older persons in Singapore, in this chapter, the author analyses the extent and notion of "active ageing", and the differences found between the older men and women in this study in relation to four areas: their contact with kin; contact with non-kin; the role of neighbourhood link centres; and physical activities among the older persons.

LIVING ALONE AMONG OLDER PERSONS IN SINGAPORE

Among the countries facing an ageing demographic trend, Singapore can be considered unique in having maintained a relatively high percentage of coresidence among older persons and their children. In 2005, 69.4 per cent of older persons in Singapore (age 65 years and above) were living with their economically independent children (Department of Statistics, Table 94, 2006). This could be attributed to the cultural norm of caring for ageing parents and the success of social policies (such as housing and tax policies) in keeping the generations under one roof.

Despite this encouraging trend, there is, however, a growing trend of older persons living alone. The numbers of elderly living alone have increased from 6.6 per cent in 2000 to 7.7 per cent in 2005, an increase from 15,000 to 22,000 in absolute number (Department of Statistics 2006). Underlying this behaviour are changing attitudes among older persons. Surveys by the Housing Development Board (HDB) have shown that while in 1998, only 15.2 per cent of older persons expressed intentions to live alone, in 2003, this figure has risen to 24.3 per cent (Tan 2005).

It is relatively difficult for average older persons who want to live alone to acquire their own living space. Because of state ideology that emphasizes family care, public housing — which houses more than 80 per cent of Singapore's population — is primarily reserved for purchase by families. Only in the recent two decades have singles age 35 and above been allowed to purchase smaller units of second-hand public flats. HDB flats are popular among the general public in Singapore because of its affordability compared to private apartments and houses. In view of older persons' desire to live independently away from their children, HDB has introduced the studio flats scheme (with a 30-year lease) in 1998 for Singaporeans age 55 and above to purchase flats under certain conditions. These flats come with elderly-friendly fixtures such as non-slip floor tiles and grab bars. Such studio flats have now been integrated into the new housing projects in response to rising demand.

For an older person with little financial means who wants or has to live alone, one may either choose to rent from the open market, usually affording only the one-bedroom flat units because of costly private rental, or rent from HDB under the public rental scheme. These are usually one- or two-room flats, ranging from 35 m² studio apartments for a one-room flat, and 45 m² consisting of a living room and a bedroom.

These units come with a kitchen area and toilet-cum-bath facilities. Because of the high proportion of older persons occupying rental flats in recent years, HDB has carried out various improvement works to the flats and blocks under Project LIFE (Life Improvement and Facilities Enhancement for the elderly). These improvements for one-room rental flats include upgrading the lifts so that they now stop on every floor, installing an alert alarm system for older residents to access help in times of emergency, and fixing non-slippery floor tiles and "sitting-style" instead of "squatting" type toilets, as well as grab bars to facilitate mobility. These housing blocks are also serviced by government–subsidized social service agencies, usually located on the first level of the housing block, to provide community-based care and support for the older people.[4]

Although the same family nucleus requirement applies for public rental flats, under the Joint Singles Scheme, a single person may combine with another single person (both must be at least 35 years old) to co-rent a one-room flat under the condition that their combined monthly income is below S$1,500. In principal, the rental flats are meant for low-income citizens who may otherwise have no roof over their heads. In his 2008 National Day Rally speech,[5] the Prime Minister spoke about the rising demand for rental flats among older persons because of mother-in-law and daughter-in-law conflicts. This situation has led many adults to apply for rental flats on behalf of their ageing parents who then move out and live alone. Among these older persons, a few are sometimes provided with a live-in domestic maid paid for also by their children to take care of their daily needs.

In part to cater to the growing need for housing among low-income older persons, as well as to serve as a safety net for low income families, HDB has plans to raise the supply of these rental flats to 50,000 in 2009 — a 20 per cent increase from the current stock (Goh 2008).

The field site: a block of one-room rental flats

The respondents in this study are typical older tenants who live in rental flats. The housing block in which these older persons live in is already more than thirty years old, but looks relatively new, having been refurbished about five years ago. The block has 319 one-room units, of which 77 units are occupied by older people living alone. There are 31 male and 46 female older residents living alone, of whom 12 are on public assistance. Even when the policy stipulates that each unit should be occupied by at least two persons, many older persons are living alone by "borrowing" a friend's identity as co-applicant while the friend need not be living in the flat or choosing not to report to the housing board officer that a roommate has passed away. In some cases, such as in a unit where a mother and child had been living, even if the mother has passed on, the adult child will be allowed to continue to occupy the unit alone. One male respondent said that he had been living alone since he moved in more than ten years ago because he had refused to accept a roommate. He told the officer that: "it's impossible (for me) to stay with a stranger. If you ask me to stay with a complete stranger, what's going to happen if we quarrel and fight?" He said that the officer has since not approached him about the matter, indicating that they are well aware of the difficulties of living with tenants when a flat is shared. Among the older persons who have tenants, although some feel that having a roommate will help alleviate the loneliness, most prefer to live alone to retain their freedom and privacy, to avoid conflicts with others, and for the safety of their belongings.

The one-room rental block is a multi-racial micro community by itself. While the residents often complain about their neighbours, and quarrels and fights sometimes arise, they also derive mutual support from each other. For example, one 88-year-old male (respondent H) heavily relies on his neighbours to help with his daily chores. The residents identify social networks among the neighbours and often gather to chat and pass time (see Chapter 6, this volume). There are also isolated cases of lone deaths in the block discovered only days after the bodies have decayed, showing the need for ways to ensure that older residents living alone are adequately monitored for their safety and well-being.

In the following discussion, the notion of "active ageing" as expressed by this group of older persons will be discussed. It will be shown that there are different dimensions to the ageing experience, each of which overlaps another to contribute to the well-being of the individuals.

"ACTIVE AGEING" AMONG OLDER MEN AND WOMEN

Contact with Kin

Among the respondents, the three older women show more contact with their kin (or fictive kin) as compared to the older men. Where contact with their own children is limited, we see older women using other forms of contact networks, such as with their siblings and/or good friends instead. The 73-year-old widow (respondent C) reports that although she stays in touch with her two sons occasionally, she only meets them and their family once or twice a year, namely during her birthday and new year; but her brothers and their wives visit her every weekend to play *mahjong*. She used to live with her younger son and helped to take care of his child but had to move out three years ago because of disputes with her daughter-in-law. Even after she had moved out, she was still asked to provide help when her youngest son's family had problems hiring a domestic maid to care for their child. For three months, she spent five nights a week at their place taking care of her granddaughter, bringing her to school, and preparing her meals. After three months, she decided not to help the family anymore and suggested that her granddaughter be sent to an after-school-care-centre. But she also revealed that the family was giving her too little money to cook the meals for the child. Although she was initially quite bitter about having to move out from her son's home, especially since she had helped finance the purchase of the home with money she earned from previously selling her own flat, she is now relieved to live alone. Moreover, when she lived in her son's home, her daughter-in-law had forbidden her from inviting friends to play *mahjong*. She now says: "[since] I have moved here, I experience no restrictions with regard to playing *mahjong*. My weekly *mahjong* sessions with my brothers serve as a get-together time for all of us, who are all in our seventies". By moving out of her son's home to live alone, she has greater control over her own social space and activities. She also managed to foster closer ties with her own siblings as a result of living alone. In fact, her life has changed to become more "active" as a result of a change in her living arrangements.

The other two older women are single and have financial support from their siblings and an income from work respectively. Respondent A, who is receiving financial support from her older sister and brother, is particularly close to her sisters' three children and grandchildren because she used to live with and take care of them. She had lived with her sister for thirty-six years and only moved out five years ago because of a lack of space in the house as her sister's grandchildren were also living there. Now, her siblings and their children visit her weekly, and her nephew brings her to the doctor regularly. She sometimes stays over at their place over the weekends too. The other older woman (respondent B), who was born in Malaysia, was abandoned by her mother at the age of five during the period of the Japanese Occupation. She was then raised by a foster family who brought her to Singapore at the age of nine when they moved from Malaysia. She in turn took care of her foster mother, who turned ill, until her eventual passing. She remained close to her foster family, and stayed with her foster sister's family for four months when she was undergoing treatment and recovering from breast cancer a few years ago. She relies on her foster sister's daughter (who addresses her as "aunt") to take her to the doctor each time. Fortunately for her, she was able to apply for concessions for her medical bills and had a full subsidy to cover her medical expenses when she was ill with breast cancer. Although the family has asked her to move in with them, she declined. However, she is treated like a family member as she has been given the key to their house. Even though she does not stay with them, the gesture of holding on to the key to their house provides her with a sense of security knowing that she has a place to go to whenever she needs to. Although she addresses her foster sister as "my closest friend" since they are not blood-related, in reality, they are her closest "family relations".

Compared to the women, the men have a lesser degree of connection with kin. For the most part, parents were the point of contact for the family. Once parents passed on, contact with siblings ceased as well. Of the seven older men, two (respondents D and F) have no contact with their siblings at all. Respondent D said that although he has many brothers and sisters, quite a few have passed away and he is probably the only one left. Respondent F said,

> "Yes, I have brothers and sisters. But I don't want to talk about them. They have money. If I visit them, they would immediately be afraid that I want to borrow money. They have no heart, that's just how I feel. So I'd rather just be by myself. Forget it."

It seems that fear of his request for financial assistance is the main reason they have lost contact.

Of the five others who expressed reservations about contacting their kin, the contact is at best minimal, usually once a year during the Chinese New Year festival when they may be invited for a feast at one of the siblings' homes, or they may have their nieces and nephews visit them usually with the intention of presenting the older person with a "red packet" containing a monetary gift. This is the experience of the divorced respondent I whose son visits him only once a year. For respondent J who is widowed and who brought up his two daughters in the same flat that he had been living in for the past thirty years, he receives occasional visits from them and his only granddaughter who is eight years old. He contacts his daughter, however, when he needs to go to the clinic. When he had an eye operation a few years ago, he stayed in his daughter's home while recovering.

The tendency for older women to keep a more active kin network compared to the older men has financial implications: the active kin network has protected the older women against financial hardship and has allowed them to stay away from public assistance because they are able to depend on their children or siblings to provide for their financial needs. Besides financial assistance, parallel to Metha's findings in her study of widowhood (this volume), the better social support networks that widows have compared to widowers also help in buffering emotional and social loneliness among the former.

Contact with Non-Kin

In terms of their social network of non-kin such as neighbours and friends, the older women also display a stronger network compared to older men. Respondent B said that she has many friends, and sometimes she stays over at their place for one or two days in a week. Respondent C whose siblings come for a *mahjong* session over the weekends said that she has a group of thirty friends from the same karaoke group she meets on some weekday nights. She sometimes goes for short weekend trips with them to neighbouring countries. Since she became more actively involved with the neighbourhood link centre, she has become busier and has less time for leisure than before.

All the older men responded that they have some friends, mostly their former colleagues, with whom they sometimes meet up. Compared to older women, older men tend to relate the extent of one's network more with one's financial status. As the childless widower (respondent G) said when asked if he had friends, "When we were young, there are many 'friends', why? We earned (money) and there were benefits. Now, we don't earn and there are no benefits." To him, the neighbours are unreliable, as "when you have money, they will treat you better. When you don't have money, they look down on you… No point knowing them".

For respondent F who does not keep in touch with his siblings, friends and neighbours are important to him.

> Sometimes, your friends are better than your own family, let me tell you. It's true. … With friends, you can depend on them for help. For example they will take you to the hospital, and see the doctor.

He has friends who are his former colleagues, whom he sometimes visits at his former workplace. He also knows most of the neighbours, and is especially grateful to one lady who together with her son, brought him to the hospital when he needed to be admitted, and visited him at the hospital. She even invited him to attend a Chinese New Year reunion dinner at her place.

Except for male respondent G, both the older men and women regard their neighbours as an essential part of their social network. Male respondent H maintains a healthy social well-being with the help of three neighbours whom he meets everyday. One female neighbour living on a different floor helps him with the cleaning of the flat and also provides breakfast and lunch. The other two male neighbours help to carry things for him and also to buy dinner for him. They also ensure his well-being by chatting with him on a frequent basis. For male respondent I, many of his neighbours were old neighbours he had known before they were all relocated together to the current block of flats he is living in from a nearby district. He often "hangs out" with them, "… they would look me up to go drink coffee (at the coffee shop). … If you do not go out to eat, drink coffee, talk with friends, it would be very boring to stay at home alone". He refers to themselves as a group who "had no money and no wives, alone. …"; they help each other financially as well, such as by lending small sums of money to each other whenever the need arises.

Female respondent B who sometimes stays over at her friend's place said that whenever she is at home, she will keep her door open "so that my neighbours can keep a look out for me. That is what neighbours are for, we help to look out for each other". She has lived in the same block of flats for twenty-five years and knows many neighbours. Even for female respondent A who has stayed in the flat for only five years, she engages actively in neighbourly exchanges to compensate for the restriction in geographical movement because of her weak legs. According to her, her Malay neighbour who lives next door usually drops by her place to ask if she needs anything whenever he is going grocery shopping. She cooks her own meals every day, but always cooks more so that she is able to pack some food to bring to an 88-year-old female neighbour living on another floor — an act she refers to as an act of a "good neighbour". She claims that she does not have any good friend, but reckons that the 88-year-old "granny" could be considered one since they meet and chat often; this older neighbour would call her on the phone to ask why she was not coming to her place whenever she did not visit her in the afternoon.

Besides casual visits to each other at their homes, they also sometimes meet to chat along the corridor outside their flats, as well as the void deck under their housing block, where benches are found. These are essential social modes for casual chatting or simply for sitting around to while away their time. Since the neighbourhood link centre was set up four years ago, it has also become a space to congregate, especially for older women who do join in the activities, use the exercise equipment available in the premises, and participate in games with the rest.

Older men mentioned spending time with a couple of friends (and neighbours) at the coffee shop, which is the cheapest place for a cup of coffee and food in Singapore. It is apparent that public places like coffee shops have become self-designated spaces for older people in the neighbourhood to spend their waking hours sometimes with a couple of friends, and sometimes alone. In a study of older persons residing in the old housing estate of Tiong Bahru in Singapore, Kong et al. (1996, p. 540) noted the significance of places like coffee shops in the neighbourhood as "physical beacons of social interactions in the elderly's community life". Such "physical beacons" play a role in active ageing of the older persons by providing a social node and enabling the presence of a loose social network among older men.

Various reasons contribute to the active neighbourly network and support in the rental block. First, as an older housing estate, many residents are already long-time residents who have developed relationships with each other over time. Second, mutual help and a supportive spirit are actively kept alive by the older residents themselves who know that as older persons living alone, they need to look out for each other so as to ensure mutual well-being. Such mutual desire for connection promotes active ageing both in terms of enhancing social and mental well-being as well as physical wellness, as it encourages one to become more physically active since they have to move physically in order to meet one another.

The Role and Impact of Social Service Providers

Although the government tries to equip rental blocks populated densely by older people with community care services and support, usually situated at the void decks, the block of rental flats in which the older persons included in this study live in has only been equipped with a neighbourhood link centre operated by a voluntary welfare organization (VWO) and subsidized by the government since 2002.

The neighbourhood link, as the name suggests, is defined to play an expanded role in the community compared to Senior Activity Centres (SACs) which have already been set up in numerous places to support older people living in one-room flats. As stated by the Ministry of Community Development, Youth and Sports, the NL "promotes integration of the older people by creating opportunities for volunteerism and for inter-generational interaction. NLs mobilise community resources to build local support networks for vulnerable and needy residents."[5] This is spelt out in the objectives of the NL, which aims to promote volunteerism in the community so that the residents, both the older and some younger ones, will remain active and engaged. They are called to mobilize community resources in building a local support network for the needy residents to assist the vulnerable residents in obtaining appropriate services to meet their needs, to promote intergenerational interaction among residents in the neighbourhood, and to manage the alert alarm system.

The NL in the field site studied serves nine blocks of flats within a residential zone, out of which only one block is made up of one-room rental flats. It runs a membership system where anyone can join the centre by paying an annual membership fee of S$10. Members can enjoy facilities such as a Health and Fitness Corner, television, newspapers and games, as well as a subsidized rate for activities and outings. Residents living in the one-room rental block enjoy free membership once they register with the NL as members. As of August 2008, the NL had 645 members. There are ten regular activities and classes conducted by the centre including morning exercise programmes, Malay conversational classes, Basic English classes, handicraft, cooking classes, as well as Chinese and Cantonese singing classes. The centre also organizes regular outings and facilitates gatherings and other opportunities for residents, such as providing a place for local groups (such as churches and schools) to interact with the older residents. A local church group, for example, organizes weekly tea gatherings for the older people. The NL also partners with YMCA to provide free lunches five times a week to the needy residents.

For older residents living in the block, the centre also functions as an information and referral point, and a social activity space. It promotes active ageing by encouraging older persons and other residents to volunteer within the community, thereby promoting mutual help and neighbourly support. The centre also runs a Home Visitation Team that is made up of senior volunteers who befriend the older residents through weekly visits. The team currently has ten members whose ages range from 60 to 80 years old. They include some of the more active older residents in the block as well, such as female respondents B and C. For respondent B, she has the 88-year-old respondent H on her list of regular older persons to visit, among others. The NL officers constantly encourage more volunteer engagements from the residents, thus, respondent C feels that she is getting busier these days as sometimes she needs to spend her Saturday mornings to help manage the reception counter of the NL. From November 2008, the NL has set up a thrift shop in the neighbouring block where volunteer workers at the shop will receive 30 per cent of the share of the income. Sixty-seven-year-old respondent D has since become one of the 11 workers who work in shifts to manage the store.

All the respondents agree that the presence of the NL is helpful to them. As the NL is in-charge of the alert alarm system, respondents mentioned specifically about the usefulness of the NL in connection with the alert alarm system. Male respondent I recounted an incident of a neighbour who fell while mopping the floor and pulled the alert alarm cord to inform the NL coordinator who then called for an ambulance to rush him to the hospital. The NL also provides a point of enquiry and help, as male respondent G said, "For example, if we want to get something done, they will help us with it. Without (the NL), who do you turn to for help?" Apart from that, other benefits of the NL include the provision of meals and organized outings and activities. Although the NL strives to promote active ageing by encouraging volunteering and a more active daily life such as to use the NL as a space for frequent gathering, exercises and leisure, the majority of the respondents do not frequent the NL on a daily basis. Only female respondents B and C are volunteering at the NL.

Among the male respondents, a couple or so may go to the centre to read the newspapers, or if they are illiterate, to ask for help in reading the letters they receive (which are usually from the authorities). Some said they sometimes attend the tea gatherings, and would go on outings when there was one. For male respondent F who works odd jobs, he participates in the activities organized by the NL whenever he is free, and he has toured various parts of Singapore as a result of the excursions organized by the NL. None of them participate actively in the regular classes. Male respondent I captures the attractiveness of the NL by saying that he will attend events when there is food provided. Otherwise they do not particularly stay around in the centre or attend regular programmes because for them, "the people are too gossipy there", and "few men are there" which makes them feel uncomfortable. Instead, older men spend time just sitting around at the void deck outside the centre, or gather with a few friends (neighbours) at nearby coffee shops.

Besides activities organized by the NL, it is also common for older persons in the block to be visited by volunteers from Lion's Befrienders. The island-wide befriending service agency aims at reaching out to older persons who are at risk of social isolation, and among the 1,700 older persons they reach out to, 64 per cent are older men. The volunteer service enhances active ageing among older persons by bringing the older persons out on occasional outings such as to watch traditional performances during Chinese New Year and "eating-out" trips.

Older persons also keep active — physically, socially and mentally — through religious activities. The respondents who are Buddhists said that they hardly visit temples, except for male respondent D who visits a Buddhist temple once in a while especially during the Chinese New Year when red packets containing cash are distributed to the older persons. He also visits a church on Sundays with other neighbours as the church provides transport for them, as well as dinner. Despite his weekly church visits, he still regards himself as a Buddhist, but thinks attending the church is interesting, "Following ... all the elderly, just for companionship. If not we sit at home and we might feel lonely".

While older persons living alone may keep active with activities provided by organizations such as Lion's Befrienders and religious organizations, it is evident that the NL plays an integral role in promoting active ageing among the older residents (see Chapters 4 and 7, this volume). Its impact on older persons, however, depends largely on their willingness to participate in the activities organized. Although the respondents in the study do not seem to be active members of the NL, observations at the NL show that older persons, mostly older women do participate in various activities and programmes organized for them such as fitness and exercise programmes, as well as English, karaoke, and art and craft programmes. They also participate in outings and gatherings. Everyday, older residents, mostly female, also gather to play Rammi-O, a foursome table game where they can challenge each other while developing their response to numbers. The NL offers a place for older residents to socialize with others but so far, older women more than older men from the neighbourhood have been found to respond more positively towards this facility.

Physical Activity

The extent of their commitment to regular exercise is one obvious indicator of how active the older persons are in keeping themselves healthy. As most respondents are affected to some extent with various types of illness and ailments, many do not refer to themselves as active in the sense that they exercise regularly. For the few who have "weak legs" or "pain in the legs" which affects their mobility, they are confined mostly in the flat and the apartment block. Female respondent A, for example, finds it hard to walk long distances and, thus, confines her activities largely within her home and visits to neighbours living on a different level of her housing block. To her, physical activities entail doing household chores around the house, such as mopping, sweeping the floor, and cooking. For others who are mobile, quite a number of them mention taking long walks in the neighbourhood in the morning, or doing light stretching exercises in the morning after they wake up. Their exercise activities are characterized by solitary activities which do not involve any group sports which may help expand their social circle. Female respondent C wakes up at five o'clock every morning and heads out for morning exercise by 7 a.m. She takes walks alone below the elevated train tracks. As a result of regular exercise, her active social lifestyle, and healthy social networks with her siblings and friends, she feels that she is still in her fifties although she is already 73 years of age.

In general, even when they are not particularly physically active, most of the respondents are aware of the need to keep an active lifestyle and to exercise, and to take care of themselves (which includes regular medication) so as to maintain their health as far as possible. They are particularly concerned with losing the ability to walk and see the problems relating to mobility as the most worrisome. As female respondent A and male respondent H have shown, a loss or deterioration of ambulatory movement restricts the ability to move out of the flat, which results in what Kong et al. (1996, p. 534) refer to as a "closing of lifespace". Mobility in movement provides the elderly with independence and the ability to get out of the house to be in touch with the outside world. Hence, the ability to walk becomes important among the respondents as a basic condition of their well-being which enables and contributes to their "active ageing".

CONCLUSIONS

At first glance, older residents living in one-room rental flats in Singapore may seem dependent, needy, and isolated. They are the most likely subjects to target individuals and organizations wanting to provide welfare services and provisions for the needy older people. Obviously, some of them tend to keep to themselves, and want little activity in their life, probably because of their state of health, their attitude, personality, and their preference to be left alone. However, a close analysis has shown that many do strive to attain active ageing within their definition of what active ageing means. They actively optimize their security, independence and dignity. The approaches they adopt, however, differ depending on individual resources, and include contacts with their children and relatives, maintaining a social network consisting of friends and neighbours, utilizing available social services, as well as accepting help from religious organizations. It is evident that mutual help and support among neighbours play an important role in enabling older persons to maintain their independence, as well as providing them with opportunities for active engagement. This reveals the importance of interpersonal dynamics within the family and community in contributing to their well-being. Their experiences of networking with friends and neighbours are well documented in the literature, which suggest the importance of friendship, and that good friends and neighbours may be more important than family in old age (Scott and Wenger 1995). Among the Chinese, the game of *mahjong* seems to play a role in promoting "active" social well-being, as it provides opportunities for older persons to get together to do something fun.

The presence of a neighbourhood link centre also plays an important role in providing opportunities for active ageing, such as introducing older residents to volunteering activities, instead of confining their role to that of receiver of assistance. One encouraging example is female respondent C, who found herself transformed from an unhappy mother-in-law to a charitable volunteer, which was one of her pursuits after moving out from her family home to live alone in a flat.

In this study, the data is limited and has a bias towards the male elderly because it is derived from a project focusing on older men living alone in Singapore. Although it is difficult to make generalizations as we studied limited cases, the study nonetheless agrees with the existing literature and with the findings reported in the other chapters in this volume which suggest that older women tend to be better connected in social networks (see Chapter 6, this volume). As a result of their prior experiences in homemaking, older women are often able to cope better with living alone with their skills in housework and cooking. This suggests that while it is generally expected that women fair less positively compared to men in old age, the situation may be reversed depending on circumstances, such as in situations where they face similar vulnerabilities. The strength of women, such as in networking with others, also helps them overcome some of their vulnerabilities and enhances their well-being.

Singapore can expect an increase in the trend towards older persons who will be living alone in the future. Among the reasons for the expected increase are demographic and social-cultural changes, such as a lower birth rate, increased family disharmony and less tolerance in mother-in-law and daughter-in-law conflicts, the increase in the rate of those remaining single in life, and the onset of globalization which has encouraged children to live and work abroad. Attitudinal changes also contribute to the desire to live alone. Findings of a focus group discussion organized by Tsao Foundation has found that more older persons are expressing the desire to live alone, and to grow old in their own home rather than move into a nursing home or live abroad with their children (Lee 2008). At the same time, new policies on housing also contribute towards this trend. On 1 March 2009, the Singapore government newly launched the Lease Buyback Scheme, allowing older Singaporeans owning three-room or smaller flats to sell their lease back to HDB for cash return in the form of a pension. As 25,000 households are said to be eligible for such a scheme, this spells a potential increase in the number of older persons living alone (Chen 2009).

The trend towards older persons living alone has several implications for policy-makers. First, there is a need for more gender-sensitive policy towards older persons, where policies should take into consideration that older men may be disadvantaged differently from older women in situations of similar vulnerabilities. For example, while older women usually cook for themselves even when living alone, older men in lone dwelling tend to rely on outside cooked food or canned food since most do not cook. Especially for older men living alone, services that provide two or three meals on a daily basis will certainly enhance their health and nutrition. Second, it is common knowledge that physical exercise helps in prolonging the functional independence of older persons. The maintenance of functional independence is important especially for older persons living alone since they have no one living with them to provide instantaneous help. Therefore, exercising is essential for these older persons in order to enable them to live alone for a longer period of time and to age gracefully. However, from the example of an NL, we know that there is inadequate emphasis on physical exercise for older persons. Most older persons know the benefits of exercising to maintain functional independence but as the respondents in the study show, they do not really adhere to a routine of doing so. Hence, there is a need to promote greater awareness of exercising during old age. A comprehensive introduction of appropriate exercises for older persons and training to equip social service providers in ageing services with knowledge on how to prolong functional independence among older persons will enable greater numbers of older persons to age gracefully with better health and a heightened sense of well-being. Third, as social services such as the NL which are in close proximity to the dwellings of older persons living alone have shown to be beneficial towards older persons in promoting their active ageing and well-being, housing policies for both older and newer housing estates should take into consideration the construction of more of such facilities in the community. The government has recently announced that 22 Senior Activity Centres will be built in rental blocks to serve the low-income and vulnerable older residents. By 2013, there will be a total number of 41 Senior Activity Centres island-wide.[6] These centres will continue to face the challenge of attracting older men to participate more actively in their daily activities and services. Thus, there is a need for a more thorough study to understand the differing needs of older men and women so that both the new and existing centres may serve the older residents more effectively.

In a study of the quality of life of older persons in Singapore, Wong (2003) emphasized the importance of financial security in old age and pre-retirement planning. However, she also found that older persons from the lowest income group and living in the smallest and cheapest housing expressed higher satisfaction levels compared to some of the older persons who were financially more well-off. Wong (2003, p. 315) suggests that "there are some elements in the quality of life that out-weigh the financial aspects". The older men and women living alone in a rental block have certainly shown that they have discovered other "elements in the quality of life" as they found ways to engage in active ageing which contribute to their well-being and quality of life within their present living environment, and financial and health limitations. Older women, however, seem to have achieved this better than older men, suggesting that there is a need to enhance opportunities for a healthier and more socially active life for some older persons living alone.

Notes

1. The data for this chapter is derived from a project collaborated with Fei Yue Community Services and funded by Mitsui-Sumitomo Welfare Fund. The author thanks Emily Lim and Letitia Thng who have assisted in collecting data for this project. Many thanks also to the staff of the Neighbourhood Link Centre for their assistance. Last but not least, my utmost gratitude to the seniors who have kindly shared with us their life experiences through the interviews.
2. "More S'poreans Eligible for Public Assistance with Relaxed Criteria", Channel NewsAsia, 5 March 2008. Available at <http://www.channelnewsasia.com/stories/singaporelocalnews/view/333089/1/.html> (accessed 20 July 2009).
3. See <http://www.getformesingapore.com/previous2005/300805_reviewofhousingoptionsfortheelderly_more.htm> (accessed 18 December 2008).
4. See <http://www.straitstimes.com/STI/STIMEDIA/pdf/20080818/rally_part2.pdf> (accessed 18 December 2008).
5. See <http://app.mcys.gov.sg/web/corp_press_story.asp?szMod=corp&szSubMod=press&qid=834> (accessed 18 December 2008).
6. "$18 Million to Develop Community-based Care Ad Support Services for Seniors and Their Caregivers", MCYS Media Release no: 04/2009, issued on 5 February 2009. Available at <http://app.mcys.gov.sg/web/corp_press_stroy.asp> (accessed 13 March 2009).

References

Chan, A., Ng T.P. and M. Niti. "The Determinants of Self-Rated Mental Health among Older Adults in Singapore". *Hallym International Journal of Aging* 8, no. 1 (2006): 65–81.

Chen, Gabriel. "HDB Lease Buyback Scheme Launched". *The Straits Times*, 2 March 2009.

Chia, Ngee Choon. "The Central Provident Fund and Financing Retirement Needs of Elderly Singaporeans". In *Ageing in Southeast and East Asia: Family, Social Protection and Policy Challenges*, edited by Lee H.G. Singapore: Institute of Southeast Asian Studies, 2008.

Chia, Ngee Choon, Shawna S.E. Lim and Angelique Chan. "Feminization of Aging and Long Term Care in Singapore". Department of Economics, SCAPE Working Paper Series, 6 March. National University of Singapore, 2008.

Available at <http://nt2.fas.nus.edu.sg/ecs/pub/wp-scape/0806.pdf> (accessed 20 July 2009).

Chou, K.L., A.H.Y. Ho and I. Chi. "Living Alone and Depression in Chinese Older Adults". *Aging and Mental Health* 10 (2006): 583–91.

Chou, K.L. and I. Chi. "Comparison between Elderly Chinese Living Alone and Those Living with Others". *Journal of Gerontological Social Work* 33, no. 4 (2000): 51–66.

Department of Statistics. *General Household Survey 2005, Statistical Release 2: Transport, Overseas Travel, Households and Housing Characteristics.* Singapore: Department of Statistics, 2006. Available at <http://www.singstat.gov.sg/pubn/popn/ghsr2.html> (accessed 26 February 2011).

Findlay, R.A. "Interventions to Reduce Social Isolation amongst Older People: Where is the Evidence?" *Ageing & Society* 23 (2003): 647–58.

Goh Chin Lian. "MPs: Plug Loopholes for Rental Flats". *The Straits Times*, 23 August 2008.

Klinenberg, Eric M. *Heat Wave: A Social Autopsy of Disaster in Chicago.* Chicago: University of Chicago Press, 2002.

————. "Dying Alone: The Social Production of Urban Isolation". In *The Sociology of Health and Illness: Critical Perspectives*, edited by P. Conrad. New York: Worth Publishers, 2005.

Knodel, J. and M.B. Ofstedal. "Gender and Aging in the Developing World: Where are the Men?" *Population and Development Review* 29, no. 4 (2003): 677–98.

Kong, L., B. Yeoh and P. Teo. "Singapore and the Experience of Place in Old Age". *Geographical Review* 86, no. 4 (1996): 529–49.

Kua, E.H. and C. Hong. "Attempted Suicide by Elderly Chinese in Singapore". *Psychogeriatrics* 3 (2003): 78–81.

Larsson, K. and M. Silverstein. "The Effects of Marital and Parental Status on Informal Support and Service Utilization: A Study of Older Swedes Living Alone". *Journal of Aging Studies* 18, no. 2 (2004): 231–44.

Lee, Hui Chieh. "Programme Ensures Elderly Voices are Heard". *The Straits Times*, 13 November 2008.

Scott, Anne and G. Clare Wenger. "Gender and Social Support Networks in Later Life". In *Connecting Gender and Ageing: A Sociological Approach*, edited by S. Arber and J. Ginn. Buckingham: Open University Press, 1995.

Tan, T. "More Elderly People Want to Live Alone". *The Straits Times*, 21 June 2005.

Tsao Foundation. "Women and Aging: Various Issues of Concern". Available at <http://www.tsaofoundation.org/incomeSecurity.html> (accessed 15 December 2008).

Wong, G.K.M. "Quality of Life of the Elderly in Singapore's Multi-Racial Society". *International Journal of Social Economics* 30, no. 3 (2003): 302–19.

World Health Organization (WHO). "Active Ageing: A Policy Framework". A contribution of the WHO to the Second United Nations World Assembly on Ageing, Madrid, Spain, April 2002. Available at <http://whqlibdoc.who.int/hq/2002/WHO_NMH_NPH_02.8.pdf> (accessed 23 June 2008).

Yap, L.K.P., S.Y.L. Au, Y.H. Ang, K.Y. Kwan, S.C. Ng and G. Chen. "Who are the Residents of a Nursing Home in Singapore?" *Singapore Medical Journal* 44, no. 2 (2003): 65–75.

9

ETHNIC PATTERNS AND STYLES OF ACTIVE AGEING AMONG WIDOWS AND WIDOWERS IN SINGAPORE[1]

Kalyani K. Mehta

The literature on widows and widowers has focused mostly on coping and adjustment aspects as well as factors that have enhanced the adaptation of the surviving spouse to the newly achieved status of widow or widower (Lopata 1973, 1987, 1996; Silverman 1986; Utz et al. 2002; Chambers 2005). It has been reiterated that gender is a mediating factor that explains different strategies of adjustment, and that socio-cultural or contextual influences have a bearing on the choices made by the surviving spouses. Against this scenario, a multi-disciplinary research project titled "Widowhood: The Asian Experience" was undertaken on widows and widowers age 50 years and above in Singapore in 1997–2000, funded by the National University of Singapore, because of a lack of research on this particular age group.[2]

THE SINGAPORE CONTEXT

According to the Singapore Census of Population 1990 and 2000, there were 127,300 widows and 129,200 widowers in Singapore

(Singapore Census of Population 1990 Release No. 1: 51 and Singapore Census of Population 2000 Advanced Release No. 8: 1). While widowhood is not related to chronological age, the demographics show that the majority of widowed persons belong to the age group 50 years and above. Two key points should be mentioned here. First, Singapore is a rapidly ageing society and the percentage of its population 65 years and above will increase from 7 per cent in 1999 to 19 per cent in 2030 (Inter-Ministerial Report on the Ageing Population 1999). Second, because of the gender differentials in life expectancy and the fact that women tend to marry men older than themselves, the phenomenon of "feminization" of ageing occurs, that is, in the older age groups women form the majority. Owing to these two demographic factors, there are a larger number of widows as compared to widowers above the age of 65 years in Singapore. The proportion ratio is about 5:1 (Singapore Census of Population 2010).

Cohort and historical factors explain the relatively high incidence of foreign-born elderly in the category above 65 years, as well as their relatively low educational levels. The educational profile of elders between 65 and 74 years shows that 89.2 per cent had primary level and below educational attainment in 1995; however, this figure was expected to decrease to 71.2 per cent in 2010 (IMC Report on the Ageing Population 1999, p. 31). Because of social and cultural attitudes, women among the current generation of elders of 65 years and above have had fewer opportunities to be educated as compared to their male counterparts.

The foresight and vision of the Singapore government led to the formulation of National Policies for the Ageing Population from 1995 with the passing of the Maintenance of Parents Act (Mehta 2002). A slew of other policies were introduced, and in 2001 the first Masterplan of Eldercare Services was released. Healthcare policies and planning have also been a high priority, as the speed of ageing of the population requires a commensurate momentum of development of healthcare services (Mehta and Vasoo 2001). Apart from acute care and medical insurance schemes, long-term care services (both family-oriented and community-oriented) were focused on, so that a multi-pronged approach could be applied. This is in keeping with the "Many Helping Hands" policy of the Singapore government, wherein family, community, and the state are partners in the eldercare industry (for more details, see Mehta 2000).

There is a strong need for more gerontological research to be conducted in Singapore, hence the impetus to conduct a study on the conditions of widows and widowers, as well as to focus on the Asian experience. The other aims of the research were to uncover: (a) what were the enhancing and hindering factors for adjustment in widowhood? (b) what strategies were used by the sample in coping with their "new" status? (c) what ethno-cultural factors influence the adjustment patterns to widowhood status? Furthermore, the research aimed to explore gender differences in the coping responses as well as the resources available to the respondents.

In view of the aims of the research, a quantitative-cum-qualitative methodology was conceived so that the experiences of the respondents could be comprehensively captured in the data. This chapter elaborates on the findings of the qualitative data, that is, the 25 interviews conducted with 7 widowers and 18 widows. The ethnic distribution is as follows: 16 Chinese, 6 Malay and 3 Indians. The youngest respondent was aged 50 years and the oldest was 80 years. The average age of the respondents was 65.3 years.

THEORETICAL PERSPECTIVE

Moving away from the discourse of coping and adjustment, this chapter aims to hone in on the "reproductive work" that widows carry out inside and outside the home. Brydon and Chant (1989, pp. 10–11) divide reproduction into three types, namely, biological, physical and social reproduction. In this regard, biological reproduction (that is, childbirth) is usually irrelevant for older widows, but physical (that is, household work and babysitting) and social reproduction (that is, maintenance of the social and economic status quo) are applicable. Can housework be classified as an "active ageing" type of activity? The WHO framework of active ageing has been adopted in many countries, including Singapore, and the Singapore government tries to encourage all older people to remain engaged socially with their family and community. Yet, can housework be considered part of active ageing? More discussion on this will be included later in the chapter.

As mentioned earlier, the aims of the research included looking at the factors that "enabled" and/or "hindered" adjustment to widowhood. Concepts that were relevant were "social support" (including formal and informal) and "civic engagement", for instance, volunteer work. It must be remembered that social support can be bi-directional and consists of different types such as instrumental, emotional, financial and informational (Gottlieb 1981). Erik Erikson's (1963, 1985) eight psychosocial stages of development may be applied in the analysis of the research, as the widowed persons were seeking a new identity for themselves, and in the process were finding meaning in relationships with new friends and the younger generation, such as their grandchildren. The crisis of "generativity versus stagnation" was faced by the respondents and their handling of this life transition reflected their choice — whether to be contented with "being" or to surge forwards towards "becoming". For those at the later age, such as above 75 years, their crisis was inclined towards "integrity versus despair". Erik Erikson emphasizes the importance of contentment/satisfaction and lack of fear of death as two important indicators of "integrity". Keeping in mind these theoretical concepts, we move on to the sample characteristics and research findings.

While there were no clear gender differences, all those who self-reported that their health was "Not Good" were women. In addition, all the widows and widowers except for six respondents, five of whom were widows, had at least one chronic illness, for example, hypertension, diabetes or arthritis.

It is to be noted that while the majority of the respondents had financial and health vulnerabilities, most of them felt satisfied with their lives. There may have been some response bias as they may have perceived the need to indicate contentment, since most of them lived with their family members. Only two were living alone, and one respondent was living with a friend. From the perspective of a non-Singaporean, the question arises of what the role of the state is in looking after widows and widowers who are vulnerable.

From the global context, there is growing pressure from grey lobby groups on governments to increase welfare spending on this fast expanding segment of the population. In Singapore, the Asian cultural values prescribe that elders should be looked after by their families, especially their adult children. The family-oriented policies of the government echo this ideological position. In the current scenario of an economic recession, are family members able to cope with the financial and other responsibilities of parental care? What about the seniors who are childless? The Singapore government negotiates this situation by providing financial schemes for the low income elders, and financial subsidies and supplements through various means such as the Central Provident Fund (CPF) (a National Provident Fund in which each working adult has an individual account, see <www.mycpf.cpf.gov.sg> for more details), Silver Medifund (an endowment fund which caters to those seniors who are unable to pay their hospitalization bills), and Parent Tax Relief for adult children caring for their parents or parents-in-law.

TABLE 9.1
Sample Characteristics of Respondents

Characteristics	% (n=25)
AGE	
50–55	16
56–60	16
61–65	24
66–70	16
71–75	8
76–80	20
RELIGION	
Buddhist	16
Christian	24
Muslim	24
Hindu	12
Taoist	20
Free Thinker	4
SELF-REPORTED HEALTH	
Excellent	16
Good	20
Fair	32
Not Good	32
LIFE SATISFACTION	
Satisfied	80
A little satisfied	16
Not satisfied	4
SOURCES OF INCOME	
Children/family	84
Savings	36
CPF	12
Salary	12
Insurance/Pension	16
Rental	4
Voluntary Welfare	4
Government aid	4

(the answers are not exclusive, hence the total is more than 100%)

SELF-REPORTED COPING LEVEL	
Very Well	16
Well	32
Just Managed	40
Not well	12

Source: "Widowhood: An Asian Perspective" (2000) (author's data).

THEMATIC ANALYSIS

Gender-Based Reproductive Activities

Across the three ethnic groups, women were more involved in household chores such as cooking, cleaning, laundry, and babysitting their grandchildren. The widowers were not chauvinistic since they performed some household tasks. They mentioned tasks that they carried out such as mopping, marketing/grocery shopping, and bringing the grandchildren to and from school. However, they did not spend as much time on these types of activities as their female counterparts. As found in much of the sociological literature, females are presumed to be more suited to the domestic life and they are seen to be more nurturing "by nature". What is interesting to note is that the widows capitalized on their lifelong skills, for example, culinary skills, and utilized them to their advantage. At a later stage in life, the significance of domestic work is revalued, and from the interviews, it seemed that the skills associated with it could become a "capital" for the seniors, as they use this capital to contribute towards their families, thus enabling the active ageing process.

In Singapore, the dual income couple is common among families. Here, the grandmother becomes a crucial figure in caregiving arrangements for young children. Other options that are available to the working couple are childcare centres and foreign guest workers or live-in foreign maids. Nevertheless, grandparents are still the favoured choice of young parents as seen by the increase in grandparents minding grandchildren from 19 per cent in 1995 (National Survey of Senior Citizens 1995) to 34.4 per cent in 2005 (National Survey of Senior Citizens 2005). As mentioned in an earlier article (Teo and Mehta 2001), widows participated as active agents who strategically planned a useful and critical role for themselves within the domestic realm. In this qualitative data set, two widows and one widower were still employed. Since they were still healthy, they felt that working outside the domestic sphere kept them active and engaged with the rest of society. As a result, they had a different lifestyle from the rest. The employed respondents played a less important role in the domestic and caregiving responsibilities, as compared to the retired widows and widowers. The former were more financially independent, spent more time with colleagues and friends, and were able to pursue their hobbies and interests.

Bereavement and grief can be very traumatic, and one of the ways the respondents coped with their journey was by keeping busy with work and family responsibilities. They contributed to their families with altruism and devotion, especially towards their grandchildren.

"When she (daughter-in-law) was pregnant, I made tonic food for her. Thus, all my grandchildren are healthy. One was even a champion in a baby contest! I told them (children) to save the money from hiring someone to take care of them after their labour. I would cook for them to eat". (Chinese widow, 69 years)

"Life is like that. You need to take things easy and be an easy-going mother. Don't worry so much. You will have less problems. If you treat a person nice such as your daughter or daughter-in-law, they will also treat you nicely". (Chinese widow, 65 years)

From the above-mentioned quotes, we can elicit the deep sense of love for family, and that relationships between family members are based on the reciprocal principle. What is exchanged may be in tangible or intangible ways, but the intention to reciprocate and respect the other is key to any supportive relationship.

Ethnic-based coping strategies

The following table summarizes the actions and activities that widows and widowers participated in to meet their needs.

TABLE 9.2
Needs and Behavioural Strategies of Widows and Widowers

Needs	Behavioural Strategy
To handle loneliness	Reading, watching TV, participate in *tai chi* or *qigong* or yoga, make handicrafts, travel, keep a pet, *mahjong*
Be productive (useful to family and society)	Looking after grandchildren, doing housework, community activities, voluntary work, teach in religious class
Financial needs	Employment, family support, approach organizations
Social and emotional needs	Family members, friends, relatives, neighbours, "adopted children", renewing friendships and making new friends
Spiritual needs	Prayer, chanting, reading religious books, singing religious verses, visiting place of worship e.g. church, mosque or temple
Family adjustment	Positive attitude, non-interference in children's and children-in-law's lives, self-reliance and self-care, grand-parenting

Source: "Widowhood: An Asian Perspective" (2000) (author's data).

Some activities were common in all the three ethnic groups. These activities were watching television, household chores, babysitting grandchildren, reading, walking, going out with friends and relatives such as siblings, handicraft making, meeting neighbours, and window shopping. However, there were also distinct culture-specific activities and these were:

(a) The Chinese were involved in health-related activities such as *tai chi* and *qigong*.

   Mahjong and calligraphy were also mentioned popularly by Chinese respondents.

   Interestingly, only the Chinese respondents mentioned gardening, senior citizen centres, Chinese opera singing, and pet-rearing as recreational activities. One widow did volunteer work in a hospital, and another in church programmes.

(b) The Malays were more concerned with spiritual pursuits such as prayer rituals five times a day, attending religious classes, and involvement in *marhaban* singing groups. Picnics and fishing were favourite pastimes.

(c) Like the Malays, the three Indian widows became more involved in religious pursuits after they were widowed, but they visited Hindu temples while the Malays, who were Muslims visited mosques. Joining yoga classes and community activities were other hobbies.

> "Since I joined the community centre I don't feel lonely. Every now and then I go there. We don't gamble. We have meetings, we decide to go. Last night we had a meeting to decide that this Sunday we are selling toys. We give the money to charity". (Chinese widow, 80 years)

> "When we feel troubles, we should say some prayers. Read the Quran. In this house, when I am tired, I would sleep. If not, I would take a walk. Religion is important. Never skip your daily five prayers". (Malay widower, 69 years)

> "Before marriage, I used to be quite active in the temple — going there and singing religious songs. But after marriage, I stopped religious singing. Then I used to go to temples with my family. After my husband's death, I started to go for religious classes in addition to the temple ... and then, slowly from there, I started teaching in religious class in temples". (Indian widow, 53 years)

The quotes above illustrate the ethno-cultural influences in the choices made by the respondents to spend their time meaningfully. As the widowers and widows tried to redefine their social identity, there was their personal identity that remained constant, that is, their cultural selves, as well as their inclinations towards certain types of pursuits. Cultural gerontologists have analysed the effects of ethnic culture on behaviour and rituals, so in our study of adaptation to one's life after the loss of spouse, it is to be expected that cultural scripts of widowhood as well as of ageing would emerge. There were no striking gender differences between the choices of activities and hobbies within the respective cultural groups. However, in relation to seeking help for their financial needs, women were more forthcoming in requesting for help than men. For widowers, perhaps the sense of pride and acknowledgement of their own failure to be self-supporting were psychological barriers in reaching out for help.

The enabling and hindering factors

Analysis of the qualitative interviews revealed the enabling and hindering factors that featured in the lives of the respondents. The reader is cautioned that these factors are not exhaustive neither are they representative of the entire older Singaporean population. This is because of the limited sample size of the study. However, they are typical of the reality faced by widows and widowers of the current cohort of older people. The case profiles illustrate the life conditions of widowed Singaporeans as well as the challenges they face.

For example, a few of the respondents expressed that they face societal stigma and may be excluded from festivities such as wedding ceremonies. For the widows in the current generation of elders, remarriage was not a real option as reflected in the quote below:

> "I follow the traditional Chinese teaching where a woman could not remarry after her husband died". (Chinese widow, 62 years)

The topic of remarriage has been discussed at length in another publication (Mehta 2002) so it will not be elaborated here in detail. Suffice to say that despite the modern and progressive Singaporean image, there are still some traditional attitudes that have a salient presence. This is the negative attitude towards remarriage of widows, but not widowers. One caveat is that in the Malay Muslim community, remarriage of widows is not frowned upon. In cultures such as among the Malays, gender differences in remarriage are not as visible as in the patriarchal cultures of the Chinese and the Indians. The research, which focused on older widows and widowers, highlighted the overlapping of culture and gender in the societal lens towards the phenomenon of remarriage of widows and widowers. We shall now turn to the enabling and hindering factors that influenced the adjustment of widows and widowers.

The enabling factors were close relationships with friends and relatives, financial stability, physical mobility, familiar neighbourhood, and a sense of satisfaction with the earlier marital life. In sum, social support and economic security are important factors that provide the "buffering effect" as the widows and widowers grappled with spousal loss. The hindering factors, in contrast, include change in residence, financial hardship, physical disability, social isolation, legal problems, and sudden death of spouse. The last factor created disturbing memories which made the journey of recovery more difficult.

It should be noted that the respondents with larger resources at their disposal such as savings, a good job, a close-knit social support network, and links with community organizations were at an advantage over those who did not have these resources, which tended to increase their vulnerability.

Gendered vulnerabilities

The accumulated effects of gender, life course, cohort and cultural contexts have resulted in the life circumstances of the 25 respondents. Gender and cohort effects explain the advantage that widowers have had in terms of higher levels of education and financial security. However, the younger widows, that is, between 50 and 58 years had higher economic resources than the older widows and, therefore, were at an advantage.

Life course trajectories have very important long-term effects in old age, as pointed out elsewhere (for example, Chambers 2005) and it is recommended that the consequences of widowhood be studied within the biography of the person. For instance, the presence or absence of social support networks, quality of family relationships, and resources available in old age are all indirectly connected to the earlier life history of the individual. O'Bryant and Hansson (1995, p. 453) state:

> The lifespan developmental orientation (Baltes 1987) might provide a useful model for understanding adaptation among widowed persons. This orientation assumes that development is a lifelong, anormative process, and the specific developmental changes are highly variable with respect to timing, magnitude and directionality of the change.

The individualization of coping styles, dispositions, and resources helps us understand how each individual's adjustment to widowhood is variable. In the sample, there was a widow who lived with a friend as she had a history of poor relationships with her adult children; in another case, the respondent was forced to stay with her son and his family as he was not willing to sell the flat which was co-owned by her and him.

It was indeed an eye-opening experience for the author to listen to the life stories of the widows and widowers, and to appreciate the second layer of cultural influence (on top of the individual experience) which was both extrinsic and intrinsic to the widowhood experience. Cultural beliefs such as filial piety and their application by adult children explained to a large extent the predominant living arrangement of the sample which was "living with family". Earlier studies on the Singapore older population (Mehta 1995; Mehta and Thang 2006; Mehta 2007) have documented the continuing pattern of multi-generational living as the most common living arrangement of Singaporean older people. However, with the passing away of one of the elderly family members, the dynamics change, and the entire family is reorganized.

> In general, older women have fewer economic resources but more social resources and richer more intimate relationships than do older men.
>
> (Hooyman and Kiyak 2002, p. 496)

The widows in the sample had better social support networks than did the widowers (see Chapters 6 and 8, this volume). This explains the higher levels of emotional and social loneliness among males. Campbell and Silverman (1996, p. 8) focused on widowers and they said, "The problem seems to be that most men lack extensive community contacts, in contrast to women who are widowed." To put it simply, men lack social resources while women lack economic resources, and each group finds ways to compensate for their deficits. However, with economic resources, men can be in a better position to assert their independence in decision-making.

Before concluding this section, I would like to emphasize that widowers may wish to extend their social networks and widows may wish to go out and find a job, but opportunities may be lacking. Lamme et al. (1996) have extrapolated on this idea in their article regarding formation of new relationships following widowhood. In their article, they also pointed out the importance of disposition together with opportunities. Globally, the concept of active ageing is premised on maximizing opportunities for work, leisure, social and recreation pursuits. This research suggests that there are constraints such as employer's attitudes, accessibility of recreational and social programmes, and societal expectations that limit the opportunities for economic and social engagement by widow(er)s.

The sociocultural context as well as political economic structure of the society open up or close opportunities for older people. In an ageist society, work or social opportunities may shrink owing to stereotypes about ageing persons and what cultural expectations hold. For instance, if adult children feel that their parents should care for the young grandchildren, then the older person would have resistance from the former if he/she wishes to be employed. Do older parents and parents-in-law contest these norms and expectations? Living in a family context implies the need for the older members to negotiate and accommodate. Each family is unique in the way it resolves intergenerational issues. Hence, in some families the older person may stop work until the grandchildren start schooling. Once the grandchildren are independent, if they still are healthy and wish to work, they may resume full-time work. In other cases, the older generation may work part-time and when they are at work, the grandchildren may go to a childcare centre. Another example is when an older person wishes to seek companionship through remarriage but fears the backlash of criticism from relatives and friends as societal attitudes do not condone remarriage by people in late life. In the sample, there was one lady who did not remarry as her adult children did not react positively to the idea. Thus, behavioural strategies of coping with widowhood are embedded in the sociocultural context and societal attitudes towards older people.

DISCUSSION

How vulnerable widows and widowers are depends on the four factors analysed above as well as the opportunities available and societal attitudes towards older persons. The most striking conclusion from the qualitative interviews was that the widows and widowers all demonstrated agency in crafting a meaningful life for themselves by applying their strengths and wisdom gained over their lifetime. They shared their personal life experiences generously, thus involving the interviewer in their struggles, dilemmas as well as achievements. The respondents in the sample shared the lessons they had gained from their lives, for example, one said:

> "I think it is about the way you take it personally and how you are going to live your life. For me, I am not going to mourn and stay at home and cry about it. ... It is fate. I consider that I am still young. If I have to be a widow, I will be a widow. It is not my choice. I leave it to God, whatever plans he has for me. I just take it a day at a time. My life now is OK. I do community work. My children are good to me".
>
> (Chinese widow, 50 years)

As mentioned earlier, the majority of widows were engaged in household chores and babysitting their grandchildren. This was to a great extent the life course and cohort effect of their social world which has been focused on the domestic sphere. Focusing their energy on the domestic sphere was also a strategy to remain useful and productive rather than becoming a burden to their families. Feminist theory has addressed this in the literature particularly from the viewpoint of political economy and gender distribution of roles within the family and societal spheres (Chambers 2005). This research found that given the limited resources that the widows had, it made good sense to capitalize on their strengths, for example, culinary skills, to carve a critical space for themselves in the household. In this way, the widows not only won the love and affection of their grandchildren, but they also wove a social safety net for their old age! One caveat is that although in most cases their efforts were appreciated, there were a couple of cases wherein their contributions were taken for granted. It is therefore the author's contention that the active ageing movement in Singapore should recognize domestic contribution by older people as part of the process of active ageing, and not relegate this kind of "work" to a less worthy status.

While the loss of a lifelong companion, that is, spouse, can be very devastating, it can also be seen as the crossroads for a new chapter wherein development and new identities are forthcoming. Whether this can be likened to the emergence of the Chrysallis (Adlersberg and Thorne 1990) or classified as "generativity" (Coleman and O'Hanlon 2004, p. 53), the outcome is that of better social and psychological well-being for the elderly. In the sample, there was one lady who had written her autobiography and had her book published. Another was very passionate about her calligraphy, while a third was working as a masseuse (she massaged ladies who had recently given birth and since the skills are very specialized, she had a thriving business!).

As mentioned in the earlier section, there were some hindering factors that prevented positive adjustment to widowhood, and we shall examine them at this point. When the widowed person is "forced" to change his/her residence perhaps because of need (for instance, the surviving spouse may have to move in with an adult child after living independently for most of her life) or had to shift residence because her adult child with whom she coresided wanted to move to a more desirable flat, the outcome tended to be negative. This is understandable as the spousal loss and the environmental change occur in close temporal proximity and the person is unable to adapt. Nair (2005, p. 110) expresses this as follows:

> Space plays an important role in an older person's life. The phenomenon of shrinking physical and social space as people age is well known. ... In many cases, the home space is where they have lived for a considerable length of time and which has much emotional and physical meaning for them. Even though some home-dwelling older people may need support from families or community care agencies for activities of daily living, they may still feel they are in control of their lives. This feeling is very important for them.

The concept of "ageing in place" has been reiterated by many scholars, but for the people entering widowhood, it takes on a new meaning. Rowles (2005) has elaborated on the concepts of "physical insideness", "social insideness" and "autobiographical insideness" (Peace, Holland and Kellaher 2005, as cited in Andrews and Phillips 2005, p. 194) reflecting that the attachment an individual has with the place in which he/she lives is beyond sentimentality. It has a direct link with the internal processes such as identity, mastery, legacy, and integration. Hence, it is very important for family members to understand the trauma of shifting residence on a widowed person, particularly at the initial stages. In the Asian context, it may be with good intentions that a filial son or daughter suggests that the surviving parent moves in with him/her but the impact on the parent has to be weighed against the potential benefit(s) of family context.

The second hindering factor, financial hardship is self-explanatory. Lack of financial resources may handicap the surviving spouse and force him/her to change one's lifestyle and even food choices. The attendant effects on physical and mental health, social life (because of cutting down on social activities and transport costs) and self-esteem do not need much elaboration. Widows have been highly represented among the poor in many parts of the world, and Singapore is no exception. It has been found in previous studies that widowhood pushes women below the poverty line especially if they lack social support and are not aware of the social services available. In some rare cases, cultural attitudes prevent the widows from seeking help from government agencies as it would 'shame' the rest of the family members. There was one case of a widow in the sample who was on government welfare assistance. She stated that she had no choice but to seek government help, as her children were also poor and she did not want to "burden" them further. Most of the other widows depended on family members, for example, siblings, friends, and religious organizations, for example, churches and non-governmental organizations for financial help.

The solace gained by the respondents in turning to their religious faith in coping with their grief was apparent in at least half of the sample. In the Asian context, religious practices, for example, prayer, visiting places of worship, chanting religious verses, attending religious classes, and reading religious books, are coping behaviours of older persons that have stood the test of time and added meaning in their lives. These were also channels by which they stayed active, as they kept in touch with others who adhered to the same religion and felt that their time was well spent. Thus, their well-being improved and their positive adjustment was supported.

CONCLUSION

Drawing from the above discussion, future research should test the enabling and hindering factors on a larger multi-ethnic sample of Singaporeans. The current research has fleshed out some insights that could be further validated or otherwise be used to push the boundaries of the stock of knowledge on this subject. It must be mentioned that the research findings are indicative but not generalizable because of the small sample size, and the exclusion of respondents from nursing homes. The study focused on community-based widowed people as the majority of this population is found outside residential institutions. However, it is suggested that in future, researchers could focus on residents in nursing homes and sheltered homes for older persons, to examine the opportunities for being active within their living environment.

A large bulk of the literature on widowhood has emerged from Western countries, where the value of independence is held to be premium. However, in Asian societies the value of "interdependence" between generations is held to be premium. This idea of whether promotion of the value of "independence" may actually lead to added pressure on the widow or widower to lead an independent lifestyle is explored by O'Bryant (1991). In contrast to the international context, the author believes that in most Asian societies, older people have been socialized to uphold the value of "interdependence" in the family sphere and that explains their choices of coping strategies, adaptation methods, and lifestyle. In the Singapore context, more research is needed to capture the fluid value changes taking place within the family arena to understand social changes.

Gender, culture, and ageing were found to be interwoven threads that flowed through the lives of the respondents in the study. The experience of widowhood in later life was a gendered reality; however, the gender differences were not the same for individuals in the three major ethnic cultures. This was particularly in regard to how society viewed the idea of remarriage for widows and widowers. Were widows more vulnerable than widowers? Upon examination of the enabling and the hindering factors to positive adjustment, it was concluded that financially the widows were worse off, but socially they were better off. Through their contributions towards their families, the widows on the whole were able to garner the love and gratitude of their family members. By capitalizing on their strengths and their life experiences, the widows used their "agency" and did not remain passive and dependent, although this was determined to a great extent by their health status and family relationships. The effects of the historical period and cohort affiliation should be kept in mind, as future cohorts of widows and widowers are likely to be better educated, and therefore their contributions would stretch beyond the family sphere. Hence, future research on the baby boomer generation's experience of widowhood is suggested, as it would be interesting to compare the findings with this study.

Notes

1. The author wishes to acknowledge research funding provided by National University of Singapore (RP 3960043) for the project titled "Widowhood: An Asian Experience" (2000).
2. A free thinker may be defined as someone who does not have a religious affiliation but believes in the existence of a supernatural being.

References

Adlersberg, M. and S. Thorne. "Emerging from the Chrysalis: Older Widows in Transition". *Journal of Gerontological Nursing* 16, no. 1 (1990): 4–7.

Andrews, Gavin J. and David R. Phillips, eds. *Ageing and Place: Perspectives, Policy, Practice.* London: Routledge, 2005.

Baltes, P.B. "Theoretical Propositions of Lifespan Developmental Psychology: On the Dynamics between Growth and Decline". *Developmental Psychology* 23, issue 5 (1987): 611–26.

Brydon, Lynne and Sylvia H. Chant. *Women in the Third World: Gender Issues in Rural and Urban Areas.* Aldershot: Edward Elgar, 1989.

Campbell, Scott and Phyllis R. Silverman. *Widower: When Men are Left Alone.* Amityville, N.Y.: Baywood, 1996.

Central Provident Fund of Singapore website. Available at <http://mycpf.cpf.gov.sg> (accessed 14 December 2008).

Chambers, Pat. *Older Widows and the Life Course: Multiple Narratives of Hidden Lives.* Aldershot, Hants, U.K.: Ashgate, 2005.

Coleman, Peter and Ann O'Hanlon. *Ageing and Development: Theories and Research.* London: Arnold, 2004.

Erikson, Erik. *Childhood and Society,* 2nd ed. New York: W.W. Norton, 1963.

———. *The Life Cycle Completed: A Review.* New York: W.W. Norton, 1985.

Gottlieb, Benjamin H. *Social Networks and Social Support.* Beverly Hills, California: Sage, 1981.

Hooyman, Nancy R. and H. Asuman Kiyak. *Social Gerontology: A Multidisciplinary Perspective,* 6th ed. Boston: Allyn and Bacon, 2002.

Inter-Ministerial Report on the Ageing Population. Singapore: Ministry of Community Development, 1999.

Lamme, S., P.A. Dykstra and M.I. Broese Van Groenou. "Rebuilding the Network: New Relationships in Widowhood". *Personal Relationships* 3 (1996): 337–49.

Lopata, Helena Z. *Widowhood in an American City.* Cambridge, MA.: Schenkman, 1973.

———. *Widows.* Durham, North Carolina: Duke University Press, 1987.

———. *Current Widowhood: Myths and Realities.* Thousand Oaks, California: Sage, 1996.

Mehta, Kalyani. "Caring for the Elderly in Singapore". In *Who Should Care for the Elderly? An East-West Value Divide*, edited by W.T. Liu and H. Kendig. Singapore: Singapore University Press and World Scientific, 2000.

———. "Perceptions of Remarriage by Widowed People in Singapore". *Ageing International* 27, no. 40 (2002): 93–107. Special Issue on New Intimate Relationships in Later Life.

———. "Multigenerational Relationships with the Asian Family: Qualitative Evidence from Singapore". *International Journal of Sociology of the Family* 33, no. 1 (2007): 63–77.

Mehta, K. and L.L. Thang. "Interdependence in Asian Families: The Singapore Case". *Journal of Intergenerational Relationships: Programs, Policy and Research* 4, no. 1 (2006): 117–26.

Mehta, K., M.M. Osman and A.E.Y. Lee. "Living Arrangements of the Elderly in Singapore: Cultural Norms in Transition". *Journal of Cross-Cultural Gerontology* 10, nos. 1/2 (1995): 113–43.

Mehta, K.K. and S. Vasoo. "Organisation and Delivery of Long-Term Care in Singapore: Present Issues and Future Challenges". *Journal of Aging and Social Policy* 13, nos. 2/3 (2001): 185–201. Special Issue on Long-Term Care in the 21st Century: Perspectives from around the Asia-Pacific Rim.

Nair, Kichu. "The Physically Ageing Body and the Use of Space". In *Ageing and Place: Perspectives, Policy, Practice*, edited by G.J. Andrews and D.R. Phillips. London: Routledge, 2005.

National Survey of Senior Citizens, 1995. Singapore: Ministries of Health, Community Development, Statistics, Labour and National Council of Social Services, 1996.

National Survey of Senior Citizens, 2005. Singapore: Ministry of Community Development, Youth and Sports, 2006.

O'Bryant, S.L. "Older Widows and Independent Lifestyles". *International Journal of Aging and Human Development* 32, no. 1 (1991): 41–51.

O'Bryant, Shirley L. and Robert O. Hansson. "Widowhood". In *Handbook of Aging and the Family*, edited by R. Blieszner and V.H. Bedford. Westport, Connecticut: Greenwood, 1995.

Peace, Sheila M., Caroline Holland and Leonie Kellaher. "Making Space for Identity". In *Ageing and Place: Perspectives, Policy, Practice,* edited by G.J. Andrews and D.R. Phillips. London: Routledge, 2005.

Rowles, Graham D. "Geographical Dimensions of Social Support in Appalacia". In *Aging and Milieu: Environmental Perspectives on Growing Old*, edited by G.D. Rowles and R.J. Ohta. New York: Academic Press, 1983.

Silverman, Phyllis R. *Widow-to-Widow*. New York: Springer, 1986.

Singapore Census of Population 1990. Release No. 1: 51. Singapore, 1991.

Singapore Census of Population 2000. Advanced Release No. 8: 1. Singapore, 2001.

Singapore Census of Population 2010. Release No. 1: 42. Singapore, 2011.

Teo, P.C.C. and K.K. Mehta. "Participating in the Home: Widows Cope in Singapore". *Journal of Ageing Studies* 15, no. 2 (2001): 127–44.

Teo, Peggy, Kalyani Mehta, Leng Leng Thang and Angelique Chan. *Ageing in Singapore: Service Needs and the State.* Singapore: Routledge, 2006.

Utz, R.L., D. Carr, R. Nesse and C.B. Wortman. "The Effect of Widowhood on Older Adults' Social Participation: An Evaluation of Activity, Disengagement and Continuity Theories". *Gerontologist* 42, no. 4 (2002): 522–33.

"WHO Framework on Active Ageing". Available at <http://whqlibdoc.who.int/hq/2002/WHO_NMH_NPH_02.8.pdf> (accessed 14 December 2008).

10

EMPLOYMENT PATTERNS OF OLDER WOMEN IN INDONESIA

Aris Ananta

LIFE OF OLDER PERSONS

It is a very hot day in an overly-crowded and polluted street in Jakarta. When the traffic light turns red, out of nowhere a group of people emerge and start approaching the cars and motorcycles, begging for money. This group includes some older men and women who have resorted to begging so as to make ends meet. In Singapore, another big city in Southeast Asia, older men and women do "odd jobs" such as cleaning dirty tables at hawker centres and public toilets. Is this the kind of employment older people are expected to take on in some parts of Southeast Asia?

In contrast, there are many older men and women in Indonesia who do not do "anything". They live in beautiful houses; they travel a lot for leisure; and they have rich children to support them. One older man works for a family business run by his son; he enjoys the work, not because of the money, but because of the nature of the job and also because it keeps him occupied. He also partakes in the profit from this business. Moreover his wife enjoys her leisure; she pursues her time exercising, visiting friends, meeting her children, children-in-law, and grandchildren. A question arises regarding the kinds of activities one would expect older persons to engage in. We could also ask if an older person who engages in wage work is better off than someone who does not? In essence, what kind of life should older persons be leading?

This chapter represents a preliminary attempt to provide the first and important step at answering that question, by analysing the employment patterns of older women in Indonesia. It provides information on what the older persons, particularly older women, do within and outside the labour market. The analysis relies on a national data set collected in 2007. Therefore, readers need to be careful when generalizing the findings in this chapter beyond 2007.

The discussion here is an extension of the research conducted by Arifin and Ananta (2009) which examined employment patterns of older persons in some countries and regions within Southeast Asia. They found a similarity between employment patterns of older persons in Southeast Asia and those in industrialized countries. Older persons were more likely to work in more flexible working arrangements. Being self-employed or working as unpaid workers seemed to be more suitable for older persons. Older persons were more likely to work as skilled agricultural and fishery workers. Moreover, they tended to work in agricultural or service sectors. Arifin and Ananta (2009) also concluded that this pattern may reflect the current labour market situation and the human capital of the older persons because advances in technology and social innovations, coupled with enhanced human capital of the older persons, produce completely different employment patterns among older persons, including that of older women, in the future.

In this chapter, the employment pattern of older women is discussed in the context of sources of support for older persons. Another feature of this chapter is the comparison between the sexes and across age groups to examine whether the patterns arising among older women are unique to them.

The published data from the 2007 National Labour Force Survey (Sakernas), collected by the Indonesian statistical agency (Statistics Indonesia 2007), provide the main source of analysis in this chapter. The publication of the results of the survey, however, does not include tabulation of occupation by age group and, as a result, this chapter does not examine the occupational patterns of older women.

This chapter starts off with a discussion on employment as one, out of many, support mechanisms for older persons. It then examines the empirical conditions of older women's employment in Indonesia in 2007. The analysis examines the gender disaggregated data related to labour force participation, including the difference in employment patterns between younger and older persons; the participation of older women in the labour force, compared with older men and younger workers; the number of work hours older women and men put in; as well as the employment sector older persons engage in and the status of older women and men. Before ending with conclusions, the chapter discusses the educational attainment of older persons by gender. It also shows the projected higher educational attainment for the future older persons by gender.

EMPLOYMENT: ONE MEANS TO FINANCE OLDER PERSONS

The issue of financing older persons has become more urgent as many countries have experienced a geriatric wave — an emergence of increasingly large cohorts of older persons demanding for geriatric care services. The demand for geriatric care services, covering both medication/medical technology and geriatric infrastructural system, has expanded. The wave will become larger as people live longer. Indonesia is no exception as it will soon experience the geriatric wave (Rahardjo et al. 2009).

Because the costs involved in geriatric care needs and services are high, this begs the question of how then can older persons be financed. As discussed in Arifin and Ananta (2009), employment of older persons is frequently used as the most important support mechanism for this group when there is limited social welfare, including old-age income security, in addition to financial support from relatives and friends. A more important issue is how much older persons are able to earn from employment such that it is sufficient to lift them out of poverty. Therefore, in this situation, being retired in the sense of not working for money at all can be seen as a "luxury" for older persons in developing economies. As mentioned in the United Nations (2007), poor people in developing economies do not have the notion of "retirement". They tend to stop working only when they are forced to do so owing to deteriorating health, unless they are financially supported by their family and friends.

Owing to the importance of productive employment for older persons, as discussed in Arifin and Ananta (2009), there are three ways to raise the productivity of this age group. First is to enhance the human capital of the older persons, including health, education, mobility, and freedom from fear. Second is to create productive jobs that are suitable for the physical condition of the older persons. Third is to eliminate discrimination against the older persons in ways such as raising or eliminating what is known as the "retirement age". In this case, older persons should not be dismissed simply because of their chronological age. Furthermore, enabling an older person to work suggests an acknowledgement of employment as a human right, regardless of age.

Nevertheless, employment is only one source of support for older persons. In general, there are three sources of support for all persons, including older women. First is income, which does not come from labour income (earning) only. Income can also be received in the form of interest on savings, rental from assets, and profits from businesses. Incomes in these last three forms are different from earnings (from employment) as individuals do not have to engage in labour to secure earnings. These three forms of income (interest, rate, and profit) may also be considered more suitable for older persons in the event they fall ill — which will take them away from work — compared with their younger counterparts. Furthermore, they may also finance their expenditure with wealth/savings accumulated when younger.

The second source of support is transfer payment, that is, money received as a "gift" from others, such as spouses, relatives, children, parents, government, and society in general. Older persons may receive transfer of payments from the government in the form of pension, which are paid by the working age population. Older persons, however, often do not receive transfer payments from their own parents because the latter would have already been deceased for some years already. However, older persons may receive transfers from their own children and grandchildren, although the reverse also occurs where some grandparents continue to make transfers to their grandchildren especially in the case where the parents of the grandchildren are unable to do so.

The third source of support includes non-monetary contributions, which can be in the form of receiving caregiving or tangible goods such as food and clothing. Living arrangements for older persons is also an example of non-monetary support.

With this wide possibility of sources of support for older persons, including older women, any discussion on financing should consider all sources of support. The discussion on employment among older women should also bear in mind these possible sources of support since the latter are also critical for enabling the elderly to sustain themselves on an everyday level.

SEX RATIO AND AGE STRUCTURE OF THE LABOUR FORCE

The working age cohort is the segment of the population that is able to work. In industrialized countries, the working age population comprises those age 15–64. People below age 15 are considered children and they are not supposed to work. In fact, in many countries, child labour is deemed as a crime. Similarly, people age 65 and above are considered old and, as a result, are generally regarded as an economic burden, and are not thought to be capable of engaging in wage work anymore. The commonly used dependency ratio is defined as the ratio between the unproductive population (age below 15 and above 64) and the productive population (age 15–64).

In Indonesia, until 1997, the definition of working age population included the entire population from age 10 and above. The assumption was that the population age 65 and above was still able to work and that the population age 10–14 were already able to work and might be working. Because of criticisms levelled against child labour, however, the definition of working age population has been restricted to those age 15 years and above since 1998. Therefore, technically, there has been no child labour in Indonesia since 1998. In contrast, statistics on Indonesia's employment recognizes older workers. In fact, the Indonesian statistical agency continues to collect data on employment of older persons, without age limit. In other words, officially, the current working age population includes the entire population age 15 years and above, with no upper limit for age. This chapter adopts the current official definition of working age population, in addition to the official definition of older persons — population age 60 years old and above.

The working population consists of those who work and those who do not. Those who are not working but are actively looking for jobs are defined as unemployed. Therefore, the unemployed does not include those who are not working and are not seeking jobs. In a country such as Indonesia where there is no unemployment compensation, being unemployed suggests that one would have to rely on financial support from relatives, friends, and the community, or even one's own savings. In other words, being unemployed implies that the individual has some form of financial support. This also suggests that the person need not necessarily be in a financial dilemma. In fact, those who are working may include those who may be in a financial dilemma, and are thus forced to work in whatever jobs they can find to meet their basic needs.

Those who are able to work but are not working nor looking for a job are categorized as "not in the labour force", rather than unemployed. As mentioned earlier, in Indonesia where there is no unemployment compensation, being "not in the labour force" can imply living a luxurious lifestyle including engaging in unpaid activities such as taking care of children/older persons, managing the household, studying, and doing charity/social work. Thus, the labour force participation rate does not necessarily reflect an improvement in one's welfare or empowerment. An increase in the labour force participation rate, in fact, can result from rising poverty such that people are forced to work. Readers, therefore, should bear these caveats in mind when interpreting the statistics.

The Indonesian working age population had almost equal numbers of males and females. In 2007, the sex ratio of the working age population, indicating number of males over 100 females, was 100.05, suggesting that the number of males in the working age population was just slightly higher than that of females. However, the labour force was very much dominated by males (169.07), indicating that there were about 169 males for every 100 females. In contrast, for every 100 females who were not in the labour force, there were only 32 males who were also not in the labour force, suggesting that women largely dominated this group (see Table 10.1).

TABLE 10.1
Sex Ratio of Older Persons and Those Below 60 Years Old: Indonesia, 2007

Age	Labour Force	Not in the Labour Force	Working Age Population
15–19	159.34	88.93	110.61
20–24	158.90	29.74	97.90
25–29	160.31	10.36	88.51
30–34	171.37	7.64	92.12
35–39	166.71	8.03	97.88
40–44	169.16	9.38	103.52
45–49	171.60	10.45	106.68
50–54	178.75	17.21	111.48
55–59	187.62	28.69	114.38
60+	192.05	49.80	96.07
Total	169.07	32.34	100.05

Source: Compiled and calculated from Statistics Indonesia, *Labour Force Situation in Indonesia, February 2007* (Jakarta: Statistics Indonesia, 2007).

That men dominate the labour force was seen especially among the older workers. With the sex ratio at 192.05, there were almost two older male workers in the labour force for every one older female worker. The sex ratio in fact increases with age, suggesting that the probability of the increasing numbers of older men participating in the labour force was higher than that for older women. The reverse is seen among the older persons who were not in the labour force — about two older women for every one older man. This finding highlights the point that gender segregation in the labour market is more significant among older persons than other age groups.

LABOUR FORCE PARTICIPATION

Gender differentials in the labour force participation rate, as shown in Table 10.2 and Figure 10.1, indicate that men more than women were more likely to participate in the labour force, regardless of age. Even among older persons, men are more than twice as likely as women to participate in the labour force. This pattern may partly reflect the traditional norms in the division of labour between men and women even in older age.

TABLE 10.2
Labour Force Participation Rate of Older Persons and Those Below 60 Years Old by Gender: Indonesia, 2007

Age	Total	Male	Female
15–19	37.92	44.37	30.80
20–24	69.04	85.65	52.77
25–29	71.97	94.40	52.12
30–34	72.88	95.98	51.60
35–39	76.32	96.44	56.62
40–44	77.92	96.28	58.92
45–49	78.47	96.05	59.71
50–54	76.92	93.57	58.36
55–59	72.34	88.44	53.92
60+	48.44	65.02	32.52
Total	66.60	83.68	49.52

Source: Compiled and calculated from Statistics Indonesia, *Labour Force Situation in Indonesia, February 2007* (Jakarta: Statistics Indonesia, 2007).

FIGURE 10.1

Labour Force Participation Rate of Older Persons and Those Below 60 Years Old by Gender: Indonesia, 2007

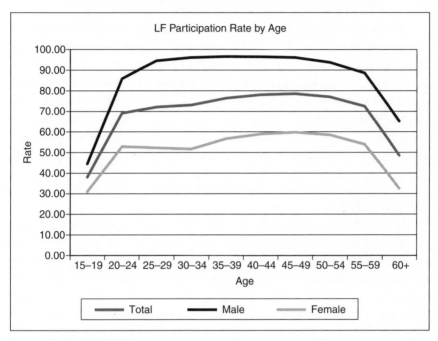

Source: Drawn from Table 10.2.

The labour force participation rate kept increasing with age, reaching the peak at age 35–39 for males and 45–49 for females. The peak of the rate was much higher for males (96.44 per cent) than for females (59.71 per cent). It then declines and a significant decline was seen at age 55–59 where the rate drops from 93.57 per cent in the age group 50–54 to 88.44 per cent in the age group 55–59 among men, and from 58.36 per cent to 53.92 per cent among women. A larger decline was seen in the age group 60+. This large decline in the labour force participation rate from age 55 may have been because of a "retirement age" — either formal or "informal". However, the significant decline in the age group 60+ may also reflect the grouping of older persons. All persons age 60 and above have been grouped into a single age group 60+. The published data do not have information for the age group 60–64. If the information is available, the decline may have been smoother, because the current grouping (60+) includes those who are very old. For example, because those age 75 years old and above may have a very low labour force participation rate, this has made the rate for 60 years and above very low.

Moreover, the labour force participation rate for male older persons was still relatively high at 65.02 per cent, which was much higher than 32.52 per cent for older women. The rates are usually high in developing countries, where there is limited, or no, social security system, and because the macroeconomic conditions have not been conducive in providing old age financing. It is these individuals who may not have other forms of income and transfer payments. Therefore, these older persons, especially the males, may not retire as they may not be able to afford retirement. For this reason, they may be forced to work so as to finance themselves and their families, including their children and grandchildren.

In 2007, the rate for the labour force participation among older persons was found to be higher than those among the youngest group. The rate among the youngest group was lower because this group, especially the male population, includes students. Table 10.3 shows that almost all males age 15–19 who were not in the labour force were school-going (99.18 per cent); however, only 78.98 per cent of the females age 15–19 were school-going. Some (16.47 per cent) of the female population who were not in the labour force did household work and the remaining (4.54 per cent) engaged in "other activities". However based on data from Statistics Indonesia 2007, it is unclear as to what exactly this "others" category constituted although we may surmise that it could include activities such as taking care of older persons, social activities, or "doing nothing".

Among the older persons, in contrast, most males who were not in the labour force were found to engage in "others" (86.99 per cent), while more than half of the females not in the labour force were preoccupied with housekeeping. In other words, when older men did not participate in the labour market, they were most likely found to be engaging in "other" activities. We may also expect that men's lack of experience on the household front may have disabled them from undertaking household work and, therefore, they may be more dependent on their wives in this regard.

The pattern among older women was different as they were found to be less likely to participate in the labour market. When out of the

TABLE 10.3
Older Persons and Those Below 60 Years Old Not in the Labour Force by Gender and Activity: Indonesia, 2007

Age	Male				Female			
	Schooling	House Keeping	Others	Total	Schooling	House Keeping	Others	Total
15–19	99.18	0.02	0.80	100.00	78.98	16.47	4.54	100.00
20–24	94.98	0.32	4.70	100.00	19.51	76.53	3.96	100.00
25–29	16.06	0.67	83.27	100.00	1.04	94.16	4.80	100.00
30–34	5.30	13.11	81.59	100.00	0.00	96.95	3.05	100.00
35–39	0.00	22.43	77.57	100.00	0.00	97.20	2.80	100.00
40–44	0.00	19.27	80.73	100.00	0.00	96.26	3.74	100.00
45–49	0.00	15.58	84.42	100.00	0.00	96.39	3.61	100.00
50–54	0.00	22.68	77.32	100.00	0.00	91.60	8.40	100.00
55–59	0.00	16.39	83.61	100.00	0.00	89.85	10.15	100.00
60+	0.00	13.01	86.99	100.00	0.00	58.40	41.60	100.00
Total	58.34	5.72	35.93	100.00	16.08	74.14	9.78	100.00

Source: Compiled and calculated from Statistics Indonesia, *Labour Force Situation in Indonesia, February 2007* (Jakarta: Statistics Indonesia, 2007).

labour market, they were most likely to engage in housekeeping although the percentage among them engaging in "others" was also relatively high (41.60 per cent).

Furthermore, when men joined the labour market, they were more likely to accept any kind of employment, rather than being unemployed (looking for work, but not doing any job). The decision to work may stem from the fact that they see it as their responsibility to work and to provide financially towards their family. For this reason, men are more likely to accept any kind of employment, rather than spending too much time seeking out for better jobs.

Because greater numbers of men engage in the labour force compared to women, conversely we can expect the unemployment rates of women to be higher than that of men. Table 10.4 shows that the rate of unemployment among women was at 11.83 per cent compared to 8.53 per cent for men. Interestingly, this pattern was seen in all age groups, except for the 50–54 and 55–59 age groups. One possibility for this exception is that among these women, they are forced to work because of declining income — income they would have received from their husbands who would have previously worked but are now unable because of declining health. Thus to help contribute to the

TABLE 10.4
Unemployment Rate by Older Persons and
Those Below 60 Years Old by Gender: Indonesia, 2007

Age	Male	Female	Total
15–19	25.62	33.92	28.82
20–24	21.33	27.11	23.56
25–29	10.92	16.17	12.94
30–34	5.87	8.72	6.92
35–39	3.68	6.02	4.56
40–44	3.41	4.20	3.70
45–49	2.95	4.04	3.35
50–54	2.76	2.63	2.71
55–59	3.10	2.12	2.76
60+	1.88	1.92	1.89
Total	8.53	11.83	9.75

Source: Compiled and calculated from Statistics Indonesia, *Labour Force Situation in Indonesia, February 2007* (Jakarta: Statistics Indonesia, 2007).

household income, these women could have been forced to accept any kind of job, simply to meet the basic needs of the family. However, further studies should be undertaken to understand this pattern in greater depth.

Nevertheless, there are several reasons for a higher unemployment rate among women. First is that women can afford to be more selective in deciding whether or not to work as compared with men because women have husbands who can finance them. The second reason is the sexual division of labour where it has become acceptable for women to depend on their husbands for financial support while they are expected to manage the household. Here, men are expected to provide for the family financially and at the same time are not expected to undertake any household chores. It is the sexual division of labour in the household which reduces the possibility of women joining the labour market and of men engaging in household chores. In keeping with this social norm, men must work and, therefore, they have recorded lower unemployment rates.

The third reason, particularly for older women, is the lack of experience in the labour market during their younger years which might have led to a difficulty in securing jobs later on. Table 10.4, which compares the rates in different age groups, shows that the unemployment rate declined with age, regardless of gender — a pattern which reflects a declining ability to be selective about employment opportunities as individuals become older. At an older age, the unemployment rates for both sexes were almost equal at very low levels, that is, less than 2.0 per cent. This very low difference in rates may indicate that those who join the labour market must accept whatever job they can secure.

HOURS WORKED

As indicated in Tables 10.5–10.7, Indonesian workers worked very hard. Around two-third worked longer than 35 hours a week and almost 15 per cent worked longer than 60 hours a week. Even the older workers worked long hours. Around half of the older workers worked more than 35 hours a week. It should be noted that the number of hours worked may not come from one job, as Indonesians often take on multiple jobs.

However, the data indicates that the number of hours they worked decreased as they become older. Among those between ages 25 and 29 and

40 and 44, about 70 per cent worked more than 35 hours a week. Beyond age 45, it was found that the percentage of those who worked 35 hours per week declined with age. While a significantly large drop was seen in the age cohort 55–59, yet an even larger drop was recorded among those in the age group of 60+. At age 60+, only half of the workers worked more than 35 hours per week.

Similar to the labour force participation rate, the significant drop in the number of hours worked as people become older may be because in the published data set all the people in the age group of 60 years and above are categorized into one age grouping such that even those 70 years and above who may work for very short hours fall under this grouping. We would instead expect the decline not to be so steep if the age grouping was broken down further into five-year age groups (that is, 60–64, 65–69, 70–74 and so on).

Interestingly, men were also more likely to work longer hours compared to women. This pattern is seen in all age groups, except the youngest group. More than half of the older men worked longer than 35 hours per week, compared to only about 40.0 per cent among older women. It is unclear whether women chose to work fewer hours or were unable to put in the number of work hours which men did because of family commitments. Nonetheless the pattern is consistent with the fact that men are more likely to stay in the labour force much longer than women.

As shown in Table 10.5, about 9.0 per cent of the workers could afford to work less than 15 hours a week. How did they support themselves by working less than 15 hours a week? Were they so productive that they could afford to work less than 15 hours a week? Were they able to support themselves because they received interest, rent, and profit or transfer payments from other sources such that they could afford to work only 15 hours a week?

The percentage was higher among female workers (12.35 per cent) compared to male workers (7.11 per cent), indicating that female workers could better afford to work less than 15 hours a week. The difference in the percentage was even larger among older workers, at 12.55 per cent among older men and 21.03 per cent among older women. How then did the older female workers manage to sustain themselves? Were these female workers receiving transfer payments from their husbands or children?

TABLE 10.5
Employment by Hours Worked of Older Persons and Those Below 60 Years Old in a Week: Indonesia, Male and Female, 2007

Age	<15 hours	15–34	35–59	>60	Total
15–19	16.72	28.70	42.65	11.92	100.00
20–24	8.38	23.64	55.17	12.81	100.00
25–29	7.57	22.27	56.03	14.13	100.00
30–34	7.64	21.67	55.35	15.35	100.00
35–39	7.15	21.82	55.05	15.98	100.00
40–44	7.47	23.09	54.68	14.77	100.00
45–49	7.97	24.64	53.46	13.93	100.00
50–54	7.96	25.94	52.71	13.39	100.00
55–59	10.17	28.64	49.54	11.65	100.00
60+	15.45	34.32	41.93	8.30	100.00
total	9.02	24.64	52.72	13.63	100.00

Source: Compiled and calculated from Statistics Indonesia, *Labour Force Situation in Indonesia, February 2007* (Jakarta: Statistics Indonesia, 2007).

TABLE 10.6
Employment by Hours Worked of Older Persons and Those Below 60 Years Old in a Week: Indonesia, Male, 2007

Age	<15 Hours	15–34	35–59	>60	Total
15–19	17.25	30.21	43.70	8.84	100.00
20–24	7.27	22.09	57.73	12.90	100.00
25–29	5.74	18.77	60.04	15.45	100.00
30–34	5.45	16.95	61.08	16.51	100.00
35–39	5.18	16.26	60.91	17.65	100.00
40–44	5.25	17.47	61.33	15.95	100.00
45–49	5.62	19.36	60.00	15.02	100.00
50–54	5.54	21.45	58.53	14.48	100.00
55–59	7.93	24.65	55.31	12.11	100.00
60+	12.55	32.68	46.30	8.47	100.00
total	7.11	20.91	57.64	14.34	100.00

Source: Compiled and calculated from Statistics Indonesia, *Labour Force Situation in Indonesia, February 2007* (Jakarta: Statistics Indonesia, 2007).

TABLE 10.7
**Employment by Hours Worked of Older Persons and
Those Below 60 Years Old in a Week: Indonesia, Female, 2007**

Age	<15 Hours	15–34	35–59	>60	Total
15–19	15.77	26.00	40.78	17.45	100.00
20–24	10.27	26.30	50.78	12.65	100.00
25–29	10.69	28.23	49.20	11.88	100.00
30–34	11.50	30.00	45.21	13.29	100.00
35–39	10.53	31.32	45.03	13.12	100.00
40–44	11.26	32.67	43.32	12.75	100.00
45–49	12.04	33.79	42.12	12.04	100.00
50–54	12.28	33.96	42.33	11.43	100.00
55–59	14.34	36.05	38.81	10.80	100.00
60+	21.03	37.47	33.53	7.97	100.00
Total	12.35	31.18	44.09	12.37	100.00

Source: Compiled and calculated from Statistics Indonesia, *Labour Force Situation in Indonesia, February 2007* (Jakarta: Statistics Indonesia, 2007).

EMPLOYMENT STATUS

Modernization is often associated with a rising percentage of workers in "formal employment" marked by more rigid workplace arrangements. Defining formal employment, however, is not an easy task. A simple definition of informal sector employment might refer to those who are not employed in the formal labour sector. In contrast, those who work in the formal labour sector are employed by permanent or regular employers as well as work with the assistance of paid or regular employees. According to Statistics Indonesia (2007), the definition of formal employment has been broadened to include "own account workers" who work in "professional, technical and related work". Hence, the number of workers employed in formal employment is much larger if we were to accept the conventional definitions (see Table 10.8 for the classification of formal employment).

Following this definition, almost two-thirds of employment in Indonesia is considered informal employment. As indicated in Table 10.9, the percentage of women engaging in informal employment was higher (66.77 per cent) than men (60.94 per cent). However, among older persons, the figure was even higher. Older women were also more likely to work in informal employment compared with their male counterparts. However, the difference was relatively small at 81.58 per cent for older men and 85.58 per cent for

TABLE 10.8
Classification of Formal-Informal Employment

Employment Status	Main Occupation									
	1	2	3	4	5	6	7	8	9	10
Own account worker	F	F	F	I	I	I	I	I	I	I
Employer assisted by temporary workers/unpaid workers	F	F	F	F	F	I	F	F	F	I
Employer assisted by permanent workers	F	F	F	F	F	F	F	F	F	F
Employee	F	F	F	F	F	F	F	F	F	F
Casual employee in agriculture	F	F	F	I	I	I	I	I	I	I
Casual employee not in agriculture	F	F	F	I	I	I	I	I	I	I
Unpaid worker	I	I	I	I	I	I	I	I	I	I

Notes:
  1 – professional, technical and related workers
  2 – administrative and managerial workers
  3 – clerical and related workers
  4 – sales workers
  5 – services workers
  6 – agriculture, animal husbandary, forestry workers, fishermen and hunters
  7 – production and related workers
  8 – transport equipment and operators workers
  9 – labourers
10 – others
  F – formal employment
  I – informal employment
Source: Statistics Indonesia, *Labour Force Situation in Indonesia, February 2007* (Jakarta: Statistics Indonesia, 2007).

TABLE 10.9
Informal Employment Rates of Older Persons and Those Below 60 Years Old by Gender: Indonesia, 2007

Age	Male	Female	Total
15–19	72.40	57.03	66.90
20–24	54.95	47.58	52.24
25–29	55.20	57.37	56.00
30–34	54.99	65.94	58.95
35–39	55.61	67.14	59.86
40–44	57.93	70.98	62.76
45–49	60.80	72.61	65.11
50–54	64.46	76.52	68.79
55–59	70.50	81.98	74.52
60+	81.58	85.58	82.95
Total	60.94	66.77	63.06

Note: Informal employment as defined by Statistics Indonesia.
Source: Compiled and calculated from Statistics Indonesia, *Labour Force Situation in Indonesia, February 2007* (Jakarta: Statistics Indonesia, 2007).

older women. The small difference and the large percentage may indicate that older workers, regardless of gender, had fewer employment choices and, therefore, chose to engage in informal employment since that might have been the only option available to them.

In fact, it could be argued that informal employment provides a financial cushion for older persons in Indonesia, especially since social security is still very limited and financial institutions and the macroeconomic environment have not been helpful for older persons. Informal employment may also have been used as a transition out of the labour force, as Karoly and Zissimopoulos (2004) have shown for older persons in the United States.

In Indonesia, the majority (44.38 per cent) of older workers worked as employers assisted by temporary workers or unpaid workers. The percentage of this group rose with age. The second largest group was own account workers (23.30 per cent), also rising with age, while the third largest group included unpaid workers (14.38 per cent), declining with age. In contrast, the percentage working as employees and casual employees outside agriculture declined with age. This is one distinguishing feature of the employment status of older workers.

EMPLOYMENT SECTOR

Three broad categories of employment sector were reflected in the data used for the analysis undertaken in this chapter. The first is "agriculture", which includes agriculture, forestry, hunting and fishery; the second is "industry", comprising mining and quarrying, manufacturing, and the electricity, gas, water and construction industries; and the third is the "service" sector.

As shown in Table 10.10, a relatively large percentage (43.66 per cent) of workers worked in agriculture, while only 18.20 per cent worked in industry. The role of agriculture in employment was much more important for older workers, with the sector providing more than two-thirds of employment for older workers. In fact, the importance of agriculture as a source of employment rose with age group; in other words, the older the age group, the more important was the role of agriculture in creating employment.

Regardless of age, industry did not seem to play an important part in providing employment for older persons compared with the younger age groups. Employment in industry did not seem to be suitable for the older workers, regardless of gender. In fact, the contribution of industry to employment initially rose in the youngest group, and then declined

TABLE 10.10
Employment of Older Persons and Those Below 60 Years Old by Industry: Indonesia, Male and Female, 2007

Age	Agriculture	Industry	Service	Total
15–19	48.08	20.10	31.82	100.00
20–24	34.17	24.60	41.23	100.00
25–29	35.82	23.47	40.70	100.00
30–34	37.39	21.18	41.43	100.00
35–39	38.33	19.36	42.31	100.00
40–44	42.06	16.72	41.23	100.00
45–49	46.30	14.93	38.77	100.00
50–54	50.69	13.27	36.04	100.00
55–59	58.21	10.98	30.81	100.00
60+	67.24	8.55	24.22	100.00
Total	43.66	18.20	38.14	100.00

Source: Compiled and calculated from Statistics Indonesia, *Labour Force Situation in Indonesia, February 2007* (Jakarta: Statistics Indonesia, 2007).

among older persons. An exception was for older women (60 years old and above) whose contribution of industry to employment was higher than that for women age 55–59.

Tables 10.11 and 10.12 show the role of agriculture in contributing to the employment of older persons. While the agricultural sector played a significant role in terms of employment for older persons, as mentioned earlier in the discussion, it must be noted that 71.52 per cent of older men were employed in this labour sector compared with only 59.01 per cent of older women. Among older women, it was found that the service sector provided a more important source of employment compared with agriculture. The service sector produced 31.58 per cent of employment for older women, but only 20.39 per cent for older men. Moreover, older women were also more likely to be found working in the service rather than industrial sector.

The relationship between age and employment in the service sector was similar to that of age and employment in the industrial sector, except that the fluctuation was smaller. It was also an inverted U-curve, first rising then declining with age. The smallest contribution of the service sector was 24.22 per cent among the older workers and the largest was 42.31 per cent among workers age 35–39. Therefore, the service sector appeared to be the second choice, after the agricultural sector, among older

TABLE 10.11

Employment of Older Persons and Those Below 60 Years Old by Industry: Indonesia, Male, 2007

Age	Agriculture	Industry	Service	Total
15–19	54.91	18.65	26.43	100.00
20–24	35.76	25.20	39.04	100.00
25–29	34.95	25.30	39.75	100.00
30–34	34.77	24.46	40.77	100.00
35–39	35.56	23.21	41.24	100.00
40–44	38.99	20.37	40.64	100.00
45–49	43.82	17.72	38.46	100.00
50–54	48.64	16.00	35.37	100.00
55–59	57.42	12.62	29.96	100.00
60+	71.52	8.10	20.39	100.00
Total	43.11	20.27	36.63	100.00

Source: Compiled and calculated from Statistics Indonesia, *Labour Force Situation in Indonesia, February 2007* (Jakarta: Statistics Indonesia, 2007).

TABLE 10.12

Employment of Older Persons and Those Below 60 Years Old by Industry: Indonesia, Female, 2007

Age	Agriculture	Industry	Service	Total
15–19	35.81	22.70	41.49	100.00
20–24	31.44	23.57	44.99	100.00
25–29	37.31	20.36	42.33	100.00
30–34	42.02	15.38	42.60	100.00
35–39	43.07	12.79	44.13	100.00
40–44	47.29	10.48	42.22	100.00
45–49	50.60	10.10	39.31	100.00
50–54	54.35	8.39	37.25	100.00
55–59	59.68	7.94	32.38	100.00
60+	59.01	9.41	31.58	100.00
Total	44.64	14.57	40.79	100.00

Source: Compiled and calculated from Statistics Indonesia, *Labour Force Situation in Indonesia, February 2007* (Jakarta: Statistics Indonesia, 2007).

workers. Both the agricultural and service sectors may provide more flexible arrangements and demand lower skills and/or physical effort although older men seemed to have a preference for working in the agricultural sector whereas older women in the service sector.

EDUCATION OF THE OLDER LABOUR FORCE

While analysing employability, taking into account the educational background of older workers becomes imperative since education to a large extent determines one's competitiveness in the labour market. The gender differentials in employment patterns among older persons of future generations may change as they are more educated than current cohorts. In 2007, the older cohort of workers in the labour force had a relatively lower educational attainment compared to the younger cohort of workers, regardless of gender. More than two-thirds of older workers in the labour force had at most only elementary education while only 1.29 per cent of this cohort had university education (see Tables 10.13–10.15).

However, the educational attainment of the older persons will soon change, as the educational attainment of the current younger persons (future older persons) is better than that of the current older persons. For example, in 2007, as shown in Tables 10.16–10.18, only 7.69 per cent of the labour force in the age group 40–59 years old had no schooling at all, which was a much smaller percentage compared with 20.81 per cent among the cohort of older persons. In contrast, 6.17 per cent of the

TABLE 10.13
Labour Force of Older Persons and Those Below 60 Years Old by Educational Attainment: Indonesia, Male and Female, 2007

Age	No School	<ES	ES	JHS	SHS	University	Total
15–19	0.99	6.53	40.12	37.22	15.04	0.10	100.00
20–24	0.85	4.27	26.33	26.39	36.41	5.74	100.00
25–29	1.19	5.13	32.18	23.98	28.20	9.32	100.00
30–34	1.68	6.65	37.45	21.42	24.95	7.84	100.00
35–39	2.88	8.75	36.45	19.48	24.46	8.00	100.00
40–44	5.22	13.20	39.14	16.10	18.48	7.86	100.00
45–49	6.99	16.98	42.26	14.99	12.22	6.56	100.00
50–54	9.97	18.39	42.37	15.16	9.35	4.77	100.00
55–59	11.16	19.29	43.51	14.08	8.22	3.74	100.00
60+	20.81	21.38	39.19	13.20	4.13	1.29	100.00
Total	5.03	10.67	36.74	20.75	20.67	6.15	100.00

Note: ES-Elementary School; JHS-Junior High School; and SHS-Senior High School.
Source: Compiled and calculated from Statistics Indonesia, *Labour Force Situation in Indonesia, February 2007* (Jakarta: Statistics Indonesia, 2007).

TABLE 10.14

**Labour Force of Older Persons and Those Below
60 Years Old by Educational Attainment:
Indonesia, Male, 2007**

Age	No School	<ES	ES	JHS	SHS	University	Total
15–19	0.86	7.37	41.69	36.62	13.42	0.04	100.00
20–24	0.65	4.50	27.85	27.92	35.59	3.50	100.00
25–29	0.69	5.02	31.32	25.64	30.10	7.24	100.00
30–34	0.93	6.07	35.65	22.83	27.53	6.99	100.00
35–39	1.66	6.89	34.57	21.21	28.11	7.55	100.00
40–44	3.17	10.92	37.29	17.79	22.52	8.31	100.00
45–49	4.73	14.58	41.73	16.31	15.57	7.08	100.00
50–54	6.76	16.41	42.98	16.58	11.79	5.48	100.00
55–59	7.64	17.61	44.96	15.23	10.22	4.33	100.00
60+	14.09	20.96	43.57	14.01	5.58	1.79	100.00
Total	3.38	9.82	36.77	21.95	22.47	5.61	100.00

Note: ES-Elementary School; JHS-Junior High School; and SHS-Senior High School.
Source: Compiled and calculated from Statistics Indonesia, *Labour Force Situation in Indonesia, February 2007* (Jakarta: Statistics Indonesia, 2007).

TABLE 10.15

**Labour Force of Older Persons and Those Below
60 Years Old by Educational Attainment:
Indonesia, Female, 2007**

Age	No School	<ES	ES	JHS	SHS	University	Total
15–19	1.19	5.17	37.62	38.19	17.62	0.21	100.00
20–24	1.18	3.90	23.91	23.97	37.71	9.32	100.00
25–29	1.99	5.29	33.56	21.33	25.16	12.67	100.00
30–34	2.98	7.65	40.53	19.01	20.52	9.30	100.00
35–39	4.90	11.83	39.58	16.59	18.36	8.74	100.00
40–44	8.68	17.06	42.26	13.26	11.64	7.10	100.00
45–49	10.87	21.10	43.17	12.72	6.46	5.67	100.00
50–54	15.70	21.92	41.27	12.63	4.98	3.51	100.00
55–59	17.75	22.45	40.77	11.93	4.47	2.63	100.00
60+	33.73	22.18	30.77	11.66	1.35	0.31	100.00
Total	7.80	12.12	36.68	18.71	17.62	7.07	100.00

Note: ES-Elementary School; JHS-Junior High School; and SHS-Senior High School.
Source: Compiled and calculated from Statistics Indonesia, *Labour Force Situation in Indonesia, February 2007* (Jakarta: Statistics Indonesia, 2007).

TABLE 10.16

**Education of Pre-Older and Older Labour Force:
Indonesia, Male, 2007**

Age	No school	<ES	ES	JHS	SHS	University	Total
35–59	4.20	12.27	39.30	17.90	19.40	6.93	100
40–59	5.12	14.25	41.04	16.69	16.20	6.70	100
60+	14.09	20.96	43.57	14.01	5.58	1.79	100

Note: ES-Elementary School; JHS-Junior High School; and SHS-Senior High School.
Source: Compiled and calculated from Statistics Indonesia, *Labour Force Situation in Indonesia, February 2007* (Jakarta: Statistics Indonesia, 2007).

TABLE 10.17

**Education of Pre-Older and Older Labour Force:
Indonesia, Female, 2007**

Age	No School	<ES	ES	JHS	SHS	University	Total
35–59	10.16	17.80	41.39	13.83	10.61	6.21	100
40–59	12.18	20.09	42.09	12.77	7.63	5.24	100
60+	33.73	22.18	30.77	11.66	1.35	0.31	100

Note: ES-Elementary School; JHS-Junior High School; and SHS-Senior High School.
Source: Compiled and calculated from Statistics Indonesia, *Labour Force Situation in Indonesia, February 2007* (Jakarta: Statistics Indonesia, 2007).

TABLE 10.18

**Education of Pre-Older and Older Labour Force:
Indonesia, Male and Female, 2007**

Age	No School	<ES	ES	JHS	SHS	University	Total
35–59	6.39	14.30	40.07	16.41	16.17	6.67	100
40–59	7.69	16.37	41.42	15.26	13.08	6.17	100
60+	20.81	21.38	39.19	13.20	4.13	1.29	100

Note: ES-Elementary School; JHS-Junior High School; and SHS-Senior High School.
Source: Compiled and calculated from Statistics Indonesia, *Labour Force Situation in Indonesia, February 2007* (Jakarta: Statistics Indonesia, 2007).

40–59 year old cohort in the labour force had university degrees, which was much higher than 1.29 per cent of the current older persons. The educational attainment, regardless of gender, is even higher among the younger labour force. The percentage among those having no schooling was only 6.39 per cent among the 35–59 year cohort, while it was

6.67 per cent among those with university education. Although educational attainment has improved for both sexes, men were still found to have a higher educational attainment compared with women.

In 2027, twenty years later, the current 40–59 year old cohort in the labour force will become older persons, replacing the current older persons. Assuming no change in the educational level of the current 40–59 year old cohort in the labour force, Table 10.19 presents the projected educational attainment of the older labour force in 2027. The percentage of no schooling will drop rapidly from 20.81 per cent in 2007 to 7.69 per cent in 2027, while the percentage with university education will rise sharply from 1.29 per cent in 2007 to 6.17 per cent in 2027.[1]

Similarly, assuming that the educational attainment of the current 35–59 year old cohort in the labour force will not change, Table 10.19 also provides the projected educational attainment of older persons in the labour force in 2032. It has been projected that the educational attainment of the older labour force in 2032 will be much improved by then compared with the current older cohort. Moreover, the percentage of the population with no schooling will decline to 6.39 per cent, and the percentage having a university education will rise to 6.67 per cent. However, gender differentials among the older cohorts in the future will

TABLE 10.19

**Projection of Education of Labour Force by Gender:
Indonesia, 2027 and 2032 (Percentage)**

Education	2027			2032		
	Male	Female	Total	Male	Female	Total
No schooling	5.12	12.18	7.69	4.20	10.16	6.39
< Elementary school	14.25	20.09	16.37	12.27	17.80	14.30
Elementary school	41.04	42.09	41.42	39.30	41.39	40.07
Junior high school	16.69	12.77	15.26	17.90	13.83	16.41
Senior high school	16.20	7.63	13.08	19.40	10.61	16.17
University	6.70	5.24	6.17	6.93	6.21	6.67
Total	100.0	100.0	100.0	100.0	100.0	100.0

Note: It is a conservative estimate, as the older group (with the least education) will have died in the future.
Source: Author's calculation.

TABLE 10.20

Annual Growth Rates of Working Age Population, Labour Force, and Not in Labour Force: Indonesia, 1998–2007

	Working Age Population	Labour Force	Not in LF
	1998–2007	1998–2007	1998–2007
Male			
Total	1.93	2.00	1.60
Older persons	2.05	1.59	2.95
Female			
Total	1.59	1.23	1.96
Older persons	1.98	0.70	2.66
Total			
Total	1.76	1.71	1.87
Older persons	2.01	1.28	2.75

Source: Calculated from Badan Pusat Statistik, *Labor Force Situation in Indonesia, August 1998* (Jakarta: Badan Pusat Statistik, 1999) and Statistics Indonesia, *Labour Force Situation in Indonesia, February 2007* (Jakarta: Statistics Indonesia, 2007).

remain, with males having an edge over females in terms of educational attainment.

CONCLUSIONS

Table 10.20 shows that the number of Indonesian older persons have been growing more rapidly (2.01 per cent) than that of the overall working age population (1.76 per cent) in 1998–2007, implying an increasingly ageing population in the country. However, the growth rate of the old labour force (1.28 per cent) is much smaller than that of the overall labour force (1.71 per cent), suggesting that when people become old, they are more likely to be out of the labour force. However, it should be noted that, from these statistics alone, it is not easy to conclude whether lower labour force participation is a good or bad thing for the older persons.

This pattern is seen among both sexes but with a difference looking at labour force participation rates. Among the male older persons, the difference between rates of growth of labour force and working population is only 0.46 percentage points (=2.05 – 1.59) — much smaller than 1.28 percentage points (=1.98 – 0.70) among female older persons. This implies that older women were more likely to be out of the labour force.

The lower labour force participation rate among women, including older women, may be attributed to several factors, two of which include social norms and education. The existing social norms posit that women bear the bulk of housework while men are expected to play the role of "rice winner". This social norm may have resulted in stronger gender segregation among the older persons because of the human capital accumulated during their younger days. The older women accumulated significant experience in household work, while the older men accumulated experience in the labour market. Nevertheless, as their health and skills deteriorated, the older men could not earn as much as they did when they were young. At the same time, the older women were also not as strong in doing household work as when they were younger.

Undoubtedly education plays a critical role in empowering women, including older women. If there is no significant change in education (or re-education) of women age 35 years and above in Indonesia today, it can be expected that future generations of older women will lag behind older men in their ability to be financially independent through labour force participation, and older men will still remain dependent on their wives for managing their households, at least until 2032. However, we cannot significantly change the educational attainment of current cohorts of older persons, including their gender differentials, as in the future cohorts (2027 and 2032, respectively) since older persons are already here today and they have already finished their educational years. Educational polices that start now with the effect of changing the gender differentials of future cohorts and their educational attainment will only affect the educational attainment of the older persons in 2062, assuming that formal education starts at 5 years old. Therefore, empowering future cohorts of older women in the labour market requires policies beyond raising educational attainment rates among women.

Nevertheless, everything can change with the advancement of technology, including modes of communication, transportation, and work environment. The advancements in technology, coupled with additional education among the older persons, will make gender segregation in jobs increasingly blurred. In this case, older women, and men, may retain and enhance their human capital, and we can expect a greater demand for older persons in the future labour market.

Furthermore, if there is an improvement in social insurance, particularly related to health, the more educated older female labour force (as well as older male labour force and the younger generations) will have better choices when they have to decide whether to work (for money) or to engage in "leisure". They may do voluntary work to help the younger generation develop the economy and by contributing to society in this way, there will be less of a "clash" between generations as the older generation will be perceived to be valuable rather than a burden. This situation may be similar to what Haider and Loughran (2001) found among the most educated, richest, and healthiest Americans, that is, that older persons were more likely to work for "leisure" than for economic necessity.

Finally, as mentioned in the beginning of this chapter, a more fundamental question should be raised on the kind of life we expect older persons to lead. While it is certain that the answers to this question will be useful towards formulating more effective policies concerning older women and men, any attempt to answer this question in its entirety is a complex undertaking, and one that is beyond the scope of this chapter.

Note

1. This is a conservative projection since the older cohort, with the lowest educational attainment, would have already died.

References

Arifin, Evi Nurvidya and Aris Ananta. "Employment of Older Persons: Diversity across Nations and Sub-Nations in Southeast Asia". In *Older Persons in Southeast Asia: An Emerging Asset*, edited by E.N. Arifin and A. Ananta. Singapore: Institute of Southeast Asian Studies, 2009.

Badan Pusat Statistik. *Labor Force Situation in Indonesia, August 1998*. Jakarta: Badan Pusat Statistik, 1999.

Chenery, Hollis B. "The Structural Approach to Development Policy". *The American Economic Review*, May 1975.

Clark, Robert, Naohiro Ogawa and Andy Mason, eds. *Population Aging, Intergenerational Transfers, and the Macroeconomy*. Massachusetts: Edward Elgar, 2007.

Haider, Steven and David Loughran. "Elderly Labour Supply: Work or Play". *Labor and Population Program Working Paper Series 01-09*. Rand Corporation, 2001.

Karoly, L.A. and J. Zissimopoulos. "Self-employment among Older U.S. Workers". *Monthly Labor Review* (July 2004): 24–47.

Rahardjo, Tribudi, Tony Hartono, Vita Priantina Dewi, Eef Hogervorst and Evi Nurvidya Arifin. "Facing the Geriatric Wave in Indonesia: Financial Conditions and Social Supports". In *Older Persons in Southeast Asia: An Emerging Asset*, edited by E.N. Arifin and A. Ananta. Singapore: Institute of Southeast Asian Studies, 2009.

Statistics Indonesia. *Labour Force Situation in Indonesia, February 2007*. Jakarta: Statistics Indonesia, 2007.

United Nations. *World Economic and Social Survey 2007: Development in an Ageing World*. New York: United Nations, 2007.

11

GENDER DIFFERENTIALS IN WORK AND INCOME AMONG OLDER MALAYSIANS

Tey Nai Peng and
Tengku Aizan Tengku Hamid

INTRODUCTION

The population of Malaysia is ageing gradually. Between 1970 and 2010, the proportion of the population age 60 and above to the total population increased from 5.2 per cent to 7.9 per cent. The number of older persons increased more than fourfold from a little more than half a million in 1970 to 2.25 million in 2010. By 2020, the number of older persons is projected to reach 3.2 million out of a population of about 32 million. The various ethnic groups in Malaysia are at different stages of ageing. In 2010, 12.2 per cent of the Chinese were age 60 and above as compared to 6.2 per cent of the other indigenous groups, 7.3 per cent among the Malays, and 7.9 per cent among the Indians.

Life expectancy at birth has gone up from 66.5 years for males and 71 years for females during the early 1970s to 71.9 years for males and 77 years for females in 2010 (Department of Statistics 2001 and 2011). According to the 2010 life tables, of those who would be alive at age 55, the number of years expected to be lived is about 21.5 years for males and 24.5 years for females. Gender differentials in life expectancy at various ages have given rise to feminization of the older population.

Despite the substantial increase in life expectancy, the retirement age remains at 55 years until recently for workers in the private sector. However, following the adoption of the Minimum Retirement Age Act 2012 by Parliament in the June/July session, the minimum retirement age of 60 for private sector workers was gazetted on 1 January 2013, and came into effect on 1 July 2013. Retirement age in the public sector was raised from 55 to 56 in 2001, to 58 in 2008 and further to 60 in 2013. With structural changes in the economy, an increasing number of workers have moved from the informal to the formal sector, and are subject to mandatory retirement. In 2005, about 73.8 per cent of the male workers and 78.5 per cent of the female workers were employees, as compared to 60.7 per cent and 52.9 per cent in 1975 (Department of Statistics 1976, 2006).

The growing awareness of the issues of population ageing in Malaysia led to the adoption of the National Policy for the Elderly in 1996. The goal of the policy was to establish a society wherein the elderly are contented, lead dignified lives, possess a high sense of self-worth, and are given the care and protection as members of a family, the society, and the nation. One of the objectives of the policy was to develop the potential of the elderly so that they remain active and productive in national development (Government of Malaysia 1996). Because older women are financially more vulnerable than older men, the feminization of the ageing population has received due attention from the government. Older persons are given financial assistance and preferential allocation for low-cost housing. Following a review of the National Policy for the Elderly, the National Policy for Older Persons (2010–15) was adopted in January 2011 to address the needs of older persons effectively and efficiently and to ensure an enabling and supportive environment for the well-being of older persons as well as to promote healthy, active, and productive ageing.

OBJECTIVES AND SCOPE

This chapter examines the gender differentials of older people in terms of work status and access to financial resources among the different ethnic groups in the country. In keeping with the objectives of the National Policy for Older Persons (2010–15) to promote active and productive ageing, we begin by analysing the work status of older men and women, which has a direct bearing on their economic well-being. Active ageing is the process of optimizing opportunities for health, participation, and security in order to enhance quality of life as people age (World Health Organization 2002). Continued work involvement has been found to have a positive effect on the physical and mental health of older people (Waddell and Burton 2006; Schwinge et al. 2009; and Zhan et al. 2009). Some older people have to work to support themselves because they do not receive financial aid from their children, who themselves may be struggling to make ends meet.

Older people have various sources of income, which can be classified as job-related income, including income from current and/or previous work (in terms of pension), investment-related income, and social income (mainly remittances from children). Specifically, this chapter examines:

(i)   gender differentials in work status;
(ii)   gender differentials in income, savings, and property ownership;
(iii) family support for older men and women; and
(iv)   gender differentials in perceived adequacy of income.

DATA SOURCES AND METHODOLOGY

The analysis in this chapter is based on data from a nation-wide survey entitled "Economic and Financial Aspects of the Older Malaysians" conducted by the Institute of Gerontology, Universiti Putra Malaysia in 2004. The survey covered a total of 2,327 respondents age 55 and above, comprising 1,178 males and 1,149 females from all thirteen states in the country. A representative sample was selected from the list of enumeration blocks and addresses maintained by the Department of Statistics, using a multi-stage sampling design. Officials from the Department of Statistics selected about 300 enumeration blocks (consisting about 100 houses each) from the 71 selected *mukim* (sub-districts). In the final stage, about one in ten houses were selected from each of the selected enumeration blocks. A more detailed description of the data can be found in Jariah et al. (2008) and Chan et al. (2010).

The sample is fairly representative of the general population, as indicated by the close correspondence of the age, sex, marital status, state, and ethnic distribution of the sample population with that of the older population age 55 and above in the 2000 population census. The socio-demographic characteristics of the sample are given in Appendix 1.

Bivariate analyses were used to examine the gender differentials in labour force participation, income and savings, family care and support, and perceived adequacy of income. Logistic regression was used to show the odds of working for an older person, within the multivariate context, and to examine the relative importance of each of the explanatory variables.

WORK STATUS

Labour Force Participation of Older Malaysians

The labour force participation rate of older people varies widely across countries from less than 2 per cent among the males and 0.5 per cent among the females in some European countries to more than 80 per cent among the males and more than 60 per cent among the females in some African countries. In less developed countries, owing to the lack of old-age support systems, many older people have to work to support themselves (United Nations 2002).

The retirement age in Malaysia, at 55 years in the private sector, and 58 years in the public sector as at 2012, is relatively young compared with a number of Asian countries. For instance, the retirement age is 60 years in South Korea, People's Republic of China, and Vietnam; and 65 years in Singapore and Japan. In spite of the early retirement age, a rather sizable proportion of older Malaysians are still working. Some retirees have continued to work on a contract basis, having found a new job, while others have started a small business. Workers in the informal sector are not subject to the mandatory retirement age.

What are the reasons for older people to continue working? In this survey, about 30 per cent of the respondents wanted to continue working and their reasons are shown in Figure 11.1. Financial consideration was by far the most important reason for older people to continue working. About two-thirds mentioned financial needs and another 14 per cent mentioned financial independence as a reason for working. Financial consideration was mentioned by 84 per cent of the males and 74 per cent of the females for wanting to continue working.

Work status, however, differs markedly between older men and women. Figure 11.2 shows that only a very small proportion of older males have never worked while more than one-third of the older women have never worked. Hence, it is no surprise that older men were three times as likely as older women to be still working (see Knodel and Chayovan, this volume). Data also show that 60 per cent of the older men and 47 per cent of the older women have retired from their previous jobs. Among those who were economically active, 83 per cent did not intend to stop working.

FIGURE 11.1

Percentage Distribution of Respondents by Reasons for Wanting to Continue Working

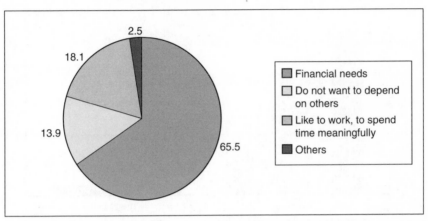

Source: 2004 Survey of Economic and Financial Aspects of the Older Malaysians (original tabulations).

FIGURE 11.2

Percentage Distribution of Older Persons Age 55 and Above by Work Status and Gender

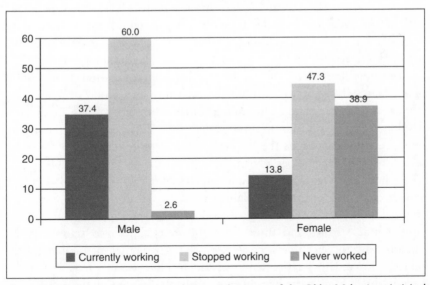

Source: 2004 Survey of Economic and Financial Aspects of the Older Malaysians (original tabulations).

FIGURE 11.3
Per Cent Currently Working by Age and Gender

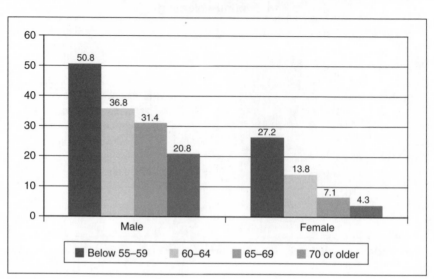

Source: 2004 Survey of Economic and Financial Aspects of the Older Malaysians (original tabulations).

Labour force participation rates for both older men and women declined sharply with advancing age. Among those age 55–59 years, about half of the men and a little more than a quarter of the women were working, but these figures declined sharply to about 21 per cent and 4 per cent respectively at age 70 and above (see Figure 11.3).

Ethnic differentials in the labour force participation rate among older men were not as pronounced as those for older women. The labour force participation rate among older men and women in the less developed states was significantly higher than their counterparts in the more developed states, as the former are much more likely than the latter to be self-employed, especially in the agricultural sector (see Table 11.1). The ethnic and regional differentials in the labour force participation rate among older people can be explained by the type of work that they were engaged in earlier on. The lower labour force participation rate among older Chinese males and those from the more developed states may be explained by the fact that they were working in the urban modern sector subject to mandatory retirement age. Indian older women have by far the lowest labour force participation rate, probably because of the lack of job opportunities for them in the formal sector in the urban areas.

TABLE 11.1
Percentage of Persons Age 55 and Above Currently Working by Sex and Selected Variables

	Sub-Groups	Male	Female
Total sample		37.4	15.3
Ethnicity	Malays and other indigenous groups	38.1	13.8
	Chinese	34.3	13.3
	Indians	40.3	4.0
Place of residence	More developed states	32.5	11.0
	Less developed states	40.9	16.5
Marital status	Never married	28.6	47.4
	Married	40.2	17.2
	Divorced	26.3	12.9
	Widowed	18.8	9.6
Educational level	No schooling	34.4	12.8
	Primary	41.1	14.2
	Lower secondary	31.3	16.1
	Upper secondary and above	33.5	19.4
Health status	Poor	16.7	8.8
	Average	32.0	12.1
	Good	46.9	17.7
Living arrangement	Alone	21.2	12.8
	With spouse only	37.6	15.7
	With spouse and children	41.1	18.0
	With children only	19.0	9.3
	Others	29.6	18.3

Note: For males, the work status is significantly related to place of residence, marital status and health status ($p < 0.05$), but it is not related with all other variables in the table. For females, the work status is significantly related to all variables in the table, except educational level and living arrangement ($p < 0.05$).
Source: 2004 Survey of Economic and Financial Aspects of the Older Malaysians (original tabulations).

The labour force participation rate is found to vary widely by marital status. Table 11.1 shows that widowed older persons were less likely to work as compared to their married counterparts. The lower labour force participation rate among the widowed elderly is partly attributed to their older age structure, as their mean age was 3 to 4 years higher than those who were currently married. Moreover, a higher proportion of the widowed persons have little or no education.

In terms of education, older men with primary schooling were more likely to be working compared to those with higher education. In contrast, older women with higher education were more likely than their less educated counterparts to be economically active. However, results from this sample survey do not show significant association between work status and educational level for both males and females (p > 0.05).

Health status was found to be a very important determinant for labour force participation of older people. Older men who perceived themselves to be in good health were three times more likely to work than those with perceived poor health, and the healthy older women were also twice as likely to work as compared to those with poor health. Studies have found that work is beneficial to physical and mental health and well-being, and not working is associated with poorer physical and mental health and well-being (Dhaval Dave et al. 2008; Waddell and Burton 2006). Zhan et al. (2009) and Cahill et al. (2005) also found that bridge employment (defined as any paid work after an individual retires or starts receiving a pension) helped protect retirees from major diseases and the decline of daily functions. Consistent with continuity theory, they argued that when retirees engaged in bridge employment, they were more likely to retain their former levels of physical and mental activities through daily work.

The survey showed that the health of the older persons deteriorated with age. Persons age 70 and above were twice as likely as those age 55–59 to report being in poor health (22 per cent versus 11 per cent). Older women were more likely than older men to report being in poor health. Given the positive correlation between labour force participation rate and health status, older persons having good health were much more likely to work as compared to those with poor health. This was true for both older men and women (see Table 11.1).

Work status is also related with living arrangements. Older persons living with a spouse and children were most likely to work, and those who coresided with children only were least likely to work. It may be that some "young-old" were still working to support their children. Owing to delayed marriage and child-bearing, many older persons still have to support school-going children.

Labour force participation rate is influenced by a host of socio-demographic variables. In order to determine the factors that explain the labour force participation rate of older men and women, separate logistic regressions were run to assess the effects of these variables in a multivariate context, and the results are shown in Table 11.2.

TABLE 11.2
Logistic Regression of Per Cent of Older Men and Women Currently Working

	Male		Female	
	Exp (B)	Sig.	Exp (B)	Sig.
Age group				
70+	1.00		1.00	
55–59	3.823	0.00	7.182	0.00
60–64	2.236	0.00	3.278	0.00
65–69	1.733	0.01	1.458	0.35
Marital status				
Widowed	1.00		1.00	
Never married	1.523	0.40	8.983	0.00
Married	2.356	0.00	1.429	0.07
Divorced	1.174	0.79	1.291	0.66
Educational level				0.38
Upper secondary and above	1.00		1.00	
No schooling	1.813	0.01	1.093	0.83
Primary	1.907	0.00	0.795	0.56
Lower secondary	1.019	0.94	0.663	0.44
Ethnic group		0.69		0.02
Indian	1.00		1.00	
Malay and others	0.816	0.49	4.628	0.01
Chinese	0.904	0.75	3.806	0.02
Place of residence				
Developed states	1.00		1.00	
Less developed states	1.453	0.01	1.480	0.05
Perceived health status		0.00		0.00
Good	1.00		1.00	
Poor	0.240	0.00	0.448	0.01
Average	0.572	0.00	0.681	0.06
Constant	0.107	0.00	0.011	0.00

Source: 2004 Survey of Economic and Financial Aspects of the Older Malaysians (original tabulations).

The "young-old" women and men were respectively seven times and four times more likely than their "old-old" counterparts to be in the labour force. However, there was no significant difference in the labour force participation rate between women age 65–69 and those age 70 and above. Moreover, currently married older men and women were much more likely to be working as compared to their widowed counterparts. There is no significant difference in the labour force participation rate between the divorced and widowed older persons.

Holding other variables constant, the labour force participation rate of older women did not vary according to their educational level. However, older men with primary or no schooling were almost twice as likely as those with at least upper secondary education to be in the labour force, net of other variables. This can be explained by the fact that the former were more likely than the latter to be engaged in the informal sector where there is no mandatory retirement age.

For older males, there was no significant difference in the labour force participation rate across the ethnic groups. However, compared to older Indian women, women of all other ethnic groups were about four times more likely to be working. The labour force participation rate of older men and women from the less developed states was about one and a half times higher than those from the developed states, as those from the less developed states were much more likely to work in the informal sector and not subject to mandatory retirement.

Health status turns out to be an important determinant for the labour force participation of older persons. Older men in poor health were about 76 per cent less likely to work compared with those in good health. Those who reported having fair health were also much less likely to work compared to those in good health. The same finding was reported elsewhere by Ng and Tey (2006).

Type of Work

Older people were involved in a variety of work. Some continued at their previous jobs, while others started on a new job. Table 11.3 shows that the majority of the older workers were engaged in agriculture or small businesses, partly because agricultural workers and the self-employed who own small businesses are not subject to mandatory retirement. Older women were more likely than older men to run their own businesses but less likely to work as labourers (see Natividad, Saito and Cruz, this volume). Few older workers (5 per cent of the total) were working as professionals or administrators and managers.

In terms of employment status, about 60 per cent of older workers were self-employed; one in three was an employee; and one in ten was an employer. There was little difference in employment status between older males and females, except that older women were more likely to be unpaid family workers as compared to older men (7 per cent versus 2 per cent).

TABLE 11.3

Workers Age 55 and Above by Occupational Categories and Gender

Occupation	Male	Female	Both Sexes
Professional	2.2	2.3	2.3
Administrative and managerial	3.5	3.0	3.3
Small business	20.4	30.1	22.8
Labourer	7.8	3.9	6.8
Semi skilled operator	3.5	2.3	3.2
Services	4.5	3.0	4.1
Agriculture	39.4	41.5	39.9
Driver	5.2	0.0	4.0
Others	13.5	13.8	13.6
Total	100.0	100.0	100.0

Source: 2004 Survey of Economic and Financial Aspects of the Older Malaysians (original tabulations).

Income Sources and Level, and Perceived Adequacy of Income

Income Sources

Access to financial resources is essential to meet the various needs of an individual, especially with the escalating cost of living and medical care. Poverty eradication has always been the priority of the Government. The poverty line income in 2004 was RM691[1] for the country as a whole, and this ranged from RM661 for Peninsular Malaysia, RM888 for Sabah, and RM765 for Sarawak (Government of Malaysia 2006). The poor, including the older people among them, have been a target group for financial assistance.

Older people have various sources of income. The sources of income of older people may be categorized as: (i) job-related income, (ii) investment-related income and savings, and (iii) social income which comprises mainly remittances from children.

In regards to the gender differentials in labour force participation rate, older men were more than twice as likely as older women to receive income from their current job and/or pension payment from previous jobs, while older women were more likely than older men to receive money from children. Older women were also more likely than older men to receive income from investments (see Table 11.4).

A more detailed breakdown of the sources of income is shown in Table 11.5. Data shown in Table 11.5 correspond closely with the mean

TABLE 11.4
Sources of Income (in Ringgit) of Older Men and Women

Sources of Income	Male		Female		Both Sexes	
	% Receiving	Amount Received	% Receiving	Amount Received	% Receiving	Amount Received
Job related	68.0	6,697	31.3	1,490	49.9	4,126
Investment related	25.2	1,765	29.7	2,408	27.4	2,082
Remittances from children	67.1	2,336	79.5	2,718	73.2	2,524

Source: 2004 Survey of Economic and Financial Aspects of the Older Malaysians (original tabulations).

TABLE 11.5
Detailed Sources of Income (in Ringgit) of Older Malaysians

Sources of Income	Male		Female		Both Sexes	
	% Receiving	Median Annual Income	% Receiving	Median Annual Income	% Receiving	Median Annual Income
Wages	30.1	4,800	10.5	2,400	20.4	4,200
Profit from business	11.1	7,200	5.3	1,080	8.3	4,500
Income from farming	11.9	1,200	7.3	600	9.6	1,111
Pension	24.6	6,426	9.7	4,800	17.2	8,000
Money from sons	53.8	1,200	67.7	1,200	60.7	1,200
Money from daughters	38.7	600	48.3	600	43.4	600
Money from grandchildren	3.8	100	4.8	200	4.3	130
Rental	4.9	3,600	3.7	3,600	4.3	3,600
Dividend	2.0	1,154	0.8	500	1.4	1,200
Bonus	3.7	600	0.5	600	2.1	600
Annuity	0.3	720	0.3	4,200	0.3	860

Source: 2004 Survey of Economic and Financial Aspects of the Older Malaysians (original tabulations).

income reported by Jariah et al. (2008), as the two studies are based on the same data set.

While older people were much more likely to be self-employed as compared to working for others, a higher proportion reported receiving wages and pension rather than income from business or farming. The inconsistency may arise because of under-reporting among those working in the informal sector. Taken at face value, engaging in business was most lucrative for older men, but older women were better off in paid employment compared with running a privately-owned business. For both older men and women, agricultural activities were the least lucrative. The low income in agricultural employment is not peculiar to Malaysia. As noted by Cervantes-Godoy and Dewbre (2010, p. 3), "people in developing countries who depend on agriculture for their living are typically much poorer than people who work in other sectors of the economy".

The main pillars of social security in Malaysia are the Employee Provident Fund (EPF, mainly for private-sector employees) and pension schemes (covering about 95 per cent of workers in the public service). These two schemes cover half of the total employed labour force. All employees, with the exception of certain categories, are entitled to join EPF. Coverage is also extended to the self-employed on a voluntary basis. In reviewing the income provision for the elderly under the auspices of the EPF, Caraher (2000) concluded that the social security scheme is inadequate to meet the needs of an increasing older population and leaves them more vulnerable to poverty in old age.

The pension scheme, which is only for public civil servants, extends to their widow/widowers. Upon retirement, a retiree (or his/her surviving spouse) will be paid half of the last drawn salary for the rest of his/her life (Jamilah and Tey 2008). Hence, pension is another form of job-related income for workers in the public sector. In this sample, almost one quarter of older men and one in ten older women were receiving pension, and the amount received was much higher than their income from current employment.

Children living elsewhere remitted money to either one or both parents. Presumably, money received by either one of the parents is meant to be spent for the household. In this survey, older women were more likely than older men to receive money from children (see Table 11.5). Older persons were more likely to receive money from sons rather than daughters (61 per cent versus 43 per cent). Among the recipients of remittances, half of them received at least RM1,200 annually from sons, and half that amount from daughters.

Few older men and women had income from rental, dividend, bonus, and annuity. However, among the few that had rental income, the amount received was more than the amount of remittances received from children.

Income Level

The mean income level of older persons was RM6,351 a year or RM529 a month. Pronounced differentials in the individual income of older men and women exist for socio-demographic sub-groups (see Table 11.6). The income of older men and women decreases with age as they withdraw from the labour market. For both sexes, the Malays have the lowest income and the Chinese have the highest. The personal income of divorced and widowed older persons was just about half that of the currently married. As expected, the income level was much higher among those who have

TABLE 11.6
Mean Annual Personal Income and Household Income (in Ringgit) by Gender and Selected Socio-Demographic Characteristics

	Individual Income			Household Income		
	Male	Female	Both Sexes	Male	Female	Both Sexes
Total	8,711	3,932	6,351	27,949	27,309	27,633
Age group						
55–59	10,430	5,547	8,213	30,683	32,964	31,718
60–64	9,029	3,813	6,492	27,349	27,849	27,592
65–69	7,120	3,069	5,034	23,973	25,559	23,245
70 and older	7,137	2,993	4,896	29,305	24,980	26,966
Ethnic group						
Malay and other indigenous	7,795	3,387	5,648	24,103	23,186	23,656
Chinese	11,318	5,670	8,629	38,943	39,896	39,397
Indian	9,620	3,961	6,127	31,595	28,951	29,963
Marital status						
Never married	3,958	6,535	5,000	11,645	18,205	14,297
Married	9,175	4,489	7,557	28,505	32,837	30,001
Divorced	3,920	3,644	3,749	13,542	29,167	23,230
Widowed	6,824	3,343	3,982	29,297	22,381	23,649
Educational level						
No schooling	4,410	2,673	3,179	19,738	20,925	20,579
Primary	7,215	4,401	6,081	22,468	30,649	25,767
Lower secondary	10,454	6,782	9,230	34,321	35,288	34,643
Upper secondary and above	17,493	10,915	15,971	50,758	62,271	53,421
Work status						
Not working	6,647	3,452	4,816	26,172	26,759	26,508
Working	12,173	6,921	10,779	30,929	30,734	30,878

Source: 2004 Survey of Economic and Financial Aspects of the Older Malaysians (original tabulations).

higher education and who were working as compared to those who have lower education and were not working.

Since couples share their financial resources, household income is a better measure of the well-being of older men and women. No discernible gender differentials in household income were observed across age, ethnicity, and work status. However, except for the widows, older women have significantly higher household income as compared to older men. Older women with primary and upper secondary education also tended to fare better than older men in the same education category in terms of household income (see Table 11.6).

The average household income of older Malaysians reported in this survey is much lower than that of the mean annual gross household income of RM38,988 for the country as a whole and RM47,472 for the urban households, but it is slightly higher than the mean monthly gross household income of RM22,500 for rural households (Government of Malaysia 2006). Nevertheless, under-reporting of household income by respondents in this survey is highly probable as many of them were not the main breadwinners. The decrease in household income with rising age may be partly explained by the fact that the relative contribution of older persons to the household economy decreases with age.

The ethnic differentials in household income among older persons are reflective of the differentials in the general population. In 2004, the Malays and other *bumiputera* groups (literally, sons of the soil) had a mean monthly gross household income of RM2,711, as compared to RM4,437 for the Chinese and RM3,456 for the Indians (Government of Malaysia 2006). Ethnic income differentials could be explained by the differences in occupation, as non-Malays are more likely to be engaged in commerce, while the Malays tend to work in the rural agricultural sector. However, the ethnic differentials in income has narrowed over time as the Government has been implementing programmes under the New Economic Policy (1970–90) and its successors, the National Development Policy (1991–2000) and the National Vision Policy (2001–10) to restructure society to reduce and eventually eliminate economic imbalances arising from the occupational identification with ethnic groups.

The mean income does not reflect income distribution which is known to be skewed. Table 11.7 presents the income distribution of respondents, which did not vary much by gender. More than half of the older persons in this survey have an annual household income of less than RM20,000, and close to 30 per cent have less than RM10,000. An examination of the percentile of income shows that 22 per cent of the older persons

TABLE 11.7

Percentage Distribution of Annual Household Income by Gender

Income Group	Male	Female	Both Sexes
<RM10,00	28.1	31.2	29.7
RM10,000–19,999	25.8	23.0	24.4
RM20,000–29,999	16.1	15.7	15.9
RM30,000–39,999	11.5	9.2	10.4
RM40,000–49,999	5.2	6.8	6.0
RM50,000+	13.2	14.1	13.7
Total	100.0	100.0	100.0

Source: 2004 Survey of Economic and Financial Aspects of the Older Malaysians (original tabulations).

were living below the poverty line of RM8,292 per year. The proportion of the elderly in this survey living below the poverty line is much higher than the incidence of poverty in the country, at 5.7 per cent.

Detailed tabulation of the data shows that more than one-third of older people from some groups have a household income of less than RM10,000 per year, and these include older men and women age 65 years and above, the never married, those who have never been to schools, and those living in the less developed states. The data also show that more than one-third of the older Malay women and divorced men were from the lowest income group. The less educated ones, however, were unaware of the government programmes that provide financial assistance to those who are in abject poverty.

Perceived Adequacy of Income

The point about perceived adequacy of income was also raised in the survey. Overall, about 16 per cent of the older people reported that their income was inadequate to meet their basic needs, and 47 per cent reported that it was just enough. Only 5 per cent of the respondents reported that they had some surplus for saving. There was no significant variation in perceived income adequacy between older men and women. However, the never married and divorcees were much more likely than the currently married and widowed older persons to report inadequacy of income (see Table 11.8).

In terms of ethnic groups, Malays and Indians were much more likely than the Chinese to report income inadequacy, and this can be attributed to their income differentials, as perceived income inadequacy is

TABLE 11.8
Percentage Distribution of Respondents by Perceived Income Adequacy by Selected Variables

		Perceived Income Adequacy				
	Inadequate	Adequate to Meet Basic Needs	Adequate to Meet Most Needs	Adequate to Meet All Needs	Have Surplus for Saving	Total
All	16.1	47.3	21.3	10.3	5.0	100.0
Gender						
Male	16.0	45.1	22.5	10.5	6.0	100.0
Female	16.2	49.7	20.0	10.1	4.0	100.0
Ethnic group						
Malay/other indigenous	16.8	49.2	21.5	8.1	4.5	100.0
Chinese	12.8	40.2	23.2	17.0	6.7	100.0
Indian	19.8	51.2	13.0	11.1	4.9	100.0
Marital status						
Never married	34.0	42.6	17.0	2.1	4.3	100.0
Married	14.4	46.7	21.6	11.6	5.6	100.0
Divorced	26.5	40.8	20.4	8.2	4.1	100.0
Widowed	17.8	49.4	20.8	8.2	3.7	100.0
Household income						
<RM10,000	23.7	54.1	14.8	5.4	2.0	100.0
RM10,000–19,999	16.8	49.8	21.0	8.1	4.2	100.0
RM20,000–29,999	13.6	47.4	24.4	10.8	3.8	100.0
RM30,000–39,999	10.8	45.2	23.7	13.3	7.1	100.0
RM40,000–49,999	15.2	35.5	23.2	18.1	8.0	100.0
RM50,000+	5.7	34.8	29.4	18.7	11.4	100.0

Note: $P < 0.05$ for ethnicity, marital status and household income, and more than 0.05 for gender. A p-value of < 0.05 means that the association between perceived adequacy of income and the specific socio-economic variable is statistically significant at 95 per cent confidence level.
Source: 2004 Survey of Economic and Financial Aspects of the Older Malaysians (original tabulations).

strongly related to income level. As expected, a higher proportion from the lower income groups were struggling to make ends meet. Nevertheless, some 6 per cent of the respondents with an annual household income of RM50,000 or more also reported that their income was inadequate to meet basic needs. This suggests that there is a need for household budget management and financial planning.

DISCUSSION AND CONCLUSIONS

The increasing number and proportion of older people in Malaysia has attracted the attention of policy-makers and researchers, especially after the launch of the National Policy for the Elderly in 1996. Research interest on the elderly has centred mainly on health and economic aspects. This chapter shows that many older persons, especially the males, are self-reliant, with income derived from current and previous jobs as well as investments. As women have lower labour force participation rates, they tend to depend more on their spouse and children for financial support in old age.

Household income rather than individual income provides a better measure of the well-being of older married men and women because it is a common practice for couples to share their financial resources. The household income of older women and men is about the same for most sub-groups of the population, although individual income varies widely between males and females. The foregoing analysis shows that older people are more likely than the general population to come from low income households. As it is the objective of the government to eradicate poverty, older men and women who have very low household income should be given special assistance.

The disadvantaged position of older women is partly the result of their low labour force participation rate. As women become better educated, more of them enter the labour market, thus narrowing the gender disparity in personal income in old age, barring any other changes. Between 1975 and 2005, female employment increased from 1.23 million persons to 3.57 million persons, and of the working women, the proportion engaged in the services sector doubled from 19.8 per cent to 38.6 per cent, while those engaged in agriculture declined from 50.3 per cent to 10.2 per cent.

The mandatory retirement age in the private and public sectors is relatively young, and many older people are willing and able to continue working. In keeping with the objectives of the National Policy for the Elderly and the new National Policy for Older Persons, effort must be made to facilitate the continued participation of older people in economic activities. As alluded to earlier, active ageing is beneficial to the health and well-being of the older people. The continued participation of older people in economic activities will also reduce their dependence on their children who are also struggling to make ends meet in the wake of rising cost of living and competing demands. Besides economic activities, older persons should be encouraged to play a more active role in the community. Many studies have found that active ageing is beneficial to the health and well-being of older people and, hence, contributes towards the reduced utilization of healthcare services.

Retirement has different implications on men and women economically, socially, and emotionally. Because women have lower labour force participation rates and are more involved in household chores, retirement does not disrupt their routine life as much as for men who are socialized into prioritizing careers and spending more time at the workplace. Not surprisingly, many older men have problems adjusting to the sudden change in role and status and shrinking social networks upon retirement.

With socio-demographic changes, especially the out-migration of the young, coresidence is becoming less common. While many older persons still receive financial assistance and care from their children, the quantum may not be sufficient. In some instances, older persons do not only have to support their school-going children, but may also have to support their own parents as well. Policies and programmes should be put in place to encourage and facilitate working couples to take care of their aged parents, especially those who do not have their own financial resources.

APPENDIX 1
Distribution of Respondents by Gender and Socio-Demographic Characteristics

		Male	Female	Both Sexes
Total sample		1,178	1,149	2,327
Ethnicity	Malay	667	629	1,296
	Chinese	274	249	523
	Indian	62	100	162
	Other indigenous groups	175	171	346
Place of residence	More developed states	668	611	1,279
	Less developed states	510	538	1,048
Age group	55–59	380	316	696
	60–64	321	304	625
	65–69	280	297	577
	70+	197	232	429
Marital status	Never married	28	19	47
	Married	1,003	529	1,532
	Divorced	19	31	50
	Widowed	128	570	698
Educational level	No schooling	256	623	879
	Primary	604	408	1,012
	Lower secondary	112	56	168
	Upper secondary and above	206	62	268

Source: 2004 Survey of Economic and Financial Aspects of the Older Malaysians (original tabulations).

Note

1. As of February 2013, the exchange rate between the Malaysian Ringgit and the U.S. dollar was US$1=RM3.1015.

References

Cahill, Kevin E., Michael D. Giandrea and Joseph F. Quinn. "Are Traditional Retirements a Thing of the Past? New Evidence on Retirement Patterns and Bridge Jobs". Working Papers 384. U.S. Bureau of Labor Statistics, 2005.

Caraher, Kevin. "Issues in Incomes Provision for the Elderly in Malaysia". Paper presented at The Year 2000 International Research Conference on Social Security, Social Security in the Global Village, Helsinki, 25–27 September 2000.

Cervantes-Godoy, Dalila and Joe Dewbre. "Economic Importance of Agriculture for Poverty Reduction". *OECD Food, Agriculture and Fisheries Working Papers*, No. 23. Doi: 10.1787/5kmmv9s20944-en, OECD, 2010. Available at <http://www.oecd.org/countries/panama/44804637.pdf> (accessed 27 December 2012).

Chan, Y.F.B., P. Laily, M. Jariah and Tengku T.H. Aizan. "The Future of Older Malaysian Employees: An Exploratory Study". *International Journal of Business and Management* 5, no. 4 (2010): 125–32.

Department of Statistics (DOS). "Labor Force Survey Report". Putrajaya: DOS, 1976.

———. "Vital Statistics Time Series Malaysia, 1963–98". Putrajaya: DOS, 2001.

———. "Labor Force Survey Report". Putrajaya: DOS, 2006.

———. "Abridged Life Tables 2008–10". Putrajaya: DOS, 2011.

Dhaval, Dave, Inas Rashad and Jasmina Spasojevic. "The Effects of Retirement on Physical and Mental Health Outcomes". Working Paper 2008-1-5, January 2008. W.J. Usery Workplace Research Group Paper Series. Available at <http://aysps.gsu.edu/usery/Papers.htm> (accessed 24 April 2009).

Government of Malaysia. Seventh Malaysia Plan. Putrajaya: Government Printer, 1996.

———. Ninth Malaysia Plan. Putrajaya: Government Printer, 2006.

Institute of Gerontology. 2004 Survey of Economic and Financial Aspects of the Older Malaysians. Selangor: Universiti Putra Malaysia, 2004.

Jamilah Ariffin and Tey Nai Peng. "Country Studies Malaysia: Social Services Policies and Family Well-being in the Asian and Pacific Region". In *Asia-Pacific Population and Social Studies Series No. 165*. Economic and Social Commission for Asia and the Pacific. Bangkok: ESCAP, United Nations, 2008.

Jariah Masud and Sharifah Azizah Haron. "Income Differences among Elderly in Malaysia: A Regional Comparison". *International Journal of Consumer Studies* 32, issue 4 (July 2008): 335–40.

Ng, S.T. and N.P. Tey. "Retirement and Perceived Health Status of the Urban Elderly". *Asia Pacific Journal of Public Health* 18 (Suppl.) (2006): 9–13.

Schwingel, A., M.W. Niti, C. Tang and T.P. Ng. "Continued Work Employment and Volunteerism and Mental Well-being of Older Adults: Singapore Longitudinal Ageing Studies". *Age and Ageing* 38, no. 5 (2009): 531–37.

United Nations. *World Population Ageing*, 1950–2050. New York: United Nations, 2002.

Waddell, Gordon and A. Kim Burton. *UK: Is Work Good for Health and Wellbeing?* London: The Stationery Office, 2006.

World Health Organization. *Active Ageing: A Policy Framework*. World Health Organization, 2002. Available at <http://whqlibdoc.who.int/hq/2002/WHO_NMH_NPH_02.8.pdf> (accessed 27 December 2012).

Zhan, Y., M. Wang, S. Liu and K.S. Shultz. "Bridge Employment and Retirees' Health: A Longitudinal Investigation". *Journal of Occupational Health Psychology* 14, no. 4 (2009): 374–89.

12

GENDER AND ECONOMIC WELL-BEING AMONG OLDER FILIPINOS[1]

Grace T. Cruz, Anna Melissa C. Lavares,
Maria Paz N. Marquez, Josefina N. Natividad
and Yasuhiko Saito

INTRODUCTION

Older women are often perceived as more vulnerable to social, economic, and health disadvantages. It is often surmised that gender discrimination is the main cause for the disadvantages they face. In situations where social structures reinforce such gender biases, particularly in education and employment opportunities, the cumulative effect of earlier life experiences render older women generally poorer than men. There are those who argue that the perceived disadvantaged position of older women may be an oversimplified global generalization which ignores the substantial variations in the relative situations of older men and women (Ofstedal, Reidy, and Knodel 2004; Knodel and Ofstedal 2003). In the Philippines, for example, the legal framework affirms equality for all citizens regardless of gender, which has helped ensure a relatively high degree of protection of its women. This is not to say that gender equality has been fully achieved, given the discrimination against women that continues to prevail in some sectors in the Philippines. It is thus important to understand the gender situation, particularly on the economic front among the older cohort, most of whom come from the generations that preceded the enactment of policies and programmes that have protected the rights and privileges of women in the country.

This chapter aims to provide an empirical analysis of the economic well-being of older Filipinos highlighting differences across gender and marital status groups. It explores the levels and differentials in economic status of older people using various objective and subjective indicators of economic well-being. The extent to which subjective and objective indicators of economic well-being interrelate with each other is likewise examined so as to generate a more appropriate measure for assessing the economic well-being of older Filipinos. This analysis is of importance in a low-income country such as the Philippines where a third of the country's population is currently living in poverty (UN OCHA, n.d.), with the older sector expected to be more vulnerable to economic liabilities. Exploring the possible interactions among economic and marital status and gender in old age is significant given that women are more likely to experience marital disruption which impinges on their economic well-being. The study findings presented in this chapter will hopefully allow new evidence needed for the formulation of appropriate programme and policy options to address the well-being of older people in general and the economically deprived older population in particular.

AGEING AND GENDER POLICIES AND PROGRAMMES

Despite the country's young population structure, the ageing issue is gaining recognition from the Philippine government. International initiatives calling attention to gender issues have likewise led to various efforts towards ensuring the promotion of gender equality in various policies and programmes. This is evident in the constitutional provisions and other policies recognizing the importance of gender and ageing, albeit as distinct rather than as linked issues.

The Philippine Constitution ensures that older Filipinos receive due care from the family and the state. It mandates the family to assume a predominant caregiving role for their elderly members and the state to adopt a comprehensive approach to health development that gives priority to the needs of the elderly (Article XIII, Section 11 of the 1987 Philippine Constitution). Accordingly, significant state efforts have been exerted to advance the welfare of the elderly, most of which have centred on the need to provide healthcare in the form of curative services. Worth mentioning are three major legislative milestones: Republic Act (RA) 7432 or the Senior Citizen's Act, whose most significant provision is the 20 per cent discount on medicines for older people age 60 and above; RA 7876 which provides for the establishment of Senior Citizens Centres; and RA 9257 or the Expanded Senior Citizens Act of 2003, which broadens the coverage of the benefits and privileges for senior citizens. More recently, RA 9994 or the Expanded Senior Citizens Act of 2010 provides additional benefits and grants senior citizens exemption from payment of value-added tax (VAT) on their purchases of qualified goods and services, allowing them to fully enjoy the 20 per cent discount on their purchases.

While policies and programmes have been in place to ensure the welfare of the elderly, evidence shows drastic differences in their implementation across the country. Generally, those residing in richer local government units (LGUs) have a better chance of accessing privileges than their counterparts from poorer LGUs. Evidence likewise shows that policy implementation works to benefit the better educated and higher income older people. For example, discounts in the purchase of medicines privilege those who have the means to purchase in the first place but have no beneficial effect on those who cannot afford to buy medication (Cruz, Saito and Natividad 2007).

Policies and programmes addressing the older people are generally gender-neutral. The constitution stipulates a clear legal framework articulating the "fundamental equality before the law of women and men" (Article II, Section 14 of the 1987 Constitution). The Philippines is also a signatory to the UN Convention on the Elimination of All Forms of Discrimination against Women (CEDAW) and recently passed the Magna Carta of Women, Philippines. This perhaps explains the relatively balanced treatment of men and women in the country, including those in the older ages, albeit there are still remaining vestiges of discrimination against women particularly in the employment and political sectors.

OBJECTIVE AND SUBJECTIVE INDICATORS OF ECONOMIC WELL-BEING

Using data from the 2007 Philippine Longitudinal Study of Aging (PLSOA),[2] this section examines the levels and differentials in economic status of older people using objective and subjective indicators of economic well-being. The discussion covers the extent to which these two classifications are interrelated with each other. Given the difficulty of measuring economic status in general, the analysis addresses multiple objective or tangible indicators of economic well-being which include the following: main sources of income, assets and liabilities, familial economic support, spouses' income, and wealth index. In the PLSOA survey, monthly income includes receipts from all possible income sources such as pension, salary, earnings from business, and money received from children and relatives. Respondents were instructed to include their spouses' income, if currently married. Although work is a major source of economic support, it is not discussed at length in this chapter since the chapter by Josefina Natividad et al. (this volume) addresses work, retirement, and the gender divide of the Filipino older people. However, this study does look at its importance as a source of income relative to other sources, as well as its relationship with perceived economic well-being.

The subjective indicator of economic well-being used in this analysis is the self-assessed income adequacy. This information was collected by asking respondents what they thought of the income of all the members of their household *vis-à-vis* all the expenses for maintaining or running the whole household.

This analysis focuses on the differences in the categories of gender and marital status. Marital status is classified into currently married and not currently married, with the former including those who are either formally married or in a living-in arrangement, including those who are separated from their spouses because of hospitalization, residence in an institution, or residence in another area for business reasons. Not currently married respondents include those who are never married, widowed, and separated.

Objective Indicators of Economic Well-Being

Main sources of income

Findings show that older Filipinos derive their income from various sources, each having an average of two sources with no significant difference across gender and marital status (see Table 12.1).

When respondents were asked to list all of their and/or their spouses' sources of income, money from children within the country, earnings from work, income from farm, pension, and money from children living outside

TABLE 12.1

Means and Percentages for Sources of Income Indicators by Gender and Marital Status: 2007 PLSOA

Indicators	Total	Gender			Marital Status		
		Male	Female	Sig.	Currently Married	Not Currently Married	Sig.
Sources of income+							
Earnings from work	28.9	37.5	22.7	***	32.3	24.4	***
Pensions	22.0	24.8	20.0	**	19.8	25.1	***
Interest on time deposits	2.1	(2.0)	2.2		2.3	(2.0)	
Rentals, savings, real estate, stocks	5.2	4.0	6.1	**	3.8	7.1	***
Income from family business	18.9	16.2	20.8	***	21.0	16.1	***
Income from farm	22.2	28.9	17.4	***	25.2	18.2	***
Money from children within the country	57.8	58.4	57.4		58.8	56.6	
Money from children outside the country	20.5	19.1	21.5		22.8	17.4	***
Money from other relatives outside the household	10.5	7.1	12.9	***	6.6	15.6	***
Mean number of income sources	1.9	2.0	1.8		1.9	1.8	
(N)	(3,095)	(1,285)	(1,810)		(1,771)	(1,324)	
Most important source of income				***			***
Earnings from work	24.7	31.9	19.6		30.9	16.3	
Pensions	19.8	18.5	20.6		18.8	21.1	
Interest on time deposits	(0.3)	(0.3)	(0.2)		(0.4)	(0.1)	
Rentals, savings, real estate, stocks	2.0	1.0	2.7		1.1	3.1	
Income from family business	8.1	6.7	9.0		8.7	7.2	
Income from farm	11.9	15.3	9.4		13.6	9.6	
Money from children within the country	21.6	17.4	24.6		17.7	26.9	

TABLE 12.1 (cont'd)

Indicators	Total	Gender			Marital Status		
		Male	Female	Sig.	Currently Married	Not Currently Married	Sig.
Money from children outside the country	8.2	6.5	9.4		7.9	8.6	***
Money from other relatives outside the household	3.6	2.4	4.4		(1.0)	7.0	
Total (%)	100.0	100.0	100.0		100.0	100.0	
(N)	(2,991)	(1,252)	(1,739)		(1,717)	(1,273)	
Second most important source of income				***			
Earnings from work	11.5	13.9	9.6		12.0	10.6	
Pensions	9.1	9.9	8.4		9.6	8.1	
Interest on time deposits	(0.4)	(0.3)	(0.5)		(0.5)	(0.4)	
Rentals, savings, real estate, stocks	2.5	(1.8)	3.0		(1.8)	(3.5)	
Income from family business	10.2	8.5	11.6		10.3	10.0	
Income from farm	10.0	12.2	8.2		11.5	7.6	
Money from children within the country	38.5	38.9	38.3		38.2	39.1	
Money from children outside the country	12.3	11.4	13.0		13.3	10.4	
Money from other relatives outside the household	5.5	(3.1)	7.4		2.7	10.3	
Total %	100.0	100.0	100.0		100.0	100.0	
(N)	(2,109)	(933)	(1,176)		(1,322)	(790)	

Notes:
+ Multiple response
*** p < 0.001   ** p < 0.01   * p < 0.05
Percentages in parentheses are based on less than 30 cases.
Source: 2007 Philippine Longitudinal Study of Aging (PLSOA) (original tabulations).

the country were the top five sources cited. Of these, earnings from work, money from children within the country, and pensions are considered the top three most important sources. Significant differences were noted across gender, with receipts from work, pensions, money from children within the country, and income from farm viewed as the main economic lifeline for the males. The corresponding categories for the females are money from children within the country, which is their most important source, followed by pension and income from work. More males than females cited earnings from work and farm as their major income source, while more females than males cited cash transfers from their children and other relatives, pensions, and income from family business.

In terms of marital status, results show a significantly higher proportion of the married than unmarried who consider their current work, family business, and farm as their most important sources of income. Significantly, more of the unmarried than married cited money from children both inside and outside of the country, pension, and money from other relatives as their most important sources of income.

The foregoing findings are consistent with their work pattern showing a higher proportion of males and married respondents who are currently working. At least 47.2 per cent of older males are currently working as compared to 33.1 per cent among the females, while the corresponding proportions for the currently married and not currently married are 42.6 and 34.1 per cent, respectively (see Table 12.2).

Remittance from children abroad is a significant source of financial support for Filipino older people. About a fifth of older Filipinos received remittances from their children abroad, significantly more so among the currently married, a higher proportion of whom have children working abroad compared to those currently not married (see Tables 12.1 and 12.2). While an equal proportion of older males and females receive monetary transfers from children abroad, more females than males (9.4 per cent vs. 6.5 per cent, respectively) consider it their main source of income. Another 13 per cent and 11.4 per cent, respectively, consider it their second most important source of income. Although a lesser proportion of those who are currently not married receive financial flows from abroad, significantly more among them consider it their most important source of income compared to the currently married. The considerable number of older people who rely on financial flows from overseas reflect the pervasive impact of the international labour migration on older people. Table 12.2 shows about 27.3 per cent of respondents have at least one child living or working abroad (with an average of 1.7 children overseas for each person).

TABLE 12.2

Means and Percentages for Work Status and International Labour Migration Indicators by Gender and Marital Status: 2007 PLSOA

Indicators	Total	Gender			Marital Status		
		Male	Female	Sig.	Currently Married	Not Currently Married	Sig.
% of older persons who are currently working	39.0	47.2	33.1	***	42.6	34.1	***
(N)	(3,103)	(1,287)	(1,816)		(1,774)	(1,330)	
% of older persons with at least one child who works abroad	27.3	27.0	27.6		29.5	24.1	***
Mean number of children who work abroad	1.7	1.7	1.7		1.7	1.8	
(N)	(2,935)	(1,224)	(1,224)		(1,748)	(1,188)	

Notes: *** p < 0.001 ** p < 0.01 * p < 0.05
Source: 2007 Philippine Longitudinal Study of Aging (PLSOA) (original tabulations).

Assets and Liabilities

Besides their income sources, the older respondents participating in the survey were asked about their assets and liabilities to examine the extent of their economic security. The majority of older Filipinos own the house that they are currently residing in, significantly more so among the males than females (79.9 per cent and 70.0 per cent, respectively) (see Table 12.3). Those who are currently married displayed a much higher proportion of home ownership relative to those not currently married (82.7 per cent and 62.7 per cent, respectively). Although the majority own the house they are currently residing in, a lower proportion of home ownership among the females and unmarried relative to their counterparts underscores the economic disadvantage of this sector of the older population.

Next to house ownership, appliances are the second most common asset of the older people with the males and the currently married registering a higher ownership rate compared to their counterparts. Besides appliances, considerably more males also own farms/fishponds and motor vehicles compared to females. More females, in contrast, own real estate properties, businesses (such as small *sari-sari* or variety stores), jewellery, and other assets. A pattern of lopsided distribution in assets emerged when controlling for marital status, with the married respondents owning more of almost all types of assets compared to those who are not currently married. Of note is the small percentage of older persons with cash and bank accounts regardless of sex and marital status. Less than 13 per cent listed cash as one of their assets and less than 6 per cent owned a bank account (see Table 12.3).

The economic wealth of the older people is likewise illustrated by their liabilities. Overall, around one in seven had liabilities, with the males incurring more than the females (18.0 per cent vs. 13.2 per cent), and the married more than the unmarried (17.4 per cent vs. 12.1 per cent) (see Table 12.3). The most common types of liabilities among the males include personal loans, loans from moneylenders, and bank loans. In contrast, females and those who are currently unmarried tend to register more personal loans, which is indicative of their tendency to incur debt from informal sources possibly because of their inability to access formal fund sources. Interestingly, less than a tenth claimed to have debts from the GSIS (Government Service and Insurance System) and the SSS (Social Security System), which is an indicator of the low social security coverage among the older population sector, regardless of sex.

TABLE 12.3
Percentages for Assets and Liabilities Indicators by Gender and Marital Status: 2007 PLSOA

Indicators	Total	Gender			Marital Status		
		Male	Female	Sig.	Currently Married	Not Currently Married	Sig.
Ownership of house that older person is currently residing in							
Older person and/or spouse	74.1	79.9	70.0	*	82.7	62.7	
Jointly by older person (or couple) and children	2.5	(2.1)	2.7		1.8	3.3	
Older person's children	9.2	5.6	11.8		5.4	14.4	
Others	14.2	12.4	15.5		10.1	19.7	
Total %	100.0	100.0	100.0		100.0	100.0	
(N)	(3,091)	(1,282)	(1,809)		(1,767)	(1,323)	
Assets of older person and/or spouse+							
Real estate	11.0	9.5	12.1	*	10.1	12.3	
Cash	12.4	13.0	12.0		12.2	12.6	
Bank accounts	5.6	5.7	5.5		6.1	4.8	
Farm/fishponds	20.8	24.3	18.3	***	22.9	17.9	***
Business (sari-sari store, poultry, etc.)	17.9	16.0	19.2	*	19.7	15.3	**
Jewellery	9.1	6.4	11.0	***	8.9	9.3	
Appliances	60.4	64.1	57.8	***	67.9	50.3	***
Motor vehicles	11.2	12.6	10.2	*	13.7	7.6	***
Others	21.1	18.4	23.0	**	15.4	28.9	***
(N)	(3,038)	(1,258)	(1,780)		(1,747)	(1,290)	

TABLE 12.3 *(cont'd)*

Indicators	Total	Gender			Marital Status		
		Male	Female	Sig.	Currently Married	Not Currently Married	Sig.
% of older person and/or spouse with any liability	15.2	18.0	13.2	***	17.4	12.1	***
(N)	(3,095)	(1,284)	(1,811)		(1,769)	(1,326)	
Types of liabilities+							
Bank loans	13.3	13.9	12.7		11.7	(16.4)	
Personal loans	49.5	40.0	58.6	***	44.3	59.1	**
Amortization for housing	(3.2)	(4.3)	(2.1)		(3.9)	(1.9)	
Loans for money-lenders	29.3	33.9	24.9	*	32.8	23.1	*
Loans from GSIS/SSS++	8.6	10.0	7.2	*	8.8	(8.8)	**
Others	(5.1)	(7.4)	(3.0)		(7.2)	(1.3)	
(N)	(467)	(231)	(239)		(308)	(160)	

Notes:

+ Multiple response

++ GSIS (Government Service Insurance System) and SSS (Social Security System) are social insurance systems for employees in the Philippines, the former for government employees and the latter for workers in the private sector and those who are self-employed.

*** $p < 0.001$ ** $p < 0.01$ * $p < 0.05$

Percentages in parentheses are based on less than 30 cases.

Source: 2007 Philippine Longitudinal Study of Aging (PLSOA) (original tabulations).

Familial Support

This section examines coresidence and family exchange of support which are viewed as the paramount social safety net, ensuring the well-being of older people. In the Philippines, where the care for older people is mainly a family rather than a state concern, an apparent manifestation of family support for its elderly is coresidence with any of the adult children. Evidence from the PLSOA shows that seven out of ten Filipino older people are currently living with at least one child regardless of sex and marital status (see Table 12.4). Quite expectedly, more of the currently married are coresiding with their children. Since most older people own the house they are currently residing in, this suggests that their children are coresiding with the older person rather than the other way around. But even where the house is owned by their children, a high level of coresidence is observed, particularly among the females (81.7 per cent) and those not currently married (84.7 per cent). This suggests that regardless of home ownership, coresidence with children is the normative living arrangement among older people in the country.

Coresidence is deemed to be an economic coping strategy that benefits all the household members including the older people. To explore the intergenerational wealth flow, we examined the living arrangement and the intergenerational flow of wealth in the older person's household. The PLSOA survey questionnaire provided an elaborate matrix containing child-specific information on the exchange of support between the elderly and their children, which allows for a closer examination of the kinds of economic support that older people receive from their family. From this extensive information, receipt of economic support in the past year from children not residing with the elderly respondent was extracted.

Table 12.4 shows that around three-quarters of older persons receive some form of economic support from any of their non-coresident children. This kind of support tends to be in the form of money, food, clothes, medicines or other gifts, although financial support was mostly reported. While there are no significant differences by gender, the currently married reported significantly greater receipt of support than their not currently married counterparts (76.8 per cent and 69.6 per cent, respectively). This finding, however, does not suggest a unidirectional flow of economic support given that previous studies demonstrate a two-way intergenerational family support system, indicating older Filipinos are active players in the intergenerational economic exchange rather than mere recipients of family support (Biddlecom, Chayovan and Ofstedal 2002; Hermalin 2003).

Despite the apparent economic dependence of the older people on their children, there is a general desire among them to be self-reliant in their old age. Although many consider money from children as one of their primary sources of income, about six in ten older people do not plan to rely on children for financial support in their old age. In contrast, about 40 per cent of the respondents, mostly females and those not currently married, indicated their plan to rely on their children for financial support in their old age (see Table 12.4).

Income

Although researchers recognize the conceptual and operational issues that beset income measurement, income is considered a prime indicator of economic well-being (Chan et al. 2002). The collection of more precise individual income data to a large extent is hampered by the informal and irregular sources of income and financial support of the elderly. Co-residential arrangement, particularly where incomes are pooled, adds to the difficulty in distinguishing the older person's own income from that of the couple or even from household income. The general reluctance of respondents to disclose income data, as well as the difficulty of quantifying income from agriculture on which a substantial proportion of respondents depend for their livelihood, also pose additional challenges in the collection of income data.

To ensure the quality of income data, respondents were first asked to identify various sources of their income and that of their spouses', if currently married, before they were asked to estimate their income for each of their identified sources. Owing to the high variability of figures collected, both the mean and median incomes are presented. Data reveal a low median monthly income for the respondent and his/her spouse at PhP3,000[3] with no significant difference across sexes (see Table 12.5).

Controlling for marital status indicates the advantageous position of the currently married, which is expected since it represents the joint income of the couple. The average income of older persons is slightly higher than the poverty threshold, which at the time of the study was about PhP1,500 per capita per month.

Wealth Index

Another objective measure of economic well-being explored in the study is wealth index. The wealth index is a composite measure of the household's

TABLE 12.4

Percentages for House Ownership, Coresidence with Children, and Familial Support Indicators by Gender and Marital Status: 2007 PLSOA

Indicators	Total	Gender			Marital Status		
		Male	Female	Sig.	Currently Married	Not Currently Married	Sig.
% of older persons coresiding with children	71.3	72.4	70.5		74.0	67.7	***
Among older persons who own house/spouse owns house:							
% who are coresiding with children	73.2	73.9	72.5		74.1	71.5	
(N)	(2,291)	(1,024)	(1,267)		(1,462)	(829)	
Among older persons whose children own the house they live in:							
% who are coresiding with children	77.5	65.3	81.7	**	63.2	84.7	***
(N)	(285)	(72)	(213)		(95)	(190)	

TABLE 12.4 *(cont'd)*

| Indicators | Total | Gender | | | | Marital Status | | |
		Male	Female	Sig.		Currently Married	Not Currently Married	Sig.
Among older persons with at least one child living outside the household:								
% who receive economic support from non-coresident child*	73.8	74.8	73.2			76.8	69.6	***
(N)	(2,753)	(1,139)	(1,614)			(1,631)	(1,121)	
Among older persons with at least one surviving child:								
% who plan to rely on children for financial support	40.4	39.0	41.4	*		37.4	45.0	***
(N)	(2,900)	(1,212)	(1,688)			(1,739)	(1,163)	

Note: *** p < 0.001   ** p < 0.01   * p < 0.05
Source: 2007 Philippine Longitudinal Study of Aging (PLSOA) (original tabulations).

TABLE 12.5

Means and Percentages for Income and Self-Assessed Income Status Indicators by Gender and Marital Status: 2007 PLSOA

Indicators	Total	Gender		Sig.	Marital Status		Sig.
		Male	Female		Currently Married	Not Currently Married	
Monthly income of R and spouse (in PhP)				**			**
Mean	5,059.7	5,325.6	4,870.0		5,628.9	4,265.8	
Median	3,000.0	3,300.0	3,000.0		3,500.0	2,400.0	
(N)	(2,767)	(1,153)	(1,615)		(1,612)	(1,156)	
Wealth index quintile				**			***
Lowest (Poorest)	16.6	18.8	15.0		14.9	18.9	
Second	17.5	18.5	16.7		17.7	17.1	
Middle	20.7	21.5	20.1		21.1	20.1	
Fourth	22.2	21.1	22.9		23.1	21.0	
Highest (Richest)	23.1	20.1	25.2		23.3	22.8	
(N)	(2,912)	(1,197)	(1,715)		(1,670)	(1,242)	
Self-assessment of the older person's current household income vs. all expenses for maintaining the whole household				**			***
There is enough income, with money left over	7.1	6.4	7.5		6.1	8.4	
Just enough to pay expenses, with no difficulty	39.7	36.8	41.8		37.9	42.2	
Some difficulty in meeting expenses	33.1	35.7	31.3		36.9	28.1	
Considerable difficulty in meeting expenses	20.1	21.0	19.4		19.2	21.3	
Total %	100.0	100.0	100.0		100.0	100.0	
(N)	(3,073)	(1,279)	(1,794)		(1,767)	(1306)	

Note: *** p < 0.001   ** p < 0.01
Source: 2007 Philippine Longitudinal Study of Aging (PLSOA) (original tabulations).

socio-economic status and was created following the procedure used in developing the widely used Demographic Health Surveys (DHS) wealth index (refer to Rutstein and Johnson 2004, for the detailed procedure). The index was constructed from data available in the Household Questionnaire which includes the household's ownership of appliances and vehicles, tenure status of the lot, types of water access and sanitation facilities, materials used for housing construction, and the type of fuel used for cooking. The principal components analysis (PCA) was used to determine the weights or factor scores for each of these variables. Based on the resulting index scores, the households were divided into quintiles from the poorest to the wealthiest. As the definition implies, wealth index is a household-level indicator of economic well-being. However, the authors assumed that the older person's economic status is the same as that of his/her household status.

Results of the study reflect a clear gender differential in the wealth index, with the females enjoying an advantage over the males. About a quarter (25.2 per cent) of the females belong to the richest quintile as compared to just a fifth of the males (20.1 per cent) (see Table 12.5). No significant difference is noted across marital status groups.

SUBJECTIVE INDICATOR OF
ECONOMIC WELL-BEING

This section provides an analysis of the respondents' subjective assessment of their economic status and examines the extent to which such a measure compares with the objective indicators. The authors examined self-assessed economic well-being by asking the respondents what they thought of the income of all the members of their household *vis-à-vis* all the expenses for maintaining or running the whole household. Response categories included the following: (1) there is enough (income), with money left over; (2) just enough; (3) some difficulty in meeting expenses; and (4) considerable difficulty in meeting expenses. Unlike the objective indicators of economic well-being discussed earlier (except wealth index), which measure the individual's or the couple's (if married) economic status, the subjective indicator is a measure of household economic well-being. This analysis examines the extent to which these various economic indicators capture various dimensions of economic status and the extent to which they correlate with each other.

Consistent with the earlier findings on the objective economic indicators, the majority of older people reported a poor self-appraisal of their household economic status. A little more than half thought they have some or considerable economic difficulty in meeting their household expenses (see Table 12.5). Only a small proportion (6.4 per cent and 7.5 per cent among the males and females, respectively) reported having enough with some money left over. Another 36.8 per cent and 41.8 per cent, respectively, reported household incomes just enough to pay for the expenses of their entire household. On the whole, females projected a better self-assessed economic well-being — a finding that hews closely to the wealth quintiles establishing the advantageous position of women.

While those currently not married have less economic resources and more liabilities relative to their currently married counterparts, significantly more of the former felt they either had enough or more than enough money to meet their household needs. The majority (50.6 per cent) of them also felt they had enough or more than enough money to meet their household expenditures as compared to 44 per cent among their currently married counterparts.

An exploration of the link between subjective and objective indicators of economic well-being shows a generally consistent pattern in the relationship across gender (see Table 12.6). Results show income, wealth quintile, most important source of income, liabilities, and intergenerational flow of support to be significantly correlated with self-assessed well-being. Only work status and assets did not register a significant correlation with subjective well-being.

Subjective assessment of their income adequacy is positively associated with actual reported incomes regardless of sex. Among the males, for instance, those who reported more than enough income for their household expenditures reported a median income of PhP7,330, which was more than three times the level reported by those who had considerable difficulty in meeting household expenditures at PhP2,000. The corresponding figures for the females were PhP6,330 and PhP2,000, respectively.

A similar pattern is evident between subjective self-assessment and wealth index. For both males and females, a higher proportion among those in the lower wealth quintiles expressed considerably more difficulty in meeting basic household needs compared to their counterparts who belong to a higher wealth quintile.

Older people whose economic upkeep is bound up with their dependence on their children within the country exhibited the poorest subjective self-assessed economic well-being, as clearly demonstrated in the highest proportion among them who reported severe income deficiency

TABLE 12.6
Perceived and Objective Indicators of Economic Well-being of Older Filipinos

Perceived Economic Well-being

Objective Economic Status Indicators	Males							Females						
	Enough Income, With Leftover	Just Enough Income	Some Difficulty Meeting Expenses	Considerable Difficulty Meeting Expenses	Sig.	Total	N	Enough Income, With Leftover	Just Enough Income	Some Difficulty Meeting Expenses	Considerable Difficulty Meeting Expenses	Sig.	Total	N
Median monthly income of R and spouse (in Philippine pesos)	7,330	4,000	3,300	2,000	***		1,146	6,330	3,500	3,000	2,000	***		1,603
Wealth index quintile					***							***		
Lowest (Poorest)	(2.2)	24.4	32.9	40.4		100.0	225	(3.1)	26.5	39.3	31.1		100.0	257
Second	(5.4)	29.9	29.0	35.7		100.0	221	(3.5)	32.9	38.2	25.4		100.0	283
Middle	(5.5)	31.9	40.9	21.7		100.0	254	(6.0)	39.5	29.3	25.1		100.0	334
Fourth	(6.5)	43.1	39.5	(10.9)		100.0	248	8.2	49.4	29.9	12.5		100.0	391
Highest (Richest)	(12.1)	52.5	30.4	(5.0)		100.0	240	12.8	53.0	26.0	8.1		100.0	430
Work status					***							***		
Currently working	6.4	35.5	37.7	20.3		100.0	605	5.6	43.0	32.7	18.6		100.0	602
Not currently working	6.4	37.9	34.2	21.5		100.0	673	8.5	41.1	30.6	19.8		100.0	1,191
Most important source of income					***							***		
Work	(4.0)	34.1	38.6	23.3		100.0	399	(6.5)	40.3	33.8	19.4		100.0	340
Pension	(10.4)	35.1	38.1	16.5		100.0	231	9.0	40.3	33.0	17.7		100.0	355
Farm	(7.8)	38.0	41.1	(13.0)		100.0	192	(4.3)	38.9	38.3	18.5		100.0	162
Children within the country	(3.7)	36.6	32.9	26.9		100.0	216	(5.0)	38.1	30.2	26.6		100.0	417
Children outside the country	(12.7)	43.0	(35.4)	(8.9)		100.0	79	(17.7)	41.5	32.3	8.5		100.0	164
Others	(7.1)	41.7	25.2	26.0		100.0	127	(8.1)	49.6	24.6	17.6		100.0	284

TABLE 12.6 (*cont'd*)

| | Males | | | | | | | Females | | | | | | |
| | Perceived Economic Well-being | | | | | | | | | | | | | |
Objective Economic Status Indicators	Enough Income, With Leftover	Just Enough Income	Some Difficulty Meeting Expenses	Considerable Difficulty Meeting Expenses	Sig.	Total	N	Enough Income, With Leftover	Just Enough Income	Some Difficulty Meeting Expenses	Considerable Difficulty Meeting Expenses	Sig.	Total	N
Assets														
R or spouse own the house currently residing in	6.6	36.3	36.9	20.2		100.0	1,046	7.6	41.6	32.6	18.2		100.0	1,309
R/spouse do not own the house currently residing in	(4.8)	38.6	31.6	25.0		100.0	228	7.3	42.0	27.8	23.0		100.0	479
Liabilities														
R or spouse have any financial liability	(5.6)	26.8	52.8	14.7	***	100.0	231	(5.4)	33.9	41.4	19.2	**	100.0	239
R or spouse do not have any financial liability	6.6	39.1	32.1	22.2	***	100.0	1,044	7.5	41.8	31.3	19.3	**	100.0	1,551
Intergenerational exchange														
Among older persons with at least one child living outside the household:														
% who receive economic support from non-coresident child	6.5	34.3	38.1	21.0	*	100.0	936	8.2	40.7	32.8	18.3	*	100.0	1,304
% who do not receive economic support from non-coresident child	(6.6)	44.4	30.1	18.9		100.0	196	(5.2)	42.9	27.7	24.2	*	100.0	289

Notes: *** p < 0.001   ** p < 0.01   * p < 0.05
Percentages in parentheses are based on less than 30 cases.
Source: 2007 Philippine Longitudinal Study of Aging (PLSOA) (original tabulations).

across main income sources. In contrast, those who mainly depend on remittances from children abroad exhibited the highest level of perceived economic well-being for both sexes, as evident in the lowest proportion among them who experienced considerable difficulty in meeting household economic needs (see Knodel and Chayovan, this volume). They also demonstrate the highest proportion who claimed to have enough income with money left over. Those who cited pension as their main income source displayed a relatively favourable subjective economic well-being. The foregoing findings point to the possible income insecurity among older women and those not currently married who cited monetary support from their children within the country as their most important source of income.

Older people's liabilities also correlate significantly with subjective well-being. Those who do not have any financial liability are more likely to say that they have enough or more than enough resources to cover their household needs, with these findings holding for both males and females.

Although economic support (in the form of money, food or material goods) from non-coresident children is viewed to help ease the economic burden of older people, about a fifth regardless of sex still claimed to have difficulty meeting their household expenses despite these intergenerational transfers. Females who receive economic support from their children perceived themselves to be slightly better off than those who do not. For the males, however, the reverse pattern is noted, with those who receive support from their children registering a higher proportion who feel considerable economic difficulty.

Work status and self-assessed income adequacy have a peculiar relationship as the data show no differential pattern, which is contrary to expectations. Regardless of their work status, most of them reported either having just enough or facing some difficulty in meeting their household expenditures. What is significant to note is that males who say that work is their most important source of income do not seem to have a positive assessment of their economic status, with almost a fourth claiming to experience considerable difficulty in meeting their household expenditures. This seems to suggest that older males continue to work in their old age, despite possible health and disability problems, in order to be able to support their economic subsistence.

As expected, those who own assets, particularly the house they currently reside in, tended to have more positive perceptions of their economic well-being, although the differences are not significant. About a fifth of older males and females who own the house they are currently residing in have considerable difficulty as compared to about a quarter among those who do not own their house.

Overall, there seems to be a significant relationship between the objective and most of the subjective indicators of economic well-being considered in the study, indicating some convergence on these two domains of economic status measurement.

DISCUSSION AND CONCLUSIONS

The study reveals the precarious economic condition of older Filipinos as shown by the various indicators of their wealth. Meagre income and assets and low levels of productive engagement and pension coverage reflect their economic insecurity. Their most common possessions are the house they currently live in and some appliances. Although each claims an average of about two income sources, the amount they receive is barely breaching poverty thresholds. A good number of them are still working or till the farm for a living, but their low earnings make many of them economically dependent on their children who are working both in and out of the country. Very few have a bank account or have cash, and at least half of them report some or considerable difficulty in meeting their household economic needs.

Objective and subjective economic indicators do not provide strong conclusive evidence to suggest the existence of a gender wealth gap. Although gender differentials are noted in selected economic indicators, there is no overwhelming evidence to indicate which gender exhibits a clear economic advantage. Income levels are generally low and comparable for both males and females. Females exhibit lower levels of home ownership, pension coverage, and employment and have incurred more personal loans. More older women consider support from their children as their most important source of income and plan to continue relying on their children for economic support in their old age relative to their male counterparts. Although women's dependence on children is associated with greater income insecurity in the sense that this is associated with most difficulty in meeting their household needs, the same women report a better profile in terms of household wealth index and overall subjective self-assessed economic status. Significantly, more women also reported owning real estate properties and jewellery and deriving income from their own businesses, mostly consisting of small neighbourhood stores. In contrast, more males are employed, receive pensions, and possess earnings from work and from their farms, making them less dependent on their children for economic support. More of them own appliances, farms/ fishponds and motor vehicles albeit registering more liabilities and lower self-assessed economic status relative to females. Notwithstanding men's seeming economic advantage, more males than females reported lower levels of self-assessed economic well-being and household wealth index.

The wealth differences across marital status groups are more defined, with the currently married registering a clear advantage. A greater proportion of married older people reported higher incomes, ownership of the homes they currently reside in as well as other assets like farms/fishponds, businesses, jewellery, appliances, and other assets. Because more of the currently married are in productive labour, they are likely to depend on their own income from work as their main source of income. There is also a higher proportion among them who coreside with their children and at the same time receive transfers from their non-coresident children. While findings show higher pension coverage among those currently not married, most of the pension recipients are the widowed who receive pension as dependents of their deceased spouses, in which case the situation cannot altogether be viewed as advantageous, considering the socio-economic implications of widowhood, not to mention the low pension rates in the country.

The study underscores the potential benefits of international migration on the economic well-being of older people, with a considerable proportion drawing mainly from remittances for their subsistence. Our findings also demonstrate that those whose main source of income is from remittances from children abroad are those who have better self-assessed economic well-being. This is not, however, without cost. The feminization of international labour migration observed in recent years is expected to negate the economic benefits of international labour migration, particularly as it affects the potential pool of caregivers of the older people. The ramifications of such movements can be measured in part by our findings which show that at least a fourth of older people have children who are currently working or living abroad. Labour migration of the older people's children, which implies absentee parents including mothers, may force older people to assume caregiving roles for their grandchildren left behind by migrant parents. While labour migration may threaten the availability of the potential pool of caregivers, the impact may be tempered in part by their high fertility level, as shown by the majority of them having at least one coresiding child. The multidimensional impact of labour migration on the well-being of older people implies the need to further examine the issue as we anticipate a sustained increase in international labour migration over time.

In terms of economic indicators, our findings demonstrate some degree of consistency between the objective and subjective indicators of economic status of the older people, suggesting some degree of convergence in capturing the concept of older people's economic well-being. Some discrepancies, indicated by the absence of a correlation between the subjective indicator and some objective indicators such as work status and assets, tend to suggest the possible differences in the criteria by which older people assess the objective and subjective dimensions of their economic status. Earlier explorations recognize the broader scope of subjective well-being that goes beyond the objective indicators of wealth, with subjective economic well-being viewed not simply as a reflection of material or objective living conditions (Hayo and Seifert 2002). It is also argued that people do not look at their own economic condition in isolation, but compare it to that of others. For instance, while a household's economic situation may be declining, it may still perceive itself to be relatively better off than others experiencing greater decline. Conversely, a stable economic situation may lead to dissatisfaction if the general economic condition is improving. People also take expectations about the future into account in their economic self-assessment (Hayo and Seifert 2002). Thus, those who are more positive about their future tend to have higher perceived economic well-being, which may explain the better self-assessed economic well-being of older females relative to their male counterparts despite the former's disadvantage in many objective economic indicators.

Our results highlight the need to further understand the comparability across different levels of measurement in assessing the economic well-being of older people. Findings demonstrate the consistency between the two household-level indicators employed in the study (wealth index and self-assessed economic well-being) but some inconsistency was found between a few individual- and household-level indicators. The observed inconsistency between these two levels of measures may be attributed to the broader context captured by household-level relative to individual-level indicators, with the household-level indicators working to one's advantage if individual economic capacities are relatively lower than the totality of their household wealth. This finding suggests the need to further explore the relationship of these two spheres of measure and to consider a multi-level analysis to capture the multiple dimensions of an older person's economic status.

The foregoing findings underscore the complexity of understanding the economic status of older people both at the substantive and quantitative levels. The assessment suggests the need to strengthen the economic safety nets for older Filipinos — safety nets that underscore marital status-specific nuances rather than gender-specific nuances, as an initial step towards ensuring successful ageing in the country.

Notes

1. This work was supported by a grant obtained by the Nihon University Population Research Institute for the "Academic Frontier" Project for Private Universities, the matching fund subsidy from the Ministry of Education, Culture, Sports, Science, and Technology (MEXT) 2006–10, and the University of the Philippines Office of the Vice-Chancellor for Research and Development Ph.D. Incentive Grant.
2. For a more detailed discussion on the PLSOA study, refer to Natividad et al., in this volume. Data analyses were performed on the weighted sample.
3. Approximately 73 U.S. dollars based on the exchange rate of 1 U.S. Dollar = 41 Philippine pesos as of January 2013.

References

1987 Constitution of the Republic of the Philippines. Official Website, Office of the President of the Republic of the Philippines. Available at <http://www.gov.ph/the-philippine-constitutions/the-1987-constitution-of-the-republic-of-the-philippines/> (accessed 20 January 2013).

Agree, E., A. Biddlecom and T. Valente. "Intergenerational Transfers of Resources between Older Persons and Extended Kin in Taiwan and the Philippines". *Population Studies: A Journal of Demography* 59, no. 2 (2005): 181–95.

Biddlecom, Ann, Napaporn Chayovan and Mary Beth Ofstedal. "Intergenerational Support and Transfers". In *The Well-Being of the Elderly in Asia: A Four-Country Comparative Study*, edited by Albert I. Hermalin. Ann Arbor: University of Michigan Press, 2002.

Cabigon, Josefina. *2000 Life Table Estimates for the Philippines and Provinces by Sex*. Manila: Commission on Population, 2009.

Chan, A., M.B. Ofstedal and A.I. Hermalin. "Changes in Subjective and Objective Measures of Economic Well-Being and their Interrelationship among the Elderly in Singapore and Taiwan". *Social Indicators Research* 57 (2002): 263–300.

Commission on Overseas Filipinos. "Stock Estimate of Overseas Filipinos as of December 2007". Available at <http://www.cfo.gov.ph/Stock%202007.pdf> (accessed 20 July 2008).

Cruz, Grace. "Health Transitions among Filipino Older People". Unpublished doctoral dissertation. University of the Philippines, 2005.

Cruz, Grace and Elma Laguna. "Overseas Labour Migration and Well-Being of Older Filipinos". In *Older Persons in Southeast Asia: An Emerging Asset*, edited by E.N. Ariffin and A. Ananta. Singapore: Institute of Southeast Asian Studies, 2009.

Cruz, G., Y. Saito and J. Natividad. "Active Life Expectancy and Functional Health Transition among Filipino Older People". *Canadian Studies in Population* 34, no. 1 (2007): 29–47.

Hausman, Ricardo, Laura D. Tyson and Saadia Zahidi. *The Global Gender Gap Report 2007*, Retrieved 20 November 2008. Available at <http://www.weforum.org/pdf/gendergap/report2007.pdf> (accessed 20 January 2013).

Hayo, Bernd and Wolfgang Seifert. "Subjective Economic Well-being in Eastern Europe". *Journal of Economic Psychology* 24 (2003): 329–48.

Hermalin, Albert I., ed. *The Well-Being of the Elderly in Asia: A Four-Country Comparative Study*. Ann Arbor: The University of Michigan Press, 2003.

Kim, I. and C. Kim. "Patterns of Family Support and the Quality of Life of the Elderly". *Social Indicators Research* 62–63, nos. 1–3 (2003): 437–54.

Knodel, J. and M.B. Ofstedal. "Gender and Aging in the Developing World: Where are the Men?" *Population Development Review* 29, no. 4 (2003): 667–98.

National Statistical Coordination Board. *2006 Philippine Poverty Statistics*, 2008. Available at <http://www.nscb.gov.ph/poverty/2006_05mar08/default.asp> (accessed 18 February 2009).

National Statistics Office. "Senior Citizens comprised Six Percent of the Population". *National Statistics Office Special Release No. 151*, 2005. Available at <http://www.census.gov.ph/data/sectordata/sr05151tx.html> (accessed 27 December 2008).

Ofstedal, M.B., E. Reidy and J. Knodel. "Gender Differences in Economic Support and Well-being of Older Asians". *Journal of Cross-Cultural Gerontology* 19 (2004): 165–201.

Ofstedal, M.B., Z. Zimmer, G. Cruz, A. Chan and Y.L. Chuang. "Self-Assessed Health Expectancy among Older Adults: A Comparison of Six Asian Settings". *Hallym International Journal of Aging* 6, no. 2 (2004): 95–117.

Rutstein, S.O. and K. Johnson. *The DHS Wealth Index*. DHS Comparative Reports No. 6. Calverton, Maryland: ORC Macro, 2004.

Sobieszczyk, Teresa, John Knodel and Napaporn Chayovan. "Gender and Well-being among the Elderly: Evidence from Thailand". PSC Research Report No. 02-531. Population Studies Center at the Institute for Social Research, University of Michigan, 2002.

United Nations. *World Population Ageing: 1950–2050*. New York: United Nations, 2001.

———. *Report of the Second World Assembly on Ageing*. New York: United Nations, 2002.

United Nations Division for the Advancement of Women. *Gender Dimensions of*

Aging, 2002. Available at <www.un.org/womenwatch/daw/public/ageing-final. pdf> (accessed 20 November 2008).

United Nations Office for the Coordination of Humanitarian Affairs (OCHA). Available at <www.unocha.org/roap/about-us/about-ocha-roap/philippines> (accessed 20 January 2013).

University of the Philippines Population Institute and Demographic Research and Development Foundation (UPPI-DRDF) *Situation Analysis of the Philippine Population and Reproductive Health.* Manila: United Nations Population Fund, 2009.

13

WORK, RETIREMENT AND THE GENDER DIVIDE IN THE PHILIPPINES[1]

Josefina N. Natividad, Yasuhiko Saito and Grace T. Cruz

INTRODUCTION

The two most common concerns of nearly all people as they reach the elderly years are their health and their economic security. These concerns are intrinsically interrelated; health problems are generally more common at advanced ages, as is diminished earning capacity resulting from retirement and the cessation of productive activity. Specifically, when health problems increase in old age, the costs incurred in seeking healthcare become a greater concern for an elderly person since the individual would more likely have to rely on savings to meet this need. In developed countries, formal support systems in the form of retirement benefits and pension plans ensure that most people who exit from the labour force in their elderly years are assured of economic sustenance, while health insurance systems take care of much of the financial burden of healthcare. In developing countries like the Philippines, formal support systems are still underdeveloped. As such, the majority of older people still rely on the traditional and informal sources of support provided by kin when they themselves are not able to ensure their own economic and health needs (World Bank 1994). One indicator of the lack of an adequate formal support system for older individuals is the higher rate of labour force participation at these ages compared with countries with formal retirement systems (United Nations 2007; United Nations 2002). Typically, in the absence of such a formal system, there is no fixed and mandatory retirement age and people continue economic activity as long as they are physically and mentally able to do so. This period can be fraught with economic uncertainty if failing health threatens the older person's capacity to continue to provide for his/her own needs and that of his/her dependents.

Another common concern is the gender dimension of work and retirement. Much of the literature plays up the potential for unequal vulnerability to adverse economic and health outcomes between men and women. Specifically, women are perceived to be more vulnerable because of a combination of lower lifetime labour force participation and, thus, they face a higher likelihood of being ineligible for pension benefits. However, in spite of enjoying a longer life expectancy, women experience higher rates of disability (Knodel and Zimmer 2009; Cruz, Saito and Natividad 2007). They also face a higher likelihood of being widowed which may leave them without economic support. Others argue that there is a tendency to overemphasize women's vulnerability at old age without acknowledging how men may be similarly disadvantaged. Knodel and Ofstedal (2003, p. 678) make the point succinctly when they write that "the possibility that older men might be the disadvantaged sex is never acknowledged except... in the curious way that men's shorter longevity is seen as a circumstance contributing to women's plight but not a problem for men". Empirical evidence from the Philippines suggests that within the same context of an inadequate formal support in old age, women's vulnerability may not be much removed from that of men's (Natividad 2005). For example, men may be forced to continue working well into their advanced years until overtaken by ill health and disability. Under these circumstances, the question that needs to be addressed, therefore, is not so much whether it is men or women who face greater vulnerability as what differences exist between the sexes in the way they face these challenges in old age.

Where there is an inadequate formal social security system, exit from the labour force is normally involuntary and contingent on health or conditions in the workplace such as layoffs or mandatory retirement policies (Hermalin 2002). But with adequate social security and pension, retirement may be more of a voluntary process involving a trade-off between work and leisure. The latter condition is more common in developed economies but even then is a fairly recent development; involuntary exit from the labour force in old age is still the norm in earlier models of the retirement process in the United States before Social Security and pension benefits began to alter motivations to retire (Quinn and Burkhauser 1994). It may be expected that workers who retire involuntarily will substantially differ from those who do so voluntarily. For one, leisure will not be a prime consideration and those who leave the workforce for good may be in worse shape than those who stay on.

In this chapter, the authors look at gender differentials in work and retirement (or the complete cessation of work) among older Filipinos age 60 and above. In this case, the assumption is that exit from the labour force in the Philippines is still largely on an involuntary basis. The chapter compares work status among elderly men and women, the reasons for stopping work, and the sources of income of those who have stopped working. We situate these differentials within the context of the available formal support system in old age in the country.

The authors then examine the correlates of work status categorized into: (1) demographic and socio-economic variables of age, education, and rural-urban residence; (2) social support variables as indicated by current marital status; (3) economic support as indicated by sources of income; and (4) health status based on self-assessed health, having at least one difficulty in an array of Nagi measures and at least one difficulty in activities of daily living (ADL). In line with the findings from other analyses conducted in Thailand, the Philippines, Singapore, and Taiwan on gender differences in the experience of work and retirement, the discussion here presents findings separately for men and women (Hermalin et al. 2002).

Old Age Social Security System in the Philippines

The Philippines has a formal system of social security coverage that covers two types of employees: the Social Security System (SSS) estab-lished in 1954 for private-sector employees and the Government Service and Insurance System (GSIS) established in 1936 for employees of government and state enterprises. Both are of the defined-benefit type. The bulk of the working population falls under the SSS; government employees constitute only a small proportion of the total labour force (Mesa-Lago et al. 2011)

Prior to 1992, the SSS covered only workers in the formal sector but a series of reforms has since made coverage under the SSS compulsory for all employees in the private sector who are not above 60 years of age, whether with permanent or provisional employment status, including domestic helpers earning at least PhP1,000 (US$20.75)[2] a month. All self-employed persons are also subject to mandatory coverage under the Regular Self Employed Program for artists, entertainers, proprietors, and professionals, and the Expanded Self Employed Program for those with monthly earnings of at least PhP1,000 regardless of trade, business or occupation (for example, unlicensed freelance workers, drivers, market vendors, and other informal sector workers). Farmers and fishermen earning at least PhP1,500 (US$31.13) a month also fall under the self-employed category.

The SSS contribution rate is equivalent to 10.4 per cent of a worker's monthly salary, shared by employer (7.07 per cent) and employee (3.33 per cent), while a self-employed or voluntary member shoulders the entire amount. There is a cap to the monthly salary subjected to the computation of the monthly contribution, from a minimum of PhP1,000 to a maximum of PhP15,000 ($311.67), except for overseas contract workers on whom a minimum monthly salary of PhP5,000 (US$103.76) is imposed. Thus, the monthly contribution per member ranges from PhP104 ($2.16) to PhP1,560 (US$32.37).

SSS retirement benefits are paid in the form of either a monthly pension or lump sum. If a member has reached 60 years of age and is separated from employment or has ceased to be self-employed, and has paid at least 120 monthly contributions prior to the semester of retirement, he/she will be eligible for monthly pension under the optional retirement scheme. For compulsory retirement, a member must have attained the age of 65, and contributed for 120 months before the semester of retirement.[3] An SSS retiree is entitled to a monthly pension for as long as he/she lives. The granting of a monthly pension to an SSS retiree below 65 years old, however, will be suspended if he/she becomes gainfully re-employed or resumes self-employment, upon which he/she is again subject to mandatory coverage until his/her compulsory retirement. SSS members who reach retirement age but are ineligible for pension are given a lump sum amount equal to total contributions plus interest.

Government employees under the GSIS, in contrast, contribute 9 per cent of their monthly salary to the GSIS while the government contributes the equivalent of 12 per cent of the monthly salary. Seven per cent of the member's contribution goes to retirement premiums while 2 per cent goes to life insurance premiums.

After the new GSIS law was passed in 1997, membership in the GSIS has become compulsory regardless of the nature of appointment of the employee. When government employees retire, they can claim two major benefits: retirement benefits/pension and life insurance benefits. To be eligible for pension, the retiree must be at least 60 years old upon retirement, must have been in the service for at least 15 years, and must not have applied for permanent total disability pension. Other retirement modes require at least three years of continuous service prior to retirement in order to qualify for benefits. This puts many females at a disadvantage because of the more sporadic pattern of their employment.

In both the private and public sectors, optional retirement age is 60 years while compulsory retirement is at 65 years. In practice, private sector employees retire at 60 while government employees work until the compulsory retirement age of 65.

The monthly pension for retirees under the SSS ranges from a minimum of PhP1,200 (US$26) to a possible maximum of PhP15,000 (US$326). This amount is not adjusted for inflation and has remained fixed since 1997. Retirees under the GSIS receive higher monthly pension because they would have paid higher premiums together with the government, and the period for eligibility for pension is longer (15 years for GSIS vs. 10 years for SSS). Nonetheless, the monthly pension under GSIS is not automatically adjusted for inflation.

Ideally, therefore, all workers who reach the optional retirement age of 60 or the compulsory retirement age of 65 could be covered by a pension scheme if they had put in contributions to the system for the required minimum time. In reality, however, a sizable segment of private sector employees are not covered by the SSS, for many reasons, chief of which is that it is often difficult for both employers and employees to be consistent with their monthly contributions to the system. Besides, many employers, especially of small establishments, opt to keep employees as non-regular workers to avoid having to pay their SSS premiums. The enforcement of contributions to the system is even more problematic for workers in the informal sector whose uneven earning capacity generally precludes their keeping up with the regular payment of monthly premiums in the face of low incomes coupled with other competing needs. Many workers in the informal sector are also unaware of the mechanisms for enrolling in the system. Therefore, overall while the SSS has been in operation since 1954 and, hence, has since then been subjected to periodic reforms to improve its coverage, much remains to be done to get workers fully protected against the hazards of old age stemming mainly from economic insecurity. Furthermore, not only is there limited coverage of the pension system, the amount of monthly pension, especially in the SSS, is low, and not nearly enough to cover living and health expenses for the older person, let alone his or her dependents.

Past studies on pension and retirement in the Philippines have established the low coverage of pension among those who left the labour force at old age (Domingo and Feranil 1990; Hermalin et al. 2002), ranging from about 11 per cent from the 1984 ASEAN survey data (albeit not from a nationally representative sample) to 29 per cent for males and 10 per cent for females from the 1996 Philippine Elderly Survey data, using a nationally representative sample of older Filipinos.

DATA

Data for this study come from the 2007 Philippine Longitudinal Study on Aging (PLSOA), the first of a proposed multi-wave panel study on ageing in the Philippines. The PLSOA is a joint undertaking of the University of the Philippines and Nihon University and is part of a three-country comparative study on ageing and health in Asia covering Japan, the Philippines, and Singapore.

While designed primarily to investigate health in advanced years in its multiple dimensions (physical, mental, emotional, and even oral health), the PLSOA also collected information on household character-istics, basic attributes and family makeup of older persons, children, grandchildren, and exchanges of support, tasks and activities, income and assets, and attitudes and beliefs. A unique feature of the PLSOA is the inclusion of anthropometric measures (height, weight, waist-hip ratio, knee length, blood pressure, blood sugar, and grip strength) among the information gathered from each elderly respondent participating in the survey.

The survey was conducted through face-to-face interviews using a structured questionnaire adopted from the multi-wave Nihon University Japan Longitudinal Study on Aging (NUJLSOA). The questionnaire was translated into the local languages in the sample areas. In all, the interviews yielded a total of 3,105 respondents age 60 and above living in households.

The study employed a multi-stage sampling design with provinces as the primary sampling units, *barangays* (villages) as the secondary sampling units, and older persons as the ultimate sampling units. The sample provinces were selected using stratified sampling with the proportion of older people in the province as of the latest Philippine census in 2000 as the stratification variable. Provinces were classified into low, medium, and high, and two provinces from each stratum were selected using simple random sampling. Metro Manila, the national capital and the most urbanized area of the country, was purposively included as one of the sample provinces. In all, a total of seven sample provinces (Metro Manila, Bulacan, Laguna, Iloilo, Negros Occidental, Eastern Samar, and Sultan Kudarat) and 78 *barangays* were covered in the study. A listing of all the older people in the sample *barangays* was undertaken prior to the survey. This list served as the sampling frame from which the survey respondents were drawn. Older people 70 years and above were over-sampled to ensure a sufficient number of cases for the second wave of data collection. To generalize from the sample to the Philippine population of older persons, a set of weights was calculated and applied to the raw data. In the analyses, the authors used the weighted sample to approximate the general population of elderly in the Philippines.

Results

The 2007 PLSOA has a total of 3,105 respondents. Table 13.1 presents percentage distributions of the characteristics of elderly Filipino based on this representative sample. In keeping with the major objective of the chapter to compare men and women, the authors present the characteristics separately for the sexes.

TABLE 13.1

Descriptive Characteristics of Filipino Elderly by Working Status and Gender

	Male			Female			All (N=3,105)
	Working (N=607)	Not Working (N=682)	Total Male (N=1,289)	Working (N=602)	Not Working (N=1,214)	Total Female (N=1,816)	
Age							
60–64	44.3	28.1	35.7	43.0	22.1	29.1	31.9
65–69	31.6	29.6	30.5	31.7	26.0	27.9	29.0
70–74	16.3	18.1	17.2	14.1	20.2	18.2	17.8
75–79	5.3	11.8	8.7	8.1	13.2	11.5	10.3
80+	2.5	12.5	7.8	3.0	18.5	13.4	11.0
Residence							
Urban	36.7	63.3	50.8	54.9	62.3	59.8	56.1
Rural	63.3	36.7	49.2	45.1	37.7	40.2	43.9
Educational attainment							
No schooling	5.6	5.3	5.5	3.5	9.0	7.1	6.4
Elementary	67.4	56.9	61.9	64.8	57.9	60.2	60.9
High school	21.1	24.1	22.6	24.3	21.1	22.1	22.3
College	5.9	13.8	10.1	7.5	12.0	10.5	10.3
Marital status							
Never married	3.5	3.4	3.4	5.6	5.8	5.7	4.8
Currently married	80.2	78.1	79.1	44.4	40.2	41.6	57.1
Widowed/separated	16.3	18.5	17.5	49.9	54.1	52.7	38.1

Sources of income

Work	73.5	5.2	37.5	63.6	2.4	22.7	28.9
Pension	11.0	37.1	24.9	14.8	22.7	20.1	22.1
Time deposit	1.3	2.6	2.0	1.5	2.6	2.2	2.1
Rentals	4.1	3.8	4.0	6.1	6.2	6.1	5.2
Family business	18.3	14.3	16.2	42.1	10.6	20.8	18.9
Farm	38.7	20.6	28.9	19.6	16.4	17.4	22.2
Children (in country)	57.1	60.2	58.8	48.1	62.9	57.4	57.8
Children (abroad)	17.6	20.9	19.3	20.1	22.5	21.5	20.5
Relatives	5.1	9.8	7.1	7.8	15.4	12.9	10.5
Self assessed health							
Good	29.4	17.9	23.2	22.9	18.9	20.2	21.5
Average	51.5	44.8	48.0	53.5	43.8	47.0	47.4
Poor	19.1	37.3	28.7	23.6	37.3	32.8	31.1
At least 1 Nagi difficulty	37.2	56.8	47.6	49.7	66.7	61.1	55.5
At least 1 ADL difficulty	4.3	18.4	11.7	9.1	22.0	17.7	15.3

Source: 2007 Philippine Longitudinal Study of Aging (PLSOA) (original tabulations).

PROFILE OF THE FILIPINO ELDERLY

In all, women comprise 58.5 per cent and men 41.5 per cent of the sample — the difference indicative of the higher longevity of women. This gender differential in longevity is further illustrated in the age distribution where the proportion of females increases dramatically after age 75 but not so for males. There are slightly more men than women residing in rural areas (49.2 per cent vs. 40.2 per cent, respectively). The difference in the educational profile between men and women is not marked unlike in other Southeast Asian countries where elderly women tend to have lower education than men (Knodel and Chayovan 2008). In addition, the overall proportion without any schooling is lower than in other countries in Southeast Asia. Slightly more women (7.2 per cent) than men (5.4 per cent) have had no schooling but with regards to the primary level, the gender difference is negligible in that there is no significant difference in distribution across education by sex. The higher longevity of women is reflected further in the marital status profile with "currently married" as the most commonly reported marital status among men (79 per cent) and widowed/separated[4] as the most common marital status among women (52.7 per cent). This difference could also be indicative of a higher remarriage rate among widowed males, although this point is not explored in this chapter. The proportion of the "never married" among women is almost twice that of men but overall the "never married" comprise a minority of 4.2 per cent, which implies that the experience of marriage is almost a universal phenomenon in this population.

For sources of income, respondents were asked in the PLSOA to indicate whether they or their spouse or both they and their spouse received income from a list of possible sources, namely earnings from work, pension,[5] interest of time deposits, income from rentals/savings/stocks/real estate, income from family business, income from farm, money from children within the country, money from children outside the country, and money from other relatives outside the household.[6] Results show differences as well as similarities in sources of income between the sexes. For both men and women, children within the country are the most commonly mentioned income source. The second most commonly mentioned is work but the proportion of men who cite this income source is much higher (37.5 per cent) than women (22.7 per cent) (see Chapters 2, 10 and 12, this volume). Also more men than women mentioned farm as an income source. This picture has not changed substantially from the findings of the 1984 ASEAN survey and the 1996 Philippine Elderly Survey (PES)

(Domingo and Feranil 1990; Hermalin et al. 2002). Pension as a source of income is reported by only about a fourth of all respondents, with no notable difference between the sexes.

In terms of health status, self-assessed health in the PLSOA questionnaire had the following response categories: very healthy, healthier than average, of average health, somewhat unhealthy, and very unhealthy. In analysing the data, the five categories were collapsed into three: very healthy and healthier than average were categorized as "good health"; somewhat unhealthy and very unhealthy were categorized as "poor health", and the category of "average health" was retained. Consistent with previous findings on gender differences in self-assessed health, the authors found that women tended to assess their health more poorly than men (Zimmer et al. 2000). With regard to self-reported physical ability/disability, more women than men (61.1 per cent vs. 47.6 per cent) reported having difficulty with at least one measure of physical ability.[7] More women than men (17.7 per cent vs. 11.7 per cent) also reported experiencing difficulty with at least one of the following measures of activities of daily living (ADL): taking a bath, dressing, eating, standing up from a bed or chair, walking around the house, going outside, and using the toilet.

On working status, the elderly who were currently working at the time of the survey tended to be younger (that is, concentrated in the age group 60–64) and had been in better health, both in terms of self-assessed health and functional health. Moreover, fewer of them had college education, and this difference holds true for both sexes. In terms of residence, there were more working men in rural areas while there were more working women in urban areas.

WORK-RELATED CHARACTERISTICS

Table 13.2 summarizes the differences between elderly men and women in work-related activities and characteristics. The authors looked at both past and current work experience and the reasons for stopping work completely among those who were no longer working but who had worked before.

As shown in Table 13.2 at the time of the survey, the proportion that had stopped working completely was about equal for men and women at a little over 50 per cent. More men than women continued to work (47.1 per cent vs. 33.1 per cent). In all, 38.9 per cent of the elderly indicated that they were currently working at the time of the survey.

TABLE 13.2
Work-Related Characteristics of Filipino Elderly by Gender

	Male (N= 1,289)	Female (N=1,816)	All (N=3,105)
Work status			
Currently working	47.1	33.1	38.9
Stopped working completely	51.4	54.6	53.2
Not working but looking for work	1.1	0.3	0.6
Never worked and not looking	0.4	12.0	7.2
Type of occupation engaged in the longest			
Executive/professional	5.4	7.4	6.6
Associate professional/technician	2.0	2.2	2.1
Clerical and services	5.8	8.3	7.3
Farmer/fishermen	46.9	21.5	31.9
Skilled blue collar	26.0	13.6	18.7
Sales and services elementary occupations	6.4	31.6	21.1
Labourers	4.7	3.1	3.7
Government official	0.4	0.4	0.4
Never worked	0.6	12.0	7.2
Reason stopped working completely	(N=660)	(N=987)	(N=1,647)
Retired	43.2	33.2	37.2
Ill health	49.5	43.4	45.8
Old age	1.8	1.8	1.8
Job-related	3.5	5.4	4.6
Family-related	1.7	14.3	9.2
Others	0.3	1.9	1.3
Type of occupation of the currently working	(N=608)	(N=607)	(N=1,215)
Executive/professional	1.8	1.6	1.7
Associate professional/technician	3.6	4.0	3.8
Clerical and services	5.9	6.3	6.1
Farmer/fishermen	57.1	22.7	39.9
Skilled blue collar	18.1	6.8	12.4
Sales and services elementary occupations	7.6	55.4	31.4
Labourers	4.4	1.8	3.1
Government official	1.2	0.7	0.9

Source: 2007 Philippine Longitudinal Study of Aging (PLSOA) (original tabulations).

Compared to earlier surveys on the elderly in the Philippines, there is a trend of decreasing labour force participation among men in the past three decades, from 55.6 per cent reported in the 1984 ASEAN Aging Survey (Domingo and Feranil 1990) to 51.4 per cent recorded in the 1996 PES (Hermalin et. al. 2002).

For women's labour force participation, the trend has been inconsistent from 35.4 per cent recorded in the 1984 ASEAN survey to 27.5 per cent in the 1996 PES. Table 13.2 further shows that about 1 in 10 (12.0 per cent) women never worked while very few men were in this category (0.4 per cent). Compared with the 1996 PES results for which comparable tabulations are available, the trend shows that the proportion of women who never worked has decreased between the two surveys. In the 1996 survey, 21 per cent of elderly women never worked (Hermalin et al. 2002).

Among those who ever worked, the type of occupation engaged in reflects the labour force profile of a less developed economy, as seen in the jobs they worked at the longest. Almost half of the men were engaged in farming/fishing while about a third of the women were engaged in elementary occupations (as market stall owners, ambulant vendors or proprietors of small home-based *sari-sari*[8] stores) (see Tey and Tengku Aizan, this volume). The second most common work for men was skilled blue-collar work (for example, carpenters, drivers, bakers, mechanics, and so forth), while for women the second most common work was farming/fishing.

For those who had exited the labour force, the dominant reason for having stopped working was ill health (49.5 per cent of men and 43.4 per cent of women), followed by formal retirement (43.2 per cent of men and 33.2 per cent of women). Of the men who left the labour force, about nine in ten stopped working because of ill health or retirement. For women, although health and retirement were highly prominent, other reasons for leaving were also mentioned. The reasons for leaving the workplace were classified into job-related reasons,[9] family-related reasons,[10] and other reasons.[11] These reasons accounted for 20 per cent of the reasons given by women for leaving the workforce permanently. While more men than women retired formally, more women than men left the labour force for family-related, job-related or other reasons.

The personal sources of income were also surveyed. The aim was to examine among those who left the labour force whether pension was a significant source of their own income — an indication that the SSS is in fact reaching its intended beneficiaries. Personal sources of income are those that the respondent reported were his own income sources, not his spouse's nor his joint source of income with his spouse. As can be seen in Table 13.3, in general, only 38.1 per cent of men and 24.9 per cent of women who left the labour force reported pension as a personal source

TABLE 13.3
Personal Sources of Income of Those Who Had Stopped Working by Reason and Gender

Personal Sources of Income	Retired Formally	Health Reasons	Too Old	Job-Related	Family-Related	Others	All
Pension							
Men	61.6	19.9	0.0	43.5	0.0	58.0	38.1
Women	36.0	17.1	22.2	31.5	19.4	31.6	24.9
Time deposit							
Men	4.6	1.5	0.0	0.0	0.0	0.0	2.7
Women	4.6	0.9	5.6	1.9	4.3	0.0	2.7
Rentals/savings/stocks							
Men	7.0	0.6	0.0	13.6	0.0	0.0	3.8
Women	10.4	2.1	0.0	13.2	9.3	0.0	6.4
Family business							
Men	14.1	15.1	25.0	8.7	0.0	0.0	14.3
Women	16.5	8.7	0.0	0.0	9.4	21.1	11.3
Farm							
Men	18.0	22.5	25.0	13.0	54.5	0.0	20.7
Women	20.4	15.5	16.7	7.5	7.1	10.5	15.4
Children (in country)							
Men	49.5	71.1	66.7	52.2	63.6	50.0	60.8
Women	55.5	63.6	44.4	61.1	65.7	72.2	60.9
Children (abroad)							
Men	19.6	24.3	9.1	8.7	18.2	50.0	21.5
Women	25.9	16.7	11.1	34.0	23.0	27.9	21.7
Other relatives							
Men	5.6	12.9	0.0	0.0	0.0	0.0	8.8
Women	16.5	17.8	11.1	11.3	15.7	5.3	16.4
N	613	755	30	76	152	21	1,647
Men	285	327	12	23	11	2	660
Women	328	428	18	53	141	19	987

Source: 2007 Philippine Longitudinal Study of Aging (PLSOA) (original tabulations).

of income. In terms of reasons for leaving the labour force, however, those who retired formally — both among men or women — had the highest proportion reporting that pension was a personal source of income.

Still, this proportion is only 61.6 per cent among men and 36.0 per cent among women. The low percentages imply that only a little over half of men and a third of women who stopped working because they retired formally were covered by either SSS or GSIS pension benefits. Overall, among those who left the labour force, more men than women were able to avail themselves of the benefits from the formal social security system, presumably because men had a longer employment period and were more likely to have worked in the formal sector (see Chapter 11, this volume).

Table 13.3 also shows that accumulated assets are the least common personal sources of income for both men and women. This indicates that few have been able to save enough for their retirement years. Table 13.3 further illustrates the prominence of the traditional support system for the elderly who left the labour force, namely children and other relatives, even in the presence of the formal system of pension. The prominence of traditional support systems is evident in the fact that even men who retired formally receive money from children, although this proportion is lower among men than women. It should also be noted that relatives (other than children) are also sources of support, although this is more common among older women than men.

The current occupational profile of the 36 per cent of the elderly who are still working was also examined (back to Table 13.2). The data revealed slight shifts in the proportions across the occupational categories when compared with the profile of the occupations that all respondents engaged in for the longest period. Among the currently working men, the highest proportion was found to remain in the occupations of fishing and farming but the proportion in this category increased to more than half of currently working men. This suggests that farming and fishing are the occupations that one tends to work in for the longest time because these occupations do not have a retirement age, and perhaps in this type of work only ill health will force one to stop working. Among women who continued to work, the most noticeable shift, when compared with the occupational profile of the longest employment, is the sharp increase in the proportion engaged in elementary occupations in terms of sales and services. This is likely the result of many older women opening small *sari-sari* stores in their homes where they would sell small items to neighbours. This is a common economic activity for house-bound workers and does not require much effort.

MODELLING WORKING STATUS

Under the general assumption that leaving the labour force is an involuntary process and mostly triggered by poor health or a mandatory retirement age, the study analysed the factors correlated with remaining in the labour force under such conditions. Because the data comes from a cross-sectional survey, the authors caution against inference of a causal relationship between these factors and remaining in the labour force. The relationships are conceived to be correlational.

Multivariate logistic regression was used in the analysis. The dependent variable is work status, coded 1 if the respondent was still working at the time of the survey and 0 if completely stopped working/never worked. As suggested in the literature, explanatory factors for working were classified accordingly: demographic (age and sex), socio-economic (residence, education), economic support (as indicated by sources of income[12]), social support (as indicated by marital status), and health status (using three measures: self-assessed health, at least one physical functioning and at least one ADL difficulty). Prior to constructing the multivariate model, the authors first looked at the characteristics of those who remained in the labour force, separately for men and women in a bivariate comparison. It was found that the direction of the relationship between some factors, for example, rural-urban residence, varies distinctly between men and women. Since the factors associated with work status may vary between the sexes, we conducted a separate analysis for men and women.

Results are presented as odds ratios which are the exponentiated regression coefficients for ease of interpretation of the results. Tables 13.4 and 13.5 present the results of the modelling exercise.

Correlates of Working Status for Men

The multivariate analysis of working among men (see Table 13.4) shows that, as expected, age is a strong predictor of working in the elderly years; the odds ratios consistently decrease as age increases. For residence, those from the urban areas are less likely to work perhaps because there are fewer opportunities for gainful economic activity for older men in urban areas. In contrast, men from rural areas have more opportunities to work, as the most prevalent occupation in rural areas are farming and

TABLE 13.4

Odds Ratios from Logistic Regression Coefficients for the Effects of Various Correlates on Working among Filipino Men Age 60 and Above

	Odds Ratio	95.0% C.I.		Sig.
		Lower	Upper	
Age 60 (reference = age 80+)	6.63	3.52	12.49	***
Age 65	4.40	2.33	8.31	***
Age 70	4.17	2.15	8.07	***
Age 75	2.15	1.02	4.53	*
Urban (reference = rural)	0.36	0.27	0.47	***
No schooling (reference = college)	2.87	1.41	5.85	**
Elementary	1.79	1.14	2.81	*
High school	1.51	0.93	2.47	ns
Never married (reference= widowed)	1.08	0.48	2.44	ns
Currently married	1.29	0.89	1.88	ns
With pension (reference= no pension)	0.26	0.18	0.38	***
With time deposit (reference = no time deposit)	0.79	0.25	2.56	ns
With rentals/savings (reference = no rentals/savings)	3.56	1.63	7.81	**
With money from children (in country) (reference = no money from children in country)	1.11	0.82	1.52	ns
With money from children (abroad) (reference = no money from children abroad)	0.80	0.51	1.28	ns
With money from relatives (reference = no money from relatives)	0.58	0.32	1.06	ns
Average health (reference = good health)	0.94	0.68	1.29	ns
Poor health	0.45	0.31	0.66	***
At least 1 Nagi difficulty (reference= no Nagi difficulty)	0.66	0.50	0.88	**
At least 1 ADL difficulty (reference = no ADL difficulty)	0.41	0.25	0.68	***
-2 log likelihood	1,428.607			

Notes: ***p ≤ .001   **p ≤ .01   * p ≤ .05   ns = not significant
Source: 2007 Philippine Longitudinal Study of Aging (PLSOA) (original tabulations).

fishing. Education is also significantly associated with working. Those who have had no education or elementary education are more likely to work in their old age compared with those with a college education. These same men are also unable to benefit from the pension system because of having low or no education and, as a result of working in the informal sector most of their working lives. Lastly, marital status is not significantly associated with working status.

Among the income sources for men, the only significant predictors of working are receiving income from pension and from rentals/savings/ stocks. Men for whom pension is a source of income are less likely to work than men who do not list this income source, while those who receive income from rentals/savings/stocks are more likely to work. This latter finding may seem counterintuitive because one would think that receiving income from such sources as rentals/savings/stocks make these individuals more economically secure and, thus, there is no need for them to work. In high probability, these older men may choose to work because their earnings from rental or stocks or, for that matter, their own savings may not be sufficient.

Moreover, the data show a link between health status and work in that those who are healthier are more likely to work compared with those who are not as healthy. All measures of health status indicate that being in poor health significantly reduces the odds of working. Men who reported being in poor health reported only half as likely to work compared with men who were in good health. Likewise, this pattern holds true for men who reported at least one difficulty with the Nagi measures of physical ability and at least one difficulty with ADL.

Correlates of Working Status for Women

The effect of age on working status of women is the same as that for men. The odds of working decreases monotonically with age (see Table 13.5). As it is with men, urban residence also decreases the likelihood of working but to a lesser degree (OR=.76 for women vs. OR=.36 for men). Education also has a significant effect but in a different way from that observed for men. Those with no education do not differ from the reference category of women with college education in terms of the odds of working. But women with elementary or high school education are significantly more likely to work compared with women with college

TABLE 13.5
Odds Ratios from Logistic Regression Coefficients for the Effects of Various Correlates on Working among Filipino Women Age 60 and Above

	Odds Ratio	95.0% C.I.		Sig.
		Lower	Upper	
Age 60 (reference = age 80+)	10.48	6.06	18.10	***
Age 65	6.40	3.73	10.96	***
Age 70	3.75	2.15	6.55	***
Age 75	3.13	1.73	5.66	***
Urban (reference = rural)	0.76	0.61	0.96	*
No schooling (reference = college)	1.43	0.76	2.69	ns
Elementary	2.22	1.50	3.28	***
High school	2.24	1.47	3.42	***
Never married (reference= widowed)	1.01	0.59	1.74	ns
Currently married	0.51	0.39	0.66	***
With pension (reference= no pension)	0.64	0.46	0.90	*
With time deposit (reference= no time deposit)	0.54	0.18	1.60	ns
With rentals/savings (reference= no rentals/savings)	1.05	0.61	1.80	ns
With money from children (in country) (reference= no money from children in country)	0.57	0.45	0.74	***
With money from children (abroad) (reference = no money from children abroad)	0.99	0.72	1.35	ns
With money from relatives (reference = no money from relatives)	0.50	0.33	0.75	***
Average health (reference= good health)	1.24	0.94	1.62	ns
Poor health	0.78	0.57	1.06	ns
At least 1 Nagi difficulty (reference= no Nagi difficulty)	0.84	0.67	1.06	ns
At least 1 ADL difficulty (reference = no ADL difficulty)	0.61	0.43	0.87	**
-2 log likelihood	2,014.347			

Notes: ***p ≤ .001   **p ≤ .01   * p ≤ .05   ns = not significant
Source: 2007 Philippine Longitudinal Study of Aging (PLSOA) (original tabulations).

education. This is probably indicative of the fact that older women continue to participate in economic activities in the informal sector such as in vending or tending a small home-based store. In contrast, older women with college education may have had the qualifications to work in the formal sector and most likely had retired formally. For women, education reduces the odds of working in the advanced ages among those with the highest (college education) and the lowest (no schooling) levels of education and increases the odds among women with elementary and high school education.

Currently, married women are significantly less likely to work than women who are widowed. While there is no difference by marital status on men's likelihood of working, currently married women are found less likely to work because there is economic support coming from spouses — a traditional arrangement wherein the primary role of men is that of breadwinner. There is no significant difference between women who are never married and those who are widowed in terms of the odds of working. This lends support to assumptions that marital status is a social support variable, working in different ways, however, for men and women (see Chapter 5, this volume).

As it is with men, pension as a source of income significantly decreases the odds of working although this tends to be less so for women than for men (OR for women=.64 vs OR for men=.26). But unlike with men, having traditional sources of support in the form of children in the country and other relatives also depresses the odds of working. This indicates that women more than men are able to rely more on traditional sources of support.

With regard to health status indicators, the relationship is not the same as that for men where poor health is clearly associated with the cessation of gainful work. For older women, being in poor health and having at least one difficulty with the Nagi measures of physical ability does not significantly affect the odds of working. Among them, it has been found that having difficulty in at least one ADL has a significant effect on taking on work. We may surmise here that the kinds of economic activity that women engage in are home-based and do not require much physical exertion. One support for this conjecture is the occupational profile of currently working elderly women which shows that a little over half are in the "sales and services elementary occupations" such as running a small home-based *sari-sari* store.

DISCUSSION AND CONCLUSIONS

The composite picture of work and retirement in the Philippines shows no clear disadvantage of one sex over the other when it comes to facing the economic uncertainty that comes with withdrawal from full participation in the labour force in the older years. While more men than women receive pension, more women are able to depend on traditional sources of support provided by children, other relatives or a working spouse. Furthermore, we found that despite a formal social security system that has been in place for a number of decades and which covers both private and public sector employees, the majority of older persons in the Philippines, even those who had formally retired, still do not report pension as a source of income since only 62 per cent of men and 36 per cent of women who retired formally report pension as a source of income (see Table 13.3). Hence, many continue to work beyond age 60 with health as the most prominent reason for leaving the labour force. Nevertheless, the kinship network as a source of economic support continues to be strong as indicated by the financial support coming from children and other relatives enjoyed by older persons. The situation between men and women are similar in these broad respects.

Still, compared with data from earlier surveys as well as United Nations data, this latest survey result is consistent with findings of a long term gradual decline in the labour force participation rate of elderly men which could be an indication that the proportion of older male workers who are able to retire with a pension from the formal social security system is gradually increasing albeit slowly (Natividad 2005). Since the policies and programmes for a formal social security system that can potentially cover all elderly people in their twilight years are already in place, what is sorely needed is the proper implementation of this plan to increase actual coverage. The main challenge is how to get workers in the informal sector, a sizable segment of the Philippine economy, enrolled into the system and to stay consistent with their contributions. This calls for creative strategies that will take into account the uncertainty in earning capacity of informal sector workers even during their most productive years. Getting the workers of today to plan for their future will go a long way in making the retirement years less burdensome for the old and their children and relatives.

The results also indicate that there are a number of notable differences between the sexes, some of which put men at more risk; others disadvantage the women more. For example, men appear to be the expected breadwinner even at old age; thus, being currently married does not affect the likelihood of working for men but decreases it for women. Men also work until they fall into poor health but women can continue to engage in economic activity even in the face of poor health because the kind of work they engage in are generally home-based store tending. This works to the advantage of women as it affords them a way to meaningfully occupy their time even if the economic returns may not be very significant. On the whole, neither sex is clearly at a more disadvantaged position relative to the other. Given evidence of low lifetime savings and few alternative sources of income, men and women are equally exposed to economic uncertainty.

Amidst these conditions, the family support network remains strong, as it does in much of Southeast Asia, and the support is extended even to those who receive pension. It is also worth noting that other relatives, not only children, contribute to the support of older people. If we project a long term trend of an increasing proportion of workers covered by pension upon retirement, it will be of interest to know what impact this might have on the informal support system now dominated by children and other kin.

Notes

1. This work was supported by a grant obtained by the Nihon University Population Research Institute for the "Academic Frontier" Project for Private Universities and the matching fund subsidy from the Ministry of Education, Culture, Sports, Science, and Technology (MEXT), Japan, 2006–10.
2. At 2009, exchange rate of US$1 = P47.93 (http://www.oanda.com/currency/converter/).
3. In the case of an SSS member who is an underground mineworker for at least five years (either continuous or accumulated) and whose actual date of retirement is not earlier than March 1998, optional retirement is at age 55 and compulsory retirement is at age 60.
4. Divorce is not legal in the Philippines. Legal separation, while allowed, is uncommon so most of those in the "widowed/separated" category are actually widowed.
5. One major limitation of the data is the lack of detailed information on the pension benefits of the elderly. This precludes a more detailed analysis of the coverage of the formal system. For this analysis, the authors assume that "pension" when mentioned as a source of income comes from the formal system (SSS/GSIS) and is the result of having worked for the requisite period to qualify for this retirement benefit.

6. Because the identified income source can be the respondent's, the spouse's, or a joint source of income, when a respondent reports pension or earnings from work, it is not necessarily from his or her own pension or work.

7. These measures include: walk 200–300 metres, climb ten steps without resting, stand for two hours, continue to sit for two hours, stoop/bend knees, raise hands above one's head, extend arms as if to shake hands, grasp with fingers, and lift a 10kg/5kg weight.

8. A *sari sari* store is a mini-convenience store selling basic household items. However, this store is located in a house, usually as a small annex to the front area facing the street. This is a ubiquitous presence in both urban and rural neighbourhoods and may be operated within metres of each other.

9. Examples of job-related reasons include the company closing, low salary, and problems at work.

10. Examples of family-related reasons include spouse not allowing the respondent to work, the need to take care of children, the parent getting sick, and children who have asked the respondent to stop working.

11. Examples of personal reasons in this case may include losing interest in a job and getting tired of working.

12. This is income derived from a specific source by respondent, respondent's spouse or both respondent and spouse.

References

Cruz, G., Y. Saito and J. Natividad. "Active Life Expectancy and Functional Health Transition among Filipino Older People". *Canadian Studies in Population* 34, no. 1 (2007): 29–47.

Domingo, Lita J., Imelda Zosa-Feranil and Associates. *Socio-Economic Consequences of the Aging Population: Insights from the Philippine Experience.* Quezon City, Philippines: Demographic Research and Development Foundation, Inc., 1990.

Hermalin, Albert I., Angelique Chan, Ann Biddlecom and Mary Beth Ofstedal. "Work, Retirement and Leisure". In *The Well-being of the Elderly in Asia: A Four-country Comparative Study*, edited by Albert I. Hermalin. Ann Arbor, Michigan: University of Michigan Press, 2002.

Knodel, John and M.B. Ofstedal. "Gender and Aging in the Developing World: Where are the Men?" *Population Development Review* 29, no. 4 (2003): 667–98.

Knodel, John and Napaporn Chayovan. "Population Ageing and the Well-Being of Older Persons in Thailand: Past Trends, Current Situation, and Future Challenges". UNFPA Thailand and Asia and the Pacific Regional Office. Papers in Population Ageing Series, No. 5, December 2008.

Knodel John and Zachary Zimmer. *Gender and Well Being of Older Persons in Cambodia: A Research Report.* Report 09-665. Population Studies Center, Institute for Social Research, University of Michigan, 2009.

Mesa-Lago, Carmelo, Verna D.Q. Viajar and Rolly C.J. Castillo. *Pensions in the Philippines: Challenges and Way Forward*. Freidreich-Ebert Stiftung-Philippine Office, 2011. Available at <www.fes.org.ph/media/PENSIONS%20IN%20THE%20PHILIPPINES_final%20for%20online.pdf> (accessed 12 December 2012).

Natividad, Josefina. "Gender and Ageing in the Philippines". *Untapped Resources: Women in Ageing Societies across Asia*, edited by K. Mehta. Singapore: Marshal Cavendish Academic, 2005.

Ofstedal, M.B., E. Reidy and J. Knodel. "Gender Differences in Economic Support and Well-being of Older Asians". *Journal of Cross-Cultural Gerontology* 19 (2004): 165–201.

Philippine Social Security Services. Available at <http://www.sss.gov.ph/sss/index.html> (accessed 12 March 2009).

Quinn, Joseph and Richard Burkhauser. "Retirement and Labor Force Behavior of the Elderly". In *Demography of Aging*, edited by L. Martin and S. Preston. Washington, D.C.: National Academy Press, 1994.

United Nations. *World Population Ageing 1950–2050*. New York: United Nations, 2002.

———. *World Population Ageing 2007*. New York: United Nations, 2007.

World Bank. *Averting the Old Age Crisis*. New York: Oxford University Press, 1994.

Zimmer, Z., J.N. Natividad, H.S. Lin and N. Chayovan. "A Cross-National Examination of the Determinants of Self-Assessed Health". *Journal of Health and Social Behavior* 41 (2000): 465–81.

INDEX